The Politics of Jurisprudence
A Critical Introduction to Legal Philosophy
Second edition

Roger Cotterrell LLD MSc (Soc)

Professor of Legal Theory in the University of London
Queen Mary and Westfield College

Members of the LexisNexis Group worldwide

United Kingdom	LexisNexis Butterworths Tolley, a Division of Reed Elsevier (UK) Ltd, Halsbury House, 35 Chancery Lane, LONDON, WC2A 1EL, and 4 Hill Street, EDINBURGH EH2 3JZ
Argentina	LexisNexis Argentina, BUENOS AIRES
Australia	LexisNexis Butterworths, CHATSWOOD, New South Wales
Austria	LexisNexis Verlag ARD Orac GmbH & Co KG, VIENNA
Canada	LexisNexis Butterworths, MARKHAM, Ontario
Chile	LexisNexis Chile Ltda, SANTIAGO DE CHILE
Czech Republic	Nakladatelství Orac sro, PRAGUE
France	Editions du Juris-Classeur SA, PARIS
Hong Kong	LexisNexis Butterworths, HONG KONG
Hungary	HVG-Orac, BUDAPEST
India	LexisNexis Butterworths, NEW DELHI
Ireland	Butterworths (Ireland) Ltd, DUBLIN
Italy	Giuffrè Editore, MILAN
Malaysia	Malayan Law Journal Sdn Bhd, KUALA LUMPUR
New Zealand	LexisNexis Butterworths, WELLINGTON
Poland	Wydawnictwo Prawnicze LexisNexis, WARSAW
Singapore	LexisNexis Butterworths, SINGAPORE
South Africa	LexisNexis Butterworths, DURBAN
Switzerland	Stämpfli Verlag AG, BERNE
USA	LexisNexis, DAYTON, Ohio

A CIP Catalogue record for this book is available from the British Library.

First edition 1989
Reprinted 1992, 1994, 1996

Not available in the United States of America

ISBN 0 406 93055 4

Typeset by Kerrypress Ltd, Luton
Printed and bound in Great Britain by The Cromwell Press, Trowbridge, Wiltshire

Visit Butterworths LexisNexis *direct* at www.butterworths.com

Preface

This book now covers a much wider range of material than it did in its first edition but it pursues the same aims, offering a critical introduction to key writings in Anglo-American legal philosophy that seek to explain in general terms the nature of law. As before, the book's critical approach is based on two kinds of inquiries pursued consistently in relation to each theoretical contribution considered. I ask (i) what that theory's relevance has been to political issues reflecting the social contexts in which it was expounded and (ii) how the aims and ideas of Anglo-American legal theory have related to the changing circumstances of lawyers as a professional group.

As an introduction written from a particular standpoint, the book makes no attempt to be comprehensive. It selects material to illustrate general approaches to legal theory and to explore professional and political uses to which that theory has been put. The book was planned as a brief supplementary critical commentary on its subject-matter. Nevertheless, it has been widely used as a general student text and because of this I have tried in this new edition to extend its approach to address the most important areas of theory that have become prominent since its original publication.

Two completely new chapters deal with the great variety of critical approaches to Anglo-American legal philosophy that have flourished in the past decade. The first edition's critique of normative legal theory hinted at a void at the heart of that theoretical tradition that needed to be filled by new approaches. Recent critical theories have not generally been intended to shore up the edifice of normative legal theory – often, perhaps, the opposite. But their emergence has made legal philosophy a much richer field than it seemed when the first edition of this book was written. The inadequacies – but also the promise – of normative legal theory, which I emphasised in concluding the first edition, have created a space for and stimulated these newer approaches, all of which in my view are to be welcomed as liberating influences in legal inquiry.

In revising the book I have benefited greatly from many constructive comments provided by reviewers of the first edition. The opportunity has been taken to adapt the text throughout to improve its clarity, to update references and to correct some errors. These changes have not altered the book's arguments but the extensive new material included, especially in Chapters 8 and 9, has given me an opportunity to test and elaborate those arguments further and illustrate them in many new ways. In the years since the book first appeared the literature of legal theory has flourished and I have tried to provide relatively full guidance to the most important recent writings across the field. As a consequence, the section of notes and further reading has been enlarged and almost entirely rewritten for this edition.

Roger Cotterrell
Queen Mary and Westfield College, University of London
January 2003

Extracts from the Preface to the first edition

This book aims to survey key theoretical contributions to the field of modern Anglo-American legal philosophy in order to outline debates about the nature of law which these contributions have provoked. In this sense it is intended as a general introduction to central areas of modern legal theory. However, it attempts something more than most such general introductions. It seeks to put the debates in the literature into a broader context than that in which they are usually presented in introductory texts. It is intended not just as a survey of central areas of the field but also, more specifically, as a discussion of what Anglo-American legal philosophy, in some of its dominant forms, is and has been *for*.

This involves examining approaches to legal philosophy in Britain and the United States in the light of conditions in which those approaches have emerged since the beginnings of modern legal professionalisation in both countries. I argue in these pages that the succession of dominant approaches in Anglo-American legal philosophy since the nineteenth century (the approaches which today make up much of modern jurisprudence) can usefully be understood, to a large extent, as responses to particular political conditions and also, especially, conditions of legal professional practice. Thus, the book suggests that this legal philosophical literature has helped to reinforce views about the nature of law which have seemed important for the legal professions' status and objectives at particular times. And this legal philosophy has also had some political significance insofar as it has promoted, reinforced or reflected wider currents of political thought. The professional and political roles of what is often seen as an esoteric region of legal thought and literature ought not to be exaggerated. But it is important to bring those roles to light.

This perspective may provide a way of showing that debates in jurisprudence which tend to be portrayed as timeless, and which often seem interminable and incapable of resolution, are better understood as reflecting specific responses in legal philosophy to pressures, developments and conditions arising in particular times and places.

Viewed in this perspective, such matters as the controversies around modern theories of sovereignty, the enduring (but problematic) appeal of legal positivism in its various forms, the ebb and flow of natural law theory and the character of certain varieties of sceptical theory in legal philosophy, appear quite differently from the way they usually appear in standard textbook treatments. This book claims that the patchwork of philosophical views of the nature of law contained in modern Anglo-American jurisprudence can be understood as a response to social and political change: but a response shaped substantially by perceived problems arising in the professionalisation of legal practice.

Such an interpretation is used here as an organising framework for an introduction to major theoretical orientations in the subject. Is it justifiable, then, to offer, as such a framework, what can be no more than a tentative sketch of a way of looking at this material? I think it is. First, this approach can suggest a structure or unity in much of the vast, unwieldy mass of modern theoretical literature on law which is not necessarily otherwise readily apparent. Second, the approach may reveal this literature as more vital and engaged in the practical affairs of law in society than it has sometimes seemed to be and, indeed, than it has often presented itself as being. The development of modern legal philosophy, at least in part, has been a kind of running commentary on the changing conditions of law in Western societies. If a limited attempt is made to put legal philosophy 'in context' – particularly by bringing to light assumptions contained within it about the social, political and professional environment of law – it may be possible to appreciate that some of legal philosophy's central issues and debates have a broader significance (for both lawyers and ordinary citizens) than is often assumed. Finally, the question of what is and what has been 'central' in this field might be clarified and even reshaped by the kind of approach adopted here. Indeed, in the case of most major writers considered in these pages the 'contextual' approach encourages a somewhat different assessment from that which represents the current orthodoxy.

No attempt at comprehensiveness is made here, even within the particular range of subject-matter highlighted. The book examines contributions to theory which have been very influential in legal philosophy in the Anglo-American common law world in the period of modern professionalisation of law. It seeks to identify the general orientations of each of these contributions, especially in the light of their professional and political relevance. It is concerned with detailed exegesis only insofar as this throws light on the central issues with which the book is concerned. Most of the theory discussed is indigenous to Britain or the United States but notably influential imports from elsewhere are included where a knowledge of them seems essential in understanding Anglo-American developments. Each contribution is discussed insofar as it offers a *theory of law*; that is, insofar as it tries to clarify theoretically the nature of law, laws, or legal institutions in general. This emphasis makes it possible to focus consistently on what I take to be a unifying thread running through much of the diverse literature of modern jurisprudence (while in no way denying the wide variety of intellectual aims attributable to the theorists whose work is discussed in these pages).

I hope that the book as thus conceived will provide a useful introduction to the areas of theory it surveys and, at the same time, a distinctive view of them. I hope also that its discussions show why this theory needs to be studied in the light of its professional and political ramifications, and how such a contextual approach – far from undermining or 'explaining away' in reductionist fashion what it examines – can actually demonstrate the enduring value of this material more clearly than can most traditional approaches to the subject. Legal philosophy, like law itself, reveals its full significance only when considered in social and political context.

I am especially grateful to my friend and colleague Dr David Nelken for reading and commenting on several sections of the manuscript, and for the stimulus of many productive conversations on questions of legal theory. Parts of this book were written while I was visiting professor and Jay H Brown Centennial Faculty Fellow in Law at the University of Texas, during the Spring Semester 1989. I benefited greatly from the research facilities and the experience of teaching jurisprudence in that environment, both of which have contributed significantly to this book. I am also grateful to Queen Mary College for a term's sabbatical leave during the early stages of research on the project; and to Dr M W Bryan of Queen Mary College and Professor W C Powers of the University of Texas Law School who also read and commented on parts of the manuscript in draft. Parts of Chapter 6 are adapted from an article which I previously published in the 1987 volume of the American Bar Foundation Research Journal (pp 509–524). The ABF's permission for reproduction of some passages from that essay is gratefully acknowledged.

Finally, I owe thanks to my children for putting up stoically with the disruption to their lives which is caused by other members of the family writing books; and to my wife, Ann Cotterrell, for her constant support and encouragement through the whole period of researching and writing this volume.

Roger Cotterrell
Faculty of Laws
Queen Mary College London
June 1989

Contents

Preface   v
Extracts from the Preface to the first edition   vii

1   Legal philosophy in context   1
Jurisprudence, legal philosophy and legal theory   1
Legal philosophy and legal practice   4
Justifying normative legal theory   6
Unity and system in law   8
Professionalisation and politics   11
Legal philosophy in social and political context   13
How should legal philosophy be interpreted contextually?   16

2   The theory of common law   21
The character of common law thought   22
The common law judge   24
Can common law thought explain legal development?   26
Common law and legislation   30
The political and social environment   32
Savigny: a theory for common law?   36
Maine's historical jurisprudence   40
Maine on politics and society   42
Historical jurisprudence and the legal profession   44
The fate of Maine's new science   46

3   Sovereign and subject: Bentham and Austin   49
The empire of darkness and the region of light   51

Positive law and positive morality   54
The coercive structure of a law   56
Sanctions and power-conferring rules   60
Sovereignty   63
Some characteristics of Austin's sovereign   65
Must the sovereign be legally illimitable?   68
The judge as delegate of the sovereign   70
Austin's theory of the centralised state   72
Austin and the legal profession   74

4   Analytical jurisprudence and liberal democracy:
    Hart and Kelsen   79
Empiricism and conceptualism   81
Hart's linguistic empiricism   83
The character of rules   87
Sociological drift   90
The structure of a legal system   92
The existence of a legal system   95
Hart's hermeneutics   96
Judicial decisions and the 'open texture' of rules   98
Kelsen's conceptualism   101
'The machine now runs by itself'   104
Democracy and the Rule of Law   107
Conclusion   111

5   The appeal of natural law   113
Legal positivism and natural law   114
Is natural law dead?   117
Natural law and legal authority   119
The 'rebirth' of natural law   121
Anglo-American lessons from the Nazi era   123
The ideal of legality and the existence of law   127
A purposive view of law   130
Fuller and the common law tradition   132
Politics and professional responsibility   136
Natural law tamed?   138

6   The problem of the creative judge: Pound and Dworkin   145
Pound's rejection of the model of rules   148
The outlook of sociological jurisprudence   150
A theory of interests   154
The search for a measure of values   156
The wider context of Pound's jurisprudence   158

Dworkin and Pound 160
Principles and policies 162
The closed world of legal interpretation 166
Politics, professionalism and interpretive communities 171

7 **Scepticism and realism** 175
Pragmatism and realism 178
Realism and normative legal theory 181
Llewellyn's constructive doctrinal realism 187
The political context of American legal realism 194
Post-realist policy-science 199
Post-realist radical scepticism 202
Legal professionalism and the legacy of realism 206

8 **A jurisprudence of difference: class, gender and race** 209
The ghost of Marx 212
Equality, difference and liberal feminism 215
Different moral voices in law 217
Radical feminism and the gender of law 221
Postmodern feminism 225
Critical race theory 229
Politics, professionalism, difference 233

9 **The deconstruction and reconstruction of law** 237
Postmodernism and deconstruction 238
Recovering minor jurisprudences 241
Law without foundations 244
Derrida, justice, autopoiesis 247
Law's empty shell 250
Reorienting legal theory 254
Theorising legal communities 257
Legal theory beyond the nation state 261
Legal theory and legal professions 264

Notes and further reading 267

References 297

Index 313

Chapter 1

Legal philosophy in context

Most lawyers have little difficulty in recognising 'law' as a clearly identifiable field. No deep reflection on the matter seems necessary. Treated as the lawyer's practical art or the special expertise of a legal profession, law seems an area of knowledge and practice with well understood unifying features and distinctive character.

In normal conditions of professional practice, there may be no need to think systematically about the character of law-in-general, or to ask broad questions about the nature of legal institutions. It may well seem enough that the lawyer has the expertise to deal with particular problems in hand, can find and interpret the specific areas of legal doctrine – rules, principles and concepts of law – needed to answer those problems, and has the 'know-how' to be able to recognise and use appropriate procedures and channels of influence to harness the legal resources of the state to clients' interests.

Given the complexities of law and regulation, this kind of understanding of law may seem as much as anyone could reasonably ask of a legal specialist. In practice, the particular, the specific and the appropriate are what count.

Jurisprudence, legal philosophy and legal theory

However, the legal realm can be looked at in ways that go beyond the immediacies of professional practice. Law is assumed to be socially significant, although the nature of this significance, and what kinds of study can best reveal it, are always controversial matters. Law has long been thought worth studying for its intrinsic philosophical or social interest and importance, which relates to but extends beyond its immediate instrumental value or professional relevance. In this sense, law is 'a great anthropological document' (Holmes 1899: 444).

In the Anglo-American world the term most often used to refer to the whole range of inquiries concerned with this broader significance of law is *jurisprudence*. Jurisprudence is not united by particular methods or perspectives. It includes work grounded in the diverse perspectives of the various social and human sciences and of many kinds of philosophy, as well as other intellectual disciplines.

Jurisprudence is probably best defined negatively as encompassing all kinds of general intellectual inquiries about law that are not confined solely to doctrinal exegesis or technical prescription. The qualification 'general' is important. If jurisprudence is unified at all it is by a concern with theoretical generalisation, in contrast to the emphasis on the particular and the immediate that characterise most professional legal practice. So it has been described as the theoretical part of law as a discipline (Twining 1984). But such a view is controversial insofar as it ties jurisprudence firmly within a conception of some overall disciplinary unity of law. Given the diversity of law and legal activity and the sheer range of material and types of inquiry that can be included in jurisprudence, this disciplinary unity may be a hypothesis to be examined rather than a postulate to be assumed (Cotterrell 1995: ch 3).

The unwieldy category of jurisprudence can be broken down into more specific fields of inquiry. For example, *legal philosophy* encompasses all philo-sophical speculation (rather than empirically-based social scientific theory) on matters related to law. So it excludes empirical social theories of law (such as those associated with sociology of law) which would be a part of jurispru-dence, as defined above.

Insofar as philosophy examines the conceptual apparatuses by which human experience is interpreted, legal philosophy's main focus is on clarifying or analysing the ideas or structures of reasoning implicated in, presupposed by or developed through legal doctrine, or which constitute the environment of thought and belief in terms of which legal processes are justified and explained. It is not concerned with the empirical inquiries about law's social effects and about legal behaviour that are pursued in sociological studies of law. But legal philosophical inquiry cannot be clearly demarcated from the kind of concep-tual inquiries with which sociology of law is concerned. The difference is primarily one of emphasis. In legal philosophy generally, conceptual clarifica-tion tends to be treated as much more important than – and sometimes independent of – systematic empirical analysis of legal institutions[1] in their historical context and social settings. By contrast, in sociology of law, analysis of law's conceptual structures is always to be undertaken only in relation to this empirical analysis.

This book is concerned with legal philosophy, but not the whole of this huge field. The following chapters deal only with the part of it that contributes to *legal theory*. Like the terms jurisprudence and legal philosophy, this term is not used uniformly by all writers. But here it can be taken to mean theoretical analysis of the nature of law, laws or legal institutions in general.

It excludes those parts of legal philosophy concerned primarily with the moral *justification* of particular aims or policies related to or expressed in legal doctrine. Legal theory does not directly address, for example, the nature of justice as a general concept, the philosophical justification of particular legal or governmental policies in relation to morally controversial matters (such as abortion), or the general question of how far the enforcement of moral principles as such is an appropriate task of contemporary criminal law. Legal theory aims to understand systematically the nature of law as a social phenomenon. While philosophical justifications of particular aims or tasks of law are not irrelevant to this concern (and may follow directly from certain types of legal theory, such as natural law theory), they are not central to it.

It follows from this definition of legal theory that both legal philosophy and sociology of law contribute to it, the latter in ways that are beyond the scope of this book (cf Cotterrell 1992). For convenience, I term legal philosophy's contributions to legal theory *normative legal theory* and sociology of law's contributions to it *empirical legal theory*. Just as the distinction between legal philosophy's conceptual inquiries and those of sociology of law is often more a matter of emphasis than of rigid demarcation, so the same is true of these two kinds of legal theory. The following chapters will be concerned, however, only with those parts of the literature of legal philosophy that have sought to contribute to legal theory and, in doing so, have powerfully influenced the shape and outlook of modern Anglo-American jurisprudence. So this book's focus is on the development of normative legal theory in this particular context.

---

1   By 'legal institutions' I mean here patterns of official action and expectations of action organised around the creation, application and enforcement of legal precepts or the maintenance of a legal order. More generally, in this book the word 'institution', in the sense of social institution, refers to a system of patterned expectations about the behaviour of individuals fulfilling certain socially recognised roles. Cf Cotterrell 1992: 3.

Legal philosophy and legal practice

Since the 1960s, Anglo-American legal philosophy has strengthened its links to academic philosophy in various ways. First, it has been developed to a greater extent than previously by scholars who see themselves as owing disciplinary allegiance to academic philosophy, or dual allegiance to law and philosophy, rather than to law. Second, issues and modes of inquiry in legal philosophy have been increasingly influenced by the wider disciplinary concerns of philosophy, rather than by issues close to the concerns of legal practice. But despite these developments, legal philosophy, in modern times in the Anglo-American context, has always been an enterprise pursued primarily by lawyers with little that today would pass for professional philosophical training. Indeed, it may be more appropriate to refer to them generally as jurists rather than legal philosophers, as legal scholars with a speculative concern, rather than members of any branch of a philosophical establishment.

There is something puzzling about this state of affairs. What have these speculating jurists, whose work makes up much of modern jurisprudence, seen as their role? What has been legal philosophy's function? What is its status as an intellectual field in relation to other such fields and in relation to the lawyer's professional knowledge of law?

Clear answers to these questions would help in understanding the nature and significance of disputes in the literature of jurisprudence or legal philosophy. Yet, very rarely are convincing answers given in general texts on jurisprudence. In this book, in considering some areas of legal philosophy that dominate the literature of modern jurisprudence, it will be necessary to try to assess legal philosophy's contribution to the wider world of political and legal activities – including especially the professional practice of law as it has developed since the mid-nineteenth century through the period during which most of the theoretical contributions discussed in this book were made.

Where could we begin to look for answers? Some relationships between conceptual inquiries in legal philosophy and the concerns of professional legal practice seem obvious. The everyday notions that lawyers use include such concepts as justice, responsibility, obligation, rights and duties, causation, validity, ownership, possession, personality – all pregnant with philosophical complexities and wide social significance. Insofar as legal philosophy focusses attention on these kinds of concepts as they relate to settings in which lawyers have to play a role, it seems merely a more general version of what lawyers do in everyday practice in interpreting legal doctrine.

Further, a concern to identify conceptual inquiries in jurisprudence specifically with issues relevant to professional legal practice may underlie the attempts by some writers to distance jurisprudence from (academic) philosophy. So Julius Stone writes that most of jurisprudence's problems are different from those of philosophy, and that jurisprudence's classifications are acceptable to the extent that they allow its concerns to be introduced to law students and discussed by lawyers generally in an orderly way (Stone 1964: 8, 16, 17). On this view, jurisprudence's main constituency is clearly a legal professional one.

On the other hand, this legal professional constituency has long distrusted many aspects of the jurisprudential enterprise, if not necessarily all of them (cf Cohen 1933: 327). Even conceptual clarification in legal philosophy may not be valued highly by those concerned with the practice of law, and sound reasons can be constructed in defence of this attitude.

First, much legal practice does not involve issues of doctrinal interpretation of sufficient depth to lead the lawyer into philosophical thickets. The conceptual puzzles of legal philosophy, insofar as they deal with issues of immediate practical significance, are usually puzzles for appellate courts, not for most office lawyers or trial judges. Issues of everyday practice are more often strategic or tactical than conceptual, routine rather than innovative, issues of fact rather than of law, and matters of care and competence rather than of doctrinal creativity. But this is not always so and some forms of legal practice undoubtedly require high levels of conceptual ingenuity and theoretical imagination.

Second, a more fundamental point can be made. Surely contemporary Western law, by its nature, does not lend itself to broad conceptual generalisation? It seems to be a mass of technicalities in no way unified by broad principle or philosophically coherent concepts.

Certainly, lawyers seek rationality and system in legal doctrine. Indeed, their ability to interpret that doctrine and predict the outcome of litigation or the effects of legal documents and transactions depends on this. But the rationality of contemporary law is a piecemeal rationality. Legal doctrine has to be organised, systematised and generalised just enough to meet the needs of the moment. Concepts are used pragmatically and not necessarily with any concern for broad consistency of meaning. In complex contemporary legal systems in which legal doctrine rapidly changes, doctrinal system and order are continually created and re-created, as far as possible, to meet practical professional needs. Conceptual clarity is produced (if at all) with the knowledge that it can be only provisional; valid until the next input of new doctrine from legislation, judicial decisions or administrative rule-making.

These conditions of legal practice are not new, although the complexity and scale of contemporary regulation has greatly increased. They certainly raise doubts, however, as to why legal philosophy should be thought significant for the professional world of law. It seems necessary to look elsewhere for the functions legal philosophy has fulfilled, at least in its contributions to legal theory, unless we are to conclude that it has served no functions in the wider world of legal activities.

If the latter were true, however, it would still be necessary to explain why an immense modern literature of the kind considered in this book exists, and why some of it has had great impact on discussion and opinion among legal and political elites. It would also be necessary to explain why legal philosophy's contributions to modern legal theory have been predominantly contributions by lawyers addressed mainly to lawyers. Despite jurisprudence's ostensibly broad, open perspectives, the part of it to be considered here has been very much a lawyer's enterprise. Its whole intellectual organisation has presupposed a single community in which legal practitioners and legal theorists are members.

Justifying normative legal theory

The justifications that Anglo-American jurists have given for their work in normative legal theory often emphasise its practical role in improving law. For Jeremy Bentham, the English legal reformer, this kind of theory was central to a science of law which would provide a secure foundation for rational reform. Bentham's less radical follower John Austin, like many later writers, put more emphasis on legal theory's systematising task – making sense of the chaotic jumble of legal materials – and its educational value in providing a 'map of the law' – a framework on which the detail of legal technicality could be arranged (Austin 1885: 1082).

For the American theorists Roscoe Pound and Oliver Wendell Holmes, legal theory could be justified in even more explicitly instrumental terms. Pound refers to its modern task as facilitating social engineering through law, with the jurist cast in the role of expert in fair and efficient governmental and judicial decision-making (see Chapter 6). For Holmes, the engineering analogy gives way to an architectural one. 'Theory is the most important part of the dogma of the law, as the architect is the most important man who takes part in the building of a house' (Holmes 1897: 1008). Theory is the ally of the scientifically-minded lawyer engaged in 'the eternal pursuit of the more exact', the establishment of law's principles 'upon accurately measured social desires' (Holmes 1899: 452, 455).

Ronald Dworkin, one of the most influential contemporary legal philosophers, sees legal theory as justifying law and so guiding and supporting judges in the task of legal interpretation: 'If a theory of law is to provide a basis for judicial duty, then the principles it sets out must try to *justify* the settled rules by identifying the political or moral concerns and traditions of the community which, in the opinion of the lawyer whose theory it is, do in fact support the rules' (Dworkin 1977: 67, emphasis in original).

Other theorists are more ambiguous in asserting practical relevance, subsuming this in wider intellectual justifications. For both the English jurist H L A Hart and the Austrian Hans Kelsen – who worked for many years in the United States and has significantly influenced modern Anglo-American jurisprudence – legal theory is justified because its conceptual inquiries help to reveal the nature of law as a social phenomenon.

Thus Hart (1961: vi) suggests that clarifying the nature of legal ideas can cast light on the social contexts in which they are used. Kelsen describes law as a 'specific social technique' (Kelsen 1941a) and sees his task as, in part, to show by examining the nature of legal knowledge and reasoning where its specificity lies. In both cases the reference to the 'social' should not mislead the reader into thinking that the theory proposed is sociological in orientation. It remains, like all normative legal theory, grounded in abstract philosophical speculation rather than in empirical examination of legal behaviour or the social and historical contexts in which law exists. Nevertheless, where serious attempts to understand the wider cultural resonance of law's conceptual frameworks are undertaken in legal philosophy, it may become sensitive to sociological dimensions of law to an unusual extent.

Finally, some other writers treat the appropriate role of legal theory as a 'debunking' or demystifying one – not to rationalise, justify, clarify or improve the conceptual structure of law, but to expose it or explain it away. Certain 'sceptical' tendencies in legal philosophy seem in their most radical manifestations to be concerned not to praise law's abstract conceptual structures but to bury them. The explicit justification for these approaches is usually that they offer 'realism'; they explain realities about law that are obscured in orthodox legal thought and other legal theory; they look behind legal doctrine to the political positions, individual and social interests, or personal value judgments (for example, of judges or other legal decision-makers) which doctrine may hide. How deep the radicalism of these approaches runs and whether they are to be seen as substantially rejecting (rather than supplementing) the more general characteristics of normative legal theory outlined in this chapter, are matters to be explored later in this book. Examples of these sceptical legal theories are discussed in Chapter 7. In recent decades they have led to analyses, drawing particularly on feminist and postmodernist theory, that consider the particular mechanisms by which legal ideas and practices reflect, sustain and constitute the environment of political, social and cultural conditions in which law exists.

Given such diverse implicit or explicit aims underlying modern Anglo-American legal philosophy's contributions to legal theory, generalisation becomes dangerous. As subsequent chapters will suggest, the relationship between particular theories and the political and legal professional environment in which they develop varies.

Jurisprudence and legal philosophy are made up of bodies of literature that have been intended to serve different purposes at different times. Further, whatever the motivations of particular theorists, any influence that their work has had on professional or political life may be equally varied. And the collecting together of this material in legal education – as part of taught jurisprudence courses – often reflects yet other considerations, expressed in such aspirations as to relate 'the law to the spirit of the time' (Laski 1967: 577) or to provide in legal education 'an orderly view of the law's "external relations"' with other fields of knowledge (Stone 1966: 30).

All these matters are important in considering the nature of legal philosophy in general and normative legal theory in particular. The latter is typically treated as a cumulating corpus of knowledge focussed on a single concern to 'theorise law'. Indeed, by definition, this is what normative legal theory is. But it would be unwise to assume more consistency of aim and effect than is implied by this purely definitional unity.

Unity and system in law

So the puzzle still remains. What, if anything, can be said, in general terms, about the significance in the practical world of affairs of legal philosophy's contributions to legal theory? What all of them have in common is that, in some way, they attempt to offer a general perspective on the nature of law.

This frequently involves trying to demonstrate some kind of *unity* of law. The search for unity can be pursued in many different ways, however. It may involve trying to identify a consistent moral or cultural foundation of legal regulation which validates and gives moral meaning and social authority to laws. It may entail trying to show how the entirety of legal rules and regulations can be seen as part of a single rational structure, or how legal reasoning entails consistent methods or epistemological assumptions, or how the diverse elements of legal doctrine applicable in a particular jurisdiction (for example, England and Wales, or the United States) link to form something that can be understood as a system of elements organised in a unified whole. It may involve a search for a purposive unity of law, so that all its elements can be interpreted and evaluated in terms of some fundamental objectives (for example, social, moral, economic or political) which they are thought to serve. Unity is sometimes sought in a common source of authority of laws, or in consistent patterns of legal reasoning which appear as law's unifying characteristics.

Unity may be sought in a universal sense, so that the law of all times and places is seen as having common foundations. In modern Anglo-American legal philosophy this approach is rare but is exemplified in the claims of the American jurist Lon Fuller that the very nature of rules as a legal mechanism of government presupposes certain universal moral criteria of their development and application in *any* social context (see Chapter 5). More typically, however, modern legal theory tries to explain how the law of a *particular* nation, state or jurisdiction can be thought of as a system, with all its diverse rules and regulations somehow rationally or purposively interconnected and yet clearly distinguished from the components of other legal systems.

These kinds of inquiries may seem highly abstract, but they are very relevant to practical legal reasoning and problem-solving. This is because they involve examining the background assumptions in relation to which those practical activities take place.

When, for example, lawyers recognise uniform general tests that determine in a legal system which rules are *valid* as (for example, English or American) law or which decisions have legal force, they seem to presuppose the distinct identity of the system as a whole; that there are conclusive means of distinguishing the legal from the non-legal and marking the boundaries of legal doctrine. Equally, some similar presuppositions about the distinctiveness of 'the legal' are entailed when it is necessary to develop a general conception of what can count as legal arguments, or justiciable issues, in contrast with non-legal or non-justiciable ones.[2] Finally, legal reasoning links rules together and presupposes that the legal relationship between them can be conclusively determined. For example, it deals with such questions as: what is the position if the rules conflict? What is their relative authoritativeness? In what circumstances can one rule determine the validity of another? In doing so, this reasoning presupposes an internal structure of the legal system, and a theory of the relationship between its elements.

It follows that unity as a practical matter entails two things. It entails predictably consistent *internal* relationships of elements (rules, principles, concepts, decisions, etc) in a legal system. Equally, it entails predictably consistent *external*

---

2   See *Council of Civil Service Unions v Minister for the Civil Service* [1985] AC 374.

relationships between the system and what lies outside it, so that the determination of the legal from the non-legal (for example, legal rules from moral rules, judicial decisions from political decisions) can be reliable.

This need to mark out what is 'internal' to law and what 'external' shows itself in many different ways besides those just mentioned. The internal-external dichotomy is complex and many-sided but closely connected with the problem of showing the unity of law or the distinctiveness of legal thought or reasoning. Indeed, the problem of the internal-external relationship pervades normative legal theory.

Thus, H L A Hart (1961; 1994) distinguishes what he calls internal and external views of legal (and other) rules. The internal view is that of legal 'insiders' who orient their thinking in terms of legal rules treated as guides for conduct – whether or not the rules are approved by such insiders. For Hart, however, the internal view is not necessarily restricted to lawyers. He defines it in such broad terms that it can encompass many different kinds of perspectives of citizens on law. The external view seems to be restricted to those who cannot really reason with rules at all or, for their own purposes, see no point in doing so (see Chapter 4).

Another way of looking at the internal-external dichotomy is illustrated in the writings of Ronald Dworkin. Dworkin sees legal questions as essentially questions of interpretation. One can understand what the law is in a particular community only by becoming involved as a participant in its interpretation. Judges and lawyers, of course, are so involved, and – according to Dworkin – so also are legal philosophers. By contrast, on the 'outside' is anyone who rejects or avoids involvement in these interpretive debates which determine the content and meaning of law. So Dworkin puts matters very differently from Hart. In particular, because for Dworkin insiders – participants in the interpretive exercise – actually determine the law, knowledge of law is essentially restricted to these participants. They can and do include ordinary citizens, as Dworkin (1977: 214–5) makes clear, but it is hard to see that the citizen will usually be able to compete effectively in interpretive debate with the professional community of lawyers and judges on the meaning of laws. Consequently, Dworkin's image of the internal-external dichotomy seems to move us closer to a parallel distinction between legal professional insiders and other outsiders (see Chapter 6).

These brief remarks on areas of theory which will be considered in later chapters at least suggest that the internal-external dichotomy can refer to several different kinds of demarcation. It may focus on the distinction of 'legal' phenomena or characteristics from 'non-legal' ones in many contexts – for example, with regard to rules, systems of doctrine, types of reasoning, institutions or decisions. It may focus on the idea of a distinctive field of legal knowledge or understanding, separable from other knowledge-fields; or on the idea of a community of legal 'insiders', distinguishable from outsiders in some consistent way; or on the idea of a distinct professional practice of law, marking lawyers off from other occupational groups or from lay citizens.

Professionalisation and politics

The concern of normative legal theory with unity, system and the internal-external dichotomy can therefore be linked not only with practical problems in interpreting law in a legal system but also with characteristics or conditions of legal *professional* organisation.

A sociologist viewing a legal profession and its members' practices might emphasise the profession's collective claim to possess special professional skills or knowledge as central to its continuing assertion of distinct professional status (eg Larson 1977: 231). The clear marking out of what count as legal knowledge, legal reasoning and legal issues might be thought of as the identification of an autonomous professional field, a field of special legal expertise, belief in which helps to ground and maintain the lawyer's professional status.

Undoubtedly, this conscious identification of a distinctive legal realm in explicit terms is not something lawyers normally need to worry themselves with. It has often been taken for granted as has the idea of a secure, distinctive and autonomous professional knowledge and expertise centred on an identifiable field of law. Equally, the idea of this autonomous legal field might not necessarily be important to all forms of legal practice, or to professional practice in all times and places. There might be more important conditions for securing and maintaining status than the acceptance of the claim to possess special, distinctive expertise and knowledge. But this claim has been, and may still be, important in some contexts.

Subsequent chapters will attempt to show that legal philosophy's varied images of law as unified or systematic have sometimes been powerful. In particular conditions and at particular times in the development of modern Anglo-American law, they have helped to reinforce the idea of a special professional knowledge and expertise that underpins lawyers' claims of professional status.

Equally, attempts in legal philosophy to explain law's unity, distinctiveness or systematic character may have a wider *political* significance. They may suggest, for example, how far law can be considered separate from politics. Obviously, some provisional conception of 'the political' is needed if this issue is to be raised. Accordingly, for this limited purpose, we can take politics to refer to the struggle to acquire and make use of power (cf Weber 1948: 78), especially through established institutions and formal processes, and without resort to direct violence. On such a view, the most widely visible and extensively organised politics centres on what is thought of as government and the state.

Law is clearly related to the political. But what is the relationship? How far are legal reasoning and judicial decisions different and distinct from policy argument and political decisions? Are legal institutions special or specialised, as regards their functions, character or controlling values, in comparison with (other) political institutions associated with government, administration and the varied activities of the state? If legal reasoning, decisions and institutions have particular unifying, distinguishing features, should law be considered a distinct *aspect* of politics or government, or should the 'legal' be *counterposed* to the 'political'? How far are legal institutions 'independent' of political institutions?

These issues are not unimportant when questions about the legitimacy or authority of a legal system, its laws and institutions, are raised. They help to define law's place in society and the degree of autonomy which law can be considered to have. Hence, the demarcations of the sphere of law which normative legal theory offers in terms of unity, system, distinctiveness and the internal-external dichotomy, might be far from insignificant in influencing views on the scope, limits and interrelations of legal and political actions and issues.

The claim that there is an important relationship between normative legal theory's concerns with unity or system in law, on the one hand, and legal professionalism and politics, on the other, provides a framework in which to consider, in the following chapters, some influential currents of Anglo-American legal philosophy.

This framework makes it possible to look at this material in a less abstract manner than is usual and to keep in mind some concrete questions:

— What practical relevance in professional and political arenas of law does normative legal theory have?

— What insights do particular theories provide for legal and political practice?

— How can we best understand the significance of debates in this literature?

— How do they relate, if at all, to particular historical conditions, to changes in Anglo-American law itself during the period in which the literature has developed, and to changes in the situations of professional practice?

— What assumptions about the nature of societies are being made in these writings that purport to clarify the nature of law?

In this way a literature that often seems very abstract and ahistorical can be confronted with the specific historical conditions that have shaped it.

Legal philosophy in social and political context

Objections might be raised to this kind of emphasis in interpreting normative legal theory. Does this theory have no intellectual significance in its own right? Why emphasise its professional or political ramifications when its explicit concerns are not normally these but are frequently expressed in terms of general philosophical curiosity, or a desire to understand law better or to interpret it in broader terms than those of everyday legal practice?

An answer might begin by noting some well recognised difficulties in interpreting normative legal theory without seriously attempting to locate it in its specific historical contexts. The first of these difficulties is often acutely felt by undergraduate students of jurisprudence. There is often a sense that in the battle of abstract arguments no-one ever wins, and, further, that there are no reliable criteria by which one could recognise victory anyway. The disputes seem timeless, the issues never resolved. Philosophy in this state of affairs leads nowhere.

The jurist Tony Honoré wrote of one such fundamental theoretical dispute: 'Decade after decade Positivists and Natural lawyers face one another in the final of the World Cup .... Victory goes now to one side, now to the other, but the enthusiasm of players and spectators alike ensures that the losing side will take its revenge' (Honoré 1973: 1–2; cf Honoré 1987: 32–3). Perhaps this interminable dispute (which will surface in subsequent chapters) reflects issues of such supreme difficulty and significance that agreement can never be reached. But if so, should the debate continue? Or should it be restructured with its elements related to particular contexts, times and places, and the *causes* and *conditions* of disagreement made the centre of attention, rather than the abstract battles themselves? Otherwise, at legal philosophy's cup finals, perhaps 'the legal theorist can only cheer or jeer, [and] label his opponent a moral leper or a disingenuous romantic' (Honoré 1987: 33).

Second, there seems good reason to suggest that the timelessness of many debates in normative legal theory is not just due to the intractability of abstract issues. Clearly legal philosophy must relate at many points to what it treats as legal experience – that is, to lawyers', judges' and (to a lesser extent) citizens' encounters with, understanding and use of legal doctrine and legal processes.

Inevitably, legal philosophy's claims are tested for plausibility against this experience. Yet, still it seems that little progress is made. Perhaps there is something suspect about the 'testing' process itself, or about the way legal experience is being interpreted.

Intellectual fashions related to the changing social context of legal development may affect the assessment of some theories, as the legal scholar William Buckland claimed in discussing John Austin's mid-nineteenth century English jurisprudence. At the age of 85, Buckland noted how attitudes in the legal world to Austin had altered since Buckland's late nineteenth century youth: 'He was a religion; today he seems to be regarded rather as a disease' (Buckland 1949: 2). Do purely intellectual arguments account for such a revolution in attitudes? And are the issues that are argued over always the same? Sometimes, as in Austin's case, a particular part of the writer's theoretical enterprise – and not necessarily that which he considered most fundamental – is treated in most later commentary as if it were his entire theoretical contribution.[3] These matters require explanation, as do consistent misrepresentations of a jurist's ideas, where the misrepresentations are sufficiently widespread to assume the proportions of myth. Again, Austin has been claimed as a victim of this kind of misrepresentation (Morison 1982: 170–177).

Problems such as these are not unique to normative legal theory. They suggest, however, that, if we are to try to understand how legal philosophy has developed and how its debates and disputes have been formed and conducted, the answers cannot be found entirely in the logic of philosophical argument. They are, in part at least, located in the wider context of ideas and activities in which theories are developed and evaluated. Reasons have already been suggested in this chapter for considering that context to be, in part, professional and political. The approach to understanding legal philosophy adopted in this book, therefore, in no way denies the significance of the substantive content of legal philosophy's debates about the nature of law. It argues, however, that that content is to be understood not as timeless but as a response to conditions and problems existing at particular historical moments in Western legal development.

By its nature, normative legal theory tends to exclude systematic consideration of the social context of law. It does so in two ways. First, unlike the empirical legal theory which is a major concern of sociological studies of law, normative legal theory, as it has been defined in this chapter, attempts to explain the nature of law almost exclusively through philosophical analysis and clarification of the values, concepts, principles, rules and modes of reasoning entailed in or

---

3   See on this eg Moles 1987; Sugarman 1986: 43.

presupposed by legal doctrine. Empirical legal theory, by contrast, relies heavily on systematic empirical analysis of legal institutions in their social environment and historical context. These behavioural and contextual inquiries are largely absent from normative legal theory.

Second, as has been seen, normative legal theory's efforts to explain the nature of law tend to entail creating some sharp internal-external dichotomy marking the legal from the non-legal. What is attempted is often a rigorous clarification of the concept of law (or laws) and this seems best attained if the concept is analysed to show how the components of the legal can be explained and interpreted without reference to non-legal criteria: law thus becomes analytically separated from its contexts. It should be said immediately that in most normative legal theory no claim is made that this can be *totally* achieved. If it could be, the result would be a total 'closure' of the legal as a self-contained realm of knowledge.

Rather than close off law analytically, legal theory should interpret it in ever-widening perspectives. As the attempt to understand law as a social phenomenon, legal theory *should* require that the limited views of law held by different kinds of participants in legal processes – for example, lawyers, judges, legislators, administrators, various categories of citizens – be confronted with wider theoretical perspectives that can incorporate and transcend these partial views and thereby broaden understanding of the nature of law. But normative legal theory has usually been produced from the perspectives of very specific kinds of legal participants – especially lawyers. So it has often served systematically to express (rather than challenge) their outlook, to confirm and refine their view of the nature of law while being influenced by their special practical needs with regard to the ordering and interpretation of legal knowledge.

Normative legal theory is often said to be concerned to answer the question 'What is law?'. But if this were really so it would look at law from many different observational and participant perspectives: not just in terms of unity and system and the internal-external dichotomy, but also in terms of law's social origins and effects; not just philosophically but also sociologically; not just as concepts but also as behaviour (cf Chapter 7); not just in terms of logical structures and rational foundations of doctrine but also through rigorous historical study of legal institutions. It would seek to embrace and understand the widest possible variety of legal experience in the widest possible range of law's sites and settings.[4] Thus, it might be said that normative legal theory in

---

4   The recent beginnings of serious efforts to force normative legal theory to embrace these wider inquiries are discussed in Chapters 8 and 9, below.

general has not seriously addressed the question 'What is law?'. It has more typically asked how it is possible to organise, in an intellectually satisfactory way, the diverse doctrinal materials and modes of juristic thought associated with legal regulation. But, in trying to answer this question it has often *implied* much about the nature of law in society.

So this book is a discussion of normative legal theory which tries to adopt a broader view of what is required for an adequate legal theory than that which normative legal theory itself has often presupposed. To remain true to that broader view the discussion seeks consistently to read normative legal theory 'in context'; to suggest the wider implications of some of this literature and what has promoted or inspired it, as well as to discuss its major claims and arguments about law.

How should legal philosophy be interpreted contextually?

The method advocated here is related to those now widely adopted in several other intellectual fields. It emphasises what one writer on social theory calls 'the non-theoretical "conditions of existence" of theory' and the importance of studying its 'external and internal history'; that is, not only the intellectual development of theory but also the events and conditions that have provided the environment and stimulus for that development (Elliott 1987: 8, 9). Equally, if the word 'legal' is substituted for 'political', Quentin Skinner's influential interpretive outlook on political theory has much relevance for an understanding of normative legal theory: '[legal] life sets the main problems for the [legal] theorist, causing a certain range of issues to appear problematic, and a corresponding range of questions to become the leading subjects of debate'. This view does not entail that theoretical ideas are to be treated as 'a straightforward outcome of their social base', but they are certainly to be read in terms of their wider intellectual context (Skinner 1978: xi).

However, more is involved than just a reading of ideas in social and intellectual context (cf Stone 1964: 5). They are also to be considered as far as possible in terms of their origins and effects. This can be a highly complex matter but one that may be integral to understanding the development of theories and their interrelations. For example, it cannot be assumed that there is a direct line of intellectual development that threads its way as a kind of triumphal progress of increasing enlightenment as one major theoretical approach is refined and eventually gives way to a later one. As suggested earlier, ideas and theoretical orientations are adopted and discarded in ways that cannot simply be explained in terms of intellectual superiority or inferiority.

The great figures of Anglo-American normative legal theory do not necessarily appear as a succession of writers diligently building on their successors' work in a continuous intellectual endeavour.[5] The wheel is sometimes re-invented. Equally, central concerns of earlier writers are sometimes simply discarded or ignored by later ones. The impression is not one of continuity. To try to link in a historical development the contributions of a few major theorists is often like trying to see a route from one mountain top to the next without casting one's gaze down to the valleys between the mountains where the travellers' tracks actually wind. This is not to deny that leading theorists explicitly relate their ideas to what they take to be the ideas of their predecessors. It is merely to assert that these relationships are much more complex than they are often made to appear.

The sociologist Karl Mannheim well expressed some aspects of this problem in writing of what he termed the 'illusion of the immanent flow of ideas'.

'The works of the past appear to the scholar as pictures in a gallery – an array of discrete entities. The temptation to construe this array as an organic and continuous growth is well-nigh irresistible to those who confine their interest to the historical records of creative expression. What is ignored in this imagery are the intervening areas in which men act and react as social beings' (Mannheim 1956: 30).

Thus, while ideas have intellectual origins and may exert intellectual influence, these relationships and lines of development are mediated by *social* factors – the acts of people as 'social beings'. In relation to legal ideas, these factors may relate – as has been suggested earlier – to professional and political considerations.

This is not, however, a book about intellectual history, but about theories that are major components of contemporary Anglo-American jurisprudence or have provided essential foundations of it. So a concern with context is solely for its contribution to a more satisfactory understanding of the nature of these theories. How then, finally, is it possible to reconcile a concern for ideas, on their own terms, with a concern to interpret them in terms of their consequences and origins?

Earlier it was suggested that normative legal theory generally propounds a sharp dichotomy between the legal and what is external to law. The clear marking out of a realm of the distinctively legal is characteristic of much of this literature. And certainly, from particular points of view – especially those of the

---

5   Cf Collini, Winch and Burrow 1983: 4, noting parallel problems in interpreting the development of what is now seen as political science.

lawyer anxious to know clearly what rules and regulations are valid as *law* – it makes good sense to treat law *as if* it can be identified as a wholly distinct realm.

It will be suggested, however, in the following chapters that normative legal theory has had only partial success in demonstrating law's distinctiveness (and in making related claims about its unity or systematic character). To the extent that it has tried to portray a distinct field of specifically legal knowledge it has often failed to show the autonomy of that knowledge from sociological, political or moral conditions or ideas. Indeed, partly because 'the legal' can never be totally separated from such matters which normative legal theory often treats as external to law, the theory itself often implies interesting ideas about the very social context which it apparently seeks to exclude from its concerns.

It will be important to highlight these ideas in subsequent chapters since they often reveal basic presuppositions on which normative legal theory is based. And we shall see that the most important current debates around legal theory (discussed in Chapters 8 and 9) now strongly emphasise the complexities of law's social context, often with dramatic, disturbing effect for these basic presuppositions.

Any study of law must provisionally identify its subject-matter. Such a marking out does not, however, require the kind of exclusory definitions of law that some normative legal theory has defended. If a rigid internal-external dichotomy is hard to accept in considering law, a productive replacement for it is an approach that tries to understand *both* the insistent attempts to defend an autonomous realm of legal knowledge *and* the conditions that equally inspire and seem to defeat those attempts. Hence, normative legal theory itself needs to be looked at from the 'inside' and the 'outside' since each kind of viewpoint is inadequate without the other. The theory should be viewed on its own terms *and* in context.

Each contribution to normative legal theory should be assessed for the persuasiveness of its particular explanation of the legal reality it chooses to emphasise. Equally, it should be viewed as reflecting and expressing a climate of thought, a particular perspective on law which is sociologically interesting insofar as that perspective has been an influential or illuminating response to developments in law as a field of practice or experience. To see normative legal theory in context is to try to relocate its perspectives on legal reality in the perspective of a 'larger' social reality, of which both the activity of philosophising about law and the particular legal experience philosophised about form only a part.

The following chapters discuss particular contributions to theory which have powerfully influenced Anglo-American ideas about the nature of law in general. Their order of treatment seems to me to correspond roughly to a progressive unfolding of the difficulties normative legal theory has faced in attempting to portray, in changing conditions, the unity, structure or autonomy of modern law, especially in the Anglo-American world.

The theory of contract

Chapter 2

The theory of common law

Any serious attempt to understand the dominant ideas that have surrounded Anglo-American law must begin by confronting the great tradition of thought and practice summed up in the words 'common law'. The mere sound of them 'thrills the hearts of all good English lawyers', according to a noted French legal scholar (Levy-Ullmann 1935: 3). However that may be, the common law tradition is rooted in centuries of English history. It emphasises the centrality of the judge in the gradual development of law and the idea that this law is found in the distillation and continual restatement of legal doctrine through the decisions of courts.

Of course, modern law is predominantly *legislative* in origin. The production or refinement of legal doctrine by judges according to time-honoured common law approaches has been increasingly subordinated to other ways of making or stating law: for example in statutory provisions, many forms of delegated legislation, administrative regulations, directives, guidelines and codes of practice. Nevertheless, common law thought as a way of conceptualising law and reasoning with it still exerts a fundamental influence in those jurisdictions that have inherited its historical legacy. Comparative lawyers still refer to a common law 'family' of legal systems. And in English legal education and scholarship, the 'common law frame of mind continues to overshadow the way we teach, write and think about law. Its categories and assumptions are still the standard diet of most first-year law students; and they continue to organise law textbooks and case-books' (Sugarman 1986: 26).

This purpose of this chapter is to establish the general theoretical ideas about the nature of law and its place in society that underpin the common law tradition. By doing so it is possible to identify some of the earliest and, in a sense, most fundamental normative legal theory from which modern Anglo-American legal philosophy has built its images of law. The theoretical problems that common law thought poses have had to be confronted in this modern legal philosophy, and, as later chapters of this book will argue, they remain to haunt it. The place of the judge in the legal and political order; the relative significance of community values and political power as foundations of law; the relationship between interpretation of law and legislative activity – these are some of the fundamental problems which the theory of common law poses and attempts to answer.

Although this book is concerned with the relevance of legal theory for the situation of law in society today, common law thought cannot be understood without taking a long historical view. Its character has been shaped by centuries of English legal practice. Consequently the picture of common law's theoretical outlook presented in this chapter has to be pieced together from ideas and events widely scattered in time and place. Classical common law thought certainly does not present a kind of legal theory comparable with the explicit, systematic theories developed in modern legal philosophy. But, as will appear, it has provided conceptual building blocks for much later legal theory.

The character of common law thought

What is common law? A limited, but direct, historical answer might be that it consists of the rules and other doctrine developed gradually by the judges of the English royal courts as the foundation of their decisions, and added to over time by judges of those various jurisdictions recognising the authority of this accumulating doctrine. Henri Levy-Ullmann notes that the expression *la Commune ley* is used, from the end of the thirteenth century onwards in the ancient reports of legal arguments known as the Year Books, 'in contradistinction to terms denoting legal rules derived from sources other than those upon which the King's judges normally based their decisions' (Levy-Ullmann 1935: 4; cf Blackstone 1809 I: 68). So common law, as the law of common jurisdiction applied by these courts, was distinguished from various kinds of special or local law. Much later, the term came to refer frequently to judge-made or judge-declared law in contrast to legislation.

But how far is this common law an affair of *rules*? Here, as in many other inquiries about classical common law thought it is important to avoid imposing on the common law tradition modern interpretations reflecting views about law derived from wholly different theoretical premises (especially those to be discussed in Chapters 3 and 4). To write of common law as a system of rules (cf Neumann 1986: 244–245) is to impose just such an alien conception on it. A commentator remarks on the surface 'chaos' of judicial decisions, underlying which is, however, 'an internally coherent and unified body of rules'. But he goes on to note that 'principles' of law stand behind these rules and, in common law thought, are more important than them (Sugarman 1986: 26). In fact, however, it is probably more true to common law tradition to see its essence not in rules at all. 'To represent it as a systematic structure of rules is to distort it; it is to represent as static what is essentially dynamic and constantly shifting' (Postema 1986: 10). The idea of common law as *principles* of law seems more appropriate for capturing this shifting, dynamic character, if only because principles suggest flexible guidelines for legal decision-making rather than rules that control.

Much more lies behind all this than a terminological quibble. As Brian Simpson has noted, if common law's existence is thought of in terms of a set of rules 'it is in general the case that one cannot say what the common law is' (Simpson 1973: 16). This is because it is impossible to mark out conclusively such a rule-set corresponding to common law. While some continental writers have interpreted the common law as a 'complete, closed and logically consistent' system (Neumann 1986: 245), Simpson seems on much firmer ground in saying: 'As a system of legal thought the common law ... is inherently incomplete, vague and fluid' (1973: 17). Thus, for Jeremy Bentham, the great English legal reformer who insisted that law should be a matter of clear rules, common law was no more than 'mock law', 'sham law', 'quasi-law'. Judicial development of law exemplified 'power everywhere arbitrary' (quoted in Simpson 1973: 16). Issues of the clarity and completeness of law therefore arise.

Common law resides in judicial decisions rather than rules. But something stands behind the decisions, justifying them, guiding them and giving them authority as law. Common law's unity has been attributed to 'the fact that law is grounded in, and logically derived from, a handful of general principles; and that whole subject-areas such as contract or torts are distinguished by some common principles or elements which fix the boundaries of the subject. The exposition and systematisation of these general principles, and the techniques required to find and to apply them and the rules that they underpin, are largely what legal education and scholarship [in the common law environment] are all about' (Sugarman 1986: 26). Indeed, a long tradition of thought sees the classical essence of common law in broad legal guidelines, as much concerned with how to reach proper judicial decisions as with their specific content. On this view it is best seen as 'a method of legal thinking' (Cohen 1933: 333) for deciding disputes and providing 'useful, just and flexible solutions to individual cases' (Lobban 1991: 15), rather than an integrated, definable body of doctrine. At the end of the nineteenth century, A V Dicey, using terms similar to those of the eminent eighteenth century jurist William Blackstone (cf Blackstone 1809 I: 67), called common law a 'mass of custom, tradition or judge-made maxims' (Dicey 1959: 23–24).

Maxims of common law symbolised the broad guidelines which could be considered to underlie and loosely direct individual decisions. One writer examining a crucial period of common law development in the first half of the seventeenth century remarks that maxims 'were the essential core of the common law, woven so closely into the fabric of English life that they could never be ignored with impunity'; as 'high level general principles or fundamental points of the law' they were used in interpreting past judicial decisions – evaluating their significance as precedents to apply to new cases (Sommerville 1999: 89–90). Maxims, indeed, were far more important than the precedents themselves. In modern times, as legal doctrine became more detailed and complex, these maxims lost their force and now have little practical significance. But they point to the enduring idea that the heart of common law is not in decisions or rules distilled from them but in broad notions, difficult to unify or systematise, which may, indeed, in some way be 'woven into the fabric of life'.

Because many of these notions are very hard to pin down, the unifying element of common law often seems mystical. Sometimes in classical common law thought it is portrayed as a vague historical destiny, a working out in history of an obscure but immanent logic of the law, or a kind of superhuman wisdom reflected in the collective work of the common law judges throughout the centuries but impossible for any single person to possess. Thus, for Blackstone, law is 'frought with the accumulated wisdom of ages' (quoted in Postema 1986: 63). And Chief Justice Coke, early in the seventeenth century, wrote:

> 'we are but of yesterday ... our days upon the earth are but as a shadow in respect of the old ancient days and times past, wherein the laws have been by the wisdom of the most excellent men, in many successions of ages, by long and continual experience ... refined, which no one man (being of so short a time) albeit he had in his head the wisdom of all the men in the world, in any one age could ever have effected or attained unto. And therefore ... no man ought to take upon him to be wiser than the laws'.[1]

The common law judge

Though such statements date from long ago they express honestly and directly a set of assumptions that underpin the classical conception of common law

---

1   *Calvin's Case* (1608) 7 Co Rep 1, 3.

judging. According to the declaratory doctrine of common law, judges do not make law.[2] They are, in Blackstone's words, 'the depositories of the laws, the living oracles, who must decide in all cases of doubt' (Blackstone 1809 I: 69). The authority of law is seen as a traditional authority.

Judges express a part of the total, immanent wisdom of law which is assumed to be already existent before their decision. The judge works from within the law which is 'the repository of the experience of the community over the ages' (Postema 1986: 32). Thus, even though he may reach a decision on a legal problem never before addressed by a common law court, he does so not as an original author of new legal ideas but as a representative of a collective wisdom greater than his own. He interprets and applies the law but does not create it, for the law has no individual authors. It is the product of the community grounded in its history. Judicial decisions, according to Matthew Hale writing in the seventeenth century, do not make law 'for that only the king and parliament can do' but are *evidence* of law, and 'though such decisions are less than a law, yet they are a greater evidence thereof than the opinion of any private persons, as such, whosoever' (quoted in Levy-Ullmann 1935: 56). Thus the judge is spokesperson for the community about its law, but a particularly authoritative spokesperson.

Such a viewpoint could lead to apparently radical conclusions. A judge could mistake the law (Postema 1986: 9–11; 194–195). Blackstone (1809 I: 70) writes: 'The doctrine of the law then is this: that precedents and rules must be followed, unless flatly absurd or unjust'. But law (wiser than any individual) is the perfection of reason, so an unjust or absurd decision cannot be declaratory of the law. It is not bad law but, in Blackstone's view, no law at all. It follows that the doctrine of precedent – the doctrine that judges must treat as binding on them the essential legal grounds of decision adopted in similar cases previously decided in courts of higher or perhaps equal status – is complex in classical common law thought. It is also perhaps much more flexible than it is typically portrayed as being (Lobban 1991: 82–89).

The judge must attach great weight to previous decisions, not only for practical and political reasons (to maintain sufficient certainty in legal doctrine and to avoid usurping the legislative function) but also for theoretical reasons. Those decisions provide, in general, the best available evidence of the collective wisdom of the common law. Judges must subordinate their own individual reasoning and values to those enshrined in the law. On the other hand, the reasoning and values of the law are greater not only than those of the presently deciding judges, but also of any of the precedent-creating judges of the past.

---

2   See eg per Lord Esher MR in *Willis v Baddeley* [1892] 2 QB 324, 326.

Hence the theory of common law does not dictate a slavish adherence to precedent. Even where prior judicial decisions are thought to state accurately the common law, a later judge is bound not by those decisions but by the principles implicit or explicit in them (Postema 1986: 194–195). Further, while classical common law thought denies that judges are creative as lawmakers, they are not merely passive as lawfinders (Levy-Ullmann 1935: 54). Judges are the privileged representatives of the community, entrusted with its collective legal wisdom and authorised to draw on it constructively to find solutions to novel issues raised before the court.

Can common law thought explain legal development?

A paradox lies at the heart of classical common law thought. Common law as the embodiment of ancient wisdom is revealed by judges, not created by them. It is, therefore, always already existent. Yet obviously it develops with the accumulation, reinterpretation and restatement of precedents and the adjustment of legal doctrine to new circumstances reflected in the never-ending succession of cases brought before courts (cf Pocock 1957: 36–37). How is the evolution of law explained in this conception? And why is it not possible to assert openly that judges *make* law, even if only within strict limits which would make them clearly subordinate to recognised legislators, such as (in the context of English history) a parliament or monarch?

The formal answer to this last question is that law embodies an ancient wisdom which may, according to some conceptions of common law, be considered timeless or, according to others, be seen as continually evolving through collective experience. On either view judges can only reflect this wisdom and not change it. In some classical common law thought the claim of timelessness is taken to fantastic lengths. Influential seventeenth century lawyers, such as Edward Coke, 'argued on the flimsiest evidence that the common laws, including their most detailed procedural provisions, dated from the earliest times': even Magna Carta was treated as declaring ancient law, confirming and making enforceable rights that had long existed (Sommerville 1999: 85, 94). Coke claimed that, in all its major parts, the law and constitution had remained unchanged since the Saxon era and even before (Postema 1986: 19). These strange views were always controversial but the reason for asserting them at times when the authority of common law was seriously challenged (as in the early seventeenth century) is not hard to see. This authority was traditional in nature. Rooting it in a distant or even mythical past emphasised that it was not derived from the present power of any monarch or other political authority.

The authority or legitimacy of common law as a legal order entitled to the highest respect was seen as residing not in the political system but in the community. If a judge *made* law this could only be as an exercise of political power. Deliberate lawmaking would be a political act. But according to common law theory, judges' authority is not as political decision-makers (certainly not as delegates of the king or parliament) but as representatives of the community. Hence they have authority only to *state* the community's law, not to impose law upon the community as if they were political rulers or the servants of such rulers. And the community is to be understood here as something uniting past and present, extending back through innumerable past generations as well as encompassing the present one.

Clearly, if the term 'community' were to be defined rigorously in this context it would be necessary to ask who exactly is in this community and what is its nature. It would also be necessary to consider the compatibility of this communitarian conception of law with the fact that the judges referred to here are judges of the *royal* courts, the instruments of a centralised justice promoted by kings. But these issues are typically absent from classical common law thought. So, for Coke, the common law is simply 'the most ancient and best inheritance that the subjects of this realm have' (quoted in Sommerville 1999: 99).

The usual way of conceptualising this apparently unchanging inheritance in classical common law thought is as *custom*. As Brian Simpson remarks, it is odd nowadays to think of law in this way because lawyers are used to treating this law as set in place by the judges. But this is another example of the tendency to impose alien modern theoretical conceptions on common law (Simpson 1973: 18). Just as common law is not strictly to be thought of, in the classical conception, as rules, neither is it decisions. To term it 'a residue of immutable custom' (Sugarman 1986: 40) is more accurate, but does not confront the fact that common law thought embraces complex notions explaining and justifying past practices (not just stating them as custom) and providing guidance for future conduct. Equally common law thought allows the development of new doctrines and ideas, so has a dynamism which custom may lack. Because of these characteristics Simpson (1973: 20) prefers to term common law customary law, rather than custom. But this does not solve the theoretical problem of its development. Customary law still has the character of custom, looking to the past rather than guiding the future. It states established practice rather than developing legal doctrine to meet changing times.

The problem is not that custom is changeless: there is no reason why it cannot be considered to change over time, so law as an expression of custom can also change. The problem is that common law thought itself cannot really address this change or explain it as a *legal* process. The mechanisms of change are in society (or the community). Law changes solely through the mysterious processes by which custom changes. To explain or even recognise explicitly processes of legal change, classical common law thought would need some kind of sociological insight. But the common lawyers were hardly sociologists. Common law thought predated any modern social science and, in any event, its practical case-by-case view of legal development would have found little room for any explicit general theory of social or cultural change. So classical common law thought emphasised continuity (which it could interpret legally in terms of precedents and principles), rather than change (for which it could find no specifically legal criteria of evaluation).

Historically, the conundrum of law as changeless yet always changing was avoided by devices made possible by cultural conditions. Common law was considered to be unwritten. Blackstone (1809 I: 67), following Hale, distinguished 'the common law, or *lex non scripta* of this kingdom' from the written law of Acts of Parliament. Even though this unwritten law was eventually reported in written form, the fact that the law itself was still considered unwritten presumably allowed individual innovation to be forgotten, subsumed in the image of a changeless collective legal knowledge. As the anthropologist Jack Goody has noted about societies lacking writing, it is not that the creative element is absent in them or that 'a mysterious collective authorship, closely in touch with the collective consciousness, does what individuals do in literate cultures. It is rather that the individual signature is always getting rubbed out in the process of generative transmission' (Goody 1977: 27). Certainly common law's unwritten character was seen as one of its strengths, making possible 'a flexible system which had developed along with the English people itself' (Sommerville 1999: 86).

In the early ages of common law the lack of writing allowed a convenient amnesia. Blackstone wrote in the eighteenth century that 'in our law the goodness of a custom depends upon its having been used time out of mind; or, in the solemnity of our legal phrase, time whereof the memory of man runneth not to the contrary. This it is that gives its weight and authority' (Blackstone 1809 I: 67). The traditional authority of common law required that its customs be shrouded in antiquity. But in the Middle Ages two or three lifetimes would be enough to make a principle of common law immemorial (Pocock 1957: 37); 'in ten or twenty years a custom was of long standing; in forty years it was "age-old"' (Gough 1955: 14). Later the flexibility of memory was less satisfactory. When, in the seventeenth century, lawyers such as Coke found it necessary to assert with the greatest possible force the traditional authority of common law against the king, the 'idea of the immemorial ... took on an absolute colouring ... It ceased to be a convenient fiction and was heatedly asserted as literal historical truth' (Pocock 1957: 37).

It can easily be seen, therefore, that common law thought eventually backed itself into a corner. First, the idea that the law was unwritten gradually became a mere fiction as the common law was recorded – preserved, explained and digested in written form in public records, law reports and 'the authoritative writings of the venerable sages of the law' (Maine 1861: 8; cf Blackstone 1809 I: 73). Second, the purely traditional authority of the law eventually demanded an utterly unrealistic claim of unbroken continuity from ancient times. And, finally, the declaratory theory of common law judging had to be maintained in the face of abundant evidence of conscious judicial innovation in legal doctrine (cf Levy-Ullmann 1935: 53).

Three responses to this situation were possible. One was to declare that common law possessed no authority by which it could develop further. Legal innovation could only come through Acts of Parliament or other legislative acts. Thus, as one judge put the matter, 'It is in my opinion impossible for us now to create any new doctrine of common law'.[3]

A second response was to embrace openly the idea that judges sometimes make law, discard all fictions and go on to ask serious questions as to *how* and under what conditions they should make it. But this pragmatic approach also involved discarding all the standard assumptions underpinning the authority and legitimacy of common law. Traditional authority would need to be replaced with something else – perhaps the charismatic authority of individual wise judges, a conception of delegated political power (see Chapter 3) or, as in the United States, the authority of a specific constitutional document providing the ultimate foundation of legal and judicial systems (Cotterrell 1992: 229–230). In any event, such a new foundation of judicial authority, if it could be found, would be something different from that presupposed in classical common law thought.

A third solution was to discard the notion of common law as custom and the formal idea of an unchanging ancient law, and to emphasise instead the complex conception of the judge as spokesperson for the community – neither individual creator of law nor mere restator of ancient truths, but representative of an evolving collective legal consciousness.[4] As will appear later, this view of common law thought, which maintains what might be considered fundamental

---

3 Per Farwell LJ in *Baylis v Bishop of London* [1913] 1 Ch 127, 137. Cf *Mirehouse v Rennell* (1833) 1 Cl & F 527, 546 (per Parke J).
4 Cf Hale's interpretation of the evolution of common law discussed in Postema 1986: 19–27.

elements in it but avoids the *cul-de-sac* of an appeal to custom, has been reflected in various forms of modern legal philosophy. It is restated in the historical jurisprudence to be discussed later in this chapter, and reworked in various ways in the writings of certain modern authors, such as Roscoe Pound and Ronald Dworkin, considered in Chapter 6.

Common law and legislation

So far legislation – the deliberate creation of new law by a formal law-making body such as Parliament – has received hardly any mention in this discussion. But in classical common law thought the relationship between legislation and the law-finding of the courts had to be settled not just as a practical and political matter, but as a theoretical one. How should legislation be viewed from the standpoint of common law theory? Nowadays, English lawyers generally have no doubt that in a conflict between statute law and judge-determined law, the former prevails over the latter. It is of superior legal authority. Equally, most lawyers (and probably most non-lawyers) have no doubt that judges in the higher courts frequently make law through their decisions, whatever classical common law theory may suggest. But there is much doubt as to how far judges are justified in doing so. We have considered the explanation of judicial authority which classical common law thought gives. How does it explain the relationship between legislation and common law?

In English history, statutes only gradually emerged as something clearly distinct from common law. In medieval times, legal opinion treated them as performing 'in a more explicit and general way, the same task which occupied the judiciary' (Postema 1986: 15) – stating customary common law. Early statute law could be regarded as part of common law (Postema 1986: 24). In an influential study, Charles McIlwain described the English parliament of the Middle Ages as a court, with its statutes considered as no more than affirmations of common law (McIlwain 1910: ch 3; Levy-Ullmann 1935: 232–233). Some of McIlwain's claims may be exaggerated (Gough 1955: ch 1) but the general picture of a slow historical separation of statute and common law and a gradual emergence of the idea of deliberate law creation by a formal body seems clear.

Concern here is not with historical events but with strands of theory related to them. As such, it is possible to see a common law theory of legislation emerging. In the seventeenth century, in the great struggle between royal and parliamentary power which culminated in the English Civil War and Revolution and its consequences, common lawyers 'elevated Parliament to a position of near-sovereignty, while at the same time insisting that unwritten custom was superior to statute law' (Sommerville 1999: 90–91).

As Parliament's supremacy in law creation was affirmed, common law thought treated the authority to enact statutes as, itself, grounded in common law. It followed that Parliament could not abolish the whole of the common law without abolishing itself (Sommerville 1999: 91), although it could obviously overrule, with legal if not necessarily moral force, particular principles of common law or decisions founded on them. So, although an Act of Parliament was 'the exercise of the highest authority that this kingdom acknowledges upon earth' (Blackstone quoted in Manchester 1980: 33), common law authority, in a sense, 'trumped' that of Parliament. Parliamentary supremacy over common law was said to be *given by* common law. Legislation could be thought of as an island or archipelago in a sea of common law (Postema 1986: 18).

This suggests why it remained possible in common law thought up to modern times to treat legislation as somehow peripheral to common law despite the ever-increasing bulk of enactments. Similarly, such a view justified a restrictive approach to legislation, which should be interpreted so that it could be integrated into the common law (Postema 1986: 17), at least where ambiguity or uncertainty of legislative meaning allowed this.

This view of legislation could hardly be satisfactory in modern times and always entailed inconsistencies. It certainly did not mean that judges were superior to Parliament (Blackstone 1809 I: 91; Levy-Ullmann 1935: 236–237). In Coke's era, for example, the threat of royal pressure on the judges would have made any such doctrine dangerous to the image of law as the defence of the subject's liberties (Sommerville 1999: 92). In any case, common law thought had to recognise that from early times 'novel law' in Acts of Parliament, ordinances, provisions and proclamations 'defeated' common law (Gough 1955: 14–15).

It seems that the common law outlook could not come to terms with modern legislation in a realistic way. It offered a powerful defence of the jurisdiction of common law judges as autonomous, while fully recognising the supremacy of Parliament. It also explained judges' role in interpreting legislation as derived from their position as declarers of the community's law, not as the servants of a political legislator. But it failed to provide an adequate theory of the political authority underlying legislation. It remained firmly rooted in a social world predating the modern legislative state. Conversely, as will appear in the following chapters, the theories that challenged common law thought and provided powerful justification for state law-making often remained ambiguous or unsatisfactory in their explanation of the sources of judicial authority. The idea of judicial authority rooted in community remains perhaps the strongest, most vibrant, contribution of common law thought. Its explanations of political law-making through legislation remain perhaps its weakest, flimsiest elements.

The political and social environment

So far in this chapter, common law thought has been presented merely as a set of abstract conceptions of law's attributes. But how does common law thought view the social and political environment of law? How might it help to define the lawyer's place in society and the relationship between law and politics? Since no attempt is being made here to present any part of the history of common law thought as such, mention of a few general contextual considerations may be sufficient to illustrate further dimensions of what has been sketched here as the classical theory of common law.

Legal knowledge and community

Common law thought has no rigorously developed conception of the nature of law's social environment. The term 'community' captures best the vague assumptions about the nature of this social setting that are presupposed in common law thought. Yet, although law is assumed to be deeply rooted in this environment and to derive essential meaning from it, the nature of the environment remains largely unelaborated. Gerald Postema sees the common law image of community as entailing a 'broad consensus and an already constituted social unity', confirmed and maintained by common law decisions but not created by them (Postema 1986: 19). But almost the only thing that can be said with certainty about social life in common law terms is that law is an *aspect* of it, inseparable from the rest.

The American jurist James Carter probably best expresses this in asserting that:

> 'Law, Custom, Conduct, Life – different names for almost the same thing – true names for different aspects of the same thing – are so inseparably blended together that one cannot even be thought of without the other. No improvement can be effected in one without improving the other, and no retrogression can take place in one without a corresponding decline in the other' (Carter 1907: 320; cf Hale quoted in Postema 1986: 73).

The common lawyers saw society through the lens of law. In a sense, society *was* the structure of relations, customs, claims and obligations expressed in legal knowledge.

But what kind of knowledge is law? In the classical conception common law is, above all, rational, excelling all other human laws in rationality (Sommerville 1999: 84, 88–91). But there are at least two conceptions of rationality at work here. Common law entailed a kind of particularistic analogical reasoning making it possible to link cases and compare precedents (Postema 1986: 31), so it could tolerate broad illogicalities arising out of particular analogical linkages of ideas or cases. Equally, however, common law is, for Blackstone, 'a rational science' of 'general and extensive principles' (Blackstone 1809 I: 2, II: 425). Therefore, such a view might permit illogicalities of detail in an overall framework of broad principle.[5] Consequently, reason could serve opposite roles in linking detailed particularities or broad tendencies in legal thought.

There is, thus, no simple key to unlock the assumed rationality of common law. In particular, there is no key which an untrained person could use. If law belongs to the community it is, nevertheless, inaccessible to most members of the community, at least in detail. According to common law thought, law is not natural reason but refined or *artificial* reason which, as Coke asserted, 'requires long study and experience, before that a man can attain to the cognisance of it'.[6] Although law is reason, reason alone will not give mastery of it. Experience of the practice of law (such as the common law judge possesses) is also essential (Postema 1986: 33, interpreting Hale), and apprenticeship is the most appropriate means of acquiring this. Thus, obviously, actual knowledge of law is denied to the community at large. This knowledge is necessarily – by its nature – the monopoly of lawyers, who appear as the community's absolutely indispensable representatives in stating, interpreting and applying its law.

The point is strengthened by aspects of the linguistic history of common law. 'Legal ideas were transmitted largely orally, and even the available literary sources were, as late as the seventeenth century, written in a special and partly private language' (Simpson 1973: 21). After the Norman conquest the language of the English common law courts became Norman French and then a unique 'Franco-English jargon', long maintained as such by the lawyers for documents, despite efforts to change the language to English by statute (Levy-Ullmann 1935: 123–124). Only in 1731 was there finally a conclusive enactment making English, rather than Latin or French, the exclusive language of court proceedings, requiring records to be made in legible writing rather than obscure 'court hand', and forbidding abbreviation of words.[7]

There is, therefore, an apparently profound inconsistency between, on the one hand, the thoroughly esoteric form in which legal knowledge existed and, on the other, the way classical common law thought understood law as having 'developed along with the English people itself' (Sommerville 1999: 86) or as 'a part of the lives of men' (Holmes 1897: 1005). The assumed link between law

---

5   Cf Lord Devlin's remarks in *Hedley Byrne & Co Ltd v Heller & Partners Ltd* [1964] AC 465, 516.

6   *Prohibitions del Roy* (1608) 12 Co Rep 63, 65. Cf Sommerville 1999: 84, 89.

7   Stat 4 Geo II, c 26.

and community has a primarily *symbolic* significance in common law thought, wholly different from any modern notions of participation or popular justice.

It would be wrong to characterise common law knowledge as 'professional knowledge' since the 'artificial reason' of the law predates the emergence of an organised legal profession in any modern sense. Nevertheless, the classical common law conception of law was undoubtedly admirably suited for the promotion of the collective status of lawyers as a group. On the one hand, the implied deep community roots of law suggested that legal knowledge was a central part of the collective wisdom of society. It was therefore of supreme social significance and the possessor of it spoke with obvious authority. On the other hand, what the historian Maitland called the 'occult science' of law (Maitland 1893: 483) was defined in such a way that no-one but legal practitioners could have access to it. Although all these claims about the community roots of common law and about the inevitable artificiality of its reason could be (and were) challenged at various times, their forceful advocacy served very well the interests of common lawyers as a group.

Common law thought and political authority

The relationship between law and politics in classical common law thought derives directly from the ambiguous relationship between law and community discussed above. Again, it will be sufficient to illustrate some aspects of the political significance of common law thought by taking a few themes from a very complex history.

How does common law thought view the political realm? Essentially, it finds great difficulty in recognising such a realm in any modern sense. English common law still has no definite and elaborated concept of the state (Maitland 1901; cf Buckland 1949: ch 7) and refers instead to the Crown. Originating in a social order in which political authority could be conceptualised as a set of private property rights held by monarchs or their subordinates (Cohen 1933: 41ff), common law thought recognised royal authority, and later parliamentary authority, as given by common law or by some fundamental principles of reason underlying it. Maitland made great play of the fact that, when the king died, 'we see all the wheels of the State stopping or even running backwards' (for example, litigation stopped and had to be restarted; military commissions had to be renewed) since there was no coherent general conception of a continuing abstract political authority (Maitland 1901: 253; cf Stoljar 1958: 27–30). Today such problems are of merely historical interest. The inadequacies of common law conceptions were marginalised long ago by legal solutions reflecting other theoretical views of law and politics, or by purely pragmatic legal developments. But they illustrate again the fact that common law thought cannot easily come to terms with the concept of the modern legislative and administrative state with its complex network of intersecting and self-renewing authorities.

Classical common law thought did not really produce a theory of the relationship of law and politics either. In the great political struggles of the seventeenth century in which common lawyers, such as Coke, sought to protect the authority of common law against the claims of monarch and parliament, the main theoretical effort was, it seems, to elaborate and extend common law's authority claims. Thus, if the roots of its authority are in an intertwining of reason and tradition, both of these elements were elevated or exaggerated in ways that emphasise their centrality for any theory of common law, and the fact that they are entirely independent of political authority.

Common law's reason was often claimed to be derived from God's reason (Sommerville 1999: 87–88). Certainly, as has been noted earlier, it was considered to transcend the reason of individuals, however wise. Thus a fundamental *natural law of reason* was held to inform common law, allowing highly controversial claims to be made in a few famous seventeenth century cases that 'when an Act of Parliament is against common right and reason, or repugnant, or impossible to be performed, the common law will control it, and adjudge such act to be void'.[8]

On the other hand, in the same period, the appeal to traditional authority became, in the doctrine of the Ancient Constitution, the mythical idea that English common law remained essentially unchanged since a time that predated all relevant *political* authorities and so had a transcendent authority unaffected by political change. Some common lawyers even denied that there had been a military conquest in 1066 that entailed any legal discontinuity. 'To admit a conquest was to admit an indelible stain of sovereignty upon the English constitution' (Pocock 1957: 53).

Thus, with what now seem bizarre claims about the authority of transcendent natural reason and the significance of myths about the sources of common law in history, common lawyers fought to maintain the independent force of common law at a time when already it was preparing to give way to types of authority rooted in political sources which it could not theoretically comprehend.

---

8   *Dr Bonham's Case* (1610) 8 Co Rep 114, 118 (per Coke CJ). See also *Calvin's Case* (1608) 7 Co Rep 1; *Day v Savadge* (1615) Hob 85; *City of London v Wood* (1701) 12 Mod 669. And see further Chapter 5, below, pp 116–117.

Savigny: a theory for common law?

The discussion so far should suggest that the legacy of classical common law thought in itself is seriously inadequate to provide a convincing legal theory. In particular, although the nature of law is seen as rooted in the nature of society, no explicit conception of society or social development exists in common law thought. One consequence is that, insofar as law is considered to be customary, it becomes very difficult to explain or even clearly identify the processes of legal development in common law. Second, the relationship between judge-declared law and legislation – the dominant source of law in modern Western societies – remains unclear. Third, the sources of law's authority frequently seem mystical: grounded in myths about history or in claims, unsupported by rigorous argument, about natural reason.

In the nineteenth century, various types of legal philosophy developed to try to address, in an explicitly elaborated legal theory, the conditions of law in the modern state, conditions which common law thought so obviously could not properly encompass. Some of these new theories reflected ideas that had been in currency long before, but all had to take account of obvious changes in the character of law and legal institutions – and especially the increasing dominance of legislation as a source of law.

The rest of this chapter will be concerned with certain theories from this period that defend and elaborate conceptions of law similar in important respects to the conception suggested in classical common law thought. In an age of extensive, deliberate law-making by political authorities aimed at reshaping society or its legal traditions, the legal philosophy that came to be known as *historical jurisprudence* can be seen as partly filling the need for a theoretical defence of common law methods. Indeed, the following discussion will argue that, today, in the Anglo-American context, the most fruitful way of interpreting historical jurisprudence in relation to normative legal theory is in these terms. But, as will appear, the scope of the rich, complex literature of historical jurisprudence extends far beyond Anglo-American common law.

The dominant original influence in historical jurisprudence is usually traced to the Prussian jurist and statesman Friedrich Carl von Savigny. Writing at the beginning of the nineteenth century, Savigny opposed the political movement of the time pressing for the codification of the law of the German states. Many of those favouring codification saw it as an instrument to promote German political unity. However, the modern idea of codification as an attempt to produce a complete statement of fundamental principles of law in some systematic arrangement suggests a culmination of legal development, the result of which can be captured in perfected, rationally elaborated legal forms and structures.

For Savigny, this idea denies the character of law as spontaneously and continually evolving with the culture, the whole way of life, of a people (*Volk*). The optimum time for codification of law would be at the peak of cultural development, but then such a fixing of law in final form would be unnecessary when law and culture are vibrant and dynamic. Codification would merely benefit 'a succeeding and less fortunate age, as we lay up provisions for winter' and such foresight is rare (Savigny 1831: 43). So, in Savigny's view, codes are usually made at the wrong historical moments: either in early phases of cultural development when legal development is lively but technical skill in distilling broad concepts and principles from this changing law is likely to be lacking, or in a time of cultural decline, as with Emperor Justinian's great codification of Roman law in the sixth century AD. Savigny notes, of the efforts of this period, that when 'all intellectual life was dead the wrecks of better times were collected to supply the demand of the moment' (1831: 51).

Immediately, these comments suggest a view of law that emphasises the pervasiveness of change and ties legal development firmly to cultural evolution. Behind all this are ideas close to those that underpin classical common law thought, although Savigny writes in a different context. Law is seen as an aspect of social life, not something distinct from other social phenomena. For Savigny, law 'has no self-dependent existence ... its essence is the life of man itself' viewed from a certain standpoint (1831: 46). In place of the ancient wisdom, rooted in a perhaps mythical past, that grounds and guides common law, Savigny makes 'the common consciousness of the people' (*Volksgeist*) the 'seat of law' (1831: 28). His descriptions of it suggest an almost exact parallel with the elusive ideas of deep communal sources of reason and authority, spanning the centuries, presupposed in classical common law thought. 'That which binds them into one whole is the common conviction of the people, the kindred consciousness of an inward necessity, excluding all notion of an accidental and arbitrary origin' (1831: 24).

Because Savigny has no hesitation about describing culture explicitly in evolutionary terms, his picture of law also is one of continuous evolution. As language develops spontaneously by uncontrolled communal processes, so law develops 'by internal silently operating powers, not by the arbitrary will of a lawgiver' (1831: 30). As in classical common law thought, legal ideas are assumed to have no individual authors. They are a wholly collective product. Legislation, as deliberate lawmaking, is treated as subordinate to the demands of the common consciousness.

Although much of the common lawyer's mystical conception of law's origins remains in this theory, a far more explicit statement of the stages of cultural change is offered and, with it, a more definite view of the role of legislation and the state in aiding the spontaneous processes of legal development. Savigny was writing at the beginning of a new age in which legislation would have a specific vocation. Although, like the common lawyers, he sees law's primary form as custom, he also recognises that modern law cannot be thought of in such terms.

He notices at least some simple sociological considerations regarding social development. With the development of societies to a certain level of complexity, social classes emerge and society fragments into different interest groups (cf Savigny 1831: 28; 1867: 14, 36). One might imagine that this recognition would lead Savigny to doubt whether a common consciousness could continue to co-exist with such social divisions. However, it leads him only to note the special role which lawyers now assume, and some special tasks of legislation. The common consciousness still exists but it is harder to focus it to produce new law directly. As the common lawyers distinguished natural reason from the artificial reason of law, so Savigny notes that law 'perfects its language, takes a scientific direction' and 'devolves upon the jurists, who thus, in this department, represent the community'. Thus it becomes 'artificial and complex' and leads a twofold existence as part of community life and also as the specialised knowledge of lawyers (Savigny 1831: 28; 1867: 36–40). This idea closely parallels the ambiguous common law view of law's relationship with community. For Savigny, as for the common lawyers, it is vital to affirm that the link with community is not broken, however complex law becomes, for where else is the source of law's utility and authority to be found?

As regards legislation, its task is explained by Savigny, in terms reminiscent of Blackstone, as that of putting settled law into systematic form and clarifying law in transitional phases where new legal principles reflecting the developing common consciousness are emerging but not yet crystallised (Savigny 1831: 33, 152–153; cf Blackstone 1809 I: 86–87). There is an important difference from classical common law ideas, however, in Savigny's recognition that legislation eventually becomes *central* to the task of developing the law, not peripheral and supplementary as it often seems to be in common law thought. The appropriate scope of legislative activity depends on the stage of development of culture that has been reached. Cultures rise, flourish and then decline. In some late phases of cultural development conditions 'are no longer propitious to the creation of law by the general consciousness of a people. In this case this activity, in all cases indispensable, will in great measure of itself devolve upon legislation' (Savigny 1867: 34). It seems to be implied, therefore, that the eventual dominance of legislation as a legal form is inevitable – though hardly to be taken as a sign of cultural vitality.

A consequence of this more definite view of the eventual pervasiveness of legislation is that Savigny is forced to make explicit the strange consequences of treating the authority of legislation as deriving from the same communal and traditional sources as other legal authority – such as, particularly, that of the law-declaring judge. The legislator must *stand in the centre* of the people or nation 'so that he concentrates in himself their spirit, feelings, needs, so that we have to regard him as the true representative of the spirit of the people' (1867: 32). This awkward and unreal formulation probably points not so much to a democratic assembly with a popular mandate as to an enlightened monarch with the common touch.

Savigny's need to address directly the legislative role at the dawn of the age of modern legal codes does, however, lead him finally to a different emphasis from that of classical common law thought. In the latter, law originated in community life and became the esoteric knowledge of lawyers as an independent occupational group, in which it found its ultimate expression. For Savigny, writing in a German context in which lawyers lacked the political independence and occupational autonomy of the common lawyers, the development could not realistically be seen to stop there. The most influential legal scholars were the university jurists. The threat of what Savigny saw as the legislative megalomania of codification hung over the Germanic 'common law' (*Gemeines Recht*) of his time (a mixture of customary law and adopted principles of Roman law). In these circumstances he felt the need to recognise legislators as central to future legal development in partnership with jurists. But, like the English common lawyers, he defines the scope of legislative authority in cultural, not political terms. In this way the power of the state to impose law is restricted by a clear obligation on the lawmaker to act as representative of the community – in Savigny's term, the *Volk*.

Savigny's writings had much influence on British and American legal scholarship in the nineteenth century, especially since the spectre of codification, the symbol of rational legislative law-making dominant over judicial law-finding, arose to challenge common law thought in both countries. Because he offers a more explicit theory of cultural development than did the common lawyers, he supplies a conception of legal development largely lacking in common law thought. Equally, the role of legislation is addressed directly in terms that clearly (if reluctantly) recognise its modern importance. But there is no hint that culture itself might be a complex, fragmented phenomenon; that cultural development might vary immensely in different societies and that cultural change itself has causes requiring explanation. Savigny's legal theory makes reference to culture, but only as a symbol which, merely by being invoked, guarantees the integrity and legitimacy of legal doctrine in evolution.

Maine's historical jurisprudence

The immense influence in England and America of the work of the English jurist Henry Maine in the second half of the nineteenth century may be partly because it helped to meet this need for a sound underpinning of common law methods in an age of legislation. But Maine wrote relatively little on common law thought as such in his most important books. His historical jurisprudence was primarily concerned with examining legal ideas and institutions in terms of their evolution in cultural history. It might appear, then, that Maine's work has little relevance to normative legal theory as it was defined in Chapter 1. But its importance here is to show one route that could be taken by efforts to develop a general legal theory compatible with basic assumptions of classical common law thought.

Maine's writings show vast geographical and chronological range. Roman law, ancient Irish (Brehon) law, Hindu law and Biblical law, as well as English law, provide his major sources. Legal concepts such as contract, property, crime and delict are traced through centuries of development or decay and across several continents. One outcome of this comparative approach is a general thesis about legal evolution expressed in his most influential book *Ancient Law*, first published in 1861.

According to Maine, law originates not as custom but from judgments handed down by human authorities (such as kings) or attributed to superhuman ones (such as gods). These judgments he terms 'themistes' (Maine 1861: 2–5; and cf Maine 1883: ch 6). The idea of a judgment thus arises in the legal history of the world before the idea of a rule. The judge predates the lawmaker.

The 'epoch of kingly rule' is succeeded, however, by 'an era of oligarchies' (Maine 1861: 6) in which the charismatic authority of particular rulers gives way to the rule of military, political, religious or other elites. At this stage the authority to make 'inspired' judgments requiring no special justification has ceased to exist. 'What the juristic oligarchy now claims is to monopolise the *knowledge* of the laws, to have the exclusive possession of the principles by which quarrels are decided. We have in fact arrived at the epoch of Customary Law' (Maine 1861: 7). Judgments are no longer considered divinely inspired but are justified as based on established custom. Customary law may, however, be seen as having a divine origin. Law, in this stage of evolution, is unwritten and so its knowledge can easily be monopolised by a juristic elite. But, Maine is anxious to assert, this unwritten law should not be confused with English common law which became written (whatever classical common law thought might suggest) once cases and legal arguments were recorded in the Year Books and elsewhere.

The third stage of legal development comes with the era of codes. Here Maine is writing particularly of the ancient codes (such as the Twelve Tables of Roman law of the fifth century BC) which Savigny had identified with the early stages of cultural development. Codes became possible with the discovery and diffusion of the art of writing and, in some contexts, gave rulers or communities a means of breaking the knowledge-monopoly of juristic elites. Maine, like Savigny, notes the generally unsystematic character and lack of technical precision of these codes. They tended to mix 'religious, civil, and merely moral ordinances, without any regard to differences in their essential character' because the separation of law from morality and from religion belongs 'very distinctly to the *later* stages of mental progress' (Maine 1861: 9; cf Cotterrell 1999: 94–95). But we should note that Maine intends in writing of the era of codes merely to mark the transition from unwritten to written law. So English common law, presented in the form of written reports and records, is 'only different from code-law because it is written in a different way' (Maine 1861: 8).

The transition to written law in the evolution of civilisations is fundamental. Without it, Maine suggests, there can be no further significant legal development. Unwritten custom may arise for good reasons but then degenerate into irrational ritual and be distorted by extension through doubtful analogies because the law exists only in collective memory, subject to many interpretations of its meaning and purpose. Reducing law to writing fixes rules so that they must be changed, if at all, deliberately. It marks the end of 'spontaneous development' of law and the beginning of the possibility of law's *purposive* development (Maine 1861: 13).

So, like Savigny, Maine sees the point at which codification occurs in the evolution of a culture as being of the utmost importance (1861: 9–10). If custom has already degenerated by the time it is codified the result will be very different from a codification of living custom animated by manifest reasons intelligible from experience. But whereas Savigny treats early codes as merely clumsy and primitive, and later systematic and comprehensive ones as valuable only to preserve legal achievements from future cultural decline, Maine treats codes – in the sense of written compilations of customs – as the keys to all future progress, as long as codification occurs while custom retains vitality.

All major civilisations, therefore, reach the era of written law. After that, 'stationary' societies show little legal development. 'Progressive' societies, however, which for Maine included those of western Europe but not many others (1861: 13–14), continue to undergo substantial social and legal change.

Three devices are available to allow modification of law to follow social change. They are: (i) legal fictions (maintenance of legal forms while hiding the fact that they operate in new ways), (ii) equity (principles distinct from ordinary law but claimed to be able to supersede it by virtue of their superior authority) and (iii) legislation (enactments deriving authority from some 'external body or person' creating them) (Maine 1861: 15–18).

Maine's use of evidence to support this general picture of legal evolution is certainly restricted. The history of Roman law looms large. But at least the need for evidence is clearly recognised and Maine's broad knowledge of legal and cultural conditions in a wide range of periods and civilisations is evidenced throughout *Ancient Law*. Culture, for Maine, has ceased to be the simple backcloth of legal development which it is for Savigny. Maine's historical jurisprudence accepts, for virtually the first time in English legal scholarship, the need for detailed knowledge of the specific cultural settings of law if the development of legal doctrine is to be understood.

Also, instead of the assertion in classical common law thought that law is merely *found* in its cultural setting, Maine tries to show the many devices by which law is *made* – not just through legislation, but also through the use of fictions, the development of equity jurisdictions and ideas of a fundamental or natural law of reason. Common law, like the law of all 'progressive' societies, is not spontaneous – merely found in culture. It is constructed by technical devices validated by long use throughout progressive societies.

Thus, Maine tries to show how law is inseparable from cultural development but (after its reduction to writing) has its *own* mechanisms for regulating legal change. It seems that the riddle of common law development is solved.

Nowadays, many of Maine's specific claims can be criticised and the overall thesis of legal evolution is hard to defend in the face of many exceptions and historical complexities. But for the first time in English legal scholarship a theory is offered that clearly links law and culture, does so with a wealth of specific empirical reference, shows processes of law-making other than legislation as of great historical significance, and emphasises the gradual pace of legal development and the roots of modern legal ideas in history.

Maine on politics and society

There is no reliable evidence that Maine was directly influenced by Savigny (Cocks 1988: 24–29), although he was certainly affected by the ideas of the German historical school generally (Kuper 1991: 104–105). Further, although *Ancient Law* was published only two years after Charles Darwin's *Origin of Species* it does not seem that Maine's innovative empirical approach to the study of legal evolution owed anything to Darwin's evolutionary theory (Feaver 1969: 46; Burrow 1966: 139, 152–153). Darwin's ideas were quickly adapted by many writers in the second half of the nineteenth century to explain social evolution in terms of some kind of natural selection or 'survival of the fittest' thesis. And this 'social Darwinism' was congenial to Maine in explaining why some legal ideas and institutions flourished and others withered. In his later writings he 'hastened to borrow new weapons from the armoury of Darwin' (Barker 1928: 161). But the source of Maine's dramatically new approach to legal scholarship first revealed in *Ancient Law* is obscure.

It is tempting to see it, in part, as a timely response to a need to put together in some orderly theory the immense baggage of history and tradition attached to legal thought in the common law environment. And Maine's work did seem to provide possible solutions to some of the problems that arise in attempting to construct a normative legal theory consistent with common law thought. It was seen earlier that, if common law is treated as judge-*made* law, serious theoretical difficulties arise. The most important difficulty is in explaining where judges get their authority to make new law, and how far that authority extends.

Maine's work implies an imaginative answer. The source of authority of judge-made law is (as classical common law thought had suggested) no different in essence from that of legislation. But Maine finds that source in historical necessity demonstrated by the lessons of comparative history. Social change in progressive societies demands that the law change to keep in step. The methods of judicial innovation (fictions, equity and natural law ideas), like those of legislation, are shown in his work to be more or less common to the entire civilised world. So the implication is that they can be treated as 'natural' elements in civilisation. Fictions, equity and legislation, emerging successively in history, reinforce each other as remedial devices to ensure law follows social progress.

The process of social change, as Maine understands it, explains not only the forms of law but also law's changing content. Progress depends on Darwinian competition. Social change is governed by the principle of the survival of the fittest (Barker 1928: 161). Thus, in progressive societies, legal rights and duties gradually cease to be based on rigid statuses of individuals (for example, as member of a clan, head of a family, wife, son or daughter) which, in general, are not freely chosen by them. Instead, law increasingly recognises the dynamic nature of social life by treating transactions, situations and arrangements as resulting from deliberate choice or decision. Status relationships cease to dominate law and society and give way to contractual relationships. Hence the dictum for which Maine is most famous: if status is taken to refer to personal situations not the direct or indirect result of agreement 'we may say that the movement of the progressive societies has hitherto been a movement *from Status to Contract*' (Maine 1861: 100).

Maine's image of modern society is, thus, clearly very different from that of the close-knit communities he associates with the past. He welcomes the individualism of the present: the movement from status to contract is progress. The proof of the naturalness of *laissez-faire* individualism is in the great evolutionary sweep of history from ancient village communities to the present.

But this conception of the nature of society also explains why, for Maine, legislation is not a specially privileged type of law-making. A critic of his ideas, in the late nineteenth century as now, could argue that legislation represents *democratic* law-making in modern states in which representative democracy flourishes. Hence it necessarily has a greater legitimacy and acceptability than judicial law-making. In Maine's view, however, this special legitimacy evaporates on examination. Society is largely composed of a mass who do not lead but only follow. Social competition for survival does not offer for most people 'any guiding thread of growing freedom' (Barker 1928: 167). Like other late nineteenth-century jurists, Maine was interested in the bases of popular obedience to authority and found them in habit and inertia rather than reason or fear (Maine 1885: 63). Thus, authoritative prescription rather than coercive command is the essential quality of law (cf Maine 1875a: ch 12). Equally, society (the mass who follow rather than lead) must be governed by elites of some kind, whether the elites are considered to be judges or legislators. Which are most appropriate as lawmakers should depend simply on which have the best expertise.

One commentator has described Maine's 'administrative' mentality: 'cool, unsentimental, honest and just, but tending always to identify with authority, and lacking in sympathy with the feelings and aspirations of the mass of mankind' (Burrow 1966: 174, 177–178). Ultimately he feared demagogues as the enemy of efficient modern state administration and his last book *Popular Government* (Maine 1885) is a polemical condemnation of democracy. Thus, just as the common law concern with community requires no popular participation in law-finding (even if a jury might find the facts), and Savigny's spirit of the people does not demand democratic institutions to express it, Maine's picture of law's evolution as part of civilisation as a whole is of an evolution to be managed by elites, not by the democratic representatives of the people.

Historical jurisprudence and the legal profession

What relevance does Maine's work have for the concerns of lawyers as an occupational group in common law systems? In considering the period when he wrote and the decades before *Ancient Law* appeared, it is certainly possible to see a modern legal profession self-consciously shaping itself and building its status, whatever may have been the nature of the occupational group of common lawyers in earlier times (Cocks 1983). In the nineteenth century, fundamental issues about legal education and training began to be seriously addressed.[9] With them arose difficult questions about the nature of the lawyer's professional knowledge and expertise, about what law students should learn so as to be well equipped as a member of a modern learned profession, about the possibility of a 'science' of law comparable with the other modern sciences then flourishing, and about whether and in what ways legal knowledge could be considered autonomous, unified and systematic.

Maine's writings are very important in this context. As has been seen, the subject matter of classical common law thought can certainly be considered to be knowledge that is both esoteric and of central social importance. But it cannot easily be considered a 'science' in the nineteenth century sense of a rational organisation of ideas. Such a rational science 'could never hope neatly to capture within its four corners the rich, living tradition of Common Law' (Postema 1986: 37). Equally, as noted earlier, classical common law thought lacked grounding in serious historical inquiry. It existed in substantial isolation from knowledge of other legal systems or legal methods (Feaver 1969: 45; Pocock 1957: ch 3). Finally, it lacked any rigorous intellectual criteria separating it from other branches of learning. Its relationship with them was parasitic yet unsystematic (Sommerville 1999: 89).

The implication of all Maine's major work is that a sound knowledge of law as an intellectual field, rather than as merely a disordered jumble of precedents and principles, demands comparative, historical and philosophical studies. Other sources of influence, such as the Select Committee appointed in 1846 to investigate the state of legal education in England and Ireland, had reached similar conclusions,[10] and Maine was active in campaigning for legal education to be developed along these lines. 'The fault of our legal system', he declared in 1855, 'is that it is exclusively practical ... with us, law is not a science' (quoted in Feaver 1969: 24). Maine's science of law was, thus, a 'new sort of empirical history that could nonetheless be fitted into a theoretical framework explaining the general evolution of legal systems' (Feaver 1969: 46).

Maine's books and their methods had immense influence in the latter part of the nineteenth century. By 1871 *Ancient Law* was widely used in the law schools of Europe and America. Maine reported that an eminent American lawyer had told him that 'he thought almost every attorney in the States had a copy' (Feaver 1969: 128, 129). The book went through eleven editions in twenty five years.

---

9 For a summary of developments see eg Manchester 1980: 54–63.
10 Report from the Select Committee on Legal Education No 686 (1846).

The impact was not just on lawyers. 'The extent and profundity of Maine's influence among the intellectual class would be hard to exaggerate ...' and his 'method dominated a whole generation's reflections on politics', reflecting 'the immense prestige and unimpeachable respectability of his achievement' (Collini, Winch and Burrow 1983: 10, 210, 252).

The reasons for Maine's success in reaching the attention of the legal profession are crucial here. He presents attractively something that looks like a genuine science of law based on sound empirical data and, moreover, that demonstrates both the impressive weight of legal knowledge and its centrality in social life and the history of civilisation. He offers ideas consistent with the in-built conservatism of common law thought and its preference for gradual legal adjustment through case law rather than wholesale legislative reform. Finally, he seems to offer the comforting message that the time-honoured methods of common law and the doctrine and institutions it has produced are validated by the natural scientific laws of social progress. And he connects legal scholarship neatly with what were in his time widely seen as the most advanced ideas in other social studies (Cocks 1988: 1–2). Thus, in the late nineteenth century, as an eminent public figure and an eloquent spokesman on legal matters he could appear as a powerful force in promoting the status of the legal profession and its knowledge in the wider world of politics and intellectual life.

The fate of Maine's new science

In 1875 Maine set out a programme for 'a new science', foreshadowed by his already published work, which would apply comparative methods, already used in other fields in illuminating the evolution of civilisation, to the investigation of 'laws, institutions, customs, ideas, and social forces' (Maine 1875b: 230). Yet, despite his popularity and renown, the new science did not produce any lasting influence on legal scholarship. Although a few eminent jurists followed Maine's lead to some extent, historical jurisprudence did not reshape legal thinking in the common law world. What went wrong?

In the previous chapter it was suggested that legal theory may serve the professional needs of lawyers by clarifying the nature of professional knowledge, demonstrating unity or system in it, and distinguishing the legal from the non-legal (the internal-external dichotomy) in definite terms. But Maine's jurisprudence is seriously defective in this respect since it does not portray legal knowledge as a well-defined, manageable field. Instead, it suggests that legal studies consistent with a scientific reworking of common law thought must embrace vast areas of cultural knowledge extending over many nations and many centuries of history.

The problem from the standpoint of professional legal education is especially clear. Maine's books were prescribed for examinations of the Inns of Court and universities in Britain and the colonies, and for the Indian Civil Service Competitive Examination. In the late nineteenth century, brief 'nutshell' books for students offered simplified versions of major law texts (Sugarman 1986: 52). The preface to one of these, dealing with Maine's works, declares:

> 'In these works there is a great deal of writing that is absolutely useless to the student for examination purposes, and page after page has to be waded through in the search for a criticism or a theory; and to discover any complete theory or criticism on any one question or theory, it is often necessary to search through not only each one of the books, but also many different chapters or lectures in each of those books. This necessitates a great waste of time and mental energy on the part of the student, there being over two thousand pages in all'.[11]

No matter that Maine's writings offered a sincere attempt to turn legal study into a pursuit of real cultural value and to escape the idea that law was no more than an 'occult science' vastly inferior to the real sciences explaining the nature and progress of civilisation. His work did not offer a conception of a manageable professional knowledge.

Thus, with the eclipse of historical jurisprudence, the problem of finding a normative legal theory compatible with common law thought seems no nearer solution. Maine's writings pointed not towards normative legal theory but instead to the need for empirical legal theory aimed at explaining the nature of law in terms of its social origins and effects. Maine is, to this day, treated as a significant figure in the history of anthropology and his work exerted major influence on the development of sociology, including sociology of law.

Even here, however, we should keep clearly in mind that he was, first and foremost, a jurist. To some extent, Maine is closer to Savigny, to whom culture appeared merely as the motif that made sense of law's claims to doctrinal integrity, than he is to modern social science. He was in no sense a 'thorough sociologist' (Burrow 1966: 151) and many writers have commented on his unreliable use of empirical evidence. Adherents of historical jurisprudence distanced themselves from the writings and outlook of sociologists (Collini, Winch and Burrow 1983: 213, 220). Equally, historical jurisprudence in England had a different orientation from anthropology. Whereas the latter appeared to take all humankind as its province, the former, as Maine established

---

11 Evans 1896: v–vi. Cf Frederick Pollock's comments, less prosaic but to similar effect, quoted in Cocks 1988: 6–7.

it, was concerned only with those peoples whose cultural history fed into what was seen as the evolution of civilisation (Collini, Winch and Burrow 1983: 212).

Historical jurisprudence traced a line of descent of civilisation, validated essentially in terms of the historical development of legal ideas and institutions and grounded in assumptions about an original Aryan family of peoples. Maine wrote: 'Civilisation is nothing more than a name for the old order of the Aryan world, dissolved but perpetually re-constituting itself under a vast variety of solvent influences' (1875b: 230). It is almost as though the seventeenth century appeal to an ultimate timeless and mystical cultural foundation of common law in the idea of the Ancient Constitution is resurrected in the idea of the timeless cultural unity of the Aryan world. The unity underpinning Maine's thought, like that of common law thought, is a unity of culture.

If such a unity is hardly satisfactory to ground a normative legal theory, where else might one look for foundations? Having followed assumptions of classical common law thought to what may seem their ultimate consequences without finding adequate solutions perhaps it might be fruitful to start from virtually opposite positions: to treat legislation as central to law and judicial law-making as peripheral and to see the foundations of law in political power rather than in community. The theory to be considered in the next chapter does exactly that. In leaving classical common law thought and historical jurisprudence it is important, however, not to lose sight of their strengths. Despite much ambiguity and some incoherence, the theory of common law, and the nineteenth century legal philosophy that developed ideas consistent with it, emphasise the vital importance of maintaining law's link with community life. By implication they pose a warning against the arrogance of legislators who treat law as no more than an affair of efficient rules organised as an instrument of coercion.

Sovereign and subject: Bentham and Austin

John Austin's wife wrote that he lived 'a life of unbroken disappointment and failure'.[1] Yet Austin, more than any other writer, provided the compact and systematic formulation of a conception of law that allowed an escape from the tradition-bound theory implicit in classical common law thought. Equally, Austin provided what historical jurisprudence could not: a clear designation of the scope of legal knowledge, an orderly theory of law that firmly distinguished the legal from the non-legal and made explicit the logical connections between legal ideas. Finally, he offered a way of looking at law that made legislation central rather than peripheral. Thus, his legal theory recognised the reality of the modern state as a massive organisation of power. It tried to show law's relationship with this centralised and extensive power structure. It seemed in tune with modern circumstances in which government, not community, was the apparent source of law.

Thus, noting Sarah Austin's comment quoted above, one of Austin's most important successors goes on to remark that 'within a few years of his death it was clear that his work had established the study of jurisprudence in England' (Hart 1955: xvi). Austin died in 1859, believing that his neglected writings and unsuccessful lectures had made no mark whatsoever. Four years later all of his most important work had been republished, largely through the efforts of his widow. Not only did it turn out to be a theory for its times, but it established or clarified ideas about the nature of law that still provide basic elements in the vocabulary of concepts used by lawyers in the Anglo-American world (cf Dworkin 1977: 16).

---

1   In a letter quoted in Rumble 1985: 56.

Austin's legal theory is contained primarily in the lectures he prepared as the first professor of jurisprudence in what was to become the University of London. Much of his legal philosophy is heavily indebted to earlier writers. It represents the packaging of a set of ideas distilled from a long tradition of political theory concerned with the concept of sovereignty, together with a selective plundering of the legal theory of Austin's original mentor, the English philosopher and law reformer, Jeremy Bentham. Today, the received wisdom is that Austin's work is much less important than Bentham's and its intellectual range is certainly much more limited. But, partly because of the accidents of publication, Austin exerted an influence on the development of legal theory and wider concerns in legal scholarship far beyond that of Bentham.

The fact that all of Austin's major work in legal theory was in print from the 1860s, whereas the major writings of Bentham which cover similar ground were not, is, however, only part of the explanation. The form of Austin's legal theory and the ordering of its concerns enable it to provide a normative legal theory particularly appropriate to the political and legal professional concerns of its time. Further, it exemplifies a certain general conception of law in an extremely concise and straightforward manner.

In fact, Austin's 'failure' in so many worldly things may have been the condition of his success in this. He pursued with apparently total singlemindedness a distinct image of how a 'science' of law might be possible. Lacking Bentham's restless intellectual curiosity – which diverted the greater writer into a vast range of projects – Austin meticulously worked on the theory of law which was merely a part of Bentham's concerns. Where his ideas differ from Bentham's it is often because he prefers a stubborn logic (for example, on the nature of sovereignty) or a hard-headed realism (for example, in discussing judicial law-making), where Bentham equivocates or tries to develop more radical analyses in the cause of legal or political reform.

For the moment there is no need to make any general judgment about the relative merits of Bentham and Austin in their development of normative legal theory. But it will be argued in the following pages that a strong defence can be made on Austin's behalf against many of the most serious criticisms that are routinely made of his legal theory. In this chapter he occupies centre stage simply because it is he rather than Bentham who has exerted by far the greater influence on later jurists and on legal scholarship generally, and he who offers a version of normative legal theory that in its clear (even dogmatic) pronounce-ments provides an effective contrast to the vague theory underpinning the common law tradition. In considering Austin's ideas and their political and professional consequences, however, comparisons with Bentham's theories will be made. And it will be necessary to trace the roots of Austin's thinking beyond Bentham to make the point that the evolution of common law thought, considered in Chapter 2, is parallelled by a long tradition of quite different thinking about the nature of law.

The empire of darkness and the region of light

A key to understanding the motivation behind and orientation of the legal theories of Austin and Bentham is to recognise the profound hostility of both writers to the methods and outlook of English common law, and the profound difference between their reactions to it. Towards the end of his life Austin may well have modified his views but his London University lectures, originally written for presentation at the end of the 1820s and the basis of his reputation in legal philosophy, are full of vitriolic comments on the absurdities of common law thought and the irrationality of a legal system, if system it could be called, developed primarily by piecemeal judicial interventions. Bentham viewed judge-made law as like waiting for one's dog to do something wrong and then beating it (cf Lobban 1991: 116). Austin, however, was not opposed to judicial law-making. What offended him was the total lack of systematic organisation or of a structure of clearly definable rational principles in common law. In his lectures he was determined to map out a rational, scientific approach to legal understanding: a modern view of law that would replace archaic, confused, tradition-bound common law thought and encompass both legislation and judge-made law.

This aim immediately distinguishes Austin from Bentham. Always the more radical thinker, Bentham has no patience in his writings with the idea that judicial decisions are an appropriate source of law. He pins his faith on the kind of codification Savigny despised. All law should be purposively, deliberately created by legislative means. As far as possible, law should be expressed in rational, systematically organised codes. Austin also favoured codification and writes extensively in his lectures of its merits and of the absurdity of most of Savigny's objections to it. But he also shows a cool realism about the possibilities. Austin's views on judge-made law will be discussed later. For the moment it is enough to say that he recognises that judge-made law is an inevitable component of a modern legal system and that, despite many disadvantages, it has some virtues and is often the only practical means of legal development at certain times and in certain fields. Codification is admirable in theory but, in practice, requires immense legislative skill, juristic knowledge and political vision. What is needed, therefore, is a view of law that can accommodate realistically all these aspects but present them in the framework of the rational, centralised governmental structure of the modern state.

Although the matter is often ignored or under-emphasised in commentaries on Austin, it is important to note that he found models of legal scholarship, to help in this task, quite outside Benthamite influences. Austin saw in Roman law (especially as interpreted and developed by continental European civil law jurists) the epitome of a rational legal order vastly superior to English common law in its logical organisation. 'Turning from the study of the English to the study of the Roman Law, you escape from the empire of chaos and darkness, to a world which seems, by comparison, the region of order and light' (Austin 1885: 58). The 'extraordinary merit' of Roman law scholarship was in the way scholars had 'seized its general principles with great clearness and penetration, ... applied these principles with admirable logic to the explanation of details, and ... thus reduced this positive system of law to a compact and coherent whole' (Austin 1832: 160–161). By contrast, English law was full of 'useless and misleading jargon' often employed inconsistently (Austin 1885: 686). While distancing himself in his writings from the legal philosophies informing Roman law and, indeed, from that law's actual content, Austin rarely fails to sing the praises of Romanist legal scholarship. He spent several months in Germany, studying the writings of the German scholars of Roman law and German legal philosophy, to prepare for his own lectures.

How important is this in understanding the orientation of Austin's legal philosophy? It suggests that, although he 'was accepted as the heir apparent of Bentham in the special department of jurisprudence' (Stephen 1900: 317) and undoubtedly saw himself, at the time he wrote his lectures, as a disciple (though a critical one) of Bentham, his model of a science of law was not wholly Benthamite. He quoted with approval other writers' praise of the 'scientific method' of the Romanists which made them 'models to all succeeding ages' (1885: 1080). This method, as Austin understood it, of identifying general principles, applying them to explain detail, and so demonstrating order and coherence in law could be used to rationalise law from many sources, including judicial decisions and custom, as well as legislation.

Certainly, Bentham had already supplied many other elements needed. He had recognised the need for a coherent doctrine to guide the rational reform of law and to dispose of common law archaism and had found this in the principle of *utility*. Utility required that law-making and legal institutions be designed to promote the greatest happiness of the greatest number of people. Utility would replace traditional, self-serving or subjectively moral evaluations with a rational evaluation of the worth of particular practices, institutions and policies. These would be judged in terms of how far they served the common good, measured in terms of maximisation of satisfaction of the actual desires of the greatest possible number of the population.

Austin's lectures presuppose the doctrine of utility as elaborated by Bentham and warmly, even fanatically, defend it. But Austin's course was devoted to the theory of law *as it is* (which he called the science of law), not the theory of law as it should or might be (which he termed the science of legislation). Consequently, although several of Austin's lectures directly discuss utility, it does not occupy the central place in the body of his writings which it does in Bentham's. Bentham's 'expository jurisprudence' (his term for the science of law), on which Austin drew extensively, was an offshoot of his concern with the working out of the principle of utility in its application to law reform. So the science of legislation (he calls it censorial jurisprudence) is central to Bentham and expository jurisprudence is a necessary basis of knowledge on which censorial jurisprudence can be pursued. By contrast, Austin is known through a set of lectures devoted to elaborating a theory of existing law. In them he apologetically justifies bringing in the principle of utility as necessary to help to explain why law has taken particular forms (Austin 1832: 58; 1885: 1078). In the particular context of Austin's lectures, therefore, the science of legislation is *subordinate* to the science of law.

This, in itself, suggests Austin's less radical view of law as compared with Bentham's, for Austin plainly considered that despite all its defects English common law had often approximated to what utility demanded. Thus, while Bentham sought an instrument to reform the law and found it in the utility principle, Austin sought, above all, a means of rationalising existing law. He wanted to organise and logically relate its elements, put it into systematic form, clarify the reasoning entailed in it and find a set of concepts through which it could be 'scientifically' understood. Such a task could be carried out in relation to a particular legal system. But a more fundamental theoretical inquiry – the real foundation of legal science – would be to carry out this task in relation to legal systems generally. Thus, what Austin calls general jurisprudence would be 'the science concerned with the exposition of the principles, notions and distinctions which are common to systems of law' or, at least, mature systems (Austin 1885: 1073). In practice, these matters can be illuminated well enough, Austin asserts, by studying the writings of his revered Romanist jurists, the modern decisions of English judges, and (with regard to arrangement and systematic organisation of law) the provisions of the French and Prussian codes (1885: 1077).

In this programme the influences of the German Roman law jurists and of Bentham come together less uneasily than is often supposed. The three sources of comparison Austin emphasises neatly summarise the three contending forces that needed to be reconciled in contemporary legal thought as he understood it: (i) the untidy raw material provided by common law judicial decisions, (ii) the Romanist example of how to rationalise order out of gradually evolved legal doctrine and (iii) the modern experience of systematic codification. But Austin's rigour made him undertake a preliminary inquiry on the basis of which the exposition of 'principles, notions and distinctions common to systems of law' could be founded as a science. That preliminary inquiry was into the meaning of the ultimate concept of 'a law' itself. Bentham, and before him, the seventeenth century English political philosopher Thomas Hobbes had provided ideas that could be developed for this purpose. In the event, it is this purely *preliminary* inquiry which has come to be treated as Austin's legal philosophy (cf Buckland 1949: 3). His contributions to the much broader 'general jurisprudence' have remained relatively neglected.

Positive law and positive morality

From one viewpoint, the most valuable contribution of Austin's legal theory is its attempt to distinguish clearly *law* from other phenomena (for example, moral rules, social customs) with which it could be confused. As has been seen in the previous chapter, classical common law thought did not do this. For Austin, clear thinking about law necessitates such a demarcation of the subject-matter of legal science. Bentham had poured scorn on the way moral notions and legal principles were mixed up in Blackstone's *Commentaries*, the famous eighteenth century treatise on English law (Bentham 1977: 3–33). To Bentham the result seemed thoroughly unscientific, allowing Blackstone to preach moral sermons or indulge his prejudices under cover of stating the law. So, when Austin – strongly influenced by Bentham's critique of Blackstone – came to write his lectures, it seemed obvious to him that the starting point for the science of law must be a clear analytical separation of law and morality. Such a strategy would in no way imply that moral questions were unimportant (although for Austin, like Bentham, they were mostly to be answered by applying the principle of utility). Indeed, the separation would make clear the independent character of legal and moral arguments and the special validity and importance of each.

So Austin's lectures begin by asserting that the subject-matter of jurisprudence, as he understands it, is positive law, 'law, simply and strictly so called: or law set by political superiors to political inferiors' (Austin 1832: 18). Immediately law is defined as an expression of power. In its *widest* proper sense a law is 'a rule laid down for the guidance of an intelligent being by an intelligent being having power over him' (Austin 1832: 18). Austin's view of law recognises it not as something evolved or immanent in community life, as in the implicit common law conception, but as an imposition of power.

The lectures then embark on a rather tedious classification, some of which, however, is of the greatest importance in understanding key points of Austin's legal theory. Austin distinguishes laws 'properly so called' from phenomena improperly labelled as law (1832: 18, 20). There are two classes of laws properly so called: *divine laws* (set by God for humankind) – which quickly appear in Austin's jurisprudence to be largely the dictates of utility – and *human laws* (set by human beings for human beings). The most significant category of human laws comprises what Austin calls *positive law*. These are laws set by political superiors acting as such or by people acting in pursuance of legal rights conferred on them by political superiors (that is, acting as the delegates of political superiors in making laws). The term 'positive' refers to the idea of law placed or laid down in some specific way and, as such, could apply to divine law, which Austin conceives as God's commands. But he wants to reserve the term positive law for human laws laid down by, or on the authority of, political superiors – the true subject of legal science. So the word 'positive' indicates a positing or setting of rules by human creators.

The other category of human law consists of rules laid down by persons having power over others but not as political superiors or in pursuance of legal rights. This seems to cover many rules which lawyers would not usually regard as law, although Austin has no doubt that the term 'law' can be used here 'with absolute precision or propriety' (Austin 1832: 123). Since he uses the word 'power' in a general sense, it seems to include the capacity of any authority figures – for example, priests or religious leaders, employers, teachers, parents, guardians or political orators – to control or influence the actions of followers, dependants or those in their charge. Austin clearly regards rule-making in such cases as significant in shaping the attitudes, opinions or moral sentiments of individuals or groups. Indeed, it forms part of what he calls *positive morality*. As morality it is distinguished from positive law; and it is positive because it is laid down by human beings for human beings. Positive morality also contains another category of rules: those without particular creators but set by the opinion or sentiment of an indeterminate body of people – that is, by public opinion or community opinion. Austin calls these authorless rules laws 'by analogical extension'; they are not laws 'properly so called' even though we sometimes talk of laws of fashion, etiquette or honour (1832: 123–124).

Finally, for completeness, he mentions one other category of laws 'improperly so called'. *Scientific laws* are not laws in the jurisprudential sense. They are the regularities of nature which science discovers but which are not laid down as laws. Austin (1832: 148–150) calls them 'metaphorical laws'.

We can say, therefore, that for Austin: (i) the term 'law' is often improperly applied to rules or regularities that are in no strict sense 'legal'; but (ii) the concept of law can properly embrace more than most lawyers would accept. Like many social scientists writing long after him, Austin considers that some rules created 'privately' outside the particular provisions or procedures of the legal system of the state can usefully be recognised as law. On the other hand, (iii) only positive law is the appropriate concern of jurisprudence.

From this dissection of the field of rules in the broadest sense what is most important is the establishment of the concepts of positive law and positive morality. As will appear, the interplay between them provides, for Austin, solutions to some of the most serious problems which his critics think they see in the elaboration of his theory of law.

The coercive structure of a law

What then is a law? Like Hobbes before him, Austin defines a law as a kind of command. Bentham, as so often, surrounds his basic assertions with a complex, exploratory excursus (in this case on various forms of expression of will) and for various reasons prefers to talk of law as 'an assemblage of signs declarative of a volition' (Bentham 1970: 1, 10). But he, too, essentially treats laws as a species of commands and the thrust of his conception turns out to be much the same as Austin's direct, straightforward characterisation. Again power is made central to law. Austin states: 'A command is distinguished from other significations of desire, not by the style in which the desire is signified, but by the power and purpose of the party commanding to inflict an evil or pain in case the desire be disregarded' (Austin 1832: 21). Thus, the power to inflict punishment (sanction) in case of non-compliance is what makes an expression a command. There is no need for any imperative form. Obviously the nature of the sanction and of the power to inflict it needs further consideration, as does the question of *whose* commands will constitute law.

However, not every command is a rule or law. Austin often uses the words 'law' and 'rule' apparently interchangeably (eg 1832: 25, 123) but is inconsistent in this since, for example, as has been seen above, he distinguishes moral rules set by public opinion from law strictly so-called.

What they have in common, however, is the requirement of *generality*. A particular command – say, a directive issued to a particular government department or administrative agency requiring that it reconsider a particular case – would not be a rule. How much generality is necessary for a law? As Austin notes, generality can be of two kinds: as to acts required or prohibited and as to persons addressed by the command. Generality as to acts indicates that the command refers to a class of actions or situations, not a single, specific action or case. Generality as to persons indicates a class of people, or people generally, as subject to the command – not a particular individual or organisation, or a number of specified individuals or organisations.

It will be seen in later chapters that this question of generality becomes important in relation to the familiar doctrine of the Rule of Law, which usually insists on both kinds of generality. It is very significant, however, that Austin sees generality as to acts is the only generality necessary for a command to be a law (1832: 27ff). Thus, law can consist of rules addressed to particular individuals, business firms or administrative agencies, as well as rules addressed to the population generally or to specific categories of it.

This is one of several aspects of his legal theory which indicate that his view of law is very different from that of many liberal theories. The latter tend to see law as a set of rules whose purpose should be to mark out a general sphere of liberty of the individual guaranteed against the risk of arbitrary state power. Austin, by contrast, sees law as a technical instrument of government or administration, which should, however, be efficient and aimed at the common good as determined by utility.

Law as government

Since the consequences of this view of law are important to many aspects of Austin's legal theory it is worth commenting further on it before considering his other claims about the idea of law as a species of command. In a sense, law *is*, for him, effective government. Certainly a directive relating to a particular occasion would not be a law. Even here, however, Austin recognises that particular commands issued by a law-making authority may, in practice, sometimes be called laws. The lectures hardly suggest that this incorrect usage raises an important issue of principle for him (Austin 1832: 25; cf Neumann 1986: 220).

When, later, he discusses civil and political liberties, the contrast with liberal theories is made very explicit. Like Bentham, Austin has no patience with ideas of natural or fundamental rights: there are no rights or laws that are somehow inherent in the human condition, in human nature, or in the very essence of social or community life. All rights and duties are created by setting down rules as an act of government. Consequently there can be nothing inherently sacred about civil or political liberties. Insofar as they are valuable they are the by-product of effective government in the common interest.

Austin's lectures are generally dry and laden with cold, precise definition and classification. But occasionally a fierceness breaks through; a vehemence that reveals deep feelings normally hidden. The discussion of liberties is one such place: 'To the ignorant and bawling fanatics who stun you with their pother about liberty, political or civil liberty seems to be the principal end for which government ought to exist'. This liberty 'has been erected into an idol, and extolled with extravagant praises by doting and fanatical worshippers' (1832: 223, 224). But, writes Austin, the purpose of government is to serve the common good. The promotion and protection of civil or political liberties is of value only insofar as it serves that end. Limiting liberty may in some circumstances be more conducive to the common good than maximising it. Austin obviously thinks that 'liberty' is a slogan that can easily get out of hand.

Several things follow from this 'governmental' view of law. One is that *duties* are more fundamental than *rights*. The individual's ability to make specific claims on others through the legal system is derivative from the law's commands. Austin's command theory produces this result analytically. Command and duty are treated as correlative terms: 'wherever a duty lies a command has been signified, and wherever a command is signified, a duty is imposed' (Austin 1832: 22). We have seen that the threat of punishment (sanction) is an essential component of the notion of command for Austin. Duty then becomes the automatic consequence of being addressed by a potentially enforceable command: 'Being liable to evil from you if I comply not with a wish which you signify, I am *bound* or *obliged* by your command, or I lie under a *duty* to obey it' (1832: 22). Duty thus appears as a fundamental component or consequence of a law. By contrast, every right presupposes a duty in someone else. Rights are derivative from duties: I can claim a right against X because the law has imposed a duty on him towards me.

Sanctions

Austin's governmental view of law is also reflected clearly in the emphasis he attaches to punitive sanctions in the structure of a law. Since sanctions are essential to the existence of commands, they are, for Austin, essential to the existence of laws. There must be 'power and purpose of the party command-ing to inflict an evil' (1832: 21) in case of *non-compliance*. There is here an important difference from Bentham's legal theory, which also treats sanctions as essential to law. Bentham (and other writers) saw no reason why legal sanctions could not include rewards as well as penalties. Austin, after consider-ing this possibility, rejects it. A reward held out for compliance would indicate a promise or inducement but not a command, on the basis of ordinary usage of the word which specifies non-optional conduct. Thus the idea of law as a species of command necessarily entails the availability of negative (punitive) sanctions.

Be that as it may, serious doubts can be raised about the direction in which Austin's view of sanctions pushes his theory. If his idea is to maintain a realistic view of modern government through law, there are good reasons for recognising a whole range of devices including positive inducements as well as negative sanctions available to support rules. Terence Daintith has written of government's powers of *imperium* – much like Austin's coercive commands – being supplemented or supported by its *dominium* powers – powers to distribute benefits of many kinds as inducements to promote compliance with its policies (Daintith 1982). Law's sanctioning techniques may involve complex combinations of both *imperium* and *dominium*.

Nevertheless, if Austin fails to recognise the variety of forms which power can take, the stress on coercive sanctions at least keeps the relationship between law and power firmly in the forefront of attention. It has even been suggested that Austin's five years of army service coloured his parade-ground view of law as negatively sanctioned command (cf Rumble 1985: 12–13). But, as will be argued later, a more satisfactory explanation of Austin's outlook is to be found elsewhere, in his wider view of the nature of society and the state.

Although every law must by definition provide for a sanction according to Austin's theory, a sanction can be 'the smallest chance of incurring the smallest evil' (Austin 1832: 23). Austin's views on the possible role of sanctions in securing obedience will be considered later but it is important to note that the prominent place sanctions occupy in his definition of law entails, in itself, no sociological claims about the significance of sanctions in ensuring compliance with law. Such claims are 'foreign to the matter in question' (1832: 23). The role of sanctions in the definition of law is purely formal.

Laws, by their nature, provide for sanctions. Sanctions are *analytically* essential to laws, whether or not they are sociologically necessary. Thus, any disadvantage formally specified directly or indirectly by a law as to be imposed in case of non-compliance can serve as that law's sanction. Mere inconvenience or the fact that a transaction or document is rendered null and void by law would count as sufficient sanctions. A sanction can also be a further legal obligation. Thus, breach of one law (say, a traffic offence) might lead to a further obligation (to appear in court to answer charges). Breach of that further legal obligation might entail the threat of a direct legal sanction or, perhaps, render the offender subject to yet another legal obligation. So a chain of obligations is possible. At the end of the chain, however, there must be a sanction (Austin 1885: 444–445). 'Imperfect laws', lacking sanctions completely, are not laws in the Austinian sense. Neither are declaratory or repealing 'laws' since they command nothing (Austin 1832: 31–32).

Sanctions and power-conferring rules

The most serious problem for Austin's conception of the relationship between laws and sanctions is usually considered to be that of so-called power-conferring rules. These include legal rules enabling people to make wills or contracts, or to enter into other desirable transactions or arrangements that would lack security without legal guarantee (private power-conferring rules). They also include rules giving powers to officials (public power-conferring rules). A now standard criticism of Austin emphasises that these kinds of rules cannot be assimilated to coercive commands. They often facilitate desirable activities. They are not concerned primarily to impose duties supported by penalties. They *enable* officials or private citizens to act. How can the command conception of law encompass these kinds of rules?

A full attempted defence of Austin must wait until his theory of sovereignty – and especially the concept of delegation entailed in it – has been outlined in the next section. Nevertheless some preliminary remarks can be made here. Austin deals directly with the question of private power-conferring rules and clearly does not see it as the problem that later writers have identified. As mentioned above, he includes nullity of transactions as a sanction. Thus, a will executed in improper form will not achieve the intended legal effect since it will be held void in whole or part. Declarations or dispositions made in breach of statutory formalities governing them may be ineffective.[2] The loss of an expected advantage is the sanction in such cases.

Critics have considered that such 'sanctions' are quite different from others Austin recognises (for example, damages, imprisonment or fines) and that to equate them distorts the radically different social functions of power-conferring and duty-imposing rules (Hart 1961: 38). But it is important to remember that Austin's analytical concern with sanctions is purely formal. The differences in social functions of laws are not pertinent here. Equally, since any disadvantage (the smallest threat of the smallest evil) is enough to constitute a sanction if it is directly or indirectly provided for by law, the difference in the character of sanctions (for example, the nullity of a transaction as against the requirement to pay a fine or monetary compensation) is not *analytically* important either in this particular context (though, of course, it may be of considerable sociological, political or other interest).

Austin's prominent critic, H L A Hart, who stresses the problem of power-conferring rules, admits that such rules can be incorporated in an overall framework of law as a coercive phenomenon. The problem Hart identifies is

---

2   See eg Law of Property Act 1925, s 53(1); Wills Act 1837, s 9.

that to force all legal rules into a single coercive model denies the variety of kinds of laws (Hart 1961: 26–42). But it is vital to recognise that Austin's position does not require such a forced distortion. His 'only claim is that the features he indicates are relevant to all laws' (Moles 1987: 66). Austin wishes to stress the coercive basis of law which he thinks is reflected in all its rules. There is no suggestion that all rules have the same functions, the same form or the same kinds of sanctions.

Where so-called *public* power-conferring rules addressed to legal 'officials' are concerned, the nullity-as-sanction argument may equally apply. The relevant sanctions in such cases are likely to be against officials in their 'official capacity', rather than in a personal capacity. So, if a judge exceeds his jurisdiction, his decision is liable to be overturned by an appellate court. An improper direction to a jury by the judge in a criminal trial is liable to result in the conviction being quashed on appeal. The legal system as a whole, by providing means of correcting legal errors, also provides for indirect sanctions because it enables (professional or social) sanctions of inconvenience, ridicule or lessening of reputation to attach to the official concerned.

As has been seen earlier, Austin's 'smallest chance' of 'the smallest evil' encompasses a wide range of possible sanctions. All that is required by the theory is that they be provided for directly or indirectly by the law (a guilty conscience would not count as a legal sanction). It would seem that in cases of public power-conferring rules where no direct penalty is attached to an official failing to comply with these rules, the legal nullity-sanction harnesses social sanctions which may be important to someone whose job security, prospects or effectiveness depend significantly on reputation.

In one sense, it is misleading to attach great significance to arguments about the sanction of nullity in considering the Austinian view of power-conferring rules. The discussion here has done so largely because, given that Austin's critics tend to make so much of this matter, it seems worthwhile to show that Austin's arguments on nullity do have something to be said for them.

In fact, however, the nullity sanction would only be relevant, if at all, to that aspect of power-conferring rules which imposes *duties* or conditions on power holders (for example, the duty of judges not to exceed their jurisdiction, of administrative officials not to act *ultra vires*, or the requirement that the testator sign the will if it is to be recognised as valid). It is absurd to seek sanctions *attaching to the power holder* with regard to the power-conferring element itself – that is, the element of *freedom* to act. But Austin's theory enables us to see where, in his view, the relevant sanctions lie. It will be recalled that, for Austin, rights in one person (which, in this context, he does not distinguish from powers or liberties) are merely the consequence of duties attaching to other people. Thus, insofar as a rule confers powers on X it is to be understood as a command to all other people concerned to recognise and respect the authority of X. So the relevant sanctions attached to the rule giving X power are those that support the duty of others to accept X as having authority within the scope of the rule.

It should be added, to complete the Austinian picture, that many procedural rules can be seen as no more than technical devices to facilitate the direct sanctioning processes of law. Thus, for Austin, 'all laws or rules determining the practice of courts, or all laws or rules determining judicial procedure, are purely subsidiary to the due execution of others' (Austin 1832: 197). The argument here, as in other contexts, is that strings or combinations of rules can link obligations to each other and ultimately connect them to some prescribed sanction. Otherwise, laws without sanctions are parts of others which do have sanctions. In fact, a difficult analytical problem is hidden in this kind of thinking: what counts as a single law or rule? Bentham wrestled with the problem of 'individuation' of laws (Bentham 1970: ch 14) but Austin largely ignores it and, again, it can be said that for him this is a detail. What is essential for him is to demonstrate the structures of power, expressed in complex legal forms, to which each crucial element in the legal order is tied by provisions for sanctioning in the event of non-compliance.

Austin's concern with power-conferring rules is merely to give them a place in a theory that sets out to portray law (in stark contrast to its portrayal in common law thought) as an expression of modern centralised governmental power. For some later writers, perhaps including Hart, power-conferring rules have become a special focus of attention for reasons that do not particularly concern Austin: reasons related to liberal legal theories and conceptions of the Rule of Law which will be discussed in Chapter 4. These theories and conceptions tend to stress law's role in marking out areas of guaranteed freedom in life (such as civil or political liberties and economic freedoms). A pre-eminently important matter for them is the freedom or power conferred by legal rules.

By contrast, Austin's legal theory stresses that these areas of freedom are only what the legally directed power of the state defines them to be through the imposition of duties on people. Thus, for him, emphasis is not on the freedoms themselves but on the coercive structure surrounding them, on which they are wholly dependent. Law gives and takes away powers: of people generally, of particular categories of people, or even (given the limited requirement of generality of rules discussed earlier) of specific individuals.

The crucial point is that Austin is not necessarily wrong because he does not share the emphases of these later writers. As the general approach of this book seeks to show, questions in legal philosophy are asked and made meaningful in the context of their time and place. Austin answers questions as to how power-conferring rules fit within the coercive model of laws and, for *his* purposes, in the context of his theoretical project, the answers are less inadequate than is often claimed.

Sovereignty

Consideration of other criticisms and possible defences of the command theory must wait until its most crucial component, the concept of the sovereign, has been discussed. If law is a type of command, the identity of the commanders and what enables them to issue legal commands must be established. If laws provide for sanctions, the authority to impose sanctions must be explained. The theory of sovereignty which Austin adapts from Hobbes' political philosophy and, to a lesser extent, from Bentham's commentaries on Blackstone is intended to serve these purposes.

What makes commands rules is the element of generality in them; what makes rules laws (in the sense of positive laws, the subject of Austin's jurisprudence) is the fact that they are direct or indirect commands of the *sovereign* of an independent political society. These commands are addressed to the members of that society, who are thus *subjects* of that sovereign. Austin writes of the sovereign as a person (for example, an absolute monarch) or a body of persons (for example, the lawmakers or electorate of a democracy, or the members of an established ruling elite). It is essential, however, to note that he always means by the sovereign the *office* or *institution*[3] which embodies supreme authority; never the individuals who happen to hold that office or embody that institution through their relationships at any given time (eg Austin 1832: 128–129, 218). Austin's sovereign is an abstraction, the location of the ultimate power that allows the creation of law in a society. As will appear later, this point is of supreme importance, since he has often been criticised for describing sovereignty, and the source of legal authority, in 'personal' terms.

Undoubtedly he felt no need to labour the matter for, in the tradition of political theory that he relies on, sovereignty is explicitly 'abstract'. Hobbes, writing in the context of Cromwellian England, describes sovereignty as the 'artificial soul' of 'an artificial man', the latter being the state or commonwealth. The sovereign is an office, not a particular person or particular people (Hobbes 1651: 9, ch 30). In the seventeenth century, Hobbes transformed English discussion of the authority of the ruler by substituting for the power of the king the abstract notion of the state as expressed in the concept of sovereignty

---

3   For the meaning I attach to the word 'institution' in this context see p 3, above.

(cf Hinsley 1986: 142); although, eventually, faced with the difficulty of locating sovereignty in England, he found it (prudently, after the royal Restoration) in the institution of the monarch (Yale 1972: 137–138).

No doubt it was Hobbes' image of sovereignty which predominantly shaped Austin's (his admiration for the earlier writer is very clear in the lectures). By contrast, Austin distances himself in important respects, as will appear, from Bentham's tentative and somewhat confusing discussion of sovereignty.

What is the sovereign of an independent political society? Hobbes had defined such a society as one that could defend itself, unaided, against any attacks from without. Austin realistically notes that few, if any, societies would qualify on this basis. Accordingly, it is the existence of sovereignty which defines indepen-dence, assuming the society is of a certain minimum size (Austin 1832: 176–177, 181). Political independence and sovereignty are correlative terms. Sovereignty exists when two conditions are satisfied: first, the bulk of the society is in a habit of obedience or submission to a determinate and common superior (whether an individual or a body of individuals) and, secondly, that individual or body is not, itself, in a habit of obedience to a determinate human superior. The idea of a habit of obedience introduces a factual, indeed sociological, criterion of the existence of sovereignty and, in this, Austin follows Bentham rather than Hobbes.

Hobbes founded the existence of sovereignty in an assumed 'social contract' by which individuals could be thought of as joining together to form a society and entrusting the absolute power of government to a sovereign who would provide peace and physical protection for them. The war 'of every man, against every man' which would exist without government would be replaced by the domination of the sovereign to whom all are subject (Hobbes 1651: 88, ch 18). But this analysis presupposed that individuals have natural rights which, by the social contract, they agree to forego so as to institute a sovereign power over them. As has been seen earlier, neither Bentham nor Austin was prepared to accept ideas of natural rights, treating them as irrational dogma. Thus Bentham, and Austin following him, discard Hobbes' social contract basis of sovereignty and replace it with the idea of a factual basis of sovereignty in actual habitual obedience. One consequence of this is that while Hobbes' social contract gave the sovereign the right to rule, both Bentham and Austin deny that it makes any sense to talk of a right in this context (Hart 1982: 221; Austin 1832: 230–234). The existence of sovereignty is a political fact, not a matter of right and wrong.

On one view, the 'weak side of the "Austinian analysis" is this transference of a legal conception to a sociological problem' (Stephen 1900: 329) and certainly the grounding of the ultimate authority to create law in a sociological consideration stores up problems for normative legal theory. Nevertheless, it is easy to see here the utilitarian attempt to be realistic, to avoid dogma and abstract talk about arbitrarily assumed natural rights, and to avoid sanctifying authority. Austin cannot resist speculating on *why* people might habitually obey but for the moment that can be left aside. Like the sociological question of how far state sanctions induce compliance with law, it is not important to the *analytical* issue of the location of sovereignty. All that is necessary for the latter is the fact that habitual obedience by the majority of the population exists. Where no such obedience exists there is either anarchy (no recognised sovereign at all) or revolution (the population is divided into groups habitually obeying different authorities).

Some characteristics of Austin's sovereign

Two important characteristics of the Austinian sovereign have already been noted. It must be common (that is, only one sovereign can exist in any single political society; the sovereign is, in that sense, indivisible although it can be made up of several components). And it must be determinate (that is, the composition of the sovereign body or the identity of the sovereign person must be clear). A further characteristic has produced more controversy than any other aspect of Austin's conception of sovereignty. This is that *the sovereign is illimitable by law.* This follows directly from Austin's definition of law. Every law is the direct or indirect command of the sovereign of an independent political society. But a sovereign cannot issue enforceable commands to itself – or at least, even if such an idea is conceivable, the sovereign can abrogate them at any time. And no laws other than the sovereign's own commands can exist to bind it. 'Supreme power limited by positive law, is a flat contradiction in terms ... Every supreme government is legally despotic' (Austin 1832: 212, 225; and see Hobbes 1651: 184).

Many critics have considered that Austin's view of sovereignty conjures up the image of a despotic monarch, an archaic and wholly inappropriate way of thinking on which to found an analysis of the authority of law in modern Western societies. But if we look more closely this is not necessarily so. First, Austin does not suggest the sovereign is free of limitations but only legal limitations. Thus positive morality (reflected in public opinion, widespread moral or political expectations, and ultimately the threat of rebellions) may provide important constraints. Second, most of Austin's discussions of sovereignty relate primarily to the conditions of representative democracies (especially Britain and the United States). Third, Austin's concept of delegation by the sovereign, which will be considered below, is used by him to express the possibility (which has become a reality in most complex modern industrialised

societies) of very extensive dispersion of legislative, adjudicative and administrative authority within the overall hierarchical framework of a centralised state.

Nevertheless, it is widely considered that Austin's conception of an indivisible
and legally illimitable sovereign quickly runs into the most serious analytical
difficulties. The problems seem to begin as soon as one seeks to identify the
sovereign in particular societies. In orthodox British constitutional law the
sovereign is said to be the Queen in Parliament: that is, the sovereign is made up
of the monarch and the two houses of Parliament. Constitutional law supports
the claim that such a sovereign is legally illimitable. Parliament cannot bind itself
or its successors by legislation.[4] Since the House of Commons is the
representative of the electorate, however, Austin (1832: 194) locates sovereignty in the monarch, the House of Lords and the electorate of the
Commons.

Many critics have seen this as either problematic or utterly misleading. In
particular, Austin has been seen as confusing legal and political sovereignty
(Dicey 1959: 76; Buckland 1949: ch 9). Popular sovereignty may well reside in
the electorate, but for legal purposes surely Parliament is sovereign. In fact,
there is no confusion. Austin does not write of *legal* sovereignty or treat
sovereignty as supreme legal competence. As C A W Manning points out,
Austin's sovereignty is not a legal but a *pre*-legal notion. It is 'the logical correlate
of an assumed factual obedience' (Manning 1933: 192, 202). In modern terms,
we can say it is the locus of legitimate ultimate political authority. It is not 'a
specified organ or complex of organs, but ... that individual or collectivity at
whose pleasure the constitution is changed or subsists intact' (Manning 1933:
192).

But if this is so how can the electorate as subjects be in a state of habitual
obedience to themselves as sovereign? The answer is that the members of an
independent political society *as individuals* can be in a state of habitual obedience
to a sovereign which is the abstract institution defined as monarch, Lords and
the *collectivity* represented by the electorate of the Commons. The distinction
between the subject population and the electorate forming part of the
sovereign (and made up of essentially the same people) is a distinction between
subject individuals and a sovereign collectivity. There is nothing incoherent in
claiming that the individual is subject to the authority of the collectivity as an
institution, or that the collectivity as a whole retains authority because the bulk
of individuals continue to accept its authority.

---

4   Eg *Vauxhall Estates Ltd v Liverpool Corporation* [1932] 1 KB 733; *Ellen Street Estates Ltd v
    Minister of Health* [1934] 1 KB 590.

What of the case of written constitutions and those where the distribution of governmental authority is especially complex, as, for example, in federal systems? Austin considers at some length the location of sovereignty in the United States to illustrate his approach. The embodiment of the sovereign as an institution must be a person or persons, but the ultimate authority of the American polity appears to be *a document*, the Constitution. Where then does sovereignty lie? Of course, in the Austinian analysis it must lie with the body of people that has ultimate authority to alter the Constitution. The Constitution itself provides in Article 5 that amendments to it must, to be valid, be ratified by the legislatures of (or conventions in) three quarters of the states. Again, in an Austinian analysis, where representatives are involved, it is the electors of these representatives who form the sovereign body (Austin 1832: 208–210).

Critics note that the Austinian sovereign in such a context is 'a despot hard to arouse', 'a monarch who slumbers and sleeps', since constitutional amendments are rare (Dicey 1959: 149). But this situation matters only if we are seeking (as Austin is not) a legal sovereign: that is, an active, ultimately authoritative lawmaker. By contrast Austin is identifying only the location of ultimate authority underlying the constitutional order; the institution recognised as having authority to confirm or amend that order.

Suppose that in a political society with a written constitution there is no such institution, no means of constitutional amendment. Sovereignty would then seem to lie in those governmental and legislative institutions that the constitution recognises as ultimately authoritative, since nothing capable of changing their authority stands behind them. In an Austinian view, however, sovereignty resides in these authorities not *because* of their designation by the constitution, but because the authorities so designated are themselves habitually accepted.[5]

---

5 Consider a further problem arising in a full parliamentary democracy in which, in Austin's terms, the electorate alone is the sovereign. The parliament may pass legislation altering the composition of the electorate (for example, by enfranchising people who previously had no legally recognised right to vote). This seems to be a case of the sovereign purporting to alter itself by law. Yet, for Austin, the sovereign is above law: its creator, not the creature of law.

Can Austinian theory be applied to explain such a situation? Austin himself provides no satisfactory solution but the matter could be argued as follows. The legislation changing the composition of the electorate is certainly law (as the sovereign's command). The issue is as to whether it is, in itself, effective to alter the sovereign. Austin must say it is not, for the sovereign's identity depends not on law but on recognition by the bulk of the population. The identification and limits of the sovereign and its authority are essentially governed by what Austin would term positive morality. But the new electoral law does, at least, have the authority of law and as such may strongly influence positive morality towards the acceptance of a redefined sovereign. Obviously the legitimacy of future law that claims authority as the commands of the redefined sovereign depends, on this analysis, on popular acceptance of

Must the sovereign be legally illimitable?

We have noted that Austin insists that by definition the sovereign cannot be subject to legal limitations. Blackstone (1809 I: 49) had earlier claimed that in every legal system there is a supreme, absolute and unlimited legislative power. Bentham, however, thought differently. While claiming that there are no *a priori* theoretical limits on sovereign power, he nevertheless considered that legal limits on such power were practically possible. Like Austin, he grounds the existence of sovereignty in the fact of habitual obedience. Hence he sees the possibility of *conditional* habitual obedience: that is, obedience might be habitually rendered to sovereign acts *within certain limits*. The 'obedience of the governed is susceptible of every modification of which human conduct is susceptible: and the rules which mark it out, of every diversity which can be clearly described by words' (Bentham 1970: 69; cf Bentham 1977: 489).

This is plausible, but seems to run into problems when it is suggested that the limitations on sovereign power are *legal*. Bentham (1970: 64) does suggest this by terming some of these limitations *leges in principem*. But where does their legal quality come from? He recognises that *leges in principem*, like all other laws, must derive from the sovereign but his explanations of how the sovereign can bind itself are far from satisfactory, relying on suggestions about the invocation of external pressures of popular opinion, religious or moral sanctions, or international relations (Bentham 1970: 67–70). For Austin, of course, these kinds of sanctions are characteristic not of law but of positive morality. It is by no means apparent how Bentham's *leges in principem* acquire their legal character.

His apparently inconclusive discussion seems motivated here primarily by a desire to recognise clearly the variety of constitutional structures which do indeed distribute authority within states in complex ways: for example, through federal arrangements, provision for judicial review of legislation, entrenched constitutional clauses or the explicit separation of governmental powers.

Austin's simpler, clearer conception of legally unlimited sovereignty is not incapable of dealing with these complexities. It has been seen that for him the sovereign is always an institution: for example, the monarch (not the person who is king at any given time) or the body that can change the constitution (not the particular individuals who may form that body). How is the institution defined or identified? It would seem that two kinds of rules may do this: rules of positive law and rules of positive morality (for example, public opinion

---

the redefinition, not on the fact that the redefinition has been enshrined in law. If the redefinition of the sovereign is accepted, however, the redefining law will, no doubt, be treated as legally expressing the new understanding of sovereign authority.

expressed in customary, moral or other rules, conventions or expectations). Only positive morality can actually bind the sovereign so as to fix its institutional character. Positive law cannot do this since the sovereign can alter this law at will.

But even if it does not bind the sovereign it can have the status of law if commanded by the sovereign and addressed to any *part* or agent of the sovereign body (for example, to the British parliament – perhaps defining its procedures; to judges – perhaps specifying jurisdiction; or to the monarch in a constitutional monarchy – perhaps defining the monarch's powers as well as the right of succession to the throne). Positive law can bind each part of such a sovereign body as 'the Queen in Parliament' since each part is not itself sovereign.

Nevertheless, the considerations that fix the nature of sovereignty in general in a particular political society must be founded in positive morality, not law. Sovereignty is, as has been seen, a pre-legal concept. In an Austinian view no law can confer or validate sovereignty. Austin asserted that much of constitutional 'law' must, in fact be merely positive morality for this reason. This is a much less unrealistic view than is often claimed, once it is appreciated that, on the basis of the arguments above, laws directed to distinct parts of the sovereign body (or, perhaps more accurately, distinct institutions through which sovereignty is expressed) can certainly be accepted as laws in Austin's terms, even though they cannot bind the sovereign as a whole.

The acceptance of the sovereign as an institution seems to remove much of the difficulty that is often thought to exist for Austinian attempts to explain the persistence and continuity of laws (cf Hart 1961: 51–66). Laws can remain in force as long as the institutional sovereign remains, perhaps for centuries. Equally, the problem of succession to authority (for example, how one king succeeds another in a recognised line of succession) and the continuity of laws may be explained in Austinian terms by the existence of rules of positive morality or positive law as described above. Where sovereignty appears to reside entirely in a single person such as an absolute monarch it would seem that the rules governing succession to the throne can only be rules of positive morality. But Austin would consider this a wholly realistic view of the matter. Whatever may be written in 'legal' form (as statutes, for example), succession in such a situation depends on political loyalties, traditional beliefs, and ideological notions which only a most narrow-minded jurist could try to reduce to purely 'legal' determinants of succession.

This defence of Austin is far from claiming that law *must* be interpreted in something like his terms. He offers only a particular partial perspective which emphasises a certain relationship between law and the modern state, viewed in terms of sovereign power. Writers who have argued forcefully against his interpretation have usually wanted to see the legal system as being governed by rules, even in its highest regions of authority, rather than – as Austin's theory so starkly claims – governed by *people*, mere human decision-makers with all their frailties and potential for arbitrary or tyrannous exercise of power. As noted earlier, Austin's theory is not a theory of the Rule of Law: of government subject to law. It is a theory of the 'rule of men': of government using law as an instrument of power. Such a view may be considered realistic or merely cynical. But it is, in its broad outlines, essentially coherent.

The judge as delegate of the sovereign

The concept of *delegation* of sovereign power is fundamental to Austin's thinking. It is obvious that the theory of sovereignty applied to modern conditions must entail such delegation among many agencies empowered to transact the business of the state in one way or another. Indeed, the idea of delegation in this sense is the element necessary to complete the discussion of power-conferring rules that was begun earlier in this chapter.

The sovereign, in Austinian terms, delegates legislative and administrative functions to many institutions – including, significantly, the judiciary. Equally, law-making power is delegated to private citizens who exercise it, for example, in creating contracts according to terms chosen by the contracting parties but which the sovereign's institutions will enforce (cf Bentham 1970: 22ff). Each dispersion of sovereign power in this way is a delegation, not a release of it. Each legitimate exercise of such power to create legal obligations (for example, when a court lays down a new rule in a case or when an official establishes a rule on the basis of statutory authority) must be treated as an exercise of the sovereign's power of command. Hence, insofar as such an act is not revoked or invalidated by higher authority representing the sovereign, it can be considered a *tacit command* of the sovereign (Austin 1832: 35–36; 1885: 642).

Many critics have claimed that this notion of tacit command, which is present also in the theory of Hobbes (1651: 187), is unrealistic as regards law-making through judicial decisions (eg Maine 1875a: 364–365; Rumble 1985: 112). Are not judges independent in such democracies as, for example, Britain and the United States? How can they be considered mere delegates of some other authority? The difficulty again arises from treating Austin's sovereign as a legal sovereign, an ultimate legislating institution. Thus, the legal doctrine of parliamentary sovereignty in Britain, which recognises Parliament as the highest law-creating authority, does not, of course, entail that judges are delegates of Parliament. Austin's theory does not, however, suggest that they are. It claims merely that they must act as representatives of the constitutional order of which they are a part. In Austinian terms that constitutional order is the consequence of the pre-legal sovereign authority embodied in monarch, Lords and the electorate of the Commons.

Logically, it follows that delegation of sovereign power, insofar as it is done by law, must be done by means of the sovereign's commands – whether as specific requirements for action or prohibitions imposing limits on action, whether addressed to officials or non-officials, and whether express or tacit.

Many important consequences follow from Austin's way of looking at the distribution of political and legal authority in the state in this way. For example, his view of the judge as delegate of the sovereign entails a straightforward recognition that judges *legislate* no less than do legislatures. Judges make law insofar as their decisions embody what can be considered to be the sovereign's tacit commands. Austin's carefully expressed views on judicial law-making have often been misinterpreted and are certainly very different from Bentham's.

Bentham sought a rational, codified legal system which would make not only judicial law-making but probably also judicial interpretation of law unnecessary and inappropriate. The role of the judge would be to decide cases not by appeal to legal precedent but by following the demands of utility in the particular case, and seeking to reconcile differences between the parties where possible (Postema 1986: ch 10). Judicial decision-making would thus be radically separated from the rational code structure of the law itself. Such a position follows from Bentham's conviction that rational law could be constructed only by purposive legislation, not by judicial pronouncements arising from the accidents of litigation. As Bentham's interpreter Gerald Postema admits, it is hard to construct a coherent theory of the place of the judiciary in the legal order from such ideas (Postema 1986: 453–459).

Austin is the model of cautious moderation beside Bentham's radicalism. But he does claim that judges 'of capacity, experience and weight' have generally been insufficiently active in developing the law (Austin 1885: 646–647). He argues against the idea that judicial law-making (or, as he calls it, 'judiciary law') is arbitrary or undemocratic, taking as his primary point that judiciary law is no different in this respect from any other form of subordinate legislation and, in all such situations, positive law and public opinion must provide the necessary safeguards. The most radical theme that emerges is that insofar as judges make law there is no reason to treat their law-making role as necessarily and essentially different from that of other delegates (officials, administrators, boards and committees) of the sovereign entrusted with rule-making functions.

So Austin's criticisms of judiciary law are entirely technical: it tends to be made in haste, it is inevitably established *ex post facto*, it 'exists nowhere in fixed or determinate expressions', it tends to be vague and inconsistent, its rules are 'never or rarely comprehensive', there is no clear test of its validity and its existence tends to make accompanying statute law 'imperfect, unsystematic, and bulky' (Austin 1885: 649–659). Hence code systems are, as Bentham had argued, better than common law systems. But Bentham rests the matter squarely on unshakeable assumptions about where perfect legal rationality resides and would, it seems, like to sweep away the law-making judge into the museum of archaic curiosities. By contrast, Austin painstakingly weighs up the practical considerations and on balance confirms the purely technical virtues of codification and legislation.

Austin's theory of the centralised state

Austin's view of the judge as just one variety of state functionary among many others leads us into a wider consideration of his image of the modern state. Austin's political and social theory is ignored in most jurisprudential discussions of his work, yet it provides the essential context in which his concept of delegation of sovereign power is given significance.

In his early political writings he made clear his belief in the virtues of political centralisation. Austin's top-down image of law reflects a top-down image of the polity. Like the other major nineteenth century writers discussed so far in this book he was far from being a democrat (though Bentham, towards the end of his life, came to advocate a kind of democratic government: see Dinwiddy 1975). Austin viewed government as a matter of rational management to be guided by principles of utility. As such (and rather like Maine) he saw it as a matter for experts. John Stuart Mill wrote that after Austin's return from Germany in 1828, 'he acquired an indifference, bordering on contempt, for the progress of popular institutions' (quoted in Dicey 1905: 163). As time went on, his views became increasingly conservative and in his last published writings he polemicised against any constitutional reforms that would extend democracy.

These views should be understood in the context of the intellectual climate of his times. When Austin wrote his lectures his view of government was undoubtedly elitist in the most literal sense. The real security for good government would be not popular participation but an enlightened population, which, understanding the rational principles that governing elites should follow, would obey government not blindly but on the basis of a critical recognition of its rational purposes.

Both John and Sarah Austin believed fervently in the need for universal education, which would make it possible for the broad population to distinguish sound policy and scientific principles (for example, of political economy) 'from the lies and fallacies of those who would use them to sinister purposes, and from the equally pernicious nonsense of their weak and ignorant well-wishers' (Austin 1832: 63). While most ordinary subjects lacked both time and inclination to master the knowledge that would make acquiescence in government a *fully* rational affair, Austin considered that they could learn at least the 'leading principles' of those matters (such as social ethics and economics) that concern government, and 'if they were imbued with those principles, and were practised in the art of applying them, they would be docile to the voice of reason, and armed against sophistry and error' (Austin 1832: 63). So Austin's view of the bases of obedience is not like that of Maine who, as noted in the previous chapter, saw reason's role as strictly circumscribed and emphasised the irrational, customary basis of the acceptance of authority.

All this suggests that to treat Austin's view of law as much like a view of mere orders backed by threats (such as those of a gunman pointing his gun at the person addressed) is misleading (cf Hart 1961: ch 2). The relation between sovereign and subject is far more than one founded on coercion. The habit of obedience to the sovereign is, according to Austin, rooted in custom, prejudices and 'reason bottomed in the principle of utility': that is, a recognition of the expediency of government (Austin 1832: 246–247). In a soundly educated people, reason would play a most important role. Equally, when we consider the significance of the sanctions attaching to law in actually securing obedience to law, Austin notes that fear of legal sanctions is not likely to be more powerful in deterring deviance than is 'the fear of public disapprobation, with its countless train of evils' (1832: 66). In forming moral character the latter is much more significant than the former.

Thus, Austin's image of the centralised state, making extensive use of coercion through law in the matter of government, is also an image of a state that can be based on reason: guided by the principle of utility and securing the allegiance of subjects to the sovereign ideally through their rational understanding and not prejudice, fear or blind habit. Nevertheless, Austin considers that it must realistically be recognised that populations are kept largely unenlightened by their rulers. Hence much government does in fact rely on irrational, habitual popular acquiescence. Universal education is thus the Austinian prescription for a sound, enlightened polity.

A need for acquiescence in unified state authority focussed on the sovereign goes along with the need for extensive delegation of sovereign powers, as has been seen. Austin praised the institutions of local government and recognised the appropriateness of judicial law-making and extensive rule-making in administrative contexts. Nevertheless, in his writings on the virtues of centralisation he insists that none of this delegation must be allowed to defeat the central co-ordination of government by which rational utilitarian policies can be consistently brought into effect.

In later life, he changed many of his political views, replacing much of his optimism about the prospects for reason in politics and social organisation with a Maine-like pessimism. Centralisation seemed less attractive to him with his fading belief in the potential of government to direct society rationally, and with a growing fear of its control by despots or mobs (Hamburger and Hamburger 1985: 185–186). Most fundamentally, Sarah Austin tells us that her husband decided some time after 1832 that 'until the ethical notions of men were more clear and consistent, no considerable improvement could be hoped for in legal and political science, nor, consequently, in legal or political institutions' (Austin 1885: 16). Apparently, education remained the key to advance but the struggle was now seen as a far harder one than originally envisaged: perhaps, indeed, an impossible one.

Austin's late, profound pessimism should not affect an assessment of the ideas contained in his lectures. It should alert us only to the fact that his 'timeless' concepts of sovereign, command, sanction and habitual obedience are not formulated in isolation from specific political conditions. Like most elements of normative legal theory they are conceptual reflections of a particular time and place, transformed in a way that gives them the potential to speak to other generations in other legal conditions. In Austin's case, however, these concepts are formulated with a clear awareness of the sociological questions they entail. This dimension of his thought has been almost totally ignored by his critics in the field of normative legal theory.

Austin and the legal profession

Austin's legal philosophy, like Maine's historical jurisprudence with which it was effectively contemporaneous, reflected the political conditions of a state gradually forming modern capacities for deliberate direction of economic and social life. But it was far more influential on professional legal thinking, in the long run, than was Maine's work.

Austin explicitly addressed his work to lawyers. His concern for systematisation and rationalisation of legal doctrine was noted at the beginning of this chapter. He seemed to offer a means of working towards the neat and 'scientific' organisation of professional legal knowledge that historical jurisprudence and the common law tradition apparently could not provide. He wrote of the possibility of supplying a 'map of a body of law' for the newcomer student: a map based on broad rational principle and demonstrating the structure of a legal system (Austin 1885: 1082). And his theory of law and sovereignty seemed to show how even the most basic notions of law could be explained in terms of their logical structure and unifying authority.

Thus, when the second edition of Austin's *Province of Jurisprudence Determined* was published, it 'was immediately welcomed as the only English work which offered a methodology for the scientific textbooks on English law required by the new courses' in legal education in the universities and the Inns of Court (Stein 1980: 85–86). Whatever its faults, Austin's jurisprudence showed a serious attempt to analyse the character of law without appeal to the vague, romantic images of common law thought. It offered a theory for the times which would explicitly recognise the modern dominance of legislation, the active law-making of the modern state, and the idea of law in flux as a purposive human creation.

But, it may be suggested, his most important professional contribution was to show, at the same time, that despite the potential changeability of law and the fact that political powers, not judges, now made the running in legal develop-ment, law could still be considered a unified field of professional knowledge. His jurisprudence, as has been seen, clearly distinguishes law from morality. It asserts also that custom is not law unless adopted as such by the courts (that is, by the sovereign's tacit command). It marks out the field of law, the province of the lawyer's concerns, with a rigour that is impossible within the framework of classical common law thought. Thus, intellectually-minded lawyers could see that Austin might be offering the basis for elaborating legal knowledge as a well organised subject respectable in the environment of university education and as the special learned expertise of a modern profession of lawyers. Law would be 'neither a trade, nor a solemn jugglery, but a science' (Pollock quoted in Sugarman 1986: 36).

Austin's work left unanswered questions about the nature and method of this science which, as will be seen in the next chapter, have troubled later writers. However, the professional needs which his work serves explain, to some extent, why it is the theory of law and sovereignty in *The Province*, and not the broader elements of Austin's 'general jurisprudence' developed in his other lectures, that has attracted continuing attention. While the latter lectures dwell on law's substance (the notions common to mature systems of law such as 'property' and its aspects and categories) the theory of *The Province* is primarily concerned with law's form and the structure of legal authority. Perhaps professional knowledge of law, in an era of continuous legislative change, could only be unified around ideas about the form and structure of law, and not around ideas about law's substantive content. The content of law was not only in constant flux but beyond lawyers' control (unlike the situation in earlier eras when judges both explained and controlled legal development). It was the result of political considerations that could not easily be brought within the professional knowledge field of lawyers.

Of course, these political considerations intrude into Austin's lectures in *The Province* in passages where he discusses the principle of utility. But, as noted earlier in this chapter, Austin's emphasis is always on rationalisation of law as it is – as a lawyer or law student needs to understand it. The science of legislation, which had been fundamental to Bentham, is portrayed by Austin as something for the ordinary student to avoid. There are passages in Austin's writings where his caution proscribes any flights of the imagination. He explains (1885: 1078) that a teacher might properly occasionally spice his exposition with references to issues of legislative policy but should do so only on matters 'which do not try the passions'. And there is always a need for a narrow focus, for limiting the range of what is studied. Most people must be content with putting together no more than the limited package of knowledge they need for immediate practice. 'I am sorry it is so', he writes (1885: 1088).

This is a far cry from Bentham's urgent commitment to legal reform and to a legal science that would continually serve the needs of legal improvement. But Austin's outlook pointed the way towards what has been called the expository tradition in legal education and scholarship. It suggested that a viable science of law could be built around the task of rationalising law as it is without much concern for how it ought to be, even in the modern era of never-ending legislative change.

On the other hand, the elements of Austin's theory discussed in this chapter also explain some primary reasons why it evokes so much hostility among many writers concerned with normative legal theory today. Discussion here has tried to suggest that it may be not the general logic of Austin's jurisprudence which is primarily at fault, for many of the matters which critics have most strongly emphasised were well understood by Austin and dealt with by him in the context of his theory. A main, if usually unstated reason for condemning Austin may be that the emphases of his thought seem *politically* inappropriate.

Austin's theory, as has been seen, does not deny the possibility of constitutional controls on government. But, as an optimistic utilitarian at the time he wrote his lectures, he, like Bentham, saw strong government as a virtue as long as that government was guided by the principles of utility. The theory of sovereignty and the political theses of centralisation and delegation which inform and fulfil it are inspired by this opinion. Equally, Austin's lack of concern for the value of liberty except as part of the utilitarian calculus of advantages offends modern sensibilities. The apparent reduction of judges, in Austin's portrayal, to merely one type of rule-creating or rule-interpreting state official among others also rankles, as does the related lack of patience with orthodox theories of the separation of governmental powers. Finally, Austin's view of international law (which will be left for comment until the next chapter) as positive morality rather than law seems inappropriate in a modern world of increasingly intricate international ties.

These political and constitutional matters are important in lawyers' professional outlook and the different view of them in some post-Austinian normative legal theory will be considered in the next chapter. The concern of discussion here has been to suggest that, interpreted in its own context and in terms of its own emphases, Austin's jurisprudence remains a valuable contribution to normative legal theory and one that grasped the problem of recognising realistically the phenomenon of centralised modern state power in a way that classical common law thought was wholly ill-equipped to do.

Chapter 4

Analytical jurisprudence and liberal democracy: Hart and Kelsen

Although Austin's legal theory may still be instructive, given its serious attempt to view law realistically as an instrument of state power, it is obvious that much has changed since he wrote. The confident utilitarianism that emphasised social benefits to be brought about by rational government and rational law was typically also an unashamedly elitist view of government.

It was seen in Chapter 3 that the virtues of democracy do not enter into Austinian calculations. To limit governmental power is not viewed as an especially important aim. Liberty is seen as a by-product of rational government, rather than as potentially threatened by state power. The doctrines of the Rule of Law and the *Rechtsstaat*, the state defined by and subject to law, are not reflected or prefigured in Austin's legal philosophy to any notable extent. Constitution building and the careful legal separation of governmental powers – matters of considerable importance to Bentham – play little part in Austin's thinking in his lectures.

In the modern Anglo-American world, however, all of these matters are regarded as politically very important. They are also, typically, matters of serious professional interest to lawyers. Thus, it is not necessarily only the defective logic of earlier legal philosophy which has inspired different approaches in the literature to be considered in this chapter. These newer writings may also reflect different concerns from Austin's, different fears, different political experiences and a changed social and legal environment.

This chapter addresses the work of two writers both of whom can be seen, in terms of the theses of this book, as trying to transcend – in radically contrasting ways – the approach to legal philosophy adopted in Austin's lectures.

One of them, H L A Hart – Professor of Jurisprudence at Oxford University from 1953 to 1968 – explicitly builds his ideas on a critique of Austin's jurisprudence. Of Hart's work it has been appropriately said that it 'provides the foundations of contemporary legal philosophy in the English-speaking world and beyond' (Hacker and Raz (eds) 1977: v).

The other major writer to be considered here is the Austrian Hans Kelsen, perhaps the most illustrious and widely discussed figure in twentieth century legal philosophy. Kelsen originally developed his theories in a continental European tradition without reference to Austinian thought, but arrived at positions which he himself recognised as having an affinity with Austin's analytical jurisprudence. Thus he wrote in the 1940s, three decades after having laid the foundations of what has become known as the 'pure theory' of law, that this theory 'corresponds in important points with Austin's doctrine' (Kelsen 1941b: 271). 'Where they differ, they do so because the pure theory of law tries to carry on the method of analytical jurisprudence more consistently than Austin and his followers' (Kelsen 1945: xv).

Kelsen's willingness to recognise these parallels is generous. His work is far wider in intellectual scope than Austin's and, outside the Anglo-American world, has been much more influential. It is based on a rigorous epistemology and a sophisticated philosophical view of the nature of legal theory: matters which Austin never seriously addressed in any comparable fashion. Kelsen's writings demonstrate his familiarity with literature in psychoanalytic theory, political and social theory and anthropology, as well as law and philosophy.

Hart's normative legal theory does not show a comparable range. As will appear, it was constructed primarily in conscious reaction to Austin's jurisprudence, and subsequently refined and revised largely in the context of commentary on and criticism of Bentham's normative legal theory. Given the contrasting intellectual contexts of Hart's and Kelsen's work it is interesting that, while Kelsen draws parallels between Austin's work and his own despite fundamental philosophical differences, Hart asserts unequivocally the need for 'a fresh start' and a total rejection of Austin's jurisprudence ('the record of a failure') to advance legal philosophy (Hart 1961: 80).

Kelsen's legal theory was shaped in a legal and cultural environment very different from that of the Anglo-American common law world. His ideas are relevant to this book insofar as they have had a significant impact on Anglo-American legal thought but also because they help to put Hart's work into a broader intellectual perspective in two ways. First, parallels between Hart's and Kelsen's ideas help to show how themes in Hart's jurisprudence may reflect wider political concerns about modern law that are not confined to the Anglo-American tradition. Secondly, a consideration of Kelsen's methods of constructing his legal philosophy – methods radically different from Hart's – helps in evaluating ideas about the nature and methods of normative legal theory that are often taken for granted in the Anglo-American context, but not necessarily shared outside it. Indeed, the root of the most basic difference between Hart's and Kelsen's theoretical approaches is in two different ideas of the very nature of theory itself. It will be necessary to outline the contrast between these ideas about theory before proceeding further.

Empiricism and conceptualism

The contrast emerges clearly from recent discussions of Austin's work. Quite apart from any particular merits or demerits Austin's jurisprudence has in clarifying the nature of modern Western law, it has apparently left a deep ambiguity at its core; one that continues to puzzle later writers. The ambiguity relates to Austin's aims and methods of analysis.

One view claims, in essence, that Austin's purpose was to produce in his general jurisprudence a systematic, orderly account of the key components of modern legal systems. Austin's concern was empirical in the sense that he wished to represent or describe theoretically the reality of actually existing legal systems, identifying elements common to these modern systems of law and organising them into a body of scientific knowledge. Thus, Austin sought, in W L Morison's words, 'to represent law empirically, as something we can readily understand in terms of observable occurrences' (Morison 1982: 2): observable at least, for example, in the form of actual statutes, judicial decisions and instances of other official action, and the habitual behaviour of subjects. So Morison argues that 'all the evidence indicates that when Austin made general factual statements about independent political communities, he believed them to be universally true' (Morison 1958: 231). They could be tested for their truth against the circumstances of particular legal systems.

The idea that theory is, in some such way, a direct representation of empirical reality, with its concepts derived from observation of and generalisation about that reality and so corresponding with it and testable for truth against it, will be called here *empiricism*.

There is, however, another view of theory which, in fact, has been more widely attributed to Austin by recent commentators on his work. It can be explained as follows. Empirical reality – the world of objects and experiences 'out there' – does not, in fact, present us with evidence which we can merely package together or generalise about to arrive at scientific truth. Concepts need to be formed in advance – *a priori* – to organise empirical evidence. The previously established concepts not only determine what is empirically relevant but also reflect a view of why it is relevant. Thus, theory aiming at a scientific explanation of any object of knowledge cannot take its concepts from observed experience but must deliberately *construct* concepts as a means of interpreting experience, of *imposing* order on it. A theory is not an attempted representation of observable reality but an intellectual construction – a logically worked out model – which can be used to organise the study of what can be observed in experience. This idea of the nature of theory will be termed here *conceptualism*.

Thus, Julius Stone, rejecting the view of Austin as an empiricist, argues that he should be understood as a conceptualist, 'presenting an apparatus for seeing as clearly as possible the aspect of a legal order with which his analytical system was concerned'; he 'sought the starting-points which would enable him to construct definitions and classifications on the basis of which he could, to a maximum extent, show the logical inter-relations of the various parts of the law to each other, and the subordination of the less general to the more general parts' (Stone 1964: 68, 69). Whereas an empiricist view would say that a theory's truth can be tested in the light of experience, a conceptualist would claim that it is usefulness, not truth, which is the issue. Do the ideas of the theory make it possible to interpret and organise what we know about actual legal systems in a clearer, more illuminating fashion?

Ultimately the methods-debate around Austin's legal philosophy is unfruitful since there are good reasons for an uncommitted reader of his lectures to conclude not only that Austin did not recognise the conceptualism-empiricism dichotomy but also that he wrote in ways that will support either interpretation of his theoretical methods. Nonetheless, the matter is important for at least two reasons.

First, some of those writers (notably Hart) who in various ways follow the empiricist approach to theory also tend to see Austin as an empiricist, and this interpretation seems to go along with an emphasis on Austin's theoretical indebtedness to Bentham and an underestimate of other influences on him. Austin's methodological ambiguity may, however, reflect the odd mixture of influences which shaped his jurisprudence: that is, on the one hand, Bentham's 'pseudo-realistic mystery-dispelling analytical technique' (Manning 1933: 212), empiricist in orientation, and, on the other, continental Roman law scholarship. In the latter tradition the deliberate construction of abstract legal concepts by jurists to organise the empirical detail of legal doctrine was an admired skill. Such an outlook on law seems compatible in various respects with a conceptualist view of theory. But this possible pull towards conceptualism in Austin's thinking tends to be ignored in the common view of him as merely a disciple of Bentham.

Second, an excessively empiricist view of Austin may make it harder to appreciate the character of some of the key concepts he uses. Thus, Hart's apparent failure to recognise the 'abstract', institutional character of Austin's sovereign may result from a too literal, empiricist interpretation of Austin's claim that the sovereign is a person or body of people. The tendency may be to assume that Austin's concept must directly represent something observable (for example, an individual person who is king) rather than operating as a means of conceptualising the ultimate authority by which positive law is made (for example, the institution of monarch). Equally, an excessively empiricist interpretation may be at the root of the common tendency of Austin's critics to seek the sovereign (and inevitably not find it) in sources of legal authority existing *within* actual legal systems (as elements of constitutional structure which a lawyer can recognise), rather than in an abstract institution 'standing behind' the constitution and legal system and presupposed by it (cf Lobban 1991: 246–247).

However that may be, the empiricism-conceptualism dichotomy in normative legal theory is important. A tendency to adhere to one approach rather than the other pushes legal theory in distinct directions. Each tends to lead to different kinds of concepts being used and certainly to different ways of evaluating these concepts. Kelsen's legal philosophy exemplifies a sophisticated and rigorous elaboration of an avowedly conceptualist approach to normative legal theory. On the other hand, Hart's 'fresh start' in legal philosophy built from his criticisms of Austin is best seen – so this chapter argues – as an attempt to adopt empiricist methods more satisfactory than those he attributes to Austin.

Hart's linguistic empiricism

Most English legal philosophy was empiricist (in the particular sense used above) in orientation between the time when Austin's jurisprudence became influential (from the 1860s) and 1953 when Hart was elected to the Oxford chair of jurisprudence. Its dominant approaches had come to be called analytical jurisprudence. They adhered to Austin's view that law and morality should be kept analytically separate and that the appropriate subject of jurisprudence was positive law. Analytical jurisprudence thus viewed law as a human creation established through political power.

A primary object of analytical jurisprudence was to clarify the meaning of legal concepts, to try to establish what such concepts represent or refer to. The idea of corporate personality, for example, although fundamental to legal thought, seemed puzzling. What does the concept of 'corporation' represent? Does it refer to a real group entity? Is it just a kind of legal shorthand form used to refer to a complex of legal rules defining certain relationships between individuals linked in some common enterprise? In an empiricist perspective, concepts arise from and represent some observable reality. Analytical jurisprudence concerned itself, therefore, with trying to discover the meaning of concepts such as possession, ownership, intention, legal personality, right and duty, generally by ascertaining what actual legal state of affairs each of these terms necessarily referred to.

It may be supposed, with hindsight, that an important reason why English legal philosophy declined in influence and interest as far as lawyers were concerned in this period was that the English empiricist approach to analysis of legal concepts appeared increasingly unrealistic and fruitless. The endless debate on the nature of corporate personality, for example, sought to fix the meaning of the concept without adequate reference to the immense variability of the circumstances in which it could be invoked, and of the legal consequences that could follow from it.

In the United States, some jurists tried to develop an approach to analytical jurisprudence that showed elements of the conceptualist, as opposed to empiricist, outlook. Wesley Hohfeld, who taught at Stanford and Yale Universities before his premature death in 1918, analysed a set of 'fundamental legal conceptions' – rights, duties, privileges, 'no-rights', powers, liabilities, immunities and disabilities – as what he called the *lowest common denominators of law*. While some of these concepts were obviously taken directly from lawyers' established usage, Hohfeld's development of them was creative. The concepts were rigorously defined theoretical constructions which, whether or not actually reflected in existing judicial practice in the way he described them, were intended by him to organise and clarify legal reasoning by giving it more precise conceptual distinctions. So analytical jurisprudence in this form was intended to aid clarification of law by devising concepts as a 'logical frame built according to specifications drawn from an actual body of law' (Stone 1964: 138).

The value of Hohfeld's work is perhaps especially in a kind of limited reconciliation between conceptualism and empiricism. It combined a deliberate, creative development of illuminating concepts – with their logical relationships precisely worked out – and an insistence that the concepts should relate directly to and be grounded in actual judicial reasoning as expressed in reported cases. Some other American writers, notably Albert Kocourek of Northwestern University, took a more clearly conceptualist approach to legal analysis

(Kocourek 1928: 228, 234, 236), inventing such new organising and interpretive concepts as 'ectophylactic', 'zygnomic' or 'mesonomic' relations and 'autophylaxis'. The danger of such an approach – a danger that Hohfeld largely avoided – is that its conceptual originality can seem as far removed from actual practical legal reasoning as does excessively broad empiricist generalisation about the meaning of lawyers' notions.

Hart's very influential inaugural lecture (Hart 1953) was clearly intended to mark a sharp break with all of these previous tendencies in analytical jurisprudence and to call in aid new resources for a more realistic analysis of legal concepts. In the lecture, Hart presents the futility of the corporate personality debates as one of several reasons why new methods are needed. Legal words, he explains, must be understood in the context of whole sentences in which they play their characteristic role. They cannot be defined in isolation as if they represented some specific entity. Their use presupposes the existence of an entire legal system and that particular rules are valid within it. Furthermore, legal statements may have a different status in different contexts: for example, a statement's status when made by a judge in the course of deciding a case in court may be wholly different from its status when made outside the courtroom in various situations. Equally, legal concepts do not necessarily relate to a uniform, invariable set of circumstances, because legal rules may attach the same legal consequences to a variety of factual situations.

The viewpoint of Hart's lecture suggests an attack on empiricism because concepts are no longer to be seen as representing anything in a one-to-one fashion. The meaning of a legal concept, according to this view, cannot be defined as if the concept represented some invariant state of affairs.

In fact, however, Hart institutes a new kind of empiricism in place of the old: an empiricism grounded in the linguistic philosophy associated especially with Ludwig Wittgenstein at Cambridge University and J L Austin (not to be confused with the jurist John Austin) at Oxford. Hart brought to jurisprudence the methods and enthusiasms of English linguistic philosophy. When appointed to the Oxford chair of jurisprudence he had no law degree but had practised at the Chancery Bar and then, after the 1939–1945 war, taught philosophy at Oxford for seven years. During the latter period he became closely involved with the Oxford development of linguistic philosophy, sometimes termed 'ordinary language philosophy'.

Hart said of this that it was:

> 'inspired by the recognition of the great variety of types of human discourse and meaningful communication, and with this recognition there went a conviction that longstanding philosophical complexities

could often be resolved not by the deployment of some general theory but by sensitive piecemeal discrimination and characterisation of the different ways, some reflecting different forms of human life, in which human language is used' (Hart 1983: 2).

Linguistic philosophy, in this form, focussed not on the meaning of words in some definitional manner, but on clarifying the way words are used in various linguistic contexts. The method could be used to illuminate 'the discourse of everyday life' or of any intellectual discipline – such as law – where a failure to appreciate its distinctive character and its differences from other discourses might result in 'perplexity or confusion' (Hart 1983: 3).

Three insights from this kind of philosophy are especially important to Hart's normative legal theory. First, language has many meaningful forms apart from empirical description or the statement of logical propositions. A significant characteristic of legal language is its 'performative' aspect, 'where words are used in conjunction with a background of rules or conventions to change the normative situation of individuals and so have normative consequences and not merely causal effects' (Hart 1983: 4). The point here is that words used in legal contexts can actually alter legal situations and all the expectations that attach to them. For example, when a contractual offer is accepted by the offeree the legal relationship between offeror and offeree is fundamentally changed. And this function of language applies not just to law. Words said in a christening ceremony, or in the making of vows, are also performatives. They change expectations, obligations and relationships through their use in a specific context.

A second important insight from linguistic philosophy is that of the 'open texture' of language. As will appear, this is basic to Hart's ideas on judicial decision-making and legal interpretation. Linguistic philosophy could not admit a *general* indeterminacy of language, otherwise philosophical study of its meaning in use could not proceed. In specific contexts linguistic meaning is asserted to be, potentially, definitely ascertainable. At the same time, however, language has a 'porosity' or partial indeterminacy so that the relationship between the core of certainty and the penumbra of uncertainty in even the most precisely stated rules requires philosophical examination.

Third, perhaps the most important claim of linguistic philosophy, as far as Hart's legal theory is concerned, is that the 'elucidation of the multiple forms and diverse functions of language' (Hart 1983: 3) is capable also of illuminating the social context in which language is used. Hart does not hesitate to make this claim about the social insights to be gained from linguistic analysis. Thus, 'the suggestion that inquiries into the meaning of words merely throw light on words is false. Many important distinctions, which are not immediately obvious, between types of social situation or relationships may best be brought to light by an examination of the standard uses of the relevant expressions and of the way in which these depend on a social context, itself often left unstated' (Hart 1961: vi).

How then would analysis proceed on such a basis? Instead of asking what the legal term 'corporation' designates we should 'characterise adequately the distinctive manner in which expressions for corporate bodies are used in a legal system' (Hart 1953: 42). And this is – although Hart never calls it such – a new kind of empiricism because what is required is 'a close examination of the way in which statements eg of legal rights or of the duties of a limited company relate to the world in conjunction with legal rules' (Hart 1983: 3). So it is necessary to examine the actual conditions under which such statements are regarded as true. The observable reality that legal statements represent is not a range of identifiable entities referred to by words such as 'corporation'. It is the reality of the linguistic practices of people living within a legal system and orienting their conduct and expectations in relation to it. In the 1953 lecture there could be little doubt that Hart was thinking of lawyers' practices. The emphasis on actual judicial and legal professional usage in all its variety and complexity seemed to breathe a healthy realism into legal philosophy.

The idea of 'performatives' entails, however, that statements can be practices in themselves. One can 'do things with words' in J L Austin's phrase; 'words are also deeds' as Wittgenstein put it (cf Hart 1970: 275). Thus, Hart's form of linguistic philosophy does not necessarily claim to be concerned with words or statements as *representations* of a social reality. The statements *are*, in themselves, the social reality. They constitute it.

Adopting this viewpoint it is not difficult to slip into the position of arguing that philosophical analysis of ordinary language use amounts to a kind of empirical explanation of aspects of social life. Thus, Hart claims in the preface of his most important work in normative legal theory, that the book is not only an essay in analytical jurisprudence but also in 'descriptive sociology' (1961: vi). This controversial claim must await evaluation later. For the moment it is enough to note that Hart's legal philosophy firmly rejects conceptualism (see eg Hart 1970: 271, 274) and seeks to find its concepts in the actual linguistic practices of lawyers, judges and citizens.

The character of rules

Given what has been said above about Hart's methods it is unsurprising that he rejects any attempt, such as Austin's, to define 'law' or 'a law' and seeks instead a concept of law that treats it as a complex of social practices. He makes no attempt to specify these practices exhaustively in a definitional manner. His concern is, apparently, only to try to clarify those that seem central to the way law is generally perceived. They are to be identified primarily by studying distinctive linguistic practices typically associated with law in ordinary usage.

These methods of proceeding are obviously very different from Austin's. Instead of defining a set of concepts (command, sanction, sovereign, habitual obedience) and exploring their relationships, Hart takes certain distinctions that seem to be drawn in everyday language, and then considers their implications. The starting point is to identify the idea of a 'rule' as the central idea in ordinary discourse about law.

Hart's method of doing this is through a critique of an Austinian model of law, which concludes that Austin's failure to examine the concept of rule and to make it central to his jurisprudence was the root cause of the inadequacies of his view of law (Hart 1961: 80). Austin's supposed inability to explain the continuity and persistence of law is traced to his inadequate acknowledgement that the sovereign is itself defined by rules, acquires and exercises authority through them and can be limited by them. The problem of power-conferring rules and the difficulty of assimilating them to commands are held to show that Austin's jurisprudence was incapable of recognising the variety of types of legal rules. Equally Austin's tracing of the source of all law to the sovereign's command is considered to ignore the fact that customary law and judge-made law may arise from and derive independent authority from sources different from that of legislation.

In Chapter 3 it was suggested that at least some of these criticisms of Austin may be misguided. Nevertheless they are important in Hart's major work *The Concept of Law* as the device by means of which the concept of 'a rule' is installed as the self-evidently appropriate starting point for an ordinary language analysis of the nature of law. As will be seen in later chapters, it is certainly possible to argue that law is best analysed theoretically as something other than, or at least involving much more than, a set of rules. Nevertheless, the lengthy attempt to demonstrate the inadequacies of a version of the command theory in the first four chapters of Hart's book (taking up a third of its text) provides a kind of tableau in which the terms of debate are set and the missing element of rules emerges to solve most difficulties.

In ordinary language we often talk of doing things 'as a rule', that is habitually: 'I play my saxophone at weekends, as a rule'. When the word 'rule' is used in other types of statement, however, it is often accompanied by expressions such as 'should', 'ought to', 'ought not' which suggest something other than the regularities of habit: 'You shouldn't make so much noise late at night. There are rules of law about causing a nuisance'. Words such as 'should' and 'ought' are normative terms: that is, they imply evaluation, criticism, or judgments regarding behaviour and not merely description or prediction as do words indicating merely habitual behaviour.

The fact that my habitual saxophone playing can also be interpreted normatively – here, in terms of its conformity or lack of conformity with legal rules about nuisance – illustrates the point that events, activities and occurrences can be spoken about in two radically different ways. They can be discussed in *predictive* terms (Am I so attached to my saxophone that I shall keep on playing it whatever happens? Will the neighbours actually sue? In practice what kind of sanction is usually imposed on people who disturb the neighbours at three o'clock in the morning?). Or these matters can be discussed in *normative* terms (Do the neighbours have a legal right to complain? According to law, ought the nuisance to stop? What order can a judge properly make if the nuisance continues and the case comes to court?).

Normative language about rules thus entails evaluations, judgments about what is proper or right according to the relevant rules, or criticism of deviations from the rule. Such deviation is considered good reason for criticism by those who accept as legitimate the rule that has been broken. Words such as 'ought' and 'should' are commonplace in normative statements. But they have no place in purely predictive statements. In the latter cases it is not a matter of what 'should' or 'ought to' be done, but what 'is' or 'will be' the situation (Will the noise stop? Will the neighbours sue? What penalties are the courts in practice imposing?).

This linguistic distinction between normative and predictive language is fundamental to Hart's concept of law. Insiders within a legal order, people who understand and act upon the normative content of the law, can reason critically with legal rules. They have an *internal view* of the rules, or view the rules in their 'internal aspect'. Equally it is possible for people to adopt a purely external or predictive view of aspects of the legal order ('It's sensible not to drive at 80 miles per hour along Mile End Road. It is very likely that you will be stopped by the police if you do'). One of the most important characteristics of rules, in Hart's analysis, is that they lend themselves to both internal and external understanding.

The internal view of rules obviously involves a certain specific mental attitude – a critical, reflective attitude to one's own conduct and that of others in the light of the rules (Hart 1961: 57) – but Hart insists that it is not equivalent to a psychological feeling of being bound by the rules. A person enthusiastically engaging in tax evasion may understand perfectly well that his activities are wrong in law and, indeed, may be well versed in the relevant rules and their legal meanings. But he may feel no compulsion to obey the law as long as he can avoid detection. Beyond this insistence on what the internal view or aspect of rules does *not* entail, Hart does not offer much further clarification of its nature.

Sociological drift

Hart's distinguishing of the two aspects of rules is important for several reasons. One is that it marks a serious attempt to break with Austin's methods. As has been seen, Austin tried to identify the field of law by defining essential elements of law as rigorously as he could in contradistinction to moral ideas or to matters 'improperly' termed legal. The field of law is marked out in descriptive fashion. Hart, however, avoids marking out the legal field as such. Instead, he distinguishes between the states of mind (with regard to legal rules) of 'insiders' of the legal system and 'outsiders'.

The outsiders (adopting an external view of legal rules) might be not just those calculating in purely predictive terms their chances of avoiding punishment or gaining some benefit, but also, for example, behavioural scientists only concerned with studying the patterned behaviour of people and unconcerned with their critical, reflective attitudes to rules. Hart argues that lawyers, judges and other legal officials must, however, take an insider's internal view of at least those rules that regulate their own official activities within the legal system. Many ordinary citizens may similarly take an internal view of some or all legal rules. People presumably may be insiders or outsiders in different circumstances or on different occasions or with regard to different legal rules.

Even before looking at the way this dichotomy is further developed in Hart's concept of law some odd features of it can be noted. The opposition Hart initially develops is between habits and rules. But it is not made clear what kinds of entities are being compared. It may be that Hart's method of linguistic philosophy prevents this (concepts only have meaning in use) but since the concept of a rule is being treated as fundamental it is surely appropriate to ask what this concept means in general use. Presumably the only way of treating habits and rules as directly comparable is to view both as impulses or motivations towards action (habits give rise to habitual behaviour, rules inspire rule-governed behaviour). So rules are, it seems, understood by Hart only in terms of their social functions or potential social effects.

That this is the way Hart views them seems to be confirmed by what he says about the concept of *obligation*. The idea of obligation presupposes rules though some rules (for example, those relating to etiquette or grammar) are not spoken of as imposing obligations (Hart 1961: 86). Obligation-imposing (or duty-imposing) rules are distinguishable from others, according to Hart, in three ways. First, in the case of obligation-imposing rules 'the general demand' for conformity is insistent and great social pressure is brought to bear against actual or potential non-conformity with them. Second, these rules are considered 'necessary to the maintenance of social life or some highly prized feature of it'. Third, compliance with them is thought of as characteristically requiring some sacrifice; duty and interest often being in conflict (1961: 86–87). The most interesting aspect of these distinguishing marks is that all relate to ideas about the relationship between the rules and the social conditions in which they exist. They are concerned with assumptions about the social function or effects of the rules or of compliance or non-compliance with them.

Thus, Hart's legal philosophy identifies the fundamental component of law, obligation-imposing rules, not by organising the familiar material of legal study in terms of concepts such as command and sovereign, but by speculating about widely held attitudes to various kinds of rules. This is, it must be said, not descriptive sociology (cf Hart 1961: vi), which should presumably be based in substantial empirical study. It is speculative philosophy not grounded in any systematic consideration of actual social conditions. The conceptualisation of obligation-imposing rules does not explain or even consider the conditions under which general agreement on the matters indicated might exist in a society; or, if agreement does not exist, which members of a population must hold the views specified; or what kind of evidence would be appropriate and sufficient to enable us to reach conclusions about these matters.

The root of the problem is this: Hart seeks to provide a general explanation of the character of law on an empiricist basis – in other words, the concepts that he seeks to link theoretically are to be drawn from actual experience or observation of law. But he rejects the idea that legal doctrine itself provides the empirical materials for theory, because there is no necessary fixity of meaning of legal ideas. They do not necessarily represent anything consistently so theory cannot concern itself exclusively with their meaning and the logic of their relationships in legal doctrine. Therefore, the empirical reality to be reflected in theory is the reality of people's (linguistic) practices, the way they talk and think around notions such as 'obligation'. But this should involve actually finding out how people talk and think and such an inquiry is not normative legal theory but sociology or social psychology.

As long as empiricist approaches in normative legal theory were satisfied with analysing legal doctrine (the concept of 'corporate personality', for example) as the relevant empirical reality (asking what is a 'corporation'), they did not lead normative legal theory's inquiries into a study of society at large. But Hart's empiricist approach leads in just such a direction. There is a kind of sociological drift (but no serious sociology) in Hart's normative legal theory. It will be necessary to return to this matter after considering further claims he makes about the nature of legal rules.

The structure of a legal system

In Chapter 3 it was noted that Hart insists that Austin's command theory cannot accommodate satisfactorily the existence of power-conferring rules in a legal system. These cannot, in his view, be treated as having essentially the same character as duty-imposing rules. Both kinds of rules are present in a legal system and the distinction and relationship between them becomes the central idea of Hart's concept of a legal system.

In a simple society it might be possible to maintain social order solely through duty-imposing rules such as rules restricting violence, protecting property, or punishing deceit. Such duty-imposing rules Hart terms *primary rules*. A regime of primary rules alone could maintain itself in practice only if the vast majority of people subject to these rules viewed them from an internal perspective, in the sense discussed earlier: that is, normatively as guides to conduct, rather than merely predictively.

Any such regime, however, is subject to obvious defects. First, the primary rules will not constitute a system but merely a set of separate standards, so doubts as to how the rules relate to each other or how far they extend cannot be resolved. They suffer from the defect of uncertainty. Second, they have a static quality since no means are available for changing them in deliberate fashion, either generally or in their applicability to particular individuals. Third, there is no means of establishing conclusively when a violation of the rules has occurred or of systematically enforcing them.

Behind this fictitious idea of what Hart terms a pre-legal society can be sensed not only a vision of some simple changeless society which an anthropologist might discover but also, perhaps, the image of unguided, culturally determined legal evolution suggested in classical common law thought, as discussed in Chapter 2. Such an image has no conception of law as *positive*, deliberately created and so subject to human interpretation and development. This conception of doctrine as subject to positive development, which Austin found in the idea of sovereignty, Hart finds in a further set of rules beyond the primary duty-imposing rules. Their introduction or evolution marks, for Hart, the transition from a pre-legal to a legal order.

These *secondary rules* are generally portrayed as parasitic on primary rules, power-conferring rather than duty-imposing, and of three kinds which correspond with the three major defects of a regime of primary rules alone.

Thus, the secondary *rule of recognition* is the simplest remedy for the uncertainty of the regime of primary rules. It specifies what particular features a rule must have to be recognised as a rule of the society. The rule of recognition may be simple or complex. An example of a complex one could be that rules are to be recognised as rules of the society if created through a certain legislative procedure, or declared by a judge in certain conditions, or supported by long customary practice. The limbs of such a complex rule of recognition could be hierarchically ordered so that the limb recognising legislative rules takes priority over those recognising customary rules and rules declared in judicial decisions.

Second, *rules of change* remedy the static quality of a regime of primary rules because they regulate procedures for creating or changing other rules or altering their operation. For example, they include rules governing the composition and procedures of a legislative body, as well as rules allowing individuals to alter their own legal circumstances: for example, by making wills or contracts.

Finally, *rules of adjudication* are needed to remedy the inefficiency in operation of a regime of primary rules. They specify means by which a final authoritative decision can be reached as to whether in a particular case a primary rule has been broken. These rules specify who has the authority to adjudicate and the procedures to be followed. They specify, for example, the jurisdiction and procedures of courts and the qualifications of judges.

When a close look is taken at the secondary rules, as Hart discusses them, considerable uncertainty is seen to surround their nature. They are identified originally as power-conferring in contrast to the duty-imposing primary rules. Hart, however, admits in effect in his later writings that the rule of recognition can be duty-imposing or power-conferring depending on how it is viewed (Hart 1982: 258–259). Other writers have noted that the distinction between primary and secondary rules is not necessarily consistent in Hart's discussions. As well as the distinction between duty-imposing rules and power-conferring rules it may be a distinction between non-parasitic rules (that can exist as meaningful social standards apart from any relationship they may have with other rules) and parasitic rules (that have meaning only in relation to others); or between rules concerning actions involving physical movement and change and others leading to the creation or variation of obligations. These varied distinctions are not necessarily mutually consistent.

Several commentators have noted that secondary rules are not necessarily power-conferring (MacCormick 1981: 106; Raz 1980: 199). Hart himself suggests that most lawyers would treat rules about appointing judges as involving two relevant types of law, one fixing the *duties* of judges (and their powers) and the other conferring on some person the *power* to appoint them

(Hart 1972: 215). Conferring powers and determining duties are thus (as Austin well understood) typically intertwined. One commentator has suggested that 'there is simply no such thing as the distinction which we may understand Hart as having made between primary and secondary rules' (Sartorius 1966: 167). Hart himself eventually referred to his 'own previous inadequate approach to the subject' and admitted that *The Concept of Law* contains 'no close analysis either of the notion of a power or of the structure of the rules by which they were conferred, save to insist that they were different from rules which imposed obligations or duties' (Hart 1972: 196).

This is, if taken at face value, extremely puzzling. Austin's failure to make the distinction between power-conferring and duty-imposing rules central to his theory is the focus of some of Hart's fiercest attacks on him. Yet the distinction remains vague and undeveloped in Hart's major work on normative legal theory. Hart accepts that some such distinction as he makes has long been recognised, but 'perhaps my claim that this distinction could throw light on many dark places in jurisprudence was novel' (Hart 1965: 358). Yet no rigorous analysis is offered to cast that light. As Hart's sympathetic critic Neil MacCormick remarks, given 'the centrality of this topic to Hart's theory of law, it is regrettable indeed that such vagueness and imprecision attends his distinction' between primary and secondary rules (MacCormick 1981: 106).

What explains this vagueness at perhaps the most fundamental part of Hart's legal theory? The explanation is surely that the need to distinguish primary and secondary rules is not dictated by considerations of analytical rigour in normative legal theory but by a *political* concern to emphasise aspects or perhaps ideals of law which Austin was thought to have under-emphasised.

Joseph Raz hints at the truth in asserting that the 'fundamental reason which moved Hart to adopt his doctrine of the rule of recognition' is his assumption that the answer to the question of whether a legal rule is valid must be found in a criterion of validity provided by *some other* rule (Raz 1980: 199–200). Putting it another way, Hart's legal theory portrays law as a self-regulating system of rules. The rule of recognition and the other secondary rules are seen as governing the entire process of production, interpretation, enforcement, amendment and repeal of rules within the legal system. In contrast to Austin's picture of a legal order as the expression and instrument of all-too-human political power (the power of the sovereign and its delegates), Hart's image of law is that of a system in which rules govern power-holders; in which rules, rather than people, govern. What is, indeed, implied here is an aspect of the deeply resonant political symbol so obviously missing from Austin's jurisprudence – the symbol of the Rule of Law, a 'government of laws and not of men' (cf Bobbio 1987: ch 7).

The concept of secondary rules can be seen, therefore, as an attempt to devise an analytical category that can serve as the umbrella under which an appropriate emphasis can be given to power-conferring *functions* of legal rules.

These secondary rules, insofar as they are 'public' in character, are the ones that typify the modern constitutional state (*Rechtsstaat*) in which the powers of officials are not arbitrary but defined by rules of law. Equally, rules conferring 'private' powers (such as rules governing the making of wills, contracts and other transactions and arrangements) allow individuals to adjust their personal legal positions in deliberate, freely chosen and purposive action. These rules mark an individual's autonomy as a *citizen* within the legal order, participating in it as a member of a legal community. To make use of such private power-conferring rules the individual presumably must be a legal 'insider', someone who adopts an internal view of the rules.

Thus, while the stress on public power-conferring rules builds the normality of the ideal of the Rule of Law (in the sense of government subject to law) into Hart's theory, the parallel stress on private power-conferring rules builds into it the normality of the ideal of autonomous citizenship, a very different perspective from that entailed in Austin's notion of subjection to a sovereign and undoubtedly a much more attractive one, politically, in a modern democracy.

The existence of a legal system

The rule of recognition of a legal system, according to Hart's concept of law, determines which other rules in the system are valid as law. It does this, of course, insofar as it is, itself, recognised or presupposed as a valid rule. One minimum condition, therefore, for a legal system to be in existence is that the rule of recognition and the other secondary rules are accepted as binding by those persons (whom Hart calls 'officials') having the task within the legal order of creating, changing, interpreting, applying, enforcing, or advising on legal rules. This acceptance is essential because the secondary rules are the means by which the legal system governs the fulfilling of these tasks. It follows that the officials must adopt an internal view (in Hart's sense) of the secondary rules. They must view them as meaningful guides for their own conduct and that of others. The other minimum condition for a legal system to exist is that citizens, in general, regularly obey the primary rules. It is not necessary that they should view the primary rules from an internal viewpoint. Obedience merely because of the fear of punishment would be sufficient. Thus, for a legal system to exist there must be general obedience to the primary rules, coupled with an acceptance by officials of the secondary rules from an internal viewpoint.

This claim about the minimum conditions of existence of a legal system is important insofar as it links, like a buckle, the two fundamental oppositions (primary as against secondary rules, internal as against external aspects of rules) around which the whole of Hart's normative legal theory revolves.

The giving of sociological hostages to fortune is, however, even more pronounced here than in the instances of sociological drift noted earlier in relation to Hart's theory. One writer refers to Hart's claims about the necessary attitudes of officials as a 'bizarre piece of prescriptive psychology' (Goodrich 1987: 48). A point reiterated frequently by Hart's more sociologically oriented critics since the first publication of his theory has been that to describe officials' views of the secondary rules in terms of a Hartian internal attitude is highly inadequate to represent the complex reality of official motivations.

A defender of Hart might insist that the idea of the internal aspect of rules is intended not to represent the complexities of official compliance with secondary rules but merely to establish an analytical distinction between the discourse of 'insiders' and 'outsiders' in relation to a rule system. That those who understand rules 'internally' can reason with them in particular ways, using normative language that makes their discourse significantly different from that of outsiders is what is important here. Motivations for obedience to the rules, and whether or not citizens or officials approve or disapprove of them, are wholly different matters.

Hart's hermeneutics

Up to a point this is a plausible answer. Hart uses his internal-external distinction to assert that law cannot be explained adequately in purely behavioural (external) terms. The essential distinguishing character of rules is that they can be understood normatively (from an internal aspect). Law is to be understood not through any purely behavioural social science (observing and measuring behaviour) but by entering its mode of discourse and its ways of reasoning. This kind of empathetic understanding is sometimes referred to as *hermeneutic* understanding.

There is, however, an ambiguity in Hart's original presentation of the internal and external aspects of rules. To understand rules from an internal standpoint must one actually be a committed insider within the legal system: that is, someone who personally accepts the rules as guides to conduct? Is the only other possible position that of the external observer who does not even recognise the normative character of legal rules? Or can one be an 'outside' observer (not actually, oneself, committed as a citizen within the legal order) who can nevertheless interpret and understand the rules, *as if* personally accepting them as guides to conduct?

Neil MacCormick has suggested the need for a third position, between the strict internal and external views of rules, to take account of the situation of an uncommitted observer who can nevertheless interpret law normatively and make what Raz has called 'detached statements' (Raz 1980: 236): that is, normative statements entailing no personal normative *commitment* to the legal system to which they relate. MacCormick (1981: 38) terms this third position the hermeneutic point of view. Various passages in *The Concept of Law* might suggest that Hart assumed all along that the internal view of rules was one that could be understood by a hermeneutic observer (a legal theorist, for example) as well as by an official or citizen adopting the rules as guides for his and others' conduct (eg Hart 1961: 89). But Hart (1982: 153–155) eventually recognised Raz's distinction between committed and detached statements as an important supplement to the ideas expressed in *The Concept of Law*. Further, he adopted MacCormick's proposed third point of view as well as the term 'hermeneutic' to describe it (Hart 1983: 14).

These apparent concessions are significant. In 1961, when *The Concept of Law* was first published, Hart saw, as the chief theoretical enemies which the idea of the internal aspect of rules was intended to address, all attempts to describe law (and especially judicial decision-making) in purely behavioural terms: that is, from a viewpoint emphasising only the external aspect of rules.[1] The idea of the internal aspect gave notice that a behavioural description of law was wholly inadequate. Yet Hart always assumed that a descriptive account of the nature of law is possible (even, as noted earlier, a 'descriptive sociology'): the point was that any such description must treat law as having both internal and external aspects. Linguistic philosophy would provide the key to understanding the internal aspects.

In 1961 it was perhaps not necessary to point out that a legal theory entailing understanding of the internal aspect of rules (the insider's perspective) could nevertheless be 'detached', uncommitted and concerned only with description, as regards the normative meaning of those rules. The only kind of analytical detachment Hart felt it necessary to argue for explicitly was the one Austin had insisted on: the analytical separation of law and morals – a matter to be considered in more detail in the next chapter. Recently, however, various writers and especially the American jurist Ronald Dworkin, have challenged the assumption that normative legal theory should aim at 'detached', objective

---

1 Some main types of theory which Hart interprets as adopting this viewpoint on law are discussed in Chapter 7, below.

description of law. An internal view of legal rules (that is, participation in the enterprise of legal interpretation) is viewed in these post-Hart theories as providing, in itself, knowledge of the nature of law. The only view of rules to be taken account of by the legal theorist thus becomes the internal view.

Dworkin's theses will be considered in Chapter 6. For the moment it is enough to recognise that the legal theory Hart advocates must now fight on a different front from that which existed when *The Concept of Law* was first published. The challenge to his approach now comes not from writers who advocate exclusive emphasis on the external (behavioural) aspect of law since it would be hard now to find any influential jurist (if ever there was one) who seriously argues that law can be understood in purely behavioural terms. The challenge now is from theories that put exclusive emphasis on the internal (normative) aspect of law (cf Hart 1987; 1994).

Hence Hart makes explicit in his later writings what was always implicit in his thinking: that the hermeneutic point of view (the view appropriate to a Hartian legal theorist) is not identical with the committed internal view of a participant in the legal system. The legal theorist is not simply engaged in legal reasoning, but tries to *describe* and *objectively explain* the nature of legal reasoning (Hart 1994: 242–244). Hart's theory is most interesting, indeed, for the balancing act it tries to sustain: the insistence that legal theory must be simultaneously 'inside' and 'outside' law as a system of ideas. In his approach, normative legal theory adopts what he sees as the perspective of a legal insider, but it does so only to enable an objective, detached view of legal activities to recognise fully the normative character of law.

Judicial decisions and the 'open texture' of rules

Unfortunately, this favourable image of theoretical balance is not the one with which we can leave a discussion of Hart's concept of law. The defence that his major categories and distinctions are purely analytical and therefore immune from sociological critique (cf Hacker 1977: 12) is unsupportable. This is because Hart's method, as has been seen, is founded on the claim of linguistic philosophy that analytical categories and distinctions are to be given meaning only in the context of actual linguistic usages which themselves reflect social practices. Hart's empiricist method entails that concepts reflect social practices. What becomes important then is to ask how successfully conceptual analysis, in illuminating linguistic practice, helps reveal aspects of social reality.

Adopting this yardstick it must be recognised that Hart's minimum conditions of existence of a legal system and the claims about officials' attitudes to secondary rules are ultimately sociological claims about the way people think and behave. Hart's minimum conditions of existence of a legal system are actually hypotheses about the sociological conditions under which a legal system maintains legitimacy or acceptance. In some of the most influential literature of sociology these matters are addressed with a wealth of historical detail and empirical illustration.[2] In Hart's writings, however, they remain at the level of brief, highly generalised and empirically unsupported philosophical speculation.

Again, therefore, it seems that Hart's empiricism directs him towards inquiries beyond the scope of normative legal theory. A further example of this tendency can be seen in his analysis of judicial decision-making and the 'open texture' of rules. Hart adopts the philosopher Friedrich Waismann's idea of the porosity or open texture of concepts to try to analyse the degree of certainty with which rules can be interpreted and applied. In considering the task of judicial decision-making this must be a vital concern for any theory such as Hart's that treats law as, in essence, an affair of rules. Surely, insofar as judges through their interpretations of law develop *new* law they cannot be *bound* by pre-existing rules? Rules may govern the means by which judicial law-making proceeds (for example, rules of precedent or jurisdiction) but the substantive content of judge-made law, by definition, is not covered by rules predating the relevant judicial decisions. So Hart's theory admits that judges in certain circumstances may and do exercise *discretion* in legal interpretation. Existing rules plus judicial discretion are, therefore, the ingredients of judge-made law.

It then becomes essential to determine the relationship between rule and discretion. If it were to be admitted that judicial discretion is very extensive, or unpredictable, the model of law in terms of rules would collapse. Hart's empirical orientation forces him to recognise that rules are often, in practice, open to widely varying interpretations. But a theorist not wedded to the idea that rules are the central element of law might suggest that legal rules are effects or consequences of judicial or other official decisions, rather than the reverse. Thus, for Austin, as has been seen in Chapter 3, law consists, strictly speaking, not of rules but of commands, and judicial decisions are a species of delegated sovereign commands. Whether these decisions embody wide or severely limited discretion they can be seen as having a uniform character. Discretion is not a fundamental problem for Austin in the way it is for a model of law in terms of rules.

Hart tries to solve the problem of maintaining the centrality of rules in his concept of law by identifying two components of them – a 'core' of settled

---

2   See Weber 1978: Part I ch 3, Part II chs 10, 11, 14 and 15.

meaning and a 'penumbra' of uncertainty (Hart 1958: 63–64). The 'life of the law consists to a very large extent' in guidance by 'determinate rules' (1961: 135). But in penumbral cases 'it is clear that the rule-making authority must exercise a discretion, and there is no possibility of treating the question raised by the various cases as if there were one uniquely correct answer to be found, as distinct from an answer which is a reasonable compromise between many conflicting interests' (1961: 132).

As with the question of whether legal theory should view law 'internally' or 'externally', Hart seeks a balanced mid-position on the question of interpretation. Law is neither the 'noble dream' of a consistent, complete set of rules whose meaning is ultimately conclusively determinable; neither is it the 'nightmare' of rule-free judicial discretion (Hart 1977). But this 'reasonable' position betrays the tension between Hart's analytical objectives and the empiricist manner in which they are pursued. His analytical model impels him to make rules central in his theory. Consequently the core of certainty in them is strongly emphasised in *The Concept of Law*: the result of the English doctrine of precedent has been to produce a set of rules 'of which a vast number ... are as determinate as any statutory rule'; the operations of courts are 'unquestionably rule-governed ... over the vast, central areas of the law' (1961: 135, 154).

On the other hand, what determines the areas of core and penumbra – certainty and uncertainty – in rules? Hart's empirical method entails that this can be determined only by actual social (linguistic) practices. Concepts, as has been seen earlier, are not considered to have meaning in isolation from the specific contexts in which they are used. Particular situations 'do not await us already marked off from each other, and labelled as instances of the general rule ... nor can the rule itself step forward to claim its own instances' (1961: 126).

Thus, certainty in rules is not a feature of rules themselves but of the social practices in which they are used. It follows that the distinction between core and penumbra is not an analytical one referring to aspects of the structure of rules: it is a representation of social practices.

The important point, then, is that it is not rules which govern and provide certainty according to this line of thinking: certainty derives from the relatively settled conventions of usage and practice which reflect a degree of social consensus. As with most aspects of Hart's legal theory, categories that are presented as analytical ultimately reveal themselves as references to presumed social facts. But there is still no concern to examine matters sociologically rather than in terms of philosophical speculation. Thus there is no real clarification of the relationship between rule and discretion, certainty and uncertainty in law.[3] While portraying the problem as analytical, Hart sets it up as sociological. Yet no sociological inquiry is made into the actual conditions (relating, for example, to the organisation and character of the judiciary) under which interpretive agreement about the meaning of legal rules becomes possible or becomes problematic.

Kelsen's conceptualism

Hart's work has had and continues to have great influence in Anglo-American legal philosophy. The prolific writings of Hans Kelsen have also had a powerful impact. Yet they have never had the same centrality despite being among the most profound contributions to legal theory during the past century.

One reason is that Kelsen's writings are informed to a considerable extent by the traditions of continental European civil law thought rather than the specific experiences of Anglo-American common law. This can be only a partial explanation, however. After fleeing from Nazi Germany to Switzerland in the 1930s, Kelsen eventually settled in the United States and spent the remaining three decades of his life there (he died in 1973), teaching at the University of California until his retirement in 1952. So he worked for a long period, writing prolifically, in an Anglo-American environment. Equally, he made great efforts to explain and interpret his ideas in relation to Anglo-American legal and political institutions and the major tendencies of Anglo-American legal philosophy.

The main reason why Kelsen has remained an outsider is that his approach to theory is thoroughly *conceptualist*, in the sense explained earlier in this chapter. In this respect it runs counter to ideas rooted in the common law tradition, as well as, perhaps, counter to broader cultural tendencies in Britain and America. Whatever view we take of classical common law thought, it remains the case that the Anglo-American common law tradition emphasises piecemeal, case-by-case legal development, and what the sociologist Max Weber termed 'empirical law-finding' (cf Weber 1978: 785–788). That is to say, concepts in common law are not imposed on the law but are assumed to be drawn from the detail of case-by-case legal experience. Legal ideas are found empirically in the practical business of deciding cases. Thus, the kind of empiricism in legal theory that has been treated as a theme of the earlier part of this chapter, actually reflects directly major underlying assumptions about common law

---

3 See the final extremely vague and inconclusive statements about the nature and value of legal certainty in Hart 1994: 251–252.

methods – even if in analytical jurisprudence it gives rise to theories that appear to supplant classical common law thought.

Yet Kelsen is a most instructive outsider. Given this book's exclusive concern with Anglo-American legal philosophy, the importance of his normative legal theory is in the contrast of its methods with Hart's empiricism. As will appear, Kelsen's conceptualism avoids some dilemmas that we have seen Hart's normative legal theory led into by its empiricist outlook. In addition, some political and professional ramifications of Hart's theory can be clarified by noting parallels in Kelsen's thinking and drawing on the rich, detailed political theory that accompanies Kelsen's legal philosophy. The following sections will be concerned with these matters.

Kelsen's conceptualism reflects the influence of continental neo-Kantian philosophy. Knowledge, according to this tradition, is not simply given by experience. We only begin to understand empirical reality by imposing concepts on it which enable us to organise as meaningful what we observe. Concepts do not reflect experience: they organise it and make it intelligible. Every science, every knowledge-field, must, therefore, create its own conceptual apparatus. Because of this necessity, each science or form of systematic knowledge is unique and distinct from all others. Consequently, legal science must have its own unique framework of concepts which cannot be shared or integrated with those of other sciences. It follows, therefore, that Kelsen wholly rejects what he calls syncretism of methods, the 'uncritical mixture of methodically different disciplines' (Kelsen 1967: 1). The unique nature of legal science is determined by its subject-matter, law, and Kelsen, like Hart, sees one of the most important characteristics of law as its normativity. Law is a matter of 'ought-propositions' or norms: 'By "norm" we mean that something ought to be or ought to happen, especially that a human being ought to behave in a specific way' (Kelsen 1967: 4). Legal science must be a normative science.

These positions immediately highlight differences from Hart's approach. Whereas, as has been seen, Hart's normative legal theory continually drifts towards sociology (yet holds back from serious sociological inquiries), Kelsen's rejection of syncretism entails that there can be no link of any kind between the legal theory he develops, as the theory of a purely legal science, and sociology. They are totally different conceptual frameworks appropriate to different subject-matter. So legal theory, as Kelsen understands it, must be purified of all foreign concepts and methods. Indeed, the name which he gives to his normative legal theory is *the pure theory of law*. It is unconcerned with law as it should or might be – for that would be the concern of politics or moral philosophy. Its subject-matter is positive law in general.

Kelsen's conceptualism entails that the purpose of the pure theory of law is to provide a set of interpretive concepts that make it possible to organise knowledge about the law of particular legal systems. The theory does not itself provide that knowledge. The pure theory of law merely provides the concepts that normative legal science can use in describing the actual norms of a particular legal system. But this task is, in Kelsen's view, nonetheless essential. It provides the framework of ideas on which law as an intellectual discipline and professional practice is based.

So there is no suggestion that the concepts of the pure theory of law are derived from or reflect empirical reality, the circumstances of actual legal systems. Empiricism, together with the syncretism of methods that tends to go with it, is firmly rejected.

In other respects, however, the thrust of Kelsen's theory is similar to Hart's. Both are committed to the idea of a legal theory that provides objective, detached explanation of the character of law and both see the recognition of law's normative character (in Hart's terms, the internal aspect of rules) as essential to that theoretical explanation.

Originally Kelsen wholly rejected behavioural (which he equates with sociological) explanations of law. Thus, in his early writings a sociology of law is treated as impossible and misguided since it fundamentally mistakes the nature of law, ignoring its essential normative character. Later, however, he adopted a view more in keeping with his neo-Kantian outlook. Treating sociology as the science whose methods and concepts are created specifically to interpret causes and effects of social behaviour, he came to recognise that a sociology of law is possible and important insofar as it concerns itself with explaining 'the actual conduct of the individuals who create, apply and obey the law'; it 'must investigate the ideologies by which men are influenced in their law-creating and law-applying activities' (Kelsen 1941b: 271). Among its most important and promising tasks, in Kelsen's view, is the critical analysis of the idea of justice as an ideology. But such investigations would be *wholly distinct* from those framed by the pure theory of law. While the latter treats law as norm and constructs concepts appropriate to that subject matter, sociology of law takes behaviour in legal contexts as its concern and constructs the entirely different concepts appropriate to causal analysis of that material (Kelsen 1991a: 301).

One important virtue of Kelsen's method is that by recognising explicitly that normative legal theory's task is to construct concepts to make possible the interpretation of law as a structure of norms he avoids the persistent ambiguities of many of Hart's conceptual formulations. Kelsen's work emphasises the need for conceptual rigour because it recognises straightforwardly that normative legal theory is deliberately *constructed* to provide a means of interpreting actual law. By contrast, because Hart's concepts are presented as discovered in actual linguistic practices or social situations they inherit the vagueness and indeterminacy of many of those practices and situations or are dogged by controversy whenever sociological evidence of the nature of the practices and situations is demanded.

'The machine now runs by itself'

In many respects, Kelsen's image of law, portrayed in his pure theory, is similar to Hart's, despite the radical differences in methods adopted by the two jurists. Frequently Kelsen remarks on the 'most significant peculiarity' of law that it regulates its own creation.[4] That is, the creation of legal norms is authorised by other legal norms. The decision of a judge, creating a norm governing the circumstances to which the decision relates, is authorised by norms defining the court's jurisdiction. Those norms may be expressed in a statute, the enactment of which was authorised by other, more fundamental norms defining the proper procedures for legislation. They may be contained in a constitution, itself established on the authority of the norms contained in an earlier constitution. Thus, 'higher' norms authorise the creation of 'lower' ones in various ways, indicating who can create them in what circumstances and within what limits (Kelsen 1991a: 257ff).

There is no suggestion that the process of norm creation is governed *only* by other norms. Just as Hart recognises judicial discretion as the 'non-legal' element that necessarily supplements the legal element of rules in judicial interpretation and development of law, so Kelsen notes that 'every law-applying act is only partly determined by law and partly undetermined' (1967: 349). Law regulates its own creation but does not determine conclusively its own content: 'There is simply no method ... by which only one of several meanings of a norm may gain the distinction of being the only "correct" one' (1967: 352). Nevertheless the non-legal determinants of new law (for Hart, discretion; for Kelsen, politics) are beyond the scope of the pure theory of law. Its concern is only to know *law*, not politics or any of the myriad considerations that may shape legal change or legal interpretation.

This is a wholly uncompromising position. Like Hart's concept of law in terms of primary and secondary rules, Kelsen's view of a structure of norms authorising their own creation, modification and destruction provides a picture of law from which human beings have almost disappeared.

---

4   See eg Kelsen 1945: 124, 126, 132, 198, 354; Kelsen 1967: 71, 221; Kelsen 1991a: 102.

At the pinnacle of Hart's legal system of rules is the rule of recognition validating all other legal rules. The actions and attitudes of officials and citizens are taken into account in Hart's theory merely to identify the system of rules as being in existence. Hart's empiricism forces him to identify the rule of recognition as an actual legal or constitutional rule or cluster of rules found in actual legal systems. Viewed externally the rule of recognition is a social fact: the observable fact that officials are acting on the basis of uniform presuppositions about what counts as valid law. Viewed internally it is the presupposition made by 'insiders' of the legal system of the validity of legal rules.

By contrast, Kelsen's conceptualism requires no such search for some ultimate legal rule in each actually existing legal system, providing validity for all other rules in the system. Kelsen postulates a 'basic norm' (*Grundnorm*) which gives validity to (authorises the creation of) all legal rules. But this is, as with all the concepts of the pure theory of law, deliberately created as a theoretical idea (not found in experience) for a specific theoretical purpose.

The purpose of Kelsen's basic norm is to portray the unity of the legal system, the fact that all its norms trace validity from a single source and must do so if they are to be considered part of the same legal system. Thus, if the sequence of authorisation of norms is traced back from a court's decision, through the statutory norms providing jurisdiction, through the constitutional norms authorising enactment of the statute, to the original constitution, the pure theory of law deliberately postulates a further single norm 'standing behind' and giving validity to the original constitution.

The basic norm is, thus, a presupposition (Kelsen 1967: 204) – a theoretical necessity. In his later writings Kelsen responds to the dilemma of how a basic norm can be the meaning of an act of will (which is the way he thinks of all norms) even though no act of will gives rise to it. He simply calls the basic norm a useful fiction (eg 1991a: 256).

It is not appropriate in a book on Anglo-American theory to discuss in detail the complexities surrounding these ideas. It is enough to note some contrasts between the basic norm and the rule of recognition which illustrate the different results of Kelsen's conceptualism as compared with Hart's empiricism. The basic norm is postulated by Kelsen as *pre-legal*, like Austin's sovereign, rather than legal as with Hart's rule of recognition. For Kelsen this is obviously the case because the basic norm is nothing more than the *assumption* on the basis of which an original constitution, or whatever is the highest legal source of the particular legal system, is treated as valid. Legal norms derive their validity from other legal norms. Eventually this process of attributing validity must come to a halt. The basic norm is the necessary theoretical postulate of the validity of the norms of the original constitution.

Because it is only a conceptualisation of the pre-legal sources of validity of law its exact formulation as a theoretical matter is not very important and is likely to be purely formal: for example, 'coercion of man against man ought to be exercised in the manner and under the conditions determined by the historically first constitution' (Kelsen 1967: 50). The content of the basic norm becomes significant only when the pure theory of law is applied to analyse an actual legal system. Then, of course, it may be important to try to identify the exact content of the normative presupposition on which the ultimate validity of the legal system depends.

For a legal system to exist its basic norm must be actually presupposed to be valid (1967: 208–212): that is, presupposed or acted upon in much the same way that Hart's rule of recognition is assumed to be. But the crucial point is that for Kelsen there is no necessity to identify an actual fundamental rule of the legal system that provides the system's unifying criterion of validity. Hart's attempt to ground concepts in empirical experience necessitates this identification. For Kelsen all that is necessary is to recognise that legal science must treat law as a unity, since legal practice and law as an intellectual discipline presuppose the possibility of relating in terms of legal logic all the norms of a single legal system. Because of this necessity the pure theory of law must create the concept of the basic norm to represent the unity of a legal system. To say that a basic norm is effective means only that this unity is actually being presupposed in legal thought and practice.

Beyond these methodological differences the parallels in Hart's and Kelsen's thinking are clear. Austin's idea of law as an expression of political power is replaced in both theories with the idea of law as a relatively self-contained system of rules or norms. Kelsen notes that mutually contradictory norms may exist in the same legal system, though the system will often provide ways to remove this 'undesirable state of affairs' (1991a: ch 29), but he denies the possibility of gaps in the law (1991a: ch 31; 1967: 245–250). Where the norms of the legal system make no provision on some matter they can be treated as permitting what they do not proscribe and if the matter is brought before a court the legal position can be determined and any supposed gap closed. Therefore, whatever their origin or content, legal norms form a unified system.

Kelsen's normative legal theory portrays law as a web of normative ideas whose essential systematic character exists independently of human agency. Neither he nor Hart deny the human, creative element in law. Indeed they both insist on it. But in neither theory is there a place to analyse it. In Hart's case this is because it is pushed outside the model of rules and designated as discretion; in Kelsen's case it is because the pure theory of law develops concepts only for the purpose of analysing law as norms and assigns all concern with human behaviour to other disciplines (such as sociology, political science or psychology) whose concepts and methods are seen as having no possibility of influencing or interacting with those of legal science.

What has appeared to happen in this twentieth century normative legal theory is well expressed by the German jurist Carl Schmitt: 'The sovereign ... the engineer of the great machine [of law], has been radically pushed aside. The machine now runs by itself' (Schmitt 1985: 48).

Democracy and the Rule of Law

Plainly, in any realistic view of law, the machine does *not* run by itself. There are, no less than in Austin's time, people in positions of power pulling its levers. What is the real significance, then, of this emphasis on the self-regulating character of modern law? Its purpose surely is to demonstrate law's integrity as an independent intellectual field and as a specialised field of professional practice.

The ideas of unity and system in law, which were noted in Chapter 1 as having considerable importance for the conception of law as a field of professional knowledge and practice, are presented in both Hart's and Kelsen's theories in ways that involve strenuous efforts to exclude political considerations or any explicit recognition that law is an expression of political power. Admittedly, neither theory is concerned to prescribe how law ought to be; both purport only to describe (in Hart's case) or provide the conceptual means of interpret-ing (in Kelsen's) law as it is. Thus, neither theory claims that law *should* be 'above' politics. They do not explicitly advocate the ideal of the Rule of Law – that governmental action should be controlled by known rules preventing arbitrari-ness – as something to guide legal and political practice. But because both theories present a de-politicised image of law and claim that such an image is appropriate for normative legal theory, they implicitly suggest that law can have a unity, system and integrity independent of politics and, therefore, that the idea of the Rule of Law is in some sense built into the very notion of law.

In Kelsen's theory this is very clear. He refuses to recognise 'the state' as an entity standing above law and creating law. The state is merely *the legal order itself* viewed from a certain standpoint. State functions, offices and jurisdictions are all defined by legal norms insofar as legitimate authority attaches to them. They have no identity apart from the content of the legal norms defining them. Thus, Kelsen makes the, at first surprising, claim that every state is a *Rechtsstaat*, a state governed by law (1967: 313). To this extent the notion of the Rule of Law is reduced to a pure issue of semantics.

There is, however, much more to the matter than that. Reading both Hart's and Kelsen's work one gains the impression that the need for legal controls on arbitrary powers of government is a matter of great political concern to both of them. When Kelsen writes (1955: 77–80) of the Rule of Law as a substantive idea of effectively controlling governmental arbitrariness he has no illusions about the difficulties of doing so. A major reason why he refuses to accept the state as an entity above law is because, when it is recognised as such, appalling things can be done in its name: 'whereas the individual as such is in no way thought entitled to coerce others, to dominate or even kill them, it is nevertheless his supreme right to do all this in the name of God, the nation or the state, which for that very reason he loves, and lovingly identifies with, as "his" God, "his" nation and "his" state' (Kelsen 1973: 67).

These sentiments, expressed in an article first published at the beginning of the 1920s, suggest a firm rejection of all supra-individual forms – such as the state – insofar as these are treated as entities possessing independent significance: that is, a significance beyond that of the individual human beings who make use of these forms in one way or another. Thus, Kelsen adds that, if the masks are stripped away from actors on the political stage and we no longer see the impersonal state 'condemning and making war', what is revealed is the reality of 'men putting coercion on other men' (1973: 67).

Such comments reveal something of Kelsen's commitment to political free-dom and his hostility to all forms of autocracy justified by appeals to an entity – state, God, nation – transcending mere individuals and claiming dominion over them. Given such an outlook it is hardly surprising that his political theory forcefully defends the ideal of democracy as government (directly or by means of representatives) by the people as individual citizens. This side of Kelsen's thinking, expressed in his political writings, is totally ignored in almost all Anglo-American discussions of his legal philosophy. Yet it provides an essential context for understanding the full significance of the methods underlying his pure theory of law.

Kelsen's conceptualism assumes, as has been seen, that each science or intellectual discipline must create its own concepts by which to secure knowledge of its subject-matter. All 'truth' is therefore relative to the particular science concerned, because knowledge-claims can only be evaluated in the context of the particular science within which they are made. Each separate science alone provides the concepts that give meaning to, and allow evaluation of, the knowledge-claims made within it. Thus, the method of the pure theory of law denies that there is such a thing as 'absolute' truth. But it asserts that the knowledge produced within particular sciences, for their particular purposes, is no less valuable as a result. And Kelsen claims that philosophical relativism of this kind, with its denial of absolutes, correlates in many important ways with political relativism – the idea that there are no absolute political values (Kelsen 1955).

Democracy is the most appropriate practical recognition of political relativism. Democracy accepts that a conflict between political values can only properly be resolved by taking the majority view for the time being. But democracy equally protects the minority's right to oppose that view because today's minority may be tomorrow's majority which will be no less entitled to insist on the 'correctness' of its views. Underlying democracy is a commitment to tolerance – an ideal to which Kelsen frequently refers. Democracy is the political embodiment of tolerance of opposed views.

Thus, the pure theory of law portrays a legal system not as the expression of supreme political values but as a framework of norms which 'always has more or less the character of a compromise' (Kelsen 1973: 76). To the extent that law forms itself as a system of norms whose integrity as a system can be recognised by an independent legal science (founded on the concepts of the pure theory of law) it is not the mere servant of politics but a structure governed by its own logic which makes possible the compromise of individual wills. To this extent, law is the essential social technique available to harness coercion to make possible civilised co-existence of individuals in a society (Kelsen 1941a).

From the point of view of the pure theory of law, therefore, the political authority of the state is a mere derivative of law. The pure theory of law dissolves away the state's legitimacy as a potential agency of intolerance. It insists that the state is properly seen as merely the effect of the structure of norms governing the relationships of individual human beings. For Kelsen the doctrine of sovereignty is harmful precisely because it asserts the existence of a supreme entity above law (1973: 71). There is no such 'superhuman organism' as the state in this sense; society's 'sole reality is the individual human being' (1991b: 526).

Equally, the pure theory of law does its best to dissolve away the *nation*, as a supreme entity, too, as far as legal science is concerned. Kelsen argues that international law and national law must be regarded as forming a single system, either because norms of national law provide for international law to be incorporated in national law, or because international law is held to validate national systems. Either way, the normative separateness of national legal systems from the international legal order is denied. Legal science attaches no particular primacy to the nation as a concept.[5] By contrast, Austin's theory of

---

5   Kelsen insists that any advocacy of the 'primacy' or 'lack of primacy' of national law over

law as the sovereign's command denied that international law should be considered law at all, but only positive morality, because only independent political societies (states) have sovereigns to command law. No sovereign of an international community exists. Kelsen's rejection of sovereignty as a concept entails not only a rejection of the claim that the state is above law but also of the claim that there can be no higher political allegiance and legal obligation than to the nation state.

As for the appeal to 'God on our side', the third source (with 'state' and 'nation') of autocracy and intolerance specifically mentioned by Kelsen in the passage quoted earlier, it is firmly excluded by the pure theory of law because, as its author never tires of insisting, the pure theory is not concerned with debates about justice. It cannot be so concerned because, in Kelsen's view, such debates do not lend themselves to scientific resolution:

> 'If the history of human thought proves anything, it is the futility of the attempt to establish, in the way of rational considerations, an absolutely correct standard of human behaviour, and that means a standard of behaviour as the only just one, excluding the possibility of considering the opposite standard to be just too' (Kelsen 1957: 21).

Again Kelsen's message is the same: a denial of absolutes, a denial which in many circumstances enjoins tolerance as the wise and courageous response to the relativity of values. The pure theory tries to provide concepts for an autonomous science of law (the systematic professional knowledge of lawyers) which is not the servant of autocracy but dignifies law by insisting on its integrity as a normative system.

No comparable explicit political theory is contained in Hart's major writings. Nevertheless a commitment to liberal individualism and an aversion to authoritarianism – attitudes not dissimilar to Kelsen's – are apparent, for example, in his writings on responsibility and the functions of criminal law (Hart 1963; 1968). Some of Hart's warmest praise for Bentham is with regard to Bentham's discussions of elements of the Rule of Law and the liberal constitutional state:

> 'One by one in Bentham's works you can identify the elements of the *Rechtsstaat* ... Here are liberty of speech, and of press, the right of association, the need that laws should be published and made widely

---

international law (and so of policies of nationalism and imperialism, on the one hand, or internationalism and pacificism, on the other) is purely political and in no way justified by legal science: Kelsen 1991b; and see Kelsen 1967: 343; 1945: 387–388. For legal science, any automatic distinction between national and international law disappears.

known before they are enforced, the need to control administrative agencies, and the importance of the principle of legality, *nulla poene sine lege*' (Hart 1958: 51).

The list might be considered a summary of the standard concerns of many lawyers in mid-twentieth century Britain, when Hart was developing his normative legal theory, about the legal framework of the interventionist welfare state.

Kelsen's pure theory purports to demonstrate the integrity of legal science – lawyers' methods of analysis of law – in opposition to the twentieth century absolutisms (for example, fascism or Stalinism) that claimed it as merely an appendage of politics. In a parallel manner, Hart provides the reassurance of a concept of law entirely in terms of rules. He gives an implicit theoretical promise that despite the proliferation of discretionary regulation and administrative structures of the modern state it is still possible to distinguish from them the rules that constitute not only the familiar stock of lawyers' knowledge, but also the formal political guarantees of autonomous citizenship and the Rule of Law.

Conclusion

How, finally, should we assess the developments in legal philosophy discussed in this chapter? In Kelsen's case it can be said that the sophistication of method that underpins his theory, the range of its reference and his single-minded devotion to explaining the possibility of an autonomous science of law, ensure that his writings address illuminatingly a host of issues that have no place in Austin's thought. The scope of Kelsen's work is simply different from that of Austin's. Yet, as has been seen, Kelsen's political theory and his particular conception of the professional and intellectual requirements of an autonomous discipline of law, may help significantly to illuminate major points at which his claims appear to conflict directly with those of Hart or Austin.

It is harder to assess Hart's advance on Austin. Most commentators today have no doubt that his theory is better, in the sense of having more explanatory power. But the content and approach of this chapter should suggest that the question of what makes a theory 'better' is a complex one in the field of normative legal theory. Hart's progress beyond Austin has been portrayed here primarily as the construction of theory that highlights a set of political and professional concerns about law that are significantly different from those of Austin.

Dicey defined the central political problem of his late-nineteenth century era (in which Austin's theory had its greatest impact) as how 'to give constitutions resting on the will of the people the stability and permanence which has hitherto been found only in monarchical or aristocratic states' (quoted in Sugarman 1983: 109). This concern to contain the potentially disruptive effects of democracy seems to explain the shape of much of Austin's theory, which puts questions of political power in central place through the concept of sovereignty, sees liberty as a by-product of rational government, and is developed in the context of a belief in the virtues of government by elites. Equally, in legal professional terms, the need Austin recognised was that of establishing a scientific foundation of legal knowledge which would replace classical common law thought and firmly relate the structure of professional legal knowledge to the reality of the political authority of the centralised modern state. The themes of liberal individualism, democracy and citizenship, and the importance of the Rule of Law as a demarcation of law from politics are not Austin's. Their reflection in Hart's (and Kelsen's) work obviously marks a significant political advance on Austin in the sense of a recognition of vitally important modern concerns.

Much of normative legal theory has 'progressed' by emphasising felt concerns of its time, rather than by providing theories that are better than earlier ones in some absolute sense. Thus, if Hart and Kelsen can be interpreted as addressing lacunae in the range of Austin's concerns, the theory to be considered in the next chapter appears, correspondingly, to address important political and professional concerns beyond those reflected in their work.

Chapter 5

The appeal of natural law

It might seem that analytical jurisprudence has made redundant the ideas and perspectives of classical common law thought with which Chapter 2 was concerned. But this book's discussion of the development of English analytical jurisprudence in the writings of Bentham, Austin and Hart and the associated development reflected in Kelsen's work has tried to show that normative legal theory does not necessarily progress through a straightforward superseding of inadequate theory by better theory addressing the same concerns. Rather, it sometimes shows important shifts of emphasis and *altered* concerns. These, in turn, may be the result of felt political or professional necessities.

Analytical jurisprudence partly reflects a demand for a systematic, rational legal science to underpin modern legal professionalism and to accommodate the political idea of law as a technical instrument of government in modern western states. Classical common law thought flourished in a different era with different preoccupations. Nevertheless, analytical jurisprudence has not necessarily provided a fully adequate perspective on contemporary Anglo-American law.

The modern so-called 'natural law' theory to be considered in this chapter can be viewed as, in part, an attempt to push the methods of analytical jurisprudence to conclusions more satisfactory than those the analytical jurists themselves typically reach. At the same time it can be seen partly as a means of recovering some themes in classical common law thought which analytical jurisprudence largely relegated to the sidelines of theoretical concern.

Legal positivism and natural law

One aspect of the aspiration towards a 'science' of law reflected in the work of such different writers as Bentham, Austin, Hart and Kelsen is the insistence on an analytical separation of law from morality. In no case does this imply that morality is unimportant. But it does entail the claim that clear thinking about the nature of law necessitates treating it as a distinct phenomenon capable of being analysed without invoking moral judgments. Hence, as Austin explains in a famous passage: 'The existence of law is one thing; its merit or demerit is another. Whether it be or be not is one enquiry; whether it be or be not conformable to an assumed standard, is a different enquiry. A law, which actually exists, is a law, though we happen to dislike it ... This truth, when formally announced as an abstract proposition, is so simple and glaring that it seems idle to insist upon it. But simple and glaring as it is ... the enumeration of the instances in which it has been forgotten would fill a volume' (Austin 1832: 157).

So Austin, like Bentham before him, criticises Blackstone for continually confusing legal and moral analysis in his *Commentaries*: for treating as law what he thought *ought* to be law, for declaring that human laws are invalid if contrary to the laws of God, for asserting that all human laws derive validity only from God's superior law (cf Blackstone 1809 I: 41).

Invoking moral precepts – whether or not linked to a supra-human authority such as the will or law of God – as part of the criteria of validity of man-made law seemed to Bentham and Austin to be dangerous. It prevented an objective, 'scientific' analysis of law as a human creation, and a clear set of indisputably objective criteria for determining which regulations should be recognised as possessing legal authority. It left such matters to ethical speculation.

Since ethical views vary, the way is opened for anyone to claim the right to 'second guess' the authority of law and state. Danger lies also in another direction, according to Bentham. To confuse legal and moral authority allows reactionaries to claim 'this is the law, therefore it must be right': existing law is assumed to possess not only legal but also moral authority. So Blackstone's primary failing in Bentham's eyes was his tendency to merge legal and moral authority, together with his complacency, implying that English law as expounded in the *Commentaries* was the best of all law for the best of all possible worlds (Bentham 1977: 498–499; Hart 1958: 53).

This chapter is concerned with the claim of the major analytical jurists that law and morality should be clearly separated for purposes of analysis, and with some important challenges to that claim. Since the term analytical jurisprudence refers only to the enterprise of analysing systematically law's conceptual structures, on the basis that they are worthy of study in their own right as distinct objects of analysis, it does not *necessarily* demand this law-morality separation. So, although writers who have considered themselves or been considered to be analytical jurists have typically subscribed to the separation of law and morality, it is convenient to use a more specific term to refer to the adoption of this analytical separation.

As has been seen, Austin treated positive law as the appropriate focus of legal science and distinguished it from all moral rules or principles not specifically 'set down' (posited) or legislated in some form but merely accepted, as well as from (religious) rules or principles attributed to some supra-human authority. Thus, the term now generally used to refer to insistence on the separation of law and morality is *legal positivism*. It is sometimes used imprecisely to refer also to a number of actual or supposed characteristics of analytical jurisprudence (cf Hart 1958: 57–58). In this chapter, however, legal positivism will be taken to mean specifically the insistence by Bentham, Austin, Hart, Kelsen and many other jurists on the necessity of analytically separating normative legal theory's inquiries into the nature of law from inquiries into its moral worth.

In contrast to legal positivism stands a tradition of thought adopting an apparently diametrically opposed position – that law cannot be properly understood except in moral terms, that it is fundamentally a moral phenomenon, that questions of law's nature and existence cannot be isolated from questions about its moral worth. This tradition is usually termed *natural law theory*. Its history extends through at least 2,500 years of Western philosophy. One of its most powerful themes (though an ambiguous one, as will appear) is expressed in the declaration that *lex iniusta non est lex* – an unjust law is no law at all. It may well be that statements like this in the history of natural law theory have never meant what they seem, at face value, to mean (Finnis 1980: 363–366). Nevertheless, they do suggest the persistent claim that questions about the nature of law and the conditions of its existence as an authoritative normative order cannot be isolated from questions about its moral foundations.

Thus typically, in many different ways throughout its long history, natural law theory has postulated the existence of moral principles having a validity and authority independent of human enactment, and which can be thought of as a 'higher' or more fundamental law against which the worth or authority of human law can be judged. This fundamental 'natural law' is variously seen as derived from human nature, the natural conditions of existence of humanity, the natural order of the universe, or the eternal law of God. The method of discovering it is usually claimed to be human reason. Natural law thus requires no human legislator. Yet it stands in judgment on the law created by human legislators.

Natural law and classical common law thought

Why might this dispute about the relations of law and morality bear on the question of whether any perspectives or concerns of classical common law thought survive their displacement by positivist analytical jurisprudence, from Bentham onwards?

As was seen in Chapter 2, classical common law thought assumed various sources of law's authority: it saw law as rooted in immemorial custom, community life, transcendent reason or an accumulation of ancient wisdom greater than that of any individual. By contrast, Bentham's and Austin's writings ground law's authority in habitual obedience to a sovereign, a purportedly objective 'test' to distinguish law from non-law. Hart and Kelsen focus on the fact of social acceptance of a rule of recognition or a basic norm as the fundamental prerequisite for determining legal authority. Positivist theories attempt to provide criteria of the 'legal' and of law's authority in specific formal conditions which avoid vague ideas of the nature of the community or of some transcendent reason. Because common law thought identified the source of legal authority not in the state or sovereign or in rule-governed procedures of legal enactment but in reason or community, it allowed at various times, as has been seen, for the possibility that – in theory, at least – some legislation or judicial decisions could be void either as abuses of legal authority or as misstatements of the law.

Given this facet of classical common law thought it is unsurprising that at times it related closely to natural law ideas (Gough 1955: ch 3; Haines 1930: ch 2), which also claimed the possibility of evaluating law's authority before the tribunal of reason. The notion of common law as something not residing in rules but in more fundamental principles expressing a transcendent reason or ancient wisdom had close affinities with natural law doctrines asserting the existence of some higher (moral) law governing and providing ultimate authority for the ordinary rules of human (positive) law.

On the other hand, natural law theory was always a two-edged sword. In English history it was used to defend the divine right of the monarch, as expressed in prerogatives, against the claims of common law (Pocock 1957: 55). Equally, it could be used to assert limits on, or a limiting interpretation of, the powers of Parliament, as in Coke's famous pronouncements in *Calvin's Case* (1608) (Gough 1955: 44–45). But appeals to natural law as a set of principles that could control the substance of human law ceased to be practically significant in England once parliamentary sovereignty was recognised. As classical common law thought had to accommodate and eventually give way to a view of law as created by political authority, so natural law thought gave way to legal positivism.

In the United States, natural law ideas proved important in the formative era of judicial interpretation of the Constitution. The temptation to fill out the meaning of a written fundamental constitutional document by appealing to an unwritten fundamental natural law may have proved irresistible to some courts (Haines 1930) or at least appeared to explain some of their decisions (Horwitz 1992: 156–159). Constitutional adjudication entrusted to a Supreme Court that assumed the authority to pronounce on the constitutional validity of legislation[1] raised special issues about the scope and bases of legal interpretation. Indeed, this may be one consideration that has made legal positivism somewhat less secure in modern American legal philosophy (as exemplified by Lon Fuller's work discussed later in this chapter, and the literature considered in Chapter 6) than it has been in Britain (but cf Fuller 1940: 116–121).

Today, in the Anglo-American setting, the fate of common law thought is not unconnected with that of natural law thought (although, outside the Anglo-American context, natural law's history must be understood in different terms). Common law thought has had to find a place, if at all, in an environment dominated by the idea that law is posited by sovereign law-makers of various kinds or their delegates or agencies. Equally, natural law theory, insofar as it has survived at all in the Anglo-American legal world, has tended to locate itself in the interstices of legal positivism, accepting much in positivist analytical jurisprudence and seeking to supplement or correct, rather than dismiss out of hand, many of the ideas that have been the concern of Chapters 3 and 4.

Is natural law dead?

Our concern is not with the long history of natural law theory in Western civilisation but with its particular appearances in the modern Anglo-American legal context. In this perspective the decline of natural law theory can be dated conveniently from Bentham's attack on natural law ideas in Blackstone's *Commentaries*. Bentham's view, that natural law was a 'formidable non-entity' and natural law reasoning a 'labyrinth of confusion' (Bentham 1977: 17, 20) based on moral prejudices or unprovable speculations about human nature, went along with a profound political distrust of resonant phrases about the

---

1 *Marbury v Madison* 1 Cranch 137 (1803).

'rights of man' enshrined in constitutional documents such as those inspired by the French Revolution of 1789.

In a single line of English positivist legal thinking, running from Bentham to A V Dicey's late nineteenth century work on *The Law of the Constitution*, specific positive rules of law providing clearly defined rights enforceable in the ordinary courts are contrasted favourably with 'practically worthless' (Dicey 1959: 256) broad declarations of the rights of man grounded in natural law conceptions but unenforced in practice.

The rise of legal positivism is often associated with the nineteenth century prestige of 'science' in general and the aspiration to produce a specific legal science which has been noted in previous chapters. But more is at stake than that. It is not a change in attitudes to science, morality or religion which should be held primarily accountable for the decline of natural law thinking and the rise of modern legal positivism but a change in the nature of law itself and its political and professional environment.

Insofar as law became seen as an instrument of state policy (and in the utilitarian view an instrument of progress, if used with caution) it was revealed as an amoral and infinitely plastic device of government. Insofar as it regulated increasingly complex and differentiated Western societies it could be seen as, above all, a means of controlling the interplay of conflicting interests. The social theorist Max Weber, writing of nineteenth century developments, noted that:

> 'In consequence of both juridical rationalism and modern intellectual scepticism in general, the axioms of natural law have lost all capacity to provide the fundamental basis of a legal system ... The disappearance of the old natural law conceptions has destroyed all possibility of providing the law with a metaphysical dignity by virtue of its immanent qualities. In the great majority of its most important provisions, it has been unmasked all too visibly, indeed, as the product or the technical means of a compromise between conflicting interests' (Weber 1978: 874–875).

Such an interpretation of law as a compromise (above all, of economic interests) could be offered even for constitutions, such as that of the United States, which expressed principles purportedly grounded in ideas of 'natural rights' – truths declared to be self-evident because founded in the nature of humankind or of human society (see eg Levy 1987).

Classical natural law theory (broadly, that developed before the nineteenth century) sought a grounding for human law in unchanging principle, derived from 'nature' in some sense (the natural order of things), and usually held to be discoverable by reason. But two legal developments in Western societies have made it especially hard to accept any such approach to understanding the general character of law. One is legal doctrine's ever-increasing technicality and complexity. This is partly the result of law's methods of compromise between conflicting interests being extended to cover more and more sectors of social life, and being invoked in support of more, and more diverse, interests within the regulated populations. The other development is the deliberate use of law as a steering mechanism in society. This presupposes that law can change rapidly and continuously but also that it does so not as a reflection of enduring principle but as a mechanism aimed at *creating* principles of social order. These principles are, however, time-bound; pragmatic principles for the moment and the context, quite unlike timeless principles of natural law. As the social theorist Niklas Luhmann has written, 'it is increasingly questionable whether principles and ultimate perspectives [such as those of natural law] withdrawn from all variation and relativity' can 'provide an apt instrument for stabilisation and control' in modern societies (Luhmann 1982: 103).

Thus, the issue is not exactly that it is impossible to agree about ultimate values; or to accept any longer that reason can discover universal 'truths' about human nature, or God's plan, or the hidden order of the universe, or any other postulated foundation of natural law. That agreement cannot be reached does not show that principles of natural law are non-existent (cf Finnis 1980: 24). As the political philosopher Leo Strauss remarks, 'by proving that there is no principle of justice that has not been denied somewhere or at some time, one has not yet proved that any given denial was justified or reasonable' (Strauss 1953: 9).

The problem is that even if there *are* universal principles of natural law they may not offer a convincing guide or grounding for complex, highly technical, ever-changing modern law. After all, legal positivism does not deny that the substance of law can be subject to moral criticism. The issue is not whether law can be morally evaluated but whether its *essential character* must be explained in moral terms. As an effort to provide such an explanation, natural law ideas are, in the view of many writers, 'devoid of any and every convincing theoretical justification' (Habermas 1974: 113).

Natural law and legal authority

None of this should necessarily lead to the conclusion that the problems that natural law theory addressed in the past have disappeared. Classical natural law theory confronted a variety of issues. Among the most important are the following:

— What is the ultimate source of authority or legitimacy of human law and of human lawmakers?
— Assuming this authority to be in essence a moral one, is it limited and, if so, what are the limits and whence do they derive?
— By what criteria is it possible to evaluate the moral worth and authority of laws?
— How should one view laws created by abuse of lawmaking authority?
— In what circumstances, if any, do governments and laws cease to command moral authority with the result that any obligation to obey them ceases?

If the word 'moral' is replaced in these questions with the word 'legal', all of them are ones that positivist analytical jurists have sought to answer in various ways. The concern that links positivist analytical jurisprudence and natural law theory is a concern with the nature of legal *authority*, with identifying its sources and its limits.

In positivist theory this concern is treated as raising technical issues. It is, above all, a matter of adequately conceptualising the highest authority of a legal system (for example, in terms of sovereignty, rule(s) of recognition, or basic norm) and determining the logical or practical relations between this authority concept and the other conceptual components of legal analysis and legal practice.

For natural lawyers, however, the issues raised are moral ones. Almost inevitably, however, they turn into – or serve as cloaks for – political issues. This is because, while moral reasoning as applied to matters of private conscience may produce a coherent ethics to govern an individual's life, moral reasoning applied to legal regulation will typically produce prescriptions as to how the power of the state should be exercised or limited in controlling citizens' actions. Natural law theory, when taken seriously, becomes a force in political struggle – usually in defence of existing legal and political systems (by demonstrating their legitimacy grounded in 'reason' or 'nature') but occasionally as a weapon of rebellion or revolution (cf Kelsen 1945: 416–417).

As regards law's authority, therefore, the primary difference between positivist theory and natural law theory is not a polar opposition but a difference as to how far inquiries about law's ultimate authority should be taken, insofar as positivists are prepared to admit that law's authority over the individual can be evaluated in moral terms and natural lawyers are prepared to recognise political authorities such as the state as having general, inherent law-making authority.

The medieval theologian Thomas Aquinas, whose writings are one of the primary sources of natural law theory, recognised the state's authority to legislate on numerous morally neutral matters about which natural law (the part of God's eternal law that can be grasped by humankind's unaided reason) would have nothing directly to say. The moral significance of this legislation would be only as part of the state's overall system of regulation which must, in Aquinas' view, serve the common good to conform with natural law.

Even in judging exercises of state authority that transgress dictates of natural law, issue is not necessarily clearly joined between classical natural law theory and legal positivism. Aquinas does not declare that all such laws lack validity or force. The philosopher John Finnis has argued that the 'central tradition of natural law theorising' – essentially that grounded in Aquinas' ideas and their antecedents – recognises the *legal* validity of unjust laws. That is, it recognises them as laws according to criteria (such as Hartian rules of recognition) that positivist theorists would emphasise (Finnis 1980: 364–365).

Certainly, where laws represent an abuse of the authority indicated by natural law (as where they are not created for the common good but for the vain whim of the lawmaker) one should, in Aquinas' view, obey God rather than the human lawmaker. But where laws are unjust merely because they do not conform to the established norms of human welfare (for example, because they impose an unjust distribution of burdens on those subject to the law) he suggests that it might be better to obey. Even if the laws do not bind in conscience one should avoid the corrupting example and civil disorder attendant on law-breaking (cf Finnis 1980: 360).

This apparent hedging of bets on the moral obligation to obey unjust laws can be understood as an attempt to work out realistically the idea that the authority of a legal system as a whole is founded on its dedication to the common good. Hence even where some laws are unjust, obligation to the system as a whole may remain insofar as it is of sufficient worth to justify its being protected against adverse effects arising from the corrupting example and disorder of law-breaking.

So the conflict between natural law and positivism tends to become a dispute as to whether the authority of a legal system as a whole can only be understood and judged in relation to some specific moral *purpose* (such as promoting the common good) for which all legal systems exist. In general, the answer of natural lawyers is yes, and of positivists, no.

The 'rebirth' of natural law

The key to the debate around natural law is thus the issue of the nature of legal authority. Natural law theory seems to become significant in debate at times when political and legal authority are under challenge. In times of stability positivist criteria of legal authority typically seem sufficient. In times of political turmoil or rapid political change they frequently seem inadequate; legal understanding seems to demand not merely technical guidance about the nature of valid law but moral or political theory. Questions as to what rules are valid as law become elements of ideological struggle; a matter of winning hearts and minds for or against established regimes.

Some of the material in Chapter 4 hinted at this dimension of the determination of legal validity. Kelsen's efforts to establish a pure theory of law are, in part, an attempt to protect law from politicisation; an attempt made in full awareness of the difficulties of doing so 'when in great and important countries, under the rule of party dictatorships, some of the most prominent representatives of jurisprudence know no higher task than to serve – with their "science" – the political power of the moment' (Kelsen 1945: xvii). Indeed, Kelsen recognises that acceptance of a positivist science of law, such as his own, may be possible only 'in a period of social equilibrium' (1945: xvii).

Thus, it is tempting to suggest that the enduring appeal of natural law arises precisely from its willingness to confront directly the moral-political issues of legality that arise in times of disorder and conflict, while positivist analytical jurisprudence presupposes a political stability that it cannot, itself, explain or even consider as a subject within the concerns of legal philosophy. However, the situation is more complex than this because modern versions of natural law theory have been developed in relatively stable societies such as those of twentieth century Britain and the United States. This suggests that legal positivism is seen by natural law writers as inadequate even where political authority is not being seriously challenged.

Perhaps the best way to understand the matter is to recognise that a degree of 'instability' as regards law-making authority is actually built into the structure of stable legal systems as portrayed by positivist analytical jurisprudence. This is because key questions about how law changes remain apparently impossible to address in modern positivist theory. This has been seen in Chapter 4 where it was noted that judicial law-making is, for Hart, the exercise of 'discretion', which his normative legal theory cannot really analyse, and is, for Kelsen, explicitly a matter of politics outside the compass of the pure theory of law.

Certain processes of law-making are, therefore, 'unstable' in the sense that what determines their outcome is a matter that positivist theory cannot subject to rational legal analysis. Given this state of affairs it is not surprising that natural law began to become a focus of attention again precisely at the time when modern legal positivism seemed to have consolidated its victories. In 1911, the American jurist Roscoe Pound wrote: 'It is not an accident that something very like a resurrection of natural law is going on the world over' (Pound 1911: 162); and Charles Grove Haines, analysing this twentieth-century rebirth, saw, as an important reason for it, the felt need to elaborate principles of 'higher law' to guide the actions of judges in developing law (Haines 1930: 323–330). In the common law world where, traditionally, the role of the judge has seemed central in the legal system, this matter is specially important. It returns us to the link, noted earlier, between common law thought and natural law theory.

Nevertheless, part of the motivation for rethinking the relative virtues of legal positivism and natural law theory has come from modern experience of tyranny and political instability, and especially from *ex post facto* reflection by jurists on the legal history of the German Third Reich (1933–1945). Here issues of the ultimate authority of law are thrown into sharp relief and the theme of the Rule of Law, identified in Chapter 4 as an important political preoccupation of modern analytical jurisprudence, is highlighted in new ways.

In this context, the Rule of Law appears not just as a matter of protecting legal structures, processes and professional knowledge against being politicised by overweening state direction, but as a defence against uncontrolled terror and arbitrary violence. In the light of the Nazi experience, professional legal knowledge founded on a separation of law and morals (the positivist science of law) can appear in a natural law perspective as, itself, a weapon of tyranny. This is because it refuses to confront ultimate questions about the necessary *moral* criteria that state regulation must conform to so as to possess authority that a lawyer or any other citizen must recognise.

The debate between positivists and natural lawyers thus becomes a debate about the meaning of the Rule of Law. Should it be understood as the positivist aspiration to remove political and moral choices as far as possible from the determination of rights and duties, or should it be seen as the natural lawyer's insistence that morally acceptable purposes must govern the unavoidably political decisions as to what rights and duties will be held to exist?

Anglo-American lessons from the Nazi era

The historical legacy of the Nazi era has explicitly influenced modern Anglo-American debates between legal positivists and natural lawyers. One of the most direct confrontations, between the positivist H L A Hart and the American natural lawyer Lon Fuller, centred in part on discussion of the way post-war German courts were apparently evaluating the legality of acts done during the Nazi period and that claimed to be lawful on the basis of Nazi law (Hart 1958; Fuller 1958).

More generally, the influence of émigré scholars, who fled from Germany during the 1930s and, in many cases, settled in the United States, helped to feed into Anglo-American legal and political consciousness insights and dilemmas about the nature and authority of legal regulation which experience of Nazi practices and policies had inspired (eg Neumann 1944, 1986; Kirchheimer 1961).

In addition, reflection on the character of war crimes trials and their basis of legitimacy and on the ultimate foundation of the principles applied to judge guilt in them, has undoubtedly made the issue of the nature and authority of Nazi regulation a matter of direct concern in the Anglo-American world and, at the same time, informed wider speculation about legal methods and reasoning (eg Shklar 1964: Part 2) and the adequacy of legal positivism (Paulson 1975).

The 1958 Hart–Fuller debate is a good starting point in considering the recent confrontation of legal positivism and modern natural law in the Anglo-American context, and especially as an introduction to Fuller's influential ideas which will be the concern of much of the remainder of this chapter. At the time of his exchange with Hart, Fuller was professor of jurisprudence at Harvard University, where he taught, with a break during the 1940s, for more than thirty years until his retirement in 1972. As his biographer notes, he was 'unquestionably the leading secular natural lawyer of the twentieth century in the English-speaking world' (Summers 1984: 151).

Hart argues that the positivists' analytical separation of law and morality aids clear thinking; it avoids confusing legal and moral obligation. To say that a rule is a valid law (judged by such positivist criteria as its being the sovereign's command, authorised by a rule of recognition or imputed from a basic norm) merely asserts the existence of *legal* obligation. Whether one ought *morally* to disobey an unjust law is a matter about which positivist analytical jurisprudence can remain uncommitted, for moral issues are not within its province.

For Fuller, however, such an approach is unrealistic and dangerous. It oversimplifies problems of obligation under a manifestly unjust regime and sets up an unreal opposition – a legal obligation to obey as against a moral obligation to disobey, as if one can keep them separate. It assumes that there can be order in a legal system without any moral content in it. In Fuller's view, the legal obligation to obey laws does not automatically follow from their enactment by a recognised formal procedure. It depends on the legal system's ability to command what Fuller calls *fidelity to law*. When certain minimum moral qualities cease to exist in a legal system, it ceases to command fidelity: that is, it ceases to have a claim to citizens' obedience. The order and coherence of a legal system (its ability simply to go on functioning) depend on a minimum moral content. Without this it ceases to be a legal system at all.

It is not very clear what is involved in this last claim. It seems to relate to the question of the definition of law, to what it is to be able to say that law *exists*. In terms of normative legal theory's concerns, therefore, the claim is that a general concept of law necessarily entails moral elements of some sort. As noted earlier, much modern regulation is technical and conventional (for example, a requirement that a will be attested by two witnesses, or the rule that in England one must drive on the left-hand side of the road). If the criticism is raised that these laws express no moral values, Fuller's answer is that law's very existence depends on its authority (its capacity to demand fidelity) and this authority ultimately depends on certain elements of moral worth.

Again, however, a positivist critic could deny that *legal* authority requires any moral component. As Austin noted: 'The most pernicious laws, and therefore those which are most opposed to the will of God, have been and are continually enforced as laws by judicial tribunals ... An exception, demurrer, or plea, founded on the law of God was never heard in a Court of Justice ...' (Austin 1832: 158). Must we say, therefore, that the positivist view offers hard-headed realism about the way legal systems actually function (with no necessary direct dependence on moral principle), whereas Fuller's thesis is merely wishful thinking about values that *ought to be*, but are not necessarily, built into law?

In his 1958 paper, as in earlier writings (1940: 101, 110; 1946), Fuller distances his thinking from classical natural law theory. As has been noted, this theory was generally vulnerable to the positivist criticism that modern law (in Weber's terms, a technical means of compromising or managing conflicting interests) is no longer usefully analysed in terms of moral absolutes and requires a 'science' explicitly recognising its human origins and instrumental political character. Fuller's strategy is to emphasise that the necessary morality of law is *procedural*, relating to the way law is created, expressed, interpreted and applied, rather than to any particular substantive content of legal rules. Looked at this way, even purely technical rules, such as the one requiring two witness attestations for a valid will, have a moral dimension. Everything depends on how the rule operates.

The historical example of Nazi Germany provides material to illustrate Fuller's thesis. To assume, as Hart does, that the only difference between Nazi law and English law was that the Nazis used their laws to achieve purposes odious to English people is, Fuller argues, to ignore the much more fundamental moral differences between legal regimes. Nazi law made frequent and pervasive use of methods that show, in terms of Anglo-American standards, a most serious perversion of procedural regularity.

For example, frequent use was made of retroactive statutes to cure irregularities. A notorious example occurred after the Röhm purge of 30 June and 1 July 1934 when, on Adolf Hitler's orders, more than seventy members of the Nazi party were shot. On 3 July, a law was passed ratifying the massacre as a series of lawful executions. Hitler apparently later declared that at the time of the purge 'the supreme court of the German people consisted of myself' (Fuller 1958: 650). Second, Fuller notes 'repeated rumours' of secret laws and regulations making it impossible for most people even to discover the rules on which officials were supposed to act. More generally, however, since 'unpublished instructions to those administering the law could destroy the letter of any published law by imposing on it an outrageous interpretation, there was a sense in which the meaning of every law was "secret"' (Fuller 1958: 652). Third, when legal formalities and procedures became inconvenient to the Nazi regime they could be bypassed by means of Nazi gangs taking action 'on the street' and achieving the required objective by violence. Fourth, 'the Nazi-dominated courts were always ready to disregard any statute, even those enacted by the Nazis themselves, if this suited their convenience or if they feared that a lawyer-like interpretation might incur displeasure "above"' (Fuller 1958: 652).

Assuming this general picture of Nazi law in action is correct (and much literature suggests it is: see eg Müller 1991), what should be said of a legal system like this? It seems less like a system of legal order than of discretions in policy-implementation organised around the furtherance of political aims of the regime in power. Not only is it inefficient, as a functioning system of *rules*, but it lacks all procedural fairness and propriety. These latter deficiencies point to a decline in what Fuller terms the *internal morality* of law. Thus, for him, they involve not just issues of efficiency but moral issues. We should be prepared to say (irrespective of the substantive content of Nazi laws) that the way the laws were applied was not merely procedurally inefficient but manifestly unjust.

Fuller argues (1958: 642) that the authority of law (its capacity to demand fidelity) derives from a moral understanding[2] between rulers and ruled, such that citizens accord moral respect to the constitution that governs them as 'necessary, right, and good'. In the 1958 paper this is inadequately analysed because there is no clear indication of the criteria to be satisfied to ensure this recognition by citizens.

The best way to support Fuller's argument about a link between the moral authority of law and its procedural proprieties would be to suggest that a gross and cynical discarding of formal and predictable procedure is a kind of fraud

---

2   In later writings Fuller refers to this, following the social philosopher Georg Simmel, as a 'kind of reciprocity': see Fuller 1969a: 39.

on those who must obey. There can be no moral understanding between rulers and ruled in such circumstances. The ruled have no chance to orient themselves to the dictates of the ruler's authority. Although they must obey, they are not given a reasonable chance to do so in an orderly, rational manner.

This is not, however, spelled out in Fuller's 1958 paper, though related arguments appear in his later writings (cf Fuller 1969a: 153, 159–162). Instead he claims, without any real justification, that a decline in the moral aims of law, which he calls law's 'external' morality and which determine the authority and respect attaching to the legal system, is likely to be accompanied by a decline in the (procedural) internal morality, and *vice versa* (Fuller 1958: 645).

The ideal of legality and the existence of law

However, the important point being made from the Nazi example is that the stable forms and procedures of law and the nature of its authority are linked and Fuller is specific in his claims about the consequence of disintegration of these forms and procedures in practice in Nazi Germany. He suggests that the decline in procedural propriety, in the internal morality of law, was so serious that a legal system, as such, *ceased to exist* in Germany during the Nazi period. Hence, post-war courts should not recognise Nazi law. Matters of legality in the Nazi period should be clarified, where necessary, by retroactive legislation.

This claim about the non-existence of law in Nazi Germany is, indeed, one that other writers had already made, and on the basis of similar arguments about the effects of the procedural arbitrariness of the Nazi regime. Franz Neumann, a distinguished jurist who practised law in Germany during the years leading to the Nazi accession to power in 1933, wrote, observing Nazi Germany from exile in America, that 'there is no realm of law in Germany, although there are thousands of technical rules that are calculable' (Neumann 1944: 468). Another eminent German scholar, Otto Kirchheimer, wrote to similar effect: 'With the access to power of National Socialism the common legal bond of a generally applicable civil law disappeared more and more ...' (Kirchheimer 1941: 89).

Obviously a specific definition of the word 'law' is involved here and Nazi regulation is being tested against it. But, in Fuller's 1958 essay, no such definition is made explicit. In Kirchheimer's and especially Neumann's writings, however, the concept of law employed is elaborated. Indeed Neumann used it in major writings of the 1930s and 1940s as the criterion for assessing general changes in the character of twentieth century regulation and as the organising concept for the most detailed historical analysis available in English of the idea of the Rule of Law (Neumann 1986).

Neumann writes bluntly: 'the National Socialist legal system is nothing but a technique of mass manipulation by terror' (1944: 458). If law is merely the sovereign's command such a system must be recognised as legal. But if law 'must be rational either in form or in content' Nazi regulation definitely does not deserve the name of law. For Neumann, law is both *voluntas* (the expression of sovereign power) and *ratio* (the expression of reason, or rational principle grounded in general ethical postulates) and the legal history of Western civilisation is a history of the attempt to reconcile these typically incompatible yet essential components of legality (Neumann 1944: 451–452; 1986: 45–46; Cotterrell 1995: ch 8). The component of *ratio* insists that law be a matter of general rules, not special individualised commands. It requires also that these general rules be clear and predictable in application, not vague general norms providing broad authority for virtually free official discretion. Hence, although Nazi regulation made considerable use of technical rules, it lacked the character of law.

Kirchheimer elaborates similar arguments. He sees Nazi regulation as guided wholly by policy demands. These necessitated technically rational norms of a purely provisional character which could be changed quickly to meet the needs of the moment, without notice and, if necessary, retrospectively. Such requirements precluded the existence of a stable body of general laws which could only hamper governmental freedom to shape, adjust and implement policy. The aim of adjudication and rule application in such a regime is not to maximise legal stability but to execute given commands 'so as to have the maximum effect in the shortest possible time' (Kirchheimer 1941: 99). Thus, the legal regime of contract is largely replaced by a system of private command and administrative order; that of family law becomes a regime of policy regarding population development and social organisation. Even the idea of the state, as the abstract source or structure of regulation, is discarded in favour of the ultimate total and all-embracing personal authority of the leader (Neumann 1944: 467–470; Müller 1991: 82–84).

For Fuller, the point of referring to evidence from a grossly pathological regulatory system is to try to show that legality is a more complex notion than legal positivism understands it to be. For rules to be legal it is not enough that they conform to the legal criteria expressed in a rule of recognition, or can be imputed from some basic norm of the legal system. Legality is a matter also of how the rules are drafted, promulgated, applied, interpreted and enforced. Neumann and Kirchheimer had already offered a broadly similar message.

Neumann, however, rejects natural law theory in his writings as a mystification usually adopted to justify the *status quo*. He is concerned only to confront positivist analytical jurisprudence with political and social realities and to demonstrate its descriptive inadequacy in failing to take account of them. Fuller, by contrast, eventually chooses the terrain of natural law on which to fight (cf Fuller 1969a: 96–97). The message of Nazi experience for him is that legal positivism cannot appreciate the moral conditions under which legality is possible. Legal order must be 'good order' so as to create conditions for fidelity to law. Good order demands conformity, at least to a minimum extent, with the internal morality of law. Legality, for Fuller, is thus a special kind of morality.

Before considering Fuller's ideas expressed in other writings it is appropriate to take stock, in a preliminary way, of this critique of legal positivism since it remains substantially unchanged in his later work.[3]

A familiar positivist reaction to Fuller is to approve all the procedural proprieties on which he insists while denying their moral character, and denying also that Fuller's conception of legality in any way undermines positivist analyses of law. The positivist claim is that the theoretical relationships between legal rules (in Hart's concept of law) and legal norms (in Kelsen's theory) are not invalidated by procedural impropriety. They exist even if denied in practice. Indeed, as has been seen, one of Kelsen's aims is to defend a rational legal science (as professional legal reasoning) in the face of political manipulation of law. The proper framing, application and interpretation of law are not moral matters for Kelsen and Hart but consequences of adhering to a coherent positivist view of a legal system and of the necessary relationships between its doctrinal elements.

Fuller's claims are symptomatic of an impatience with legal positivism's *silences*, with what it refuses to say about law, rather than with its explicit tenets. In Chapter 4 it was noted that modern analytical jurisprudence contributes to lawyers' professional concerns by attempting to establish a coherent concept (Hart) or science (Kelsen) of law which adequately reflects the normative view of rules or norms held by legal 'insiders': in other words, above all, by lawyers. At the same time, a political dimension to these theories was noted. They suggest an image of the Rule of Law as in-built in the very concept of law or legal system, because they portray law as a self-regulating system. But Fuller's procedural natural law theory seeks to show the inadequacy of this formal Rule of Law conception.

Legality is typically reduced in the implicit positivist conception to a professional understanding of the doctrinal consequences of a logically integrated system of rules. The actual operation of rules is ignored and, indeed, is largely irrelevant to this conception. But Fuller, passionate about the evils of Nazism

---

3   And see generally the extensive criticisms of positivism in Fuller 1940.

(Summers 1984: 7, 152), insists on the inadequacy of any such abstract, formal view of legality and the Rule of Law and emphasises the need to examine the practical conditions of making and applying rules.

Nevertheless, if the legal professional concern for a coherent portrayal of doctrine in its logical relationships is the concern which analytical jurisprudence is attempting to meet, its failure to address wider political and ethical dimensions of law in action is not necessarily inimical to the achievement of its objectives. Its silences on the moral issues of Nazi law do not, in themselves, invalidate its theses or render them incoherent. On this view, Fuller's natural law approach merely strains at the limits of normative legal theory as a rationalisation of legal professional knowledge: it asserts a need to infuse a more profound political awareness into normative legal theory. As will appear later, even legal positivists have realised that this might be desirable.

A purposive view of law

Fuller's other writings make it clear, however, that his main concerns about law's morality are not with questions of legal pathology such as whether Nazi law was too evil to be law, but with constructive issues as to how to infuse the highest legal virtues into systems, such as those of Anglo-American law, which he regarded as far from pathological. The internal morality of law (the procedural criteria by which Nazi legal tyranny is measured in the 1958 essay) are discussed in Fuller's most influential book, *The Morality of Law* (Fuller 1969a), as criteria also of possible legal excellence.

In *The Morality of Law* Fuller distinguishes between two kinds of morality or moral judgment. The *morality of duty* refers to the basic moral demands of order without which existence (whether of a society or of a legal system) becomes impossible. The *morality of aspiration*, by contrast, refers not to a moral minimum, but a maximum. 'It is the morality of the Good Life, of excellence, of the fullest realisation of human powers' (1969a: 5). Duty and aspiration are opposite ends of a moral scale that rises from the bare moral necessities for any human achievement, through to the highest moral ideals.

Moral demands can be pitched at various points on this scale. For example, a judgment about the morality of gambling could stress that extensive gambling directly harms society, the individual and the individual's family in economic, psychological and other ways. These 'duty' considerations might suggest that gambling should be legally prohibited. On the other hand, gambling on a small scale and for low stakes might not seem harmful in these basic ways but only a matter for regret that the individual can find no better use of time and energy.

The aspiration that people should live 'good lives' is not something to which they should be compelled. We assume that law should require the moral minimum, not try to force citizens to become saints.

This idea of a moral scale enables Fuller to pose, as a fundamental problem of all legal regulation, that of deciding where the pressures of duty stop and the excellences of aspiration begin. Law's impositions must be sufficient to sustain duty but they become tyrannous if they seek to impose excellence. Hence one of the most important arts of law-making is that of judging for each issue, each law and each activity or situation, what level of moral demands law should operate with. But the demand for legality is itself a moral demand. Therefore, it is necessary to decide how far it relates to the morality of duty and how far to that of aspiration. Where on the moral scale is the internal morality of law to be located?

In *The Morality of Law*, law's internal morality is first presented negatively as 'eight ways to fail to make law'. These are: (i) a failure to achieve rules at all, so that every issue must be decided on an *ad hoc* basis; (ii) a failure to publicise the rules to be observed; (iii) the abuse of retroactive legislation 'which not only cannot itself guide action, but undercuts the integrity of rules prospective in effect, since it puts them under the threat of retrospective change'; (iv) a failure to make rules understandable; (v) enactment of contradictory rules or (vi) enactment of rules requiring conduct beyond the powers of the affected party; (vii) introducing such frequent changes in the rules that those addressed cannot orient their conduct by them; and (viii) a failure of congruence between the rules and their actual administration (Fuller 1969a: 39).

Total failure in any one of these directions, or a pervasive general failure in them (as with Nazi regulation) would, for Fuller, result in the non-existence of a legal system (1969a: 39). At this basic level, therefore, the internal morality of law provides a minimum morality of duty without which the existence of a legal system is impossible.

Beyond such rare pathological cases, however, the internal morality of law is primarily a morality of aspiration, the aspiration to maximise legality, to make legal order as good an order as can be. The internal morality can then be expressed as eight excellences which are the reverse of the 'eight ways to fail to make law': government always by rules, which are always publicised, prospective, understandable, non-contradictory, etc. Yet Fuller stresses that it would be counterproductive to try to realise fully all eight excellences in a working legal system. No system of rules could function on such a basis but would collapse in chaos or paralysis. For example, retroactive laws are sometimes inevitable, not all legal disputes can be solved by existing rules, and rules cannot achieve perfect clarity in advance of all applications of them.

So the achievement of legality is not merely the acceptance of a set of moral principles. It is a matter of judging the point on the moral scale between duty and aspiration where each component of legality, as related to each concrete problem of legal regulation in the particular legal system concerned, should be set. And the point on the scale will vary with circumstance and time. The achievement of legality is thus a task requiring all the skills of legislator and jurist. It is the heart of 'the enterprise of subjecting human conduct to the governance of rules' (1969a: 91, 96).

The use of this last mentioned phrase is the closest Fuller comes to defining law (cf 1969a: 106) but the definition, such as it is, is instructive. It emphasises that law is a purposive activity (not merely rules or norms which are the product of the activity). Equally Fuller's definition reflects his view (readily acceptable to many legal sociologists but sometimes less so to lawyers and legal philosophers) that the term 'law' need not be limited to refer only to rules enforced by state agencies. Fuller's purposive concept of law allows it to be applied to rule structures governing numerous social institutions – such as schools, hospitals or business corporations – and social groups. The internal morality of law provides criteria of legality by which rule systems of many kinds can be judged. Indeed, this concept of legality has been used in sociological studies in such fields as industrial relations (Selznick 1969) and policing (Skolnick 1975).

There is much of value in these ideas. Nevertheless, it is clear that we have moved on to different terrain from that of positivist analytical jurisprudence. What is now offered by Fuller no longer appears as a direct critique of legal positivism but as a different enterprise concerned with the examination of law in purposive terms. Although Fuller presents his ideas as an attack on legal positivism, they cannot be defended as a critique of the logic of positivist analytical jurisprudence but only of the inappropriateness, narrowness or political and social irrelevance of its projects. His claims are strong. But they amount to saying: you should have devoted your researches to this rather than that. And the positivist can still reply: maybe so, but your arguments are no criticism of what I *have* done in seeking to rationalise the legal knowledge that is important to lawyers.

Fuller and the common law tradition

One further line of attack on legal positivism presents itself in Fuller's work and, though it is usually the least discussed, it is the strongest attack mounted in his writings. In an important article, Fuller attacks positivist analytical jurisprudence at what has already been identified in this and earlier chapters as one of its weakest points: its understanding of the judicial process and the practice of judicial development of case law.

Using a dichotomy very similar to Neumann's contrast between *ratio* and *voluntas*, he argues that judicial development of law necessarily involves both reason and fiat or 'order discovered and order imposed' and 'to attempt to eliminate either of these aspects of the law is to denature and falsify it' (Fuller 1946: 382). Classical natural law theory cannot convince us that law can actually be pure reason; it cannot supplant the need 'for authority, for a deciding power' (1946: 388).[4] But, equally importantly, positivism cannot convincingly portray law as pure fiat (that is, a formal structure of authority) because the legal outcomes of judicial decisions cannot be understood except in the light of reasons for the decisions. In case law, reason and fiat are inseparably intertwined. The judicial decision is an exercise of authority but also a search for, and attempt to construct, reason in legal doctrine. Common law method entails an appreciation of both fiat and reason in case law. At its best, it keeps these aspects of law in balance.

Thus, Fuller suggests that an extreme positivism, which sees law only as fiat, is 'essentially alien to the American spirit' (1946: 394). It cannot adequately represent the common law method of legal development. Hence the emphasis on 'reason', which in Fuller's later writings develops into the procedural version of natural law represented by the internal morality of law, connects with a defence of common law methods.

There is, however, more to this defence than a device for attacking legal positivism. In Chapter 2 the image in classical common law thought of law's deep roots in community life was discussed. Fuller, also, asserts in his writings that the case law of the common law tradition projects its roots 'more deeply and intimately' into the actual patterns of human interaction than does statute law (Fuller 1969b: 26). His concern to understand these social patterns and their relationships with legal procedures and institutions gradually led him to deeper study of sociology, anthropology and social psychology. What resulted was a body of writing examining the social roots and consequences of particular forms of law and of particular kinds of legal procedures and institutions.

The most interesting aspect of all this for the concerns of this book is the way in which Fuller's researches led him to a kind of restatement of elements of

---

4   No doubt it is this point which, several years later, makes Fuller in *The Morality of Law* (now explicitly accepting the label natural law for his own theory) address that theory directly only to the procedural forms by which the deciding power expresses and implements its decisions, rather than to the substance of the decisions (as classical natural lawyers typically have done).

classical common law theory, but in a sophisticated form that replaces the mystical images of community encountered earlier in Chapter 2 with specific sociological claims about law in society. For Fuller, the necessity of human interaction is what gives purpose to law, and the principle of reciprocity is a major foundation of social interaction and social institutions (1969a: 20–21, 61). His writings portray social life as a kind of collective endeavour, a matter of co-operation (for example, in maintaining legality: 1969a: 91) and ideally, the collaborative working out of a reasoned view of human affairs.

The overriding task of law is, thus, to keep open lines of communication between members of society (1969a: 185–186), by means of which disputes can be resolved, projects planned, and individual and group objectives achieved. Fuller's image of social life is one in which a network of free individual initiatives sorts most matters out. Governmentally-imposed solutions to social problems may often be of limited use. Thus, for Fuller, negotiation, arbitration and mediation are specially important means of resolving social difficulties. He served for twenty years as an industrial relations arbitrator of grievances under collective bargaining agreements and devoted much energy to this role (Summers 1984: 7).

Such a view of social life and its ordering does not, therefore, lead to the simplistic conclusion, so often associated with classical common law thought, that the wise judge as repository and distiller of communal knowledge and custom is always the ideal regulator. Fuller plainly considers this *often* to be the case (Fuller 1940: 131–138). But courts cannot, for example, deal well with polycentric problems – those where the interconnections of the problem posed with other problems of practical social ordering are sufficiently complex to make attempted solutions counterproductive unless their ramifications in a variety of contexts are systematically considered.[5]

Beyond this, the criteria of legality – the internal morality of law – are not necessarily appropriate to all kinds of government action, for example in economic planning and allocation (Fuller 1969a: 171), or to private rule-making by negotiation between the parties. Different kinds of social order and organisation require different kinds of regulation and regulatory mechanisms and procedures. Much of Fuller's later work is concerned with exploring the relationships between the inherent character of various means of regulation (for example, custom, contract, adjudication, legislation, managerial direction, and democratic collective decision-making) and the types of social order for which they are appropriate (cf Summers 1984: ch 6).

---

5   Fuller 1978. Allison 1999 argues that Fuller's analysis of adjudication in this context is culturally biased; and see also p 220, below.

Nevertheless, Fuller's later writings attach special significance to a kind of social order which seems close to that suggested by the idea of the community in classical common law thought. Fuller terms it the relationship of 'friendly strangers' (1969b: 27). It is neither the relationship of intimacy which is the ideal of family life, nor that of antagonism as between hostile nations. It seems to be the social order in which individuals pursue their own objectives in a spirit of co-operation through social relationships of reciprocity.

In discussing the ideal legal framework for such a social order, Fuller distinguishes between three types of law. *Customary law* derives directly from patterned interaction between individuals and it changes as the patterns of interaction change. What Fuller calls *enacted law* is any officially imposed law. Between these two categories stands *contractual ordering*, or the 'law of the contract'. This refers to the rules that interacting parties make between themselves and for themselves by negotiation: the rules of private ordering which lawyers would call terms of the contract.

Contractual ordering is ill-suited to the ordering of intimate or hostile relations but ideally suited to 'the habitat of friendly strangers, between whom interactional expectancies remain largely open and unpatterned' (Fuller 1969b: 27, 29). Customary law can operate across the whole spectrum of social contexts from intimacy to hostility, but enacted law (the kind of regulation that must demonstrate legality in the sense of Fuller's internal morality of law) is, like contractual ordering, most appropriate within the social order of friendly strangers. Its task is, indeed, for Fuller, above all that of facilitating contractual ordering of relationships.

Striking similarities with the orientation of classical common law thought can be seen in these ideas. First, there is the somewhat unclear legitimacy of enacted law which, as in classical common law thought, is seen as in partnership with and even subordinate to other regulatory structures that emerge in the conditions of everyday social life (contractual negotiation, custom). For Fuller, even enacted law must find its roots in the changing conditions of human interaction (Witteveen 1999). The internal morality of law (legality) helps to ensure this since it expresses the moral relationship of reciprocity between rulers and ruled (Fuller 1969b: 24).

Second, customary law, which Austin did not even recognise as law (Austin 1832: 35) and which plays little role in positivist legal thinking, re-emerges in Fuller's later writings with all the centrality which classical common law theory gave it. Customary law, for Fuller, consists of the established patterns of social interaction that provide the stable structure of expectations within which people can co-operate, negotiate, plan and act. Social science shows how important these stable structures are – often much more important than those provided by enacted law.

Finally, Fuller's writings emphasise the autonomous, spontaneous processes by which regulation (especially contractual ordering and custom) develops. They challenge the positivist emphasis on creation of law by fiat. Again this is strongly reminiscent of the evolutionary picture of law offered in classical common law thought.

Thus, a sociological perspective on regulation allows Fuller to demystify some old themes of common law thought. In the modern dress of social science they confront the legal science of positivist analytical jurisprudence.

Politics and professional responsibility

In earlier chapters, an attempt has been made to show why positivist analytical jurisprudence has been potentially significant as the basis of a science or a concept of law demonstrating the intellectual autonomy and unity of professional legal knowledge. Fuller's theories seem to have none of the qualities that would make them professionally useful in this respect: they deny any sharp demarcation between law and non-law and claim instead that the existence of law (as measured by the criteria of legality) can be a matter of degree (Fuller 1969a: 122). Equally, Fuller refuses to see 'lawyers' law' as uniquely distinctive and is happy to apply the term 'law' to the rule systems and processes of social groups and social institutions of many kinds. None of this seems very promising as support for the thesis that influential varieties of legal theory have been relevant in clarifying problems of legal professionalisation. Yet a colleague of Fuller wrote that he 'reached more American law students and stimulated more speculative thought about the law than any other American law teacher' (quoted in Summers 1984: 15).

In fact, it is not necessary to read far into Fuller's work to see that his concerns are very strongly organised around the dilemmas and responsibilities of legal professional practice.[6] This is, for example, obviously the case with his attack on legal positivism in relation to the Nazi regime. A failure of positivism, as seen by Fuller, is that of not making clear the moral responsibilities of legal practice. Lawyers are *not*, because of their professional allegiance to the legal system as a part of the state apparatus, absolved from moral responsibilities to other individuals; or from a political responsibility to defend the liberty of others,

---

6   For Fuller, 'the task of the legal philosopher is to decide how he and his fellow lawyers may best spend their professional lives': Fuller 1940: 2. See generally Fuller 1940: 2–4, 12–15.

which is the price to be paid for the privilege of living in a democracy. Yet German legal positivism, in Fuller's view, encouraged lawyers to accept as law anything that called itself by that name, was printed at government expense, and seemed to come from higher authority (Fuller 1958: 659).

Fuller has no doubt that such passive views of legality helped the rise of Nazi tyranny. 'The first attacks on the established order were on ramparts which, if they were manned by anyone, were manned by lawyers and judges. These ramparts fell almost without a struggle' (1958: 659). The notion that legal positivism blinds lawyers and others to moral issues that surround governmental action when that action is dressed in the garb of 'law' is a common theme in discussion of the Nazi period and the years preceding it. The Protestant theologian Emil Brunner wrote: 'The totalitarian state is simply and solely legal positivism in political practice ... the inevitable result of the slow disintegration of the idea of justice'. And he adds: 'If there is no justice transcending the state, then the state can declare anything it likes to be law; there is no limit set to its arbitrariness save its actual power to give force to its will' (Brunner 1945: 15–16). To similar effect, Neumann (1944: 47) writes of Kelsen's theory that 'it is virginal in its innocence ... it paves the way for decisionism, for the acceptance of political decisions no matter where they originate or what their content, so long as sufficient power stands behind them'.

The issue seems to come down to whether the separation of law and morality necessarily, in practice, leads to a neglect of the moral aspects of regulation. As noted earlier, *in theory* there is no reason why it should and some legal positivists have claimed that the fusion of legal and moral issues can be a weapon of reactionaries or authoritarians (claiming 'this is the law; therefore, it must be right'). Nazi writers did, indeed, claim that a fusion of law and morality had finally been achieved in Germany by National Socialism (Kirchheimer 1941: 88). And Kelsen sees the totalitarian state as founded on an assertion of 'absolute' values that are inseparable from its law (Kelsen 1955: 42).

By contrast, legal positivism can co-exist (as in Kelsen's own work) with a relativistic approach to values which requires the individual to face the dilemmas of conscience autonomously, without solutions 'legislated' by moral authorities (whether the state, the nation or the churches) considered to be absolute and infallible. Equally, legal positivism can co-exist with a belief in moral absolutes as long as legal analysis is seen as in no way dependent on these absolutes. Either way, positivism today is defended as a means of keeping 'the final sovereignty of conscience' separate from claims of legal validity (MacCormick 1985: 10).

Thus, there is nothing in positivist analytical jurisprudence as such that guarantees moral myopia (see Campbell 1996: ch 5). But there is a sense that positivism does not actively *encourage* a concern with the moral responsibilities of legal practice. Fuller's belief in a humanistic, broad approach to legal scholarship and legal education is part of his reaction against narrowness of moral vision. He wrote extensively on questions of legal education, supported broad curricula, loathed mechanical rule manipulation by the 'black-letter mind', and emphasised that basic problems of law and government can be solved by 'reason' (Summers 1984: ch 11). Reason, the lodestar of classical natural law, remains an object of faith. The lawyer should always refuse to accept fiat without reason.

Fuller's dissatisfaction with positivist analytical jurisprudence may, thus, be inseparable from a rejection of the limited technocratic image of legal professionalism which it seems to support. Excluding moral issues from the professional sphere of legal knowledge is unsatisfactory, from a standpoint such as Fuller's, if it make these issues seem of *less* concern to the lawyer than to other citizens. Further, treating law as wholly distinct from non-law is unsatisfactory if it disguises the fact that lawyers are in the job of *creating* legality, of building law from non-law and preventing legality declining or slipping away into arbitrariness. Finally, criteria of legal validity provided by definitions of the sovereign's command, by rules of recognition or a basic norm, are inadequate if they make lawyers think that the practice of law does not involve them in a *political* responsibility when they recognise the formal authority claimed for laws and regulations.

Fuller's image of the requirements of legal professionalism in modern conditions does not, therefore, deny the image that legal positivism sets up or implies. His position is, in essence, that positivism is not enough, and that twentieth century history should have warned us clearly of its inadequacy.

Natural law tamed?

No other natural law theory in the Anglo-American context in modern times has been widely seen as posing a stronger challenge to modern positivism than has Fuller's. And this despite the fact that his claims constitute only a modest, cautious version of natural law theory – essentially related to the procedural proprieties of law and not, as in most classical natural law theories, the substance of its rules. Has, therefore, natural law really become obsolete, as Weber seemed to suggest at the beginning of this century?

Certainly, in recent times, natural lawyers' demonstrations of legal positivism's apparent inadequacies when a broader understanding of law is required in modern political and ethical conditions have been influential. They have contributed to a growing sense among positivists that their legal theory needs in some way to reach out more firmly towards moral issues or moral foundations of law. Thus, Neil MacCormick has seen a convergence between natural law and legal positivism and argued that positivists should recognise 'the essential moral aspiration of lawgiving' and that laws 'are fully intelligible only by reference to the [moral] ends or values they ought to realize' (MacCormick 1992: 113, 118; cf MacCormick 1981: 161–162). Tom Campbell has recently insisted that legal positivism implies 'foundational moral views about what law and politics should be all about' and that it necessarily assumes these 'ethical aspects' as prerequisites of its practice (Campbell 1996: 1). Campbell makes these ethical implications explicit in what he calls a 'legal theory of ethical positivism'.

Quite apart from developments such as these, many legal positivists, recognising the frequency of appeals to broad values or standards in many legal processes, are now prepared to emphasise, following Hart's lead, that a Hartian rule of recognition might specifically invoke *moral* criteria of legal validity (Hart 1994; Waluchow 1994).

Long before any of these recent explicit 'moralisations' of legal positivism's outlook, Hart (1961: 199) had been prepared to accept a 'core of good sense' in the doctrine of natural law, recognising that the very conditions of all human existence necessitate certain kinds of social rules in any society if it is assumed that its members have a common aim of survival.

In Hart's view, five features of the human condition (vulnerability, approximate equality of physical power, limited altruism, limited resources and limited understanding and strength of will) ensure than any society must have *some* rules protecting persons, property, promises and exchanges, and providing for sanctions to ensure compliance (Hart 1961: 193–200). This minimum content of natural law, as Hart calls it, is far from the natural law that has been discussed in most of this chapter. It provides no significant criteria for criticising or justifying the substance or procedure of positive law (since survival may be achieved 'even at the cost of hideous misery': Hart 1961: 192), but only a set of truisms indicating broad areas in which some kind of regulation must exist.[7]

---

7 Interestingly, in his posthumous postscript to *The Concept of Law*, Hart (1994: 249) declares it 'quite vain to seek any more specific purpose which law as such serves beyond providing guides to human conduct and standards of criticism of such conduct'. But his 'minimum content of natural law' postulates just such a specific purpose. Perhaps this apparent forgetfulness of his earlier claim emphasises how unimportant the 'minimum content' ultimately is in Hart's thinking: a concept that damns natural law with faint praise but has no implications for substantive legal debates.

Tendencies among legal positivists towards rapprochement with natural law typically amount to a recognition that principles to guide or structure legal development are necessary but (unless specifically incorporated in positive law) are not to be found through positivist analysis of legal doctrine alone. Indeed, the increasing technicality of modern law and its tendency to appear as a mere compromise of interests may make the identification of guiding principles seem more relevant and important, not less.

Thus, Hart came to treat the influential modern natural law theory of the Oxford philosopher John Finnis (1980) as 'in many respects complementary to rather than a rival of positivist legal theory' (Hart 1983: 10). This seems fair. Finnis' theory rejects any claim to judge the legal validity of rules and so avoids any confrontation with legal positivism. It essentially offers a moral philosophy to give guidance as to what law's substance and purposes *should be*, rather than a normative legal theory to explain the doctrinal components or characteristics of particular legal systems. So Finnis' theory cannot be central to the concerns of this book. But some of its features are important here as illustrating the role that natural law theory seems to be coming to play as an adjunct to positivist analytical jurisprudence.

Finnis is concerned with what he understands, following Aristotle, as a 'focal' conception or 'central case' of law. This focal conception is an ideal or pure form, of which actually existing forms are mere derivatives or imperfect examples. Hence Finnis is less interested in the law present in actual legal systems than in the law (in a focal sense) that can be philosophically deduced as necessary and appropriate from certain moral postulates revealed by speculative analysis.

It is this method of analysis which is Finnis' most important contribution to modern natural law theory. As noted earlier, most earlier natural law theory sought to reason out philosophical consequences from observed characteristics of the human condition, or to deduce moral principles from rational argument, or from imagined states of nature existing before societies or governments came into being. These approaches have usually been vulnerable to the criticism that an unacceptable sleight of hand is involved in seeking to deduce what morally *ought* to be from speculation about what *is* (for example, what the state of nature or the human condition actually is). Indeed, as has been seen, even in Fuller's procedural version of natural law theory the procedural criteria that *ought* to govern a legal system are derived by speculating on what a working (efficient) system of rules *actually* involves.

Finnis' approach appears to bypass these traditional difficulties by grounding natural law not in reason but in intuition: in what is 'self-evident', requiring no rational justification. In this, his method follows and develops that of Aquinas.

Thus, For Finnis, seven objects of human striving are self-evidently good (1980: chs 3 and 4). These basic human goods are (i) *life* (every aspect of vitality that makes possible human self-determination); (ii) *knowledge* (for its own sake and not merely as a means to an end); (iii) *play* (activity with no purpose beyond the activity itself); (iv) *aesthetic experience* (the appreciation of beauty); (v) *sociability* or *friendship* (acting for the sake of friends and their wellbeing); (vi) *practical reasonableness* (being able to bring one's intelligence and judgment to bear in choosing how to live one's life); and (vii) *religion* (understanding something of what life is for).

It is not necessary here to assess Finnis' claim that these are indeed self-evident and that all other goods can be understood as combinations or derivatives of them. But his attempt to avoid the derivation of 'ought' from 'is' marks a methodological advance over many other expositions of natural law. The basic human goods are not derived from rational speculation on what *is* the case in nature. As intuitively recognised goods they are already normative in effect: because they are self-evidently 'good' it is equally self-evident that they should be pursued and promoted. Practical reasoning (itself one of the basic goods) provides, in Finnis' view, general prescriptions of reason ('basic methodological requirements') which should guide the pursuit of these goods. Further, since they can only be sought in communal life, in interaction with other people, a legal system to secure them is necessary.

From Finnis' detailed filling out of this analytical framework, three matters, related directly to the themes of this chapter, can be mentioned. They are the discussions of 'community', 'authority' and the Rule of Law.

A link between the idea of community implicit in classical common law thought and the purposive view of law reflected in natural law theory has been noted earlier – as has the appeal to reason which characterises them both. Indeed, modern literature on the basis of moral authority often strongly emphasises the concept of community (cf Weinreb 1987: 249–259). So it is not surprising that Finnis, like Fuller, attaches much importance to analysing the nature of the moral community (in Fuller's case the collectivity of 'friendly strangers') to which law relates most directly. Finnis notes that part of the unity of community is physical and biological (for example, in family ties), part in intelligence and shared modes of understanding, part in common technology and cultural unity, and part in common action or interaction. While the last of these is most relevant to the analysis of practical reasoning in human communities, it presupposes the other elements.

Finnis notes the different character of business, play and friendship relationships and that political communities combine elements of all of these (1980: 149). This complex variety of relationships is typical of 'complete' communities – the ones to which law in its focal sense relates. A complete community is thus 'an all-round association' in which are co-ordinated 'the initiatives and activities of individuals, of families, and of the vast network of intermediate associations'. Its point is 'to secure the whole ensemble of material and other conditions, including forms of collaboration, that tend to favour, facilitate, and foster the realisation by each individual of his or her personal development' (Finnis 1980: 147). This is obviously, for Finnis, a philosophical ideal. But like any group, a community in this sense has definite conditions of existence. It can be said to exist 'wherever there is, over an appreciable span of time, a co-ordination of activity by a number of persons, in the form of interactions, and with a view to a shared objective' (1980: 153). It is enough to note here that, like the exponents of classical common law thought, Finnis sees the moral and rational strength of law as grounded in its purposive contribution to the continuance and fulfilment of a complete community. Unlike the classical common lawyers, however, he also sees the need to make some effort to elaborate rigorously what this concept entails.

Finnis' ideas about authority and the Rule of Law can be considered together. Influenced here, as elsewhere, by Max Weber, he sees the basis of the authority of rulers not, for example, in the consent of the governed nor in a notional social contract such as Hobbes or John Locke described, but merely in the likelihood of compliance by those over whom authority is claimed (1980: 249). The existence of constitutional structures and the issue of whether the ruler has the consent of the governed are relevant in asking whether someone guided by practical reason ought to obey the claimed authority. But this does not derogate from Finnis' surprisingly Austinian position that authority depends on the 'sheer fact' of likely obedience (1980: 250).

On the other hand, a Fullerian view of the Rule of Law and its demands is built on to this positivist conception of political authority. Acknowledging Fuller's influence, Finnis stresses reciprocity between rulers and ruled as the foundation of the moral demands of legality (1980: 274). Elaborating the main features of legal order, Finnis produces a general picture strikingly like Fuller's. Thus, law is a coercive structure but, more fundamentally, a system of rules. It brings clarity and predictability to human interactions, regulates its own creation and modification, allows individuals to adjust their circumstances rationally in a rule-governed environment, provides reasons for future actions, and postulates a gapless framework of regulation.

Finnis' descriptive emphasis on these characteristics seems to reflect a recognition of the importance of technical imperatives in the application of legal rules that no modern legal positivist could quarrel with. The Rule of Law, then, as in Fuller's characterisation of legality, is the requirement to make these elements of rule-governed reliability and predictability as pervasive as possible in a legal order. And, like Fuller, Finnis emphasises the reciprocal relationship between ruler and ruled (and the virtue of maximising the dignity of individuals as free, responsible agents) as the foundation of the Rule of Law and the conditions that make it a component of political virtue.

At the point at which Finnis' natural law theory meets legal positivism's direct concern with working systems of legal rules, it restricts itself, like Fuller's theory, to elaborating and lauding the virtues of the Rule of Law. But, whereas Fuller attacks positivism at this point, Finnis offers no challenge to positivism on its own ground. Natural law has, it seems, become an ally and supplement to legal positivism. In times of social and political stability it does not displace the reassuring picture that positivist analytical jurisprudence offers of orderly legal knowledge and uncontroversial, professionally understood structures of authority in legal systems. But if Western political arrangements become significantly less stable, perhaps natural law theory will become powerful again, enlisted for or against the *status quo*.

Only in one area has modern natural law theory found a general and major analytical weakness in the theories it opposes. The judicial function still remains problematic in the tradition of modern analytical jurisprudence. In the common law world, lawyers and non-lawyers alike are reluctant to accept that the judge is merely the delegate of an Austinian sovereign and that judge-made law is merely what Fuller terms fiat. But post-Austinian legal positivism, represented by Hart's and Kelsen's theories, offers little or no analysis of how judges reach decisions in controversial cases and of the nature of their authority as legal innovators. Fuller's work, echoing older common law conceptions, at least reopens this question, while Finnis' re-examination of community points towards sources of legal authority independent of political structure. But different approaches, free of the controversies of natural law and firmly focussed on felt professional concerns of lawyers, have emerged to take these inquiries further. They will be considered in the following two chapters.

Chapter 6

The problem of the creative judge: Pound and Dworkin

Looked at in relation to legal environments beyond Britain, legal positivism as embodied in analytical jurisprudence has sometimes seemed ridiculous. How can law be understood in isolation from politics and social values when so much of it is a matter of judicial interpretation (of legislation, constitutional provisions, or earlier judge-made law) and of interpreting what judges say? Surely law, in this sense, is a moral or political *practice* of some kind, not just a set of distinctive concepts to analyse?

Throughout the Anglo-American legal world this question is significant but in the United States it has seemed especially pressing (cf Hart 1958: 49–50). The American legal environment (which has inspired much of the theory to be considered in this chapter and the next) is framed by a written constitution explicitly recognised as the repository of fundamental political values, and by a heritage of common law which, it is assumed, 'must continually reflect currently held social attitudes'; in this context a recognised role of judges is 'to integrate constitutional principles with changing social attitudes and values' as manifested in common law and other legal doctrine (White 1976: 18). Law seems hardly recognisable by applying litmus-like tests but is rather argued over, or teased out of judicial pronouncements by creative interpretation.

Classical common law thought, however, seems no more able than positivist analytical jurisprudence to take account of this reality of creative legal development. Seeing law as reason, classical common law thought ignored the 'fiat' side of the equation (to use Fuller's terms). Denying that judges make law, it portrayed legal processes not as purposive, innovative and creative, but as passive, responsive and evolutionary. Whether or not judges legislate, they are clearly significant actors in managing the processes of legal development.

Neither positivist analytical jurisprudence nor classical common law seems capable of explaining the nature of this activity and the principles governing it.

The problem of developing a normative legal theory explicitly recognising, as a principled enterprise, the activity of judges and other officials in developing law is the focus of this chapter. Although this is a task of normative legal theory in relation to any legal system, it should be a special concern in the context of Anglo-American law where the tradition of common law thinking makes the judge central in the legal system. But, in England, as has been seen, positivist analytical jurisprudence met legal professional needs to rationalise legal knowledge while reflecting the political realities of a centralised state in which law-making power was concentrated and all special jurisdictions absorbed (Arthurs 1985).

Perhaps the only fully explicit political theory of the judge's role offered by English positivist analytical jurisprudence is Austin's explanation of the judge as the sovereign's delegate, an official theoretically much like any other charged with governmental decision-making. This theory, however inadequate, does at least purport to explain the character of the activity in which a judge is involved in creating new law and the (sovereign's) authority that justifies this law-making.

Hart's theory, by contrast, explains (in terms of secondary rules) the legal powers and constraints within which the judge operates, but treats the exercise of judicial discretions (the activity itself) as beyond the concern of legal theory. Both Hart and Kelsen explain what makes a judge's decision binding as law, but not where the judge obtains authority specifically to develop law. To stress, as Kelsen and – by implication – Hart do, that law regulates its own creation does not solve the problem since while law regulates this process it does not control it. Human agencies are at work reaching beyond the presently stated rules of law. What directs and impels them?

Two American writers, whose work is rarely compared, are the most important modern contributors to the attempt to solve this problem in Anglo-American normative legal theory. Despite major differences in methods and approaches to theory construction, the writings of Roscoe Pound and Ronald Dworkin show similar practical concerns and a fundamentally similar restructuring of common law thought in defence against positivist analytical jurisprudence. Yet very little attention has been paid in jurisprudential literature to the parallels between them (cf Burnet 1985). A partial explanation lies in the fact that, despite important parallels in the broad aims of their writings in legal theory, the form in which the substance is presented differs very greatly between them and is influenced by very different intellectual climates.

Pound, who was Dean of Harvard Law School from 1916 to 1936 and whose immensely prolific writings span almost the entire period from the first years of the twentieth century until his death in 1964, directed his criticisms broadly against a wide range of competing approaches to legal thought in the Anglo-American context. Constructively, his writings seek to develop a self-proclaimed 'sociological' jurisprudence presented as an amalgam of largely continental European influences and indigenous American tendencies in philosophy. Pound's theories thus appear as syntheses marshalling the strengths of many pre-existing legal philosophies (Hull 1997: 9ff). This apparent Catholicism and openness carries the risk of producing a hotchpot of ideas lacking unity and rigour (what Kelsen castigates as syncretism of methods). Indeed the criticism that Pound failed to integrate and systematise the diverse trends of his thought has often been levelled against his contributions to legal theory.

By contrast, Dworkin elaborated his original theory by systematically developing a sustained attack on positivist orthodoxy as represented in Hart's work, but with little direct reference to other major theoretical predecessors. Until recently, Dworkin's main institutional position was, indeed, that which Hart previously held. He replaced Hart as professor of jurisprudence at Oxford University after the latter's retirement in 1968 and held that post together with other academic responsibilities in the United States.

Interestingly, while Dworkin is now one of the most widely discussed contemporary legal philosophers, Pound's intellectual reputation, once unassailable as that of the unquestioned doyen of American legal scholarship (cf Wigdor 1974: ix), has fallen considerably so that his ideas no longer play a significant role in the mainstream of debate in normative legal theory.

In this chapter it will be necessary to account for this dramatic change in evaluation of Pound's significance, as well as for the immense disparity between the present statuses of Pound's and Dworkin's theories.

The situation is only partly explicable in terms of the unquestionably greater rigour and philosophical sophistication of Dworkin's work. This chapter will argue that the explanation lies, in part, in a widespread misunderstanding of the nature of Pound's enterprise, which obscures both his achievement and the true nature of the problems of his theory. This, in turn, raises the possibility that Dworkin's normative legal theory (though not his wider moral, legal and political philosophy which is beyond the scope of this book) actually retraces by different means some ground which Pound travelled and that a somewhat similar ultimate assessment of the broad practical import of their legal theories will emerge with time. But Dworkin's work is still developing so that any general assessment of it can only be provisional.

Pound's rejection of the model of rules

It is customary to approach Pound's writings by taking seriously the label he himself gave to his theoretical outlook. He called it sociological jurisprudence and it is true that – especially in the first decade of the century, when he taught in Chicago at Northwestern University and the University of Chicago – he was significantly influenced by social scientists working in the city, and by the sociologist Edward Ross who had been a colleague at the University of Nebraska (Wigdor 1974: 111–113, 141–146). Ross and others offered ideas about the organic nature of social development and about the nature of social control (of which law could be considered one aspect) which aided Pound's efforts to escape the constraints of both positivist analytical jurisprudence and traditional common law thinking.

Nevertheless, if the main themes of Pound's normative legal theory – those that make him a significant figure in the progression of legal ideas with which this book is concerned – are to be understood, it is necessary to discount heavily any suggestion that his major theoretical work is sociologically informed to a significantly greater degree than that of other writers so far discussed in these pages.

In essence, for Pound, the label 'sociological'[1] was a banner to symbolise and rally serious efforts to view law in a broader, more dynamic perspective than that which positivist analytical jurisprudence offered, and in a more realistic, practically oriented and reformist perspective than that which much other legal philosophy (such as classical natural law theory) provided.[2] A prerequisite for establishing a dynamic view of law, one that could recognise it as in continuous flux, would be to discard the idea that it could be understood merely as rules or norms. For Pound, the concept of law must include not only the 'static' elements of law expressed as rules, but also those elements that direct and propel legal development. He writes: 'Law, as distinguished from laws, is the system of authoritative materials for grounding or guiding judicial and administrative action recognized or established in a politically organized society' (Pound 1959 II: 106).

Law, in this broad view, is not merely a model of rules but a doctrinal system in movement. Thus, even if we consider only legal doctrine in a strict sense (what

1   He had early doubts about attaching the word to his approach, but thought it important simply because it suggested in a challenging way the need to escape old, sterile methods in legal scholarship: Hull 1997: 84–85.

2   Holmes J in *Lochner v New York* 198 US 45 (1905) refused to follow the mechanistic reasoning of the majority of the United States Supreme Court in striking down as unconstitutional a statute limiting employees' working hours. Pound hailed Holmes' dissent in the case as 'the best exposition of ... sociological jurisprudence' extant in America. Cf White 1972: 1004.

Pound terms 'precepts' of law), this is not exhausted by rules ('precepts attaching a definite detailed legal consequence to a definite detailed state of facts or situation of fact'). Precepts also include *principles* ('authoritative starting points for legal reasoning'), *conceptions* ('authoritatively defined categories', such as trust, sale, bailment) and *standards* ('defined measures of conduct, to be applied according to the circumstances of each case', such as the standard of due care, or of fiduciary responsibility). Beyond this, however, law in Pound's broad sense includes also 'an authoritative technique of developing and applying the precepts, and a body of received ideals as to the end or purpose of the legal order, and hence to what legal precepts ought to be and how they ought to be applied' (Pound 1941: 256–257).

It might seem that this includes not only what positivist analytical jurisprudence typically treats as legal, but also much of what natural lawyers would wish to include in an understanding of law. But Pound's writings show little sympathy for classical natural law. They emphasise that law is an affair of values, and of techniques for elaborating and applying values to solve particular problems. The values themselves are, however, never timeless and universal as classical natural law sought to prove. They are values only for the time and place, related to the conditions of a particular legal system and to the kinds of claims brought to it to be recognised and satisfied.

Pound was sometimes prepared to see an affinity between natural law ideas and his emphasis on values underlying law, but the latter would be a 'practical natural law'. Insofar as he approved of the revival of natural law thought in the twentieth century this was because it brought a renewed emphasis, like his own, on values in law, and only to the extent that (as a natural law with a 'changing or a growing content') it denied that any *absolute* values underlie law (Pound 1923: 149). On this matter, unlike much else, Pound's views remained fairly constant throughout his career.[3]

What inspires Pound's very different approach to normative legal theory as compared with that of positivist analytical jurisprudence? His early writings show an obvious impatience to reform archaic legal procedure and extend professionalisation of law. The impatience is strangely like Austin's, half a century earlier in England: the irritation of an able and imaginative, if conservatively minded lawyer at the unsystematic, irrational practices of his own profession. Like Austin's, Pound's reform impulses were limited, largely aimed at making existing legal institutions work better, and tended to evaporate with the passing years.

---

3   Cf Wigdor 1974: 167, 274, 276.

Both men saw their legal theory as an aid in developing and guiding a modernising legal profession. When Pound was a boy of ten in Nebraska in 1880 the American legal profession was relatively unorganised. During the nineteenth century the public image and status of the legal profession had fluctuated greatly. Wigdor claims that '[t]hroughout the country, no legitimate profession had a more tarnished reputation' and in Nebraska, when Pound entered practice in 1890, 'almost anyone willing to read law for a few weeks could become a lawyer' (Wigdor 1974: 81; cf Stevens 1983: 25). Elsewhere, legal professionalism had strongly reasserted itself but had not yet put behind it a nineteenth century history of decline and disorder. There was an urgent need for a strong rational foundation of legal education and scholarship to aid professional consolidation (Stevens 1983: chs 1 and 2).

Parallels with Austin end here, however, for Pound saw Austin's kind of legal science as a wholly inadequate theoretical basis for professional development and institutional reform in the legal system. As will appear, Pound's odyssey in legal theory is, in essence, an effort to secure, purify and develop the tradition of common law which Bentham and Austin had so impatiently brushed aside.

In a country just emerged from pioneer times when Pound's ideas were being first formulated, it plainly made sense to treat courts (dispersed widely through states and territories) as the focus of legal authority, rather than to think in terms of lines of authority delegated from a centralised Austinian sovereign. But, even much later, his most illuminating legal theory aimed at revitalising common law techniques in the face of challenges presented by the immense legislative and administrative power of modern states. He also defends the common law conception of reason in law in the light of modern forms of systematic knowledge (especially social science) which have become increasingly important in shaping legislative and judicial policy. Pound's sociological jurisprudence, seen as a serious attempt to refurbish common law thought in modern conditions, is an important contribution to the themes of this book, however misleading the label 'sociological' which he gave it.

The outlook of sociological jurisprudence

An attempt to explain the basis on which judges develop law could move in one of two directions – emphasising either *instrumental* or *organic* aspects of the judicial role. David Wigdor has demonstrated clearly Pound's original ambivalence between these directions of analysis and explanation (Wigdor 1974: ch 9).

An *instrumentalist* approach would argue that the determinants of judicial creativity derive from outside law or legal doctrine as such: in various policy considerations, social pressures, political factors or economic imperatives. Pound's use of the adjective 'sociological' to describe his jurisprudence in contrast to analytical jurisprudence (which he tended to associate with mechanical, blindly deductive legal reasoning), and his frequent advocacy of social science as an aid in developing the law, suggest an instrumentalist outlook. So does his reiterated view that law's task is 'social engineering'. When a closer look is taken at what is being suggested in his writings, however, and especially when his ideas are viewed in the light of their evolution over the decades, a different conclusion is justified. It becomes clear either that, as Wigdor argues, Pound deserted the instrumentalist ideas of his early career, or (the reading I prefer) that instrumentalism was never for Pound more than a minor supplement to, or perhaps a useful rhetoric in aid of, a clearly *organicist* view of law.

This organicist view can be expressed in the following ideas:

(i) law contains within itself the doctrinal resources for its own development in the form of values and principles that can give content and shape to evolving law (rather than relying inevitably on inputs of change from 'outside' in the form of deliberate political action resulting in legislation or administrative rule-making);

(ii) law has a natural momentum for change, an in-built tendency to develop (it is inherently dynamic rather than static);

(iii) legal development is a matter of orderly adjustment within the legal system to the changing patterns of human demands being registered in it (a process of adjustment to be managed primarily, if not exclusively, by lawyers and judges using established legal techniques and principles); and

(iv) the task of the jurist is to keep these orderly processes of legal development working freely.

To think of the lawyer's task as one of social engineering did not mean, for Pound, engineering reforms, as such, except where the fourth of the above principles required it (Wigdor 1974: 230). But in his early writings he is much concerned with the failure of lawyers and others to keep the orderly processes of legal development working. These are seen by him as natural processes much like those assumed by classical common law thought. Hence *procedural* reforms in the legal system are urgently advocated.

Pound made his name, ironically, as a radical critic of the legal profession with a hugely controversial address to the American Bar Association (ABA) in 1906 on 'The Causes of Popular Dissatisfaction with the Administration of Justice'. The central concern of his famous paper is, indeed, with practical defects of procedure and organisation in administering justice. But it notes that in *all* legal systems, causes for popular dissatisfaction exist. They include the mechanical operation of legal rules, the inevitable divergences of law and public opinion, the popular assumption that administering justice is an easy task not requiring high professional skills, and popular impatience with legal restraints.

Equally, the Anglo-American common law system (leaving aside procedural and organisational problems) is not blameless. Its individualist spirit 'agrees ill with a collectivist age'; it arouses impatience and resentment by turning great social or economic issues into private legal disputes; it lacks general ideas or legal philosophy and so encourages 'petty tinkering where comprehensive reform is needed'; the adversary system 'turns litigation into a game'; and 'defects of form' arise because 'the bulk of our legal system is still case law' (Pound 1906: 185).

These remarks caused a storm in the American legal profession at a time when blunt, even if carefully modulated, criticism of law's inadequacies was unusual. And they show that Pound's original defence of common law, and his critique of the conception of law as fiat which positivist analytical jurisprudence suggested, is not an attempt to turn the clock back. Some of his early writings strongly defend legislation against mindlessly destructive interpretations by courts, castigate the sterility of case law, and argue that only legislation can provide a new starting-point for legal development (Pound 1908: 614, 621). Austinian analytical jurisprudence is criticised not because it seems to make legislation central to its conception of law but because it considers only the formal authority by which law is made and not the purposes for which that authority should be exercised.

On the other hand, Pound's defence of legislation has *some* Savignian overtones. Legislation is implied to be the handmaid of spontaneous legal development through the courts: clarifying doctrine where it has become confused, consolidating it and suggesting lines of development where none clearly emerges from current case law. Legislation is needed to provide a restatement of the law 'from which judicial decision shall start afresh' (Pound 1908: 622). But this involves 'new rules, then new premises, and finally a systematic body of principles as a fresh start for juristic development' (1908: 612), so there is no suggestion that legislation is restricted merely to consolidation. For Pound its role is dynamic: to move law forward in the light of modern social needs when other forces of legal development are failing.

Pound's early essays make the reader see legislative action as a kind of shock treatment to get the heart of common law beating regularly again. It follows that, given this importance of legislation, lawyers must become knowledgeable in its techniques and effective professional advocates in debates about its content. According to Pound, such a role demands lawyers' attention to social science which provides important material in these debates.

It is also clear from these essays that, for Pound, the reason why legal doctrine as developed by the courts has reached an impasse is that the essence of common law method has not been followed. Courts have adopted blindly deductive reasoning, 'mechanical jurisprudence', antithetical to the common law concern with precepts in relation to their 'conditions of application' (1908: 611–612). The time-honoured methods of common law require in modern conditions that lawyers use the sources of knowledge of community values and needs that social science can provide.

The ABA address, although atypical of Pound's work in its sharp criticism of professional practices, usefully highlights some of his early, central, reformist concerns which help to explain the direction his normative legal theory takes. The address notes criticism of common law methods for their individualist emphasis in a society that attaches increasing attention to broad social interests. It seems to follow, then, that a theory in defence of common law methods in modern conditions should direct attention systematically to these social interests and show how they are and should be taken into account in the adjudicative and lawmaking processes.

Equally, if a cause of dissatisfaction is the distortion of broad social issues into matters of private dispute, it is surely necessary to show how individual and social concerns can be kept analytically distinct, considered on their own separate planes: individual against individual, social against social, with disputes of broad consequences being considered primarily in terms of the social issues raised, rather than confused with private or individual concerns.

Again, if litigation seems too much like a game, perhaps what is needed is a theory of adjudication emphasising its objective character as a balancing process in which opposing interests are systematically identified, weighed and compared.

Finally, if common law is a bewildering mass of case law, what is surely required is a theoretical scheme by which its contents can be systematically ordered: not just in terms of the chaotic doctrine thrown up by the mechanical jurispru- dence of modern courts,[4] but in terms of the interests of individuals, groups and society, reflected in case law and recognised and protected by law. A theory for common law must presumably be true to the ideal character of this law as a legal expression of the life of the community. Hence it must be a theory of law's substance – of the elements of community life expressed in legal claims

---

4   Though Pound also cautiously supported the project of the American Law Institute to produce Restatements of the law in the form of codifications of principles distilled from systematic analysis of case law: Stevens 1983: 136; Hull 1997: 135.

and conflicts, not (as with positivist analytical jurisprudence) a formal theory of law's structure.

Whether or not there is a direct link between the complaints set out in the ABA address and the central tenets of Pound's sociological jurisprudence as it gradually took shape, it is easy to see the general ideas sketched above (all of which are, as will appear, integral to Pound's legal theory) as a natural outcome of the list of practical dissatisfactions that caused such a sensation in the American legal profession in 1906.

A theory of interests

Pound's programme for sociological jurisprudence, reiterated many times in his writings, involves a set of juristic tasks that ally jurist, judge and practising lawyer in the same enterprise of making the legal system work with (to use one of Pound's favourite phrases) the minimum of friction and waste.

The first task is to list and classify all interests (claims, demands or expectations that people individually or collectively seek to satisfy) pressing for legal recognition, so that in the task of deciding which should be protected, and to what extent, none will be ignored. At first sight this appears to entail a definite sociological basis for Pound's project. Surely the identification of interests in society is a task for the social scientist. But here, as in all other aspects of Pound's theoretical outlook, social science is firmly subordinated to the lawyer's professional skills.

Pound sees social scientific surveying of interests as impractical, at least for the foreseeable future. Interests are to be identified by noting the claims actually brought before courts (and so reflected to some extent in case law) or lobbied before legislatures. Legal and legislative records thus reveal the presence of interests, whatever the extent of legal protection of these interests. So, in Pound's outlook, pressures for change in law arising from changing social needs become relevant to the legal system, its theorists and practitioners only when the pressures are registered in legislative or judicial processes. The picture offered is one of a legal system waiting for change to be brought to it, not used as an engine to promote or direct social change.

It was suggested in the previous section that an emphasis on interests as the basic units of legal theory reflects the need to keep central the common law idea of law's intimate relationship with community needs and problems. It is important to notice that for Pound these basic units are only *potentially* legal in a strict sense. Once interests are legally protected they become legal *rights* but as claims pressed upon the legal system for recognition they are merely the raw material of law. They express patterns of social interaction and structures of social relationships, and changes in the interests pressing for legal recognition reflect changes in the patterns of social interaction and relationships. Thus, it can be argued that interests are the practical components of the idea of community identified in earlier chapters of this book as at the heart of classical common law thought.

Pound's writings contain exhaustive classifications and taxonomies of interests. Three kinds (social, individual and public) are identified. Social interests are those generalised as claims of society as a whole, treated as a collectivity. They include interests in the moral health of society, in general security and the security of social institutions, the conservation of social and natural resources, and in economic, political and cultural progress. Public interests are those asserted by the state as the legal embodiment of politically organised society. Individual interests include all interests in private security of the person, of transactions, of property, family relations, privacy, reputation and belief. Since there is, according to Pound, a social interest in the maximisation of individual wellbeing it follows that the general promotion, as far as possible, of individual interests is a social interest too – perhaps the most important social interest of all.

Pound seemed to delight in elaborating this scheme of interests, classifying and sub-classifying, and documenting the categories with a mass of illustration from Anglo-American case law. But what is it really for? The objective is, it seems, to demonstrate order and unity in law (an objective seen in earlier chapters to be central to normative legal theory) in a way compatible with the common law outlook. Such an approach requires, as Austin suggested, a 'map of the law', but not – as he understood this – a map of its formal structures demonstrating the top-down patterns of authority conveyed by the idea of sovereignty.[5] The map should presumably rather be of law's content in relation to actual community needs: the interests reflected in and constituting social life.

Once such an overall view of legal concerns is in place the rest of the programme of sociological jurisprudence can be attempted. Pound (1941: 261) sets this out explicitly as: (i) selecting the interests law should recognise; (ii) fixing the appropriate legal limits of protection of those interests; (iii) deciding how and to what extent law can effectively protect them; and (iv) formulating principles of valuation by which the three previously stated tasks are to be accomplished.

All these tasks are clearly very different from the descriptive objectives of analytical jurisprudence. They are prescriptive – specifying how legal develop-

---

5   Cf Chapter 3, above, p 75.

ment *should* take place. At the same time they can be understood as explaining the prescriptive guidelines *actually* adopted in a working common law system. In that sense the enterprise is also descriptive. Hence an ambiguity is written into Pound's project. Prescription and description of legal processes and adjudicative practices go together: it becomes difficult to distinguish one from the other. What is becomes inseparable from what ought to be. Again, this position is closely compatible with that of classical common law thought (custom being simultaneously what is and what ought to be), although wholly opposed to the outlook of positivist analytical jurisprudence.

Interests are to be balanced 'on the same plane' (Pound 1943: 2): that is, individual against individual, and social against social (public interests eventually seem to disappear from Pound's major concerns). Individual interests are never to be balanced directly against social interests, and, where possible, interests are to be compared in 'their most generalised form': that is, as social interests (Pound 1943: 3).

It can be inferred that what really lies behind Pound's insistence on this point is his wish to enable the adjudicative processes of common law to deal effectively with clashes of social interests, and so avoid the criticism of common law as excessively individualistic. At the same time, since Pound sees protection of the individual life and its aspirations as perhaps the pre-eminent social interest, the new theoretical elevation of social interests does not destroy the traditional particularistic focus of common law case development but affirms its importance within a larger field of social conflicts and the balancing of social interests.

The search for a measure of values

Viewed in this way, Pound's sociological jurisprudence in its overall shape and emphasis is a not-unsophisticated refurbishment of the common law outlook in the light of modern conditions. Looked at in detail, however, as a practical (prescriptive) guide for legal development or as an explanatory (descriptive) theory of the way Anglo-American law evolves, it reveals serious problems which go to the heart of the project being attempted in this kind of normative legal theory.

Pound's theory is a kind of 'bootstraps' theory of law, by which I mean that to explain the character of law it relies on concepts that are themselves constructed from what is to be explained. This is true of the concept of interests itself. What counts as a distinct interest for the purposes of the theory is far from clear (Llewellyn 1930a: 14) and depends on possibly controversial interpretations of the body of existing legal doctrine (which is what the theory is meant to illuminate). The identification of the 'measure of values' which the theory demands to guide the balancing of interests (that is, deciding how far interests should be recognised, and how far legally protected in each particular case when they conflict with others) is equally problematic. Like classical common law thought, Pound sees this measure of values as somehow implicit in law itself – secreted in the developing patterns of legal doctrine.

A great deal of Pound's writing is devoted to the search for this elusive evaluative measure that can guide future legal development. In Chapter 2 it was noted that classical common law thought avoided the difficulty by assuming legal change to be merely an aspect of cultural change: expressed in the idea of custom as evolving spontaneously without direction by any explicit guiding principle. But this position remains wholly unsatisfactory as a basis for legal theory appropriate to common law since it suggests no legal basis for change and removes the evolutionary development of law (central to the common law concept of law) entirely from the ambit of legal explanation. Pound's theory tries to replace this mystical core of classical common law thought with an explicit set of evaluative principles.

Following the German jurist Josef Kohler, he terms them the *jural postulates* of the time and place. They are 'ideas of right to be made effective by legal institutions and legal precepts' (Pound 1923: 148). They are in no sense absolute values, but merely those recognised or implied in a particular society at a particular time. Kohler saw the postulates as underlying values of civilisation. Pound (1923: 148) asserts:

> 'There is no eternal law. But there is an eternal goal – the development of the powers of humanity to their highest point. We must strive to make the law of the time and place a means towards that goal in the time and place, and we do that by formulating the presuppositions of civilisation as we know it. Given such jural postulates, the legislator may alter old rules and make new ones to conform to them, the judges may interpret, that is, develop by analogy and apply, codes and traditional materials in the light of them, and jurists may organise and criticise the work of legislatures and courts thereby'.

But where are the jural postulates to be discovered? The answer for Pound is in law itself. Legal doctrine reveals its immanent values. Again, although the postulates are theoretical devices to enable us to understand law better, we rely on studying law itself to understand its postulates.

This is less absurd than it appears. Pound sees the jural postulates as merely the most abstract and generalised normative components of a particular legal system at a particular time. As such they provide its fundamental internal structure of values, reflected in many detailed decisions made in the system. For example, Pound originally identified the postulates of Anglo-American law early in the twentieth century as affirming generally: (i) the wrongfulness of intentional aggressions; (ii) the importance of good faith in a wide variety of contexts; (iii) the sanctity of private property; (iv) the importance of due care to avoid injury to others; and (v) the obligation to prevent potentially dangerous things which one owns from getting out of hand (cf Pound 1942: ch 4).

In many ways the list of postulates Pound elaborates is odd: a strangely cramped, myopic view of the scope of civilised values, seen through the prism of professional legal practice. That, however, is less important than the point that the postulates have little explanatory or prescriptive power. They generalise from the doctrine of a legal system at a certain time. Yet, as Pound recognised, they need continual revision as law and civilisation evolve and change their character (Pound 1959 III: 11–14; 1940: 83); and this revision can only be in the light of legal change that is already complete, not legal change to come. Because of this, the postulates cannot reliably guide or explain the future development of law because no theoretical explanation is offered as to how they themselves alter or are developed. And in an age of rapid change it may be impossible to discover what existing postulates are (Pound 1942: 133–134; 1959 III: 14–15).

In defence of Pound it can be said that there is no suggestion that the jural postulates are the key to understanding all present and future legal development. The vague aim of avoiding friction and waste in human affairs is offered as the primary key (Pound 1942: 133–134). 'No matter what theories of the end [ie purpose] of law have prevailed, this is what the legal order has been doing, and as we look back we see has been doing remarkably well' (1940: 76).

Stating the postulates is just an effort to identify law's most abstract, intractable components and to do so within the broad, multifaceted idea of the legal field that Pound counterposes to positivism's restricted conception of law as rules or norms. The postulates are the product of a serious effort to identify those components of the inherently dynamic character of common law that are located in legal doctrine itself. That the product is so limited might suggest, however, that the attempt to explain law's processes of development in terms of the character of legal ideas themselves (that is, as something internal to law, rather than imposed upon it by external forces, as an instrumentalist might argue) is, itself, misguided.

The wider context of Pound's jurisprudence

Pound's continual reference to the avoidance of friction and waste as a basic aim of legal ordering suggests an enduring instrumentalist tinge to his thinking, despite the dominance of the organic common law conception of law. But his failure to devote any serious attention to elaborating theoretically what might count as friction and waste and what would actually be entailed in avoiding them confirms that this strand in his thought, for all its prominence, is essentially a rhetorical supplement to an organicist view of legal development.

Wigdor is no doubt correct to argue that in Pound's early career his outlook appeared, to himself and to others, as fully compatible with various political positions and reform movements sympathetic to instrumentalist views of law (Wigdor 1974: chs 8 and 9). He supported the Progressive movement in American politics early in the twentieth century. This advocated rational, deliberate government action for social reform within the framework of and in support of what were considered fundamental established values of American life. The Progressives adopted a broadly pragmatic outlook 'in which rational men could work out their differences' with 'facts and good faith' (Hull 1997: 29).

The then new philosophy of pragmatism also appealed to Pound and his early writings support it as a basis for modern legal thought. This too, has misled some commentators into overemphasising the instrumentalist aspects of his jurisprudence and the compatibility between his ideas and those of younger American scholars who wholeheartedly adopted instrumentalist approaches to law. Pragmatism implied a distrust of absolutes and a belief that values (including the value of truth) are realised only in practice, as the successful means of achieving deliberately chosen ends.[6]

But, for Pound, the word 'pragmatism' is, it seems, no more nor less useful than the word 'sociological'. Both are labels for approaches that emphasise law's purposes rather than its abstract logic: 'The sociological movement in jurisprudence is a movement for pragmatism as a philosophy of law; for the adjustment of principles and doctrines to the human conditions they are to govern rather than to assumed first principles; for putting the human factor in the central place and relegating logic to its true position as an instrument' (Pound 1908: 609–610). For Pound, that instrument is to be used not, as jurists unequivocally inspired by pragmatism would later insist, for planning and social reform through government and law, but for realising the destiny of common law as a continuous expression of the changing patterns of community life. Indeed, the clearest proof of Pound's outlook is in the fact that as soon as it became clear to him that pragmatism was being taken seriously as a basis for thoroughly instrumentalist views of law, he opposed this tendency with a fervour reserved for few other objects of his criticism (Pound 1931; cf Hull 1997: 189–195).

---

6   See further, below, pp 178–179, 252–254.

Through the nine decades of Pound's life his view of the destiny of common law methods changed very significantly. In his early writings the problem is seen as one of freeing these methods from the stagnation that mechanical jurisprudence (formalistic, abstract legal logic) produced. Legislation and administrative action are seen as aids in solving the problem and Pound's writings have an open, progressive tone in advocating modern methods of legal development and the use of resources from the social sciences to set law on an appropriate course to meet contemporary challenges.

In his later work the tone is quite different. Administrative rule-making is seen as a fundamental threat, part of the broader threat of political 'absolutism': uncontrollable governmental power (Pound 1940: ch 1) which eventually, for Pound (1950: ch 3), comes to include most governmental programmes of social reform. Law is portrayed as embattled, threatened from all sides by governmental legislative and administrative action inimical to the natural processes of common law development. Judges appear no longer in Pound's writing as objects of criticism but as heroic defenders of legal reason (eg Pound 1963). It is frequently implied by his acts (for example, in opposing the appointment of social scientists to law faculties: cf Wigdor 1974: 223–224, ch 10) and in his writings that lawyers must close ranks against threats to the professional world of law, which has the judiciary at its centre and is defined by its custody of the immanent reason of common law.

On such a gloomy note, Pound's modern rethinking of common law thought evaporates, with the conservatism of age and perhaps under the sheer weight of the positive law and administrative regulation created by the modern state, into a narrow defence of old professional prerogatives.

Dworkin and Pound

Dworkin's writings hardly refer to Pound,[7] yet have many similar concerns. However, they adopt methods that hold out the possibility of avoiding many of the thickets into which Pound's sociological jurisprudence falls.

Much of Dworkin's early writing, which began to become influential in the late 1960s, a few years after Pound's death, is concerned to attack the positivist model of rules in a much more rigorous and systematic manner than Pound

---

7   There is a brief discussion in Dworkin 1967. Of Dworkin's major books on normative legal theory only the first (Dworkin 1977) contains index references to Pound. These identify two brief and peripheral comments, one of which (p. 4) seems to indicate that Dworkin thinks of Pound primarily as an instrumentalist.

adopted. While Pound merely asserted that law should be understood in the broad sense of precepts (including rules, principles, conceptions and standards), techniques and ideals, Dworkin tries to show exactly why the model of rules is inadequate. Ultimately, however, the demonstration comes down to an assertion of much the same truths about law as those that Pound, at his best, tried to emphasise. Analysis in terms of rules alone, Dworkin insists, cannot explain the full range of legal materials that a judge uses in deciding a 'hard' case: that is, one for which an answer is not given merely by logical application of existing rules.

On the other hand, Dworkin's worries about the model of rules are significantly different from Pound's. Dworkin's focus is not on interests (the elements that for Pound are the key to understanding those communal roots of law ignored by positivist analytical jurisprudence) but on *rights*. This emphasis signals Dworkin's preoccupation with positivism's inability to give a clear legitimacy to judicial decision-making. According to positivist analytical jurists, judges in hard cases cannot apply law to reach their decisions but necessarily exercise discretion. Since the authority for this exercise of discretion cannot easily be explained in legal terms, the judge as 'legislator' is a highly problematic figure unless seen in Austinian terms as the delegate of a sovereign electorate. Such a judge must, in a democracy, defer always to the democratic will as expressed in legislation. Consequently, judges' tendencies will always be to favour the majority will so expressed. They will lack the authority to protect minorities through the exercise of creative discretion *against* the majority (cf Dworkin 1971: 158–159). Yet rights are precisely those legal entitlements that should be enforceable against anyone – even an opposed majority. Must it be said that in hard cases there are no rights to be relied on?

Looked at in this way, Dworkin's concern to escape the limitations of positivism is part of a strategy to affirm law's capacity to defend broad liberal values of individual freedom and autonomy, if necessary against majority wishes reflected in government policies. Like many earlier writers he sees a central task of law as to prevent, not aid, the 'tyranny of the majority' (cf Mill 1859: ch 1). Pound's preoccupations are, as has been seen, with the professional autonomy of the common lawyer faced with the threat of imposition of law by political authorities: a threat especially great because in the contemporary Anglo-American environment these authorities possess the unquestionable (and, therefore, absolute) legitimacy of democracy (or 'King Demos' as Pound sometimes refers to it: cf Wigdor 1974: 227, 230).

Dworkin does not share Pound's general suspicion of democracy although he is obviously concerned at its tyrannous possibilities. Nor does he share Pound's belief in government by (legal) experts (cf Wigdor 1974: 199). Equally,

Dworkin's position is not so explicitly framed as a defence of common law thought. His emphasis is on the protection of rights and on the moral autonomy of the citizen. Pound seemed to recognise the former, if at all, only in terms of a general defence of common law methods and the latter in terms of the professional autonomy of the lawyer.

Rights, for Dworkin, are thus antecedent to and give meaning to legal rules. His rejection of the model of rules is not expressed, like Pound's, as a claim that law contains more than rules. It is a claim that law is *more fundamental* than rules and that rules are incomplete and problematic expressions of the content of law. This position is very close indeed to that of classical common law thought. As noted in Chapter 2, the classical common law conception recognises the essence of law in principles expressing the reason of law, not in rules.

Dworkin's ideas on the place of principles in law will be elaborated below. For the moment it is important to note that, once the task of the judge has been defined as to enforce 'rights and obligations whose present power is independent of the majority will' (Dworkin 1971: 159), judges are for Dworkin (and contrary to the positivist analytical jurists' view) in no sense legislators. They do not derive authority, like a democratic legislature, from their representing the will of the majority. Nor is it the judge's task to implement that will, however it is to be understood. Judicial authority, for Dworkin, must derive from a different source and support a different role from that of a legislature.

Like Pound, he sees the judge as deriving both the authority to develop law and the resources to do so from *within* law itself, not from some external source such as an Austinian sovereign whose policies define this authority and the resources available to the judge in the task of interpreting hard cases. As will appear, however, Dworkin's explanation of what it is, internal to law, that provides resources and authority for the judge's interpretive activities is significantly different from, and richer than, Pound's discussion in terms of precepts, techniques (left vague in his discussions) and a measure of values centred on the jural postulates of the time and place.

Principles and policies

In the rare general comments that Dworkin offers on Pound's work, he praises the earlier writer's recognition of the legal significance of principles but criticises Pound for having stopped short of an effective critique of legal positivism since he fails to show that principles are a part of law 'in the *sense* that particular rules are, that they in fact control and regulate officials' (Dworkin 1967: 217). Without this demonstration, positivist analytical jurists could agree that principles and other general ideas associated with law are significant in interpreting rules but deny that the model of rules needs amendment to accept these elements as essential components of law. In effect, much of what Pound treats as precepts other than legal rules could be seen by positivist analytical jurists as merely a segment of the discretionary (non-legal) considerations that judges or other officials take into account in making decisions in hard cases. The positivist image of law would remain inviolate. The judge's creative role would remain legally inexplicable and legally unjustifiable.

Dworkin's strategy is, therefore, to show that principles, which cannot be reduced to legal rules, are treated in practice by courts as legal authorities which cannot be ignored: that they are essential (not optional or discretionary) elements in reaching decisions in hard cases. Indeed, Dworkin seeks to argue that in all cases a structure of legal principles stands behind and informs the applicable rules. The only difference, then, between a hard case and a simple case is that in the latter the relationship between applicable principles and relevant rules is seen by the deciding court and by interpreters of the court's decision as clear and unproblematic.

A favourite illustration, in Dworkin's writings, of legal principles is the case of *Riggs v Palmer*[8] in which the New York State Court of Appeals refused to allow Elmer Palmer to inherit property as a beneficiary under the will of his grandfather, whom he had murdered by poisoning. The applicable legal rule appears to be that legacies contained in legally valid testamentary dispositions are to be guaranteed by law in accordance with the wishes of the testator. Yet the court in *Riggs v Palmer* consciously decides not to apply the rule and does so by relying on a general principle that a wrongdoer should not be allowed to profit from his own wrong. It is not judicial discretion which operates to defeat the ordinary rule as to legacies but an interpretation of the rule in the light of a governing principle. And the principle here is legal since it is not taken out of the air as a purely discretionary invention of the court but is one that has its own legal history as something developed, applied and interpreted in earlier cases and in relation to different legal rules and circumstances.

This is not to say that because law contains principles as well as rules, the former are to be equated with the latter. While legal rules may be identifiable by using some positivist test expressed in terms of rules of recognition, basic norm or sovereign command, legal principles cannot be so identified. They emerge, flourish and decline gradually by being recognised, elaborated and perhaps eventually discarded over time in the ongoing history of the legal system concerned. As such, they reflect and express the legal system's underlying

---

8   115 NY 506 (1889). See Dworkin 1977: 23; 1986: 15–20.

values or traditions: in a sense, its underlying political philosophy. Constitutional principles, and principles underpinning the basic structures of private law (for example, expressing the basic values of the enforceability of agreements or good faith), show these characteristics. Because they defy positivist tests that neatly distinguish law from non-law they cast doubt on the whole structure of positivist explanation. And this is fundamental because, as *Riggs v Palmer* shows, principles *control* the applicability of rules – those elements of the legal system that, according to positivist analytical jurisprudence, lend themselves to definite tests of legal validity.

The direction of Dworkin's argument at this point might suggest the conclusion that the internal-external dichotomy dividing law from non-law, or (in another aspect) legal insiders from legal outsiders, is to be discarded. But this is far from his position.[9] The recognition that principles governing cases can be *legal* principles merely enlarges law's scope but does not, in Dworkin's view, make the idea of law as a distinct phenomenon incoherent. Equally, as will be seen later, he maintains a sharp distinction between legal insiders and outsiders. Insiders are those participating in the interpretation of legal rules and principles and so involved in determining creatively (rather than mechanically through the application of positivist tests) what is and is not law, while outsiders are those uninterested in or unable to play the interpretive game.

Principles differ from rules in other fundamental ways. They do not apply in an all-or-nothing fashion, as rules do (Dworkin 1977: 24). Rules are either applicable or not; principles have what Dworkin calls a dimension of weight. Legal rules cannot logically conflict – if they seem to do so one rule must be an exception to the other and can be written into it. Otherwise one of the rules must be invalid (1977: 25). But there may be conflicting principles applicable in the same case. The task of legal interpretation then involves weighing the principles against each other as they relate to the case in hand. The parallel with Pound's balancing of interests in the specific case is obvious. One might consider equitable principles as examples. The maxims 'equity regards as done that which ought to be done', 'equity will not perfect an imperfect gift' and 'equity will not allow a statute to be used as an instrument of fraud' might suggest different results when applied to the same case. The judge's task would be to assess their relative weight in the particular circumstances, so as to reach a conclusion by applying them.

Why should we not say, as a positivist would, that a judge merely exercises discretion or adopts a certain policy in making such a judgment? Dworkin does

---

9　Cf Dworkin's critique as 'illogical' of Fuller's idea that the existence of law can be a matter of degree: Dworkin 1965: 677–678.

not deny the need for 'weak' discretion – by which he means merely creative judgment in the application of legal doctrine, whether rules or principles. But he denies the existence of 'strong' (that is, legally uncontrolled) judicial discretion in essentially the same way that classical common law thought would deny it. Judges do not *make* law because all the resources for their proper decisions are provided by the existing law as correctly understood. A judge does not decide a case in a legal vacuum but on the basis of existing rules which express, and, at the same time, are informed by, underlying legal principles.

The task of the judge faced with a hard case is, therefore, to understand what decision is required by the whole doctrinal structure of existing law. Even if rules, understood in positivistic fashion, seem to give the judge no guidance, a broader understanding of the patterns of values that have gradually developed in the legal system and are expressed in the combination of rules and principles, does offer that guidance. Judges must understand the content of the legal system in this broad sense and give effect to it in their judgments to the best of their ability. Their task is undoubtedly creative. Yet it is not legislative. Properly understood, the judicial role is not the dynamic one of making law like a legislator, nor is it the purely passive one of 'finding' law. The judge must make the law the best that it can be through *creative* interpretation of existing legal resources. But, according to Dworkin, no non-legal materials are used in doing this. Thus, Dworkin is able to make the claim, which has long puzzled many of his critics, that existing law provides an answer for every hard case (although judges and lawyers may argue interminably as to what that answer is). There is simply no room for the exercise of strong judicial discretion (Dworkin [R] 1985: ch 5).

While the application of principle is fundamental to the judicial function, this is, for Dworkin (1977: 22; 1986: 221–224), to be distinguished clearly from the invocation of *policies* – standards setting out economic, political or social goals to be reached. The latter are normally not a matter for judges, but for legislatures. While the law that Dworkinian judges are required creatively to apply will have been influenced by policy matters, policy should not shape their legal judgments in the way that principles – the expression of the community's moral and political values reflected in law – must (Dworkin 1986: 244).

Many critics have doubted that principle and policy can be clearly distinguished in the manner Dworkin requires, but the distinction is fundamental to his thinking. The reason for this can best be understood by referring back to the controversy surrounding the organicist and instrumentalist dimensions of Pound's thought. While ultimately, as has been seen, Pound's conception of law is thoroughly organicist, his failure to distinguish principle from policy leaves ambiguities which have misled some commentators. In Dworkin's writings there is no such ambiguity. He never expresses the matter in terms of the organicist-instrumentalist opposition; nevertheless, by making principle central to adjudication Dworkin affirms implicitly that judges must operate with an organicist conception of law, developing it from within. Through its own resources, creatively interpreted, law can 'work itself pure', according to the strange phrase of classical common law thought.[10]

Policy, by contrast, is a matter for instrumentalists. It relates to pressures from outside the legal system directing law towards specific goals. Dworkin's position is here considerably clearer and less conservative than Pound's, for there is no suggestion that law must essentially develop itself by its own 'internal' resources of common law reason, with legislation (reflecting policy) no more than a handmaid. Dworkin has no doubt of the necessity for instrumentalist approaches to law providing essential policy input.[11] His position, however, asserts a clear division of labour between a policy-driven legislature and a principle-driven judiciary. For Dworkin, in effect, Pound's type of common law outlook holds good for courts and their responsibilities. But there is no reason why it should hamper wide-ranging legislative activity to promote social change.

The closed world of legal interpretation

Such a neat reconciliation of organicist and instrumentalist conceptions of law is, unfortunately, ultimately unstable and illusory, because Dworkin, like Pound, must decide between two opposite views. Can law control its own destiny from its own resources – is it morally and politically autonomous in that sense? Or is it essentially an instrument of political power, subject to control and direction from beyond its own doctrinal resources?

In Dworkin's later writings it is made clear that the organicist conception triumphs. In other words, for him, as for Pound, the common law judge should still dominate the legal system. One might be forgiven for thinking that as long as rules can be distinguished from principles and understood in positivist fashion, they import into the arena of judicial interpretation normative material which judges cannot but give effect to: the material controls them. Thus, insofar as law consists of policy-shaped legislative rules, the judge can only be an instrument of policy without independent creativity. Yet, as has been seen, for

---

10 *Omychund v Barker* (1744) 1 Atk 21 at p 33 (argument of Solicitor-General Murray, later Lord Mansfield). See Dworkin 1977: 112; 1982: 187; 1986: 400.

11 As a liberal he favours considerable government intervention to protect, extend and realise in practice the promise of equality of citizens' rights: see eg Dworkin [R] 1985: ch 14.

Dworkin, principles control the interpretation of rules. Hence, the rule-principle distinction has lost much significance in his later writings. Principles are expressed through rules; rules derive their meaning from principles. Law is entirely a matter of interpretation.

In this specific sense, no law is *imposed* on the judge. All law that comes out of judges' decisions is the result of their creative interpretation, whether of legislation, prior case law or ultimate constitutional provisions (such as in the written United States Constitution).

It follows that, in a sense, principle trumps policy because the interpretation of law derived from policy considerations must be conducted in accordance with the judge's obligation to fulfil the elements of principle in law. There is no law other than that which results from creative interpretation of existing legal materials guided by the attempt of the interpreter to make the law the best it can be.

Law as interpretation

In his writings since the 1980s Dworkin has used analogies with literary interpretation to explain the judge's obligation in creative legal interpretation (eg 1982: 166–168; 1985: ch 6; 1986: 228–238). A judge is like a writer trying to continue a story started by earlier writers. The writer must make the story as good as it can be. This necessitates that what he adds must be consistent with what went before (the requirement of 'fit'), and must make the best of that existing material by interpreting it in the most plausible and attractive way and then adding a contribution that will further enhance it. Since the task of the writer is to continue the story, he cannot simply go off on a personal literary frolic but must create a contribution in a way that is consistent with the best interpretation of the meaning of what went before.

Of course, the writer must supply that interpretation. What will determine whether it is the best possible? Ultimately this will be a matter of whether it shows the previous contributions plus his own as an integrated whole, consistent and rich in meaning and clear in development. Similarly, a judge must tell the best story, construct the best legal meaning, from the work of previous contributors to legal doctrine. In adding his own contribution (the new decision in the case before him) he is constrained by the need for 'fit' with existing legal materials. Some interpretations that he might as a matter of personal preference like to adopt and act on are ruled out because they would not be consistent with the need to portray law as an integrated, principled whole.

Thus, Dworkin claims that his theory does not give judges the freedom of legislators, as the positivist idea of judicial discretion seems to do. They are constrained by the entire structure of values that the legal system represents. They are required to decide cases in ways that will further those values and portray legal doctrine as a whole, as an integrated and consistent expression of them. The need for consistency requires that a judge will put a high value on precedent and on the need to give effect to clearly expressed legislative provisions, quite apart from the fact that the legal system may well have principles of *stare decisis* and of deference to the will of democratic legislatures as part of the fundamental structure of legal values which the judge must recognise (Dworkin 1986: 401).

At the same time, as in classical common law thought,[12] Dworkin's theory allows judges to assess critically the work of their predecessors even to the extent of declaring, and refusing to follow their 'mistakes'. Similarly, legislative provisions are to be considered in relation to the whole environment of relevant legislative history. In some instances this approach could lead a judge to conclusions about legislation that would be very much more than a straightforward application of statutory words (Dworkin 1986: 343–350).

The overall shape of Dworkin's theory is, therefore, remarkably like that of classical common law thought, as described in Chapter 2. Pound's sociological jurisprudence can be seen as prescriptive but also presents itself as an attempt to describe the common law system in objective terms as a set of balancing operations and procedures informed by a measure of values. As has been seen, the attempt at description runs into serious difficulties when the measure of values has to be objectively identified, and, perhaps, even when the initial task of identifying, listing and classifying interests is attempted. Classical common law thought was, however, never a descriptive theory of law but always a set of prescriptions and expectations as to how judges should go about their job. From this standpoint Dworkin's theory is more in harmony with classical common law thought than is Pound's because Dworkin effectively discards any claim to be offering objective description of law from some detached observer's standpoint.

Once it is recognised that law is entirely a matter of interpretation it follows that all who are involved in discussing it must be engaged in the same interpretive exercise. Otherwise they cannot communicate information about law amongst themselves. The judge, the lawyer and the legal philosopher thus become, for Dworkin, participants in the same 'game' of interpretation. They are all involved in debates about what law is (whether for the purposes of arguing a particular case, understanding a line of precedents, or developing a theory of a specific legal field or of the legal system as a whole). But what law is depends on

---

12 See Chapter 2, above, pp 25–26.

how the values understood as informing a legal order are to be interpreted. Thus, all participants in legal interpretation, according to Dworkin, are concerned also with what law ought to be. They cannot be *describers* of some objectively existing datum of law. They must be full participants in the discourse of legal argument of the particular legal system with which they are concerned.

One great advantage of this approach over Pound's is that the problem of objectively identifying a measure of values in the legal system disappears. Instead it is recognised that this measure is continually being constructed and reconstructed by participants in the system and makes sense only from a participant perspective. It is to be understood as the ongoing interpretive project of participants in the legal order and not as a set of postulates to be described from some external theoretical standpoint.

Law's community

But there is a price to be paid for this apparent theoretical advance. What happens, for example, to the relationship between law and community that has been identified in this book as central to classical common law thought? It becomes, for Dworkin, what it is for classical common law thought: something that cannot be examined empirically but only taken for granted as the ongoing collective pursuit of legal interpretation. This is because the theory offers no external or detached standpoint from which law's relationship with community can be analysed. Here is an illustration of the inherent and admitted limitations of Dworkin's theory arising from its wholly internal, insiders' perspective on law. All the other major theorists so far considered in this book have sought to hold open the possibility of an external, uncommitted view of law, even if (as with Hart's concept of law) the quest for objective description of a legal system is combined with a proper insistence that an understanding of the internal, insiders' viewpoint on law is essential to any such objective description.

Dworkin writes extensively about community as the basis of law and about how it can be conceptualised (1986: 195–215), yet within the terms of his legal theory he can offer no analysis of the sociological conditions under which a community can exist, or of the meaning of the concept of community as a characterisation of empirically observable patterns of social life, or of the historically specific political and social circumstances in which it is useful to think of law as expressing community values.

Previous chapters in this book have sought to suggest that these are important questions and more sociologically sensitive theorists such as Fuller (pp 133–136, above) have made valuable efforts to address them. Dworkin's silence about the empirical significance of a concept which is inevitably important to his theory is frustrating because, without some such analysis, postulating the existence of a community whose collective interpretations and understandings produce law seems no more than a fiction.[13]

Ignoring such problems and pursuing a purely philosophical analysis of the concept of community, Dworkin sees it as a moral-political structure of human interaction in which the collective development and fulfilment of values of justice, fairness and integrity are sought. But this seems merely a projection of his image of what it is to participate in a legal system. Just as the classical common lawyers glimpsed community as an extension or projection of what they understood law to be, so for Dworkin the image of community is seen through a legal prism, as something implicit in the outlook of legal insiders participating in legal interpretation. For Dworkin, participants in legal interpretation in a legal system *are*, by virtue of their participation, the community. But many questions about what it means to participate (By whom? In what ways? In what processes? Subject to what limits?) seem to be begged.

This can be contrasted with Finnis' consideration of community which, although equally lacking empirical grounding in a study of actual social conditions, does proceed philosophically from first principles.[14] The contrast here between Finnis and Dworkin is easily understood. Like Hart, but unlike Dworkin, Finnis asserts the possibility of a descriptive, rather than prescriptive or committed, legal theory (Finnis 1980: ch 1), even though it must accept the inevitability of moral evaluations and be founded on assumed universal moral intuitions. Hence Finnis' starting point is not Dworkin's wholly internal legal perspective but one in which both law and morals can be viewed from a standpoint that is not just that of particular participants in practical legal interpretation. Community is, therefore, something that can and should, for Finnis, be analysed for its moral significance as such. It does not appear merely as a projection of the outlook of legal 'insiders' on their law.

For Dworkin, therefore, the attempt to explain judicial creativity, in terms of law itself, leads to the conclusion that this can be done only by becoming a participant – adopting the standpoint of a lawyer or judge – in interpreting law in the particular legal system concerned. But it will be seen in the final section of this chapter that ultimately Dworkin's approach leads to serious problems for normative legal theory as an explanation of judicial decision-making and processes of doctrinal development.

---

13 On all of these matters see further Chapter 9, below, pp 257–261.
14 See Chapter 5, pp 141–142, above.

Politics, professionalism and interpretive communities

Throughout this book normative legal theory has been presented as, in part, a response to specific problems of legal professionalisation. There is little difficulty in interpreting Pound's defence of common law methods and the role of legal experts in these terms. But Dworkin makes some determined efforts to avoid his theory becoming a defence of professional prerogatives or of the intellectual or moral autonomy of professional legal knowledge. Thus he insists that the community of participants in legal interpretation is not just a community of lawyers. Anyone living in a society and actively committed to the values – the moral and political foundation – of its legal system is properly seen as a participant in the task of interpreting that society's law.

It follows that a citizen can properly disagree with the interpretation of the law offered by the highest court of the legal system. 'A citizen's allegiance is to the law, not to any particular person's view of what the law is, and he does not behave unfairly so long as he proceeds on his own considered and reasonable view of what the law requires' (Dworkin 1977: 214). What is reasonable is a matter of interpretive debate, like everything else entailed in deciding what the law is. But lawyers and judges have no necessary monopoly of such judgments.

Thus, Dworkin provides a justification for civil disobedience; not one justifying *breach* of law, but one that justifies following a reasonably held interpretation of law that happens to differ from that made by official legal authorities. For Dworkin, this is not a licence to disobey but an assertion that there can be cases where the meaning of law – judged not just as rules, but as the whole structure of legal doctrine including the particular moral and political values crystallised in the doctrinal and institutional history of the legal system – is a matter of legitimate dispute. In such cases the view of citizen dissenters ought to be respected and their acts, based on such a view, should be judged with official tolerance.

Dworkin has consistently maintained this view (see Dworkin [R] 1985: ch 4). Yet it seems profoundly unrealistic to ask for official toleration of acts that will be seen, by those who control the coercive power of a legal system, as law-breaking, not as alternative legal interpretation. It is also profoundly unrealistic to consider non-lawyer citizens, on the one hand, and lawyers or judges, on the other, as part of the same community of legal interpreters. For example, can the views expressed in scholarly law review articles on the meaning of current legislation be somehow seen as part of a debate with the opinions of, say, homeless people, asylum seekers, mental patients, or other groups who urgently need law's help, as to whether the fundamental values and principles of the legal system are accurately expressed in recent judicial pronouncements? This image of community is entirely unconvincing.

If law is to be understood as interpretation, it is important to recognise clearly in legal theory that lawyers (who may be representative, in some sense, of wider social groups) almost entirely monopolise that interpretation. Any other view seems either naïvely idealistic or a wilful refusal to recognise evidence from social experience. And it is tempting to suggest that Dworkin's strange lack of realism here derives from what was noted in the previous section – the impossibility of seriously examining the actual conditions of existence of a community within the terms of a theory purporting to express only the perspective of participants in that community. Since the participant perspective is inevitably that of the lawyer within a community of legal interpreters it becomes hard to see realistically, in terms of such a theory, the position of other sections of society in their relationship with the professional group of lawyers.

Despite Dworkin's wish to defend a basis of citizen participation, his major writings in normative legal theory are almost entirely concerned with judicial interpretation of law. They consistently assume the judge to be the central figure in the interpretive community. Interpretation of legal meaning is treated as a matter for professionals. Hence we can consider what Dworkin's theory tells us about this *professional* interpretive community and the way it works. Here surely are to be found the answers to questions about the principles that guide legal development and judicial creativity?

But the theory does not provide these answers. If law is entirely a matter of interpretation, as Dworkin now insists, the meaning of legal provisions cannot be controlled by any objective historical documents, conditions or events. This uncompromising position allows Dworkin to deny that any objectively existing legal or social conventions (such as Hart's rule of recognition or any other positivist criterion of law) determine what is valid as law. Equally, it avoids Pound's problem of needing to identify jural postulates as objectively existing components of a legal system. But, of course, *something* must control legal interpretation.

One radical answer as to what that might be is given by the literary theorist Stanley Fish in a law review debate with Dworkin. Fish agrees with Dworkin that law, like any literary text, is a matter of interpretation. He goes on to argue, however, that what is interpreted (a literary text or historical legal materials) cannot be distinguished from the interpretation itself: that the interpretation *constitutes* what is interpreted (Fish 1982; 1983).

On Fish's view the controls that operate to limit possible interpretations are in no way given by the item interpreted itself (the statute or the precedent case, for example, does not, 'by its nature', rule out certain interpretations). The actual controls on interpretation arise from the conventions, expectations, shared understandings and structure of the interpreting community (for example, a legal profession, or a judiciary) and the skill in argument of the interpreters. Thus, it would seem to follow that to understand law-as-interpretation we must understand the social structure of the interpretive community and the pressures, constraints, modes of consensus formation and conditions of conflict that actually exist in it and determine how the business of interpretation of law actually goes on. In other words, what seems to be required is a sociological view of the interpretive community of legal professionals and of their practices.

Although Fish's view preserves the idea of law as interpretation it appears to entail that constraints on interpretation can only be understood sociologically. But this denies the utility of what Dworkin advocates: a normative legal theory developed entirely from a legal insider's perspective. A sociological view of lawyers patently refuses to be restricted to such a perspective. Thus, Dworkin rejects as 'extravagant' Fish's view that interpretation constitutes what is interpreted (Dworkin [R] 1985: 176). In some way the historical legal record must be the foundation of legal interpretation, not the other way around. Therefore, he relies on the requirement of 'fit'. Legal interpretations must fit the historical materials of the legal system – the body of existing constitutional provisions, statutes, judicial precedents, etc. But this begins to look like legal positivism. What can determine the legal significance of these materials except some objective positivist criteria of law? Finally, therefore, to escape this positivist conclusion Dworkin is forced to the position that what constrain judicial interpretations are not historical legal materials in some objective sense but the judges' *convictions* about fit – again a matter of interpretation.

In what sense do these convictions constrain? Dworkin cannot rely, like Fish, on claims about the *collective* constraints exercised on judges (and lawyers) by their membership in the professional community. To understand why and how those constraints are collective (that is, arise within the professional group) it would be necessary, again, to understand the sociology of the interpretive community.[15] Thus, Dworkin's position is that the constraint on judges arises from their *personal* need as individuals to integrate their convictions about fit with their convictions about whether the interpretation they plan to adopt will show the interpreted legal practices or doctrine in the best light. The constraint

---

15 Cf Karl Llewellyn's discussion of 'steadying factors' in judicial interpretation arising out of judges' professional and institutional environment: Llewellyn 1960, and see Chapter 7, below pp 192–193.

is 'a structural constraint of different kinds of principle within a system of principle' (1986: 257).

But is this a constraint at all? Dworkin does, at least, recognise the obvious question: Will a judge's convictions as to which interpretation shows legal practices and doctrine in the best light shape that judge's convictions about fit so that no constraining tensions between these two sets of convictions arise? (cf Dworkin 1986: 236–237). But he gives no answer except to suggest that this depends on the complexity and structure of the individual judge's pertinent opinions as a whole. We are thus pushed into a realm of speculation about judges' personal philosophies in which realistic examination (for legal participants no less than for sociological observers) of the nature and effects of general constraints on judicial interpretation becomes impossible. The reason lies in Dworkin's refusal to abandon his vision of a self-contained arena of legal philosophical discourse that preserves intact a watertight separation of 'internal' (legal insiders') and 'external' (sociological) perspectives.

The lesson to be learned from this is surely that the search for legal principles governing judicial creativity can lead to at least three distinct projects. The most modest is Pound's: a rather unsystematic attempt to observe and describe the value elements and other considerations that, according to settled legal practice, the judge should take into account in deciding a hard case. Much more ambitious is Dworkin's attempt to see law and rationalise its components exclusively from the perspective of the conscientious judge and lawyer. Once it appears, however, that such an exclusively 'inside' perspective reduces to purely personal judicial convictions, only one possibility seems to remain open. This is to examine sociologically the structure and environment of the interpretive community which may determine how collective professional interpretations of law are possible. It is this remaining possibility which will be the central focus of the next chapter.

Chapter 7

Scepticism and realism

Previous chapters have related developments in Anglo-American normative legal theory to a search for theoretical unity and system in law as a body of knowledge and as a professional practice. In that perspective a kind of progression appears.

We have observed classical common law theory struggling to come to terms with the emergence of the modern sovereign state and its centralised law-making authorities (Chapter 2). Historical jurisprudence offered support to the common law outlook in the nineteenth century through its attempts to specify theoretical links between law and culture. But this hardly solved the difficulties and positivist analytical jurisprudence appeared as a more realistic framework for confronting the relationship between law and political power.

Later, as the utilitarian faith in rational government waned or assumed more complex forms, legal philosophy was pressed into service to explain law not as the consequence of political power but as its master or controlling normative framework. The assumed theoretical problems of sovereignty and, more fundamentally, the need to portray law in terms fitting for democratic government, in which regulatees are to be citizens rather than subjects, inspired, at least in part, the transformations of analytical jurisprudence noted in Chapter 4.

But the problem of the role of the judge remained in this theory and its inadequacy encouraged efforts, exemplified in different ways by main themes in Fuller's, Pound's and Dworkin's work, to find a justification and explanation of judicial creativity (and legal interpretation more generally) in values inherent in Anglo-American law.

In one sense the wheel turns full circle because the virtues of classical common law thought (its insistence on the inseparability of law from an idea of community or communal values, its concern with underlying principle as much as with technical rule, its image of law as continuously and steadily developing) are now apparently what the writers considered in the previous two chapters are especially concerned to recapture. It seems as though the positivist revolution in legal thought in the nineteenth century failed: that it did not *replace* classical common law thought but merely confirmed the inadequacy of the common law outlook.

At the same time, what might be called neo-classical common law thought, of which Dworkin's legal philosophy is the best example, raises difficulties of its own, explained in Chapter 6. Above all, it seems forced to give up any prospect of a science of law, in the sense of a search for something more systematic and objective than the participant perspective of a practical legal interpreter. Yet it was precisely that search for systematic theoretical explanation of the nature of law as a body of professional knowledge and as a distinctive professional practice which, as has been seen, first inspired and gave original legitimacy to modern Anglo-American legal philosophy in Bentham's and Austin's work.

Is there a way out of this impasse? Suppose we were to retrace our steps and go back to Austin's original starting point for legal science: the idea that a law is the result of a distinctive *action* (in his theory the act of commanding), and is to be understood in terms of those who perform the action (for Austin, the sovereign or sovereign body) and the means available to make the action effective (sanctions).

Suppose that, without becoming embroiled again in arguments about sovereignty or the specific form of law, we were to treat these *behavioural* dimensions of law as the focus of scientific inquiry in legal theory. And suppose further, finally, that to avoid the problems encountered in Chapter 6 about identifying values and traditions in a legal system that determine appropriate judicial development of doctrine, it were to be assumed as a starting point for analysis that innovations in legal doctrine are nothing more nor less than expressions of the wishes, policies, or preferences of the decision-makers (for example, judges) who create law. What would follow from such positions?

At least initially, taken without qualification or elaboration, these points of departure suggest a profound *scepticism* about normative analysis of law. They suggest that doctrine is less important than those who create it; that what judges do is more important than the reasoning with which they justify their decisions; that values are relevant to legal analysis only insofar as they represent the particular preferences of influential decision-makers; that legal outcomes reflect configurations of political power, not overarching social or political values. But this approach might also be called *realistic*, and seen as adopting the only starting points that make it possible to respect fully the original motivating assumption of the analytical jurists: that law is a human creation, to be understood as it is and not as it might or should be. On this view then, law is a matter of people doing the jobs of governing, resolving or containing disputes, allocating benefits or detriments and channelling state power to achieve specific purposes. It is not 'a brooding omnipresence in the sky' (Howe (ed) 1953 II: 822).

In such a 'realist' perspective it can be recognised that political authorities such as legislatures and administrative agencies are primary producers of legal rules and doctrine. At the same time the full extent of judicial power to develop law through creative interpretation can also be recognised, as a practical matter. Indeed, judges and courts viewed merely as decision-makers determining disputes might not look very different in character from administrative regulators or legislative rule-makers (cf Llewellyn 1930a: 29–31). It will be recalled that Austin, too, was not convinced that the distinction between courts and other political agencies concerned with legal interpretation, adjudication and application of doctrine should be as sharply drawn as many lawyers and others claim.[1]

Anglo-American legal scholarship has produced a broad current of writing that adopts such sceptical or realist premises as those suggested. This chapter will be concerned with the relevance of this literature, and its 'post-realist' legacy, for normative legal theory. But in discussing 'legal realism' it becomes necessary, for the first time in this book, to recognise a development in Anglo-American legal philosophy occurring on one side of the Atlantic which has had virtually no parallel on the other.

In the literature of Anglo-American legal thought legal realism is almost exclusively *American* legal realism, and is known by that name. Although, in Britain, attention has been paid, alongside discussion of American developments, to the writings of Scandinavian jurists who developed ideas comparable in some respects with those of the American realists, no similar realist movement in legal thought emerged in Britain as a significant indigenous development.

Indeed, it has often proved difficult for British legal scholars to understand the immense significance of the realist movement in the United States. What, in America, became for a time (especially during the 1930s and 1940s) a set of presuppositions pervading legal scholarship and a tradition of thought that still

---

1   See Chapter 3, above, pp 70–72.

informs much of the intellectual context of legal debate in the United States, has appeared to many legal philosophers in Britain as an almost incomprehensible naivety in thinking and writing about law: something thoroughly alien and to be accounted for only by unique features of American law and legal history, of little relevance for legal philosophy in Britain.

Pragmatism and realism

This situation needs explanation and there is no shortage of analyses of the social, economic and political conditions that provided the context for the loosely identifiable, broad and diverse American realist movement to flourish. Unlike much of the theory considered earlier in this book, legal realism actually encourages a contextual interpretation of itself and has been developed with *explicit* reference to its political and professional context.

The reasons for this are clear. An attempt to explain law in behavioural terms entails examining its causes or origins in the decisions or directives of human actors, and its effects in terms of social consequences of those decisions or directives. Law is to be viewed *instrumentally*, not as doctrine deriving worth from its integrity or normative unity as a system of abstract ideas but as a means to practical ends, an instrument for appropriate governmental purposes (Llewellyn 1930a: 25–27). If law is understood in these terms, it should follow that legal scholarship and legal theory are also, in a realist conception, means to the ends of explaining and improving law as an efficient technology of regulation in its time and place. Hence a realist view of legal theory is likely to view developments in legal philosophy in terms of their functional relevance, or lack of relevance, to the legal needs of the time and place.

A particular philosophy, usually called *pragmatism*, underpins this outlook. In an orthodox pragmatist conception knowledge is 'true' to the extent that it is useful: that is, validated in experience. Indeed, there may perhaps be no better criterion of truth, in a pragmatist perspective, than the practical success of ideas in action: in this sense, knowledge *is* successful practice. Early in the twentieth century, such American philosophers as William James and John Dewey developed pragmatist philosophy in forms that seemed immediately relevant to legal issues (cf Dewey 1924).

Consider, for example, the problem of the nature of corporate personality raised earlier in Chapter 4. As noted there, H L A Hart, in his Oxford inaugural lecture, takes this issue as illustrating the sterility of much conceptual analysis in legal philosophy. His solution, as has been seen, is to consider legal statements in their specific linguistic contexts. Hence the legal meaning of 'corporation' can be understood only by considering linguistic contexts in which the concept is invoked. There is no 'thing' that can be identified with what law treats as a corporation or as corporate personality. Instead there are usages of legal language which lawyers can examine and (usually) make sense of in practical legal discourse.

From a realist-pragmatist perspective this is not sufficient. Legal discourse is not to be treated as self-validating. What determines legal usage? What is really meant when a court declares that a corporation has 'moved' its location from one city or state to another? What, in terms of actual practices, must have happened for the statement to be correct or meaningful? What is actually taking place when a corporation (not individual human beings such as its directors or employees, but the abstract entity itself) is held liable for a tort, crime or breach of contract? For lawyers none of these ideas or situations is necessarily odd or difficult, but if one seeks to consider law in terms of behaviour, as ideas which gain their validity as successful *practice* – that is, instrumentally – the particular forms of legal language may be intelligible (if at all) only as peculiarly complex and oblique ways of organising and expressing certain policies in regulatory form.

In one of the classic essays of legal realism, Felix Cohen reconsiders issues of corporate personality in just this way (Cohen 1935). Cohen's main point is that although legal language has significance and meaning only as a means to practical ends, much of it is expressed in forms that almost wholly obscure this instrumentality.

Hence, instead of asking how particular social or economic goals are best to be served through a certain regulatory decision – for example, whether a trade union should be subject to liability in tort for the actions of its members – courts in Britain and the United States considered whether a trade union is a 'person' in law,[2] an issue that, phrased in abstract terms, is akin to the apocryphal scholastic dispute as to how many angels can stand on the point of a needle (Cohen 1935: 35, 38). The abstract question of personality is apparently treated as determining whether or not there can be liability.

Frequently, other concepts fill what Cohen sees as similar roles. They include the notions of 'property right' (serving as a kind of red light against interference with a private benefit or the *status quo*), 'fair value', 'due process', 'title', 'contract', 'conspiracy', 'malice' (all suggesting objective conditions rather than policy evaluations) 'and all the rest of the magic "solving words" of traditional jurisprudence' (Cohen 1935: 45).

---

2   *Taff Vale Railway Co v Amalgamated Society of Railway Servants* [1901] AC 426; *United Mine Workers of America v Coronado Coal Co* 259 US 344 (1922).

What is in issue here? Can it not be said that what Cohen castigates in his 1935 paper as 'transcendental nonsense' is merely the special discourse of law, which is not that of politics or policy? Is it not absurdly naive to assert, as Cohen does, that all concepts 'that cannot be defined in terms of the elements of actual experience are meaningless' and to demand as an ultimatum of jurisprudence that any word 'that cannot pay up in the currency of fact, upon demand, is to be declared bankrupt, and we are to have no further dealings with it' (Cohen 1935: 48, 52)? Critics of realism among analytical jurists lost patience long ago with any such reductionist view of concepts and have usually treated statements such as Cohen's as textbook illustrations of legal realism's naive inability to appreciate the specific character of law's normative language. Why should legal ideas somehow be defined in terms of actual experience? And what is 'actual experience' for this purpose? A strict behaviouralist view ignores the reality of ideas: the possibility that legal reasoning should, in itself, be treated as part of social reality.

Although these criticisms are powerful they do not address the central questions raised. *Why* should the distinctiveness or autonomy of legal reasoning and language be accepted as appropriate or natural? *Why* should any line of demarcation between legal reasoning, on the one hand, and policy argument, on the other, be treated as self-evidently realistic or justifiable?

Suppose we were to accept, with Cohen and other realists, that a judge is a type of policy-maker or policy-implementer; suppose we were to refuse to treat as self-evident that judges are *not* merely gowned politicians or administrators; suppose we remain unconvinced that when a judge decides a 'hard case' the decision is anything other than a legislative act (and not, as in Dworkin's view, something specially judicial and non-legislative in character); and suppose, finally, that we see the judge not as a delegate (as Austin suggested) of any identifiable sovereign, but rather (especially, perhaps, in the United States) as a functionary exercising power as part of a complex political system – a system characterised less by centralisation and delegation than by a network of law-making and law-applying jurisdictions offering considerable leeway to many judicial decision-makers.

On the basis of such suppositions it makes sense to ask *why* legal language is expressed in forms that often obscure policy choices and present them as technical issues in the elaboration of legal logic. Requiring legal words to 'pay up in the currency of fact' then means requiring legal doctrine to reveal its politics on its face. And the dramatic, if philosophically clumsy, way in which the demand is made is perhaps a reflection of how urgent it seemed to many American lawyers that courts, as political agencies, should be seen to act as *responsible* political agencies, providing reasoned, intelligible policy-grounds for decisions having significant impact on American society.

At another level, what is in issue is a matter much stressed by members of the Critical Legal Studies movement, a modern descendant of realism to be considered later in this chapter. Cohen's discussion highlights the aspect of language and thought (especially legal language and thought) that critical legal scholars term *reification* (Gabel 1980). Legal ideas seem to take on a life of their own. They appear reified, 'thing-like', and are treated as having a reality distinct from the social, political or other functions that first gave them life and meaning. Hence legal reasoning becomes a kind of mystification. It becomes possible to theorise about the meaning of 'corporate personality', 'title' or 'contract' without considering as a central matter the policy, functions or settled practices that these concepts reflect, or, at least, once reflected in their origins.

Realism and normative legal theory

Beyond a certain point, quickly reached, it becomes counterproductive to generalise about American legal realism. One of its most prominent figures, Karl Llewellyn, then a professor at Columbia University, declared in 1931: 'There is no school of realists. There is no likelihood that there will be such a school. There is no group with an official or accepted, or even with an emerging creed ... There is, however, a *movement* in thought and work about law' (Llewellyn 1931a: 53, 54). Llewellyn himself claimed to have introduced the term 'realistic jurisprudence' in 1930 (Llewellyn 1930a; 1960: 512), and asserted three decades later that realism had always been merely a method or technology, not a legal philosophy. It embraced diverse work linked only by the vague injunctions 'see it fresh', 'see it as it works' (Llewellyn 1960: 509–510).

Llewellyn's 1931 defence of realism against Roscoe Pound (cf Pound 1931) and other critics summarised the realists' 'common points of departure' as:

(i)   a conception of law in flux, and of judicial creation of law;

(ii) a conception of law as a means to an end, and not an end in itself;

(iii) a conception of society in flux and of the need to re-examine law to keep it up to date with social need;

(iv) temporary separation of study of law as it is from speculation as to what it should (ethically) be;

(v)   'distrust of traditional legal rules and concepts insofar as they purport to *describe* what either courts or people are actually doing';

(vi) distrust of the idea that rules as expressed in the form of legal doctrine 'are *the* heavily operative factor in producing court decisions';

(vii) 'belief in the worthwhileness of grouping cases and legal situations into narrower categories than has been the practice in the past';

(viii) insistence on evaluating law in terms of its effects and on the importance of trying to discover these effects; and ←

(ix) insistence on 'sustained and programmatic attack' on legal problems in these various ways (Llewellyn 1931a: 55–57).

Despite the vagueness of several components of this list, it usefully indicates not only important preoccupations of Llewellyn himself, to which special attention will be devoted in the following pages, but also the divergent paths realist scholarship could take and the resulting possibility that different realist approaches could have differing relationships with normative legal theory.

If normative legal theory is theory attempting to explain the nature of law as a structure of legal ideas or legal doctrine (that is, in terms of the unity, autonomy, rationality, moral justification or systematic character of legal doctrine) it might appear that legal realism would necessarily deny the whole project of normative legal theory. In some of the most radical realist writing this is the case: law is to be considered in terms of behaviour *and not* doctrine.

Item (viii) on Llewellyn's list indicates the realist concern with law's effects. Indeed, some legal realists concerned to examine seriously the social and economic effects of particular laws and legal institutions (for example Charles Clark on civil and criminal procedure, William Douglas on business failures and bankruptcy, and especially Underhill Moore on banking law and practice) did take very seriously a social science model of legal scholarship in which doctrinal analysis sometimes appeared relatively insignificant beside 'fact research' on the behaviour of lawyers and laypersons.

Nevertheless, as J H Schlegel has shown, this serious activity of legal realists in conducting empirical research on law as a cluster of governmental activities and social and economic practices was relatively shortlived and very much a minority concern (Schlegel 1995). For those realists most sympathetic to social science, research on legal institutions and practices came to be seen (with Moore remaining perhaps the only significant exception: Schlegel 1995: ch 3) as an aid to realistic policy analysis, to guide and justify legal doctrine. It would not displace lawyers' practical concerns with systematic doctrinal analysis and the rational development of legal thought but would bring those concerns into appropriate relationship with policy debate and pressing social need.

This entailed a recognition that policy as an essential component of law imported social, economic and political concerns into any realistic analysis. But it did not necessarily lead to a commitment to what was called in Chapter 1 empirical legal theory – theory concerned to explain systematically the character of legal doctrine and institutions in general in terms of historical and social conditions. Policy-oriented realism suggested the inadequacy, for any realistic understanding of law, of all orthodox forms of normative legal theory, but not necessarily their replacement with any other coherent theoretical view of law.

At the same time, items (v) and (vi) on Llewellyn's list, representing what are often seen as the core propositions of realist thought, suggest either a radical challenge to the whole enterprise of normative legal theory or, at least, a significant attack on the approaches to it that have been the concern of most previous chapters of this book. They suggest a greatly reduced significance of legal doctrine and its analysis as a basis for any serious understanding of law's nature. Item (v) foreshadows Cohen's concern with the 'unreality' of legal concepts and implies that doctrine may provide little help in a realist enterprise concerned to explain or describe law as socially significant practices. Item (vi) suggests legal doctrine's limited relevance for predicting behaviour – especially for predicting how judges will decide cases, not just in recognised 'hard cases' but even when they purport to follow or be bound by established legal rules or precedents.

These elements of the realist outlook suggest not only the need to supplement normative, doctrinal inquiries about law with reliable data about law's effects, but the apparently limited relevance of doctrine for understanding judicial practice or social order. Thus, elsewhere, Llewellyn (1930a) contrasts 'paper' rules (expressed in judicial opinions, statutes and law books) with 'real' rules (the actual patterns of decision by courts: what judges do as a matter of regular practice, as opposed to the doctrinal rationalisation of their decisions). 'One seeks the real practice on the subject, by study of how the cases do in fact eventuate. One seeks to determine how far the paper rule is real, how far *merely* paper' (1930a: 24). Llewellyn claims that, if matters are viewed in realistic, behavioural terms, judges have numerous opportunities, at least in the higher levels of judicial systems in appeal courts, to narrow or extend, apply or distinguish, restate or rephrase precedent and apparently established rules. The significance of legal doctrine and its analysis as a basis for understanding law is thus seriously put in issue.

An explicit, central concern with *predictability* of judicial decisions, which is a pervasive theme in much of Llewellyn's work and in many other realist writings, is not generally found in the theoretical writings considered earlier in this book. The theme is often traced to an 1897 speech in Boston by Oliver Wendell Holmes, later an Associate Justice of the United States Supreme Court and, in Llewellyn's (1931b: 103) words, the man 'from whom we [realists] all derive'. Holmes polemically declared: 'The prophecies of what the courts will do in fact, and nothing more pretentious, are what I mean by the law' (Holmes 1897: 994) and he explained this as the realistic standpoint of a 'bad man' who cares nothing for ethical rules but merely wants to know what, if any, consequences will follow from law for him.

Holmes' 'bad man' standpoint was useful for deflating legal rhetoric and focussing on practical outcomes of law but it should not mislead a student of legal realism into thinking that the focus of concern is with lay rather than professional views of law, or that ultimately the focus on predictability reflects concerns any different from those that have been seen in earlier chapters as underpinning the development of normative legal theory.

The predictability of judicial decisions sought by Holmes' realist followers is generally that required by professional lawyers: first, so that they can interpret – and thus, to a reasonable extent, control – judicial development of law; and, second, so that they can claim convincingly to possess a body of systematic legal professional knowledge capable of providing reliable, practical guidance on the legal consequences of specific situations and transactions. The concern here, as for other theory discussed earlier in this book, is with convincingly maintaining a claim to a secure corpus of distinct professional knowledge in a situation in which law threatens to dissolve away into no more than the exercise of governmental discretions.

Llewellyn's concept of paper rules emphasises that analysis of legal doctrine cannot produce knowledge of law without corresponding analysis of judicial behaviour. At no point, however, does he deny that rules or other elements of legal doctrine are important matters for analysis. The essay in which paper rules are put in their place also contains the statement:

> 'that I feel strongly the unwisdom, when turning the spotlight on behaviour, of throwing overboard emphasis on rules, concepts, ideology, and ideological stereotypes or patterns ... a jurisprudence which was practically workable could not have been built in terms of them if they had not contained a goodly core of truth and sense' (Llewellyn 1930a: 37).

This statement alone should invalidate the still common caricature of Llewellyn as a behaviouralist denying the importance of legal doctrine. But the threat here posed to normative legal theory is the equally forceful assertion that no reliable knowledge of law can come from examining doctrine alone – as if it constituted or reflected the reality of law as practical activity.

Some realists, however, notably Jerome Frank, appeared virtually to abandon concern with legal doctrine in some of their theoretical writings. While

Llewellyn's early work emphasised behavioural factors that ensured that rules and precedents alone could not ensure certainty and predictability in appellate courts' decision-making (Llewellyn 1989: 73–84), Frank found a more fundamental source of uncertainty in trial courts' fact-finding processes.

Declaring himself a 'fact sceptic' in contrast to 'rule sceptics' such as Llewellyn (Frank 1930: x–xi), he asserted that the rule sceptics' focus on appeal courts' interpretations of legal doctrine blinded them to the more basic uncertainties arising in trial courts' ascertainment of facts. The fallibility of witnesses, the prejudices or preconceptions of judges or jurors, the relative persuasiveness of counsel, and many other aspects of the courtroom environment made the process of fact-finding unscientific and unpredictable, with the result that unpredictability affected the establishment of material facts even before the trial court came to apply rules of law to them. In such circumstances appeal courts could generally do little to correct this fundamental source of unpredictability (Frank 1949: ch 3).

Frank's frequent claims that certainty was impossible to achieve in the judicial process were accompanied by the assertion that the childish quest for certainty should be replaced with an explicit concern for a clearly articulated justice of outcomes (eg Frank: 1930: xi). Yet Frank's legal philosophy seems to suppose that such justice can exist in isolation from certainty, and to ignore the possibility that the former might be no less elusive than the latter. Given these views it seems somewhat amazing that he became in 1941, after a series of significant governmental positions during the New Deal era of the 1930s, a judge of the United States Second Circuit. The appointment was likened in some quarters to the appointment of a heretic to serve as a bishop in the Roman Catholic Church (White 1988: 275).

Three kinds of realism

So at least three contrasting types of realist thought in relation to normative legal theory can be identified. The first, which I shall call *policy-science realism*, emphasises 'fact research' – empirical social scientific or behavioural studies – to inform and supplement doctrinal analysis, and puts a related stress on the need to guide doctrinal development with a more sophisticated understanding of policy matters. Such an approach does not necessarily deny the utility of normative legal analysis or normative legal theory as long as policy can be treated as something objectively recognisable or discoverable and incorporated into legal doctrine as a set of ideas susceptible (like rules) to rational interpretation and elaboration.

A second type of realist orientation, which I shall call *radical scepticism*, is profoundly dubious about the value of orthodox doctrinal analysis. It suggests that this kind of analysis offers merely rationalisations or mystifications of legal reality as embodied in the actual practices of officials such as judges and other participants in legal processes. In this view, judicial decisions or other legal outcomes may seem fundamentally unpredictable because grounded in unfathomable, or at least unfathomed, personal characteristics or preferences of the decision-maker; or they may appear intelligible only by treating them as political decisions uncontrolled by legal doctrine or institutional or procedural constraints.

Third, a 'moderate' position, which I shall term *constructive doctrinal realism*, does not deny the significance of analysis of legal doctrine in gaining an understanding of the nature of legal reality. But it asserts the hopeless inadequacy of any such understanding that does not take account of behavioural factors determining how and to what extent legal doctrine is significant in the production of judicial and other official decisions.

The crucial variable by which I distinguish these three realist orientations here is their attitude to normative legal analysis: that is, to the rational interpretation of legal doctrine. Policy-science realism could adopt any of a variety of positions: for example, that legal doctrine is (i) socially insignificant or merely uninteresting or (ii) indeterminate in its effects and therefore of unknown instrumental significance or (iii) significant but harmful in its effects or (iv) significant but created and applied in ignorance of its specific social consequences. On the basis of any of these positions the importance of social scientific 'fact research' on law could be asserted.

By contrast, radical sceptical realism is directly concerned with doctrine but in a negative, sceptical way, denying explicitly the traditional claims made for doctrinal rationality and its significance. Its concern is to demystify or debunk legal doctrine and traditional forms of legal reasoning. Law in this radical view is, in essence, *not doctrine* but policy, politics, personal preferences of powerful decision-makers – or (ideally) justice.

Finally, from a constructive doctrinal realist position, doctrine is viewed as important and (at least potentially) socially valuable yet its character is asserted to be greatly misunderstood by orthodox doctrinal analyses and normative legal theory. New ways should be found to make normative analysis of law realistic by examining the institutional settings and social, economic and political contexts in which legal doctrine operates and is developed and by reorganising or reinterpreting doctrine in the light of these inquiries.

It should be noted, also, that policy-science realism is compatible with either of the other two realist orientations, but, as noted earlier, serious social scientific policy research was always very much a minority pursuit among realist legal scholars. On the other hand, radical sceptical realism and constructive doctrinal realism are plainly mutually incompatible, although some realists might be considered to have wavered between the two, and some may have matured (or, from another viewpoint, weakened) from a radical to a constructive outlook over time.

In the remaining sections of this chapter aspects of the development of these three positions in realist and post-realist American legal thought will be traced. In important respects the third (constructive doctrinal) position (especially represented by the evolution of Llewellyn's jurisprudence) offers the most direct and sustained engagement with orthodox forms of normative theory (neither polemically dismissing it in favour of purely behavioural inquiries as Frank's fact scepticism sometimes seemed to advocate, nor merely supplementing or elaborating it through policy analysis of the actual or potential content of legal doctrine).

Consequently, while the policy-science and radical sceptical approaches are, as will appear, the foundation of important modern attempts in legal scholarship to come to terms with the legacy of realist thought, constructive doctrinal realism, exemplified in Llewellyn's work, has generally been treated, by serious scholars of realism concerned with legal theory, as the variety of realist thought offering the most direct and productive confrontation with orthodox forms of normative legal theory.

Llewellyn's constructive doctrinal realism

Hart (1961: 136) refers to 'rule scepticism' as 'the claim that talk of rules is a myth, cloaking the truth that law consists simply of the decisions of courts and the prediction of them'. If, as seems likely, this is intended to refer to Llewellyn's theories (cf Hart 1961: 277, 298; Twining 1968: 6), it is a serious distortion, yet typical of the misunderstandings of realism often found, at least until recently, among analytical jurists in Britain.

Llewellyn expressed regret that a single sentence ('What these officials do about disputes is, to my mind, the law itself') in one of his early works, taken out of context, 'was enough to characterise a whole man and his whole position' for many critics of realism.[3] As noted earlier, Llewellyn's belittling of paper rules in

---

3   See Llewellyn 1951: 8–10, 12; 1960: 511; Twining 1973: 148–150; cf Hart 1977: 124.

1930 was accompanied by a firm insistence in the same essay (Llewellyn 1930a) that an emphasis on legal behaviour certainly did not make the study of legal doctrine unimportant. In Llewellyn's view, however, a sensitivity to what courts are doing (decisions and their practical consequences), as well as to the way judges rationalise their actions through legal rules and principles, ought to make legal scholars view doctrine much more cautiously and critically.

Llewellyn's writing does not usually show the kind of cynicism about orthodox conceptual thought in law that is suggested by Felix Cohen's essay on the 'transcendental nonsense' of legal ideas, Thurman Arnold's analogies between legal reasoning and theological debate (Arnold 1935: 59–67) or Frank's deliberately provocative talk of 'modern legal magic' (Frank 1949: chs 4 and 5). Instead, Llewellyn consistently emphasises the need to narrow the scope of legal concepts, using more specific, particularised categories in doctrinal classification which reflect actual distinctions patterned in judicial practice but not necessarily recognised in paper rules and textbook concepts (Llewellyn 1930a: 27–28; 1931a: 56–57).

Thus, his influential *Cases and Materials on the Law of Sales*, first published in 1930, breaks down the concept of 'title' by reference to doctrinal categories reflecting specific stages at which distinct sales issues arise. And he makes explicit the way behavioural study should be integrated with study of the paper rules: 'study of the actual use of the title concept by the courts in contracts for future sale results in the conclusion that the allocation of title is in fact determined repeatedly by features of the contract which serve equally well to solve the problem without recourse to the title concept itself' (Llewellyn 1930b: xiv; cf Wiseman 1987: 476–477). This does not mean that the paper legal concept is to be discarded in a behavioural view but that 'the student can come to see title for what it really is: a concept historically conditioning the etiquette of sales discussion; a wholly unnecessary major premise introduced as a matter of inertia or of etiquette in perhaps half the cases; in other cases, a convenient bridge for moving from one aspect of the contract to some other in regard to which the contract is not equally explicit; lastly, a concept so hallowed by tradition that it must be reckoned with as sometimes obscuring a sensible solution of the case in hand. To get along without the title concept, to get along without learning to use it, reason with it, argue from it is impossible', but to treat it in isolation from its actual practical use (or non-use) 'is to lose perspective on modern developments' (Llewellyn 1930b: xiv–xv).

This goes beyond Hart's insistence that concepts are to be understood in their legal linguistic context. Llewellyn requires that concepts be interpreted not just as elements in specific statements made by judges or lawyers. They are to be understood in relation to the outcomes that they may aid or obstruct. Doctrine may constitute a practical problem, no less than a solution, in official decision-making.

The general issue of the relationship between judging as a problem of efficient administrative behaviour and legal doctrine as an ideal structure of rational guidance for conduct is the central focus of much of Llewellyn's most important work both as a legal theorist and as an eminent American commercial lawyer, who was primarily responsible for determining the original shape and structure of the United States Uniform Commercial Code which now provides the general framework for much American commercial law.

His method 'is to take accepted doctrine, and check its words against its results ... If a doctrine [legal rule, principle, concept] does not, in and by itself do all that it purports to do, then [it is necessary to ask] *what else* is at work helping the doctrine out' (1940: 135). So Llewellyn's predominant emphasis is not (as was Frank's) on the factors promoting uncertainty and unpredictability in law, but on those producing a remarkable predictability of legal outcomes, *despite* the 'leeways of precedent', the indeterminacy of doctrine or its inability to remove the human and subjective character of judging.[4] Equally, Llewellyn has a specific answer as to 'what else is at work' helping doctrine out. 'There is the tradition of the judge's craft, stabilising the work of our judges, and guiding it; and there are the ideals of that craft, which also stabilise and guide' (1940: 135; and see 1989: 77–81).

Llewellyn's behavioural perspective on law becomes a perspective on courts and judiciaries (and other components of the legal world) as *institutions* (Llewellyn 1941; cf Twining 1973: 176–177) – stable patterns and structures of behaviour operating within a set of normative expectations about, for example, the right way to do the job of judging, the right way to organise a court and a hearing, the right way to read precedent cases, the right way to reach and justify decisions. In the writings of the last two decades of Llewellyn's career, and especially in his richly imaginative book *The Common Law Tradition* published just over a year before his death in 1962, this institutional view of judging is elaborated in depth.

He gained very important insights into the social and institutional conditions under which judicial craftsmanship could be developed through his collaboration in the 1930s and 1940s with the anthropologist E A Hoebel in studying social control and dispute resolution processes in several native American

---

4　Cf Frank 1949: 31; Llewellyn 1960: 4, 45. This view is present early in his work. In lectures first published in 1933, he emphasises that, if judicial processes are understood realistically, 'the outcome of a dispute concerning the law is predictable to a truly amazing degree' (Llewellyn 1989: 76).

tribes. Of these studies the most important in its general influence on his theoretical ideas about legal institutions was that of the Cheyenne Indians (Llewellyn and Hoebel 1941). Though most of the fieldwork was done by Hoebel, Llewellyn developed a very strong sympathy with the communally based judicial wisdom that he saw reflected in the case histories of problem-solving in traditional Cheyenne life collected by the researchers. The study of a small scale society in its past glory[5] was of profound concern to Llewellyn, otherwise devoting much of his time as an American commercial lawyer to intricate problems of regulation in one of the world's most complex and advanced societies.

In what he and Hoebel portrayed as well-ordered traditional Cheyenne society, Llewellyn thought he saw the simple essence of juristic method – not as the rational organisation and application of legal doctrine but as performance of a social task of good government: 'the search for serviceable forms and devices ... the quest for their skilful use ... the seeking to keep vital and vigorous under any form, any formula, any "rule", its living reason, its principle' (Llewellyn and Hoebel 1941: 307).

For Llewellyn, doctrine is the product of a certain way of working. As such it reflects a particular behavioural style pervasive in the legal institutions of the time and place. 'Juristic method is not dissimilar in nature from style in art – an extremely complex and subtle set of somethings which affect in varying degree a whole range of craftsmen at once, yet allow huge divergencies' (Llewellyn and Hoebel 1941: 308). And because the style of working and its social context is more fundamental than the doctrine to which it gives rise, legal doctrine alone does not express the whole of legal life or even its most fundamental elements.

Period-style

In *The Common Law Tradition*, published nearly two decades after the Cheyenne study, Llewellyn develops in detail, and specifically in relation to American appellate courts, the idea of a behavioural style of judging pervasive among judiciaries in a certain time and place: 'It is the general and pervasive manner, over the country at large, at any given time, of going about the job, the general outlook, the ways of professional knowhow, the kind of thing the men of law are sensitive to and strive for, the tone and flavour of the working and of the results. It is well described as a "period-style"' (Llewellyn 1960: 36).

---

5   Much of the case material consisted of informants' recollections of events and practices from at least half a century earlier.

The importance of this idea in relation to the critique of orthodox forms of normative legal theory is that it makes possible for Llewellyn (and justifies as absolutely essential) a fusion of behavioural analysis of judicial work and normative analysis of legal doctrine (Llewellyn 1941). Doctrine is the expression and reflection of a style of working: not the cause of it but the consequence. It makes no sense to try to understand law as a structure of ideas without analysing the institutional settings and wider social and professional environments that, in determining the general period-style of the judiciary, shape the form and content of those ideas. At the same time, period-style is revealed most clearly in the judicial reasoning preserved in law reports. Indeed, *The Common Law Tradition* relies on the examination of vast numbers of cases from many American state jurisdictions to plot changes in period-style over time.

Llewellyn identifies two contrasting period-styles. *Grand Style* judging (or the Style of Reason) treats precedents as welcome and very persuasive but tests them against (i) the reputation of the opinion-writing judge, (ii) principle, which is understood as 'no mere verbal tool for bringing large-scale order into the rules' but 'a broad generalisation which must yield patent sense as well as order', and (iii) policy 'in terms of prospective consequences of the rule under consideration' (1960: 36). Grand Style allows 'on-going renovation of doctrine' but (at its best) with no hint of revolution in the law or even of campaigning reform. It involves a constant quest for the best law for the future but the 'best law is to be built on and out of what the past can offer; the quest consists in a constant re-examination and reworking of a heritage' (1960: 36).

Parallels with Dworkin's description of appropriate judicial methods (see Chapter 6) are clear, and it is unsurprising that Llewellyn explicitly associates Grand Style with what he sees as the ideal tradition of common law judging. But, unlike Dworkin, Llewellyn does not characterise this judicial approach as in-built in the value system and doctrinal traditions of Anglo-American law (as something internal to law as a system of ideas). Instead, he portrays it as a style that waxes and wanes in American legal history as a result of complex historical causes. These operate as institutional pressures on behaviour which (presumably) demand sociological explanation. The legal theorist needs to understand not just how to participate in interpretative practice at any given time but also the dynamics of change in the overall outlook and structure of the community of interpreters itself.

In contrast to Grand Style stands *Formal Style* (or Authoritarian Style), which Llewellyn describes as 'the orthodox ideology' in the American context since the late nineteenth century (1960: 38), though displaced to some extent by a renaissance of Grand Style from the early decades of the twentieth century. In Formal Style,

> 'the rules of law are to decide the cases; policy is for the legislature, not for the courts, and so is change even in pure common law. Opinions run in deductive form with an air or expression of single-line inevitability. "Principle" [here meaning something quite different from what it means in Grand Style judging] is a generalisation producing order which can and should be used to prune away those "anomalous" cases or rules which do not fit, such cases or rules having no function except, in places where the supposed "principle" does not work well, to accomplish sense – but sense is no official concern of a formal-style court' (1960: 38).

Much of *The Common Law Tradition* is taken up with plotting the historical movement in actual judicial practice in various American state jurisdictions between these two styles. Later writers have challenged Llewellyn's periodisation and offered more sophisticated accounts of processes of transition between styles of legal thought. What is important here, however, in examining the progress of debates in normative legal theory in the Anglo-American context is that Llewellyn's writings not only express realism's behavioural critique of 'pure' doctrinal analysis in law (and of normative legal theory that presupposes that law can be explained as a system of ideas). They also suggest means of viewing law behaviourally (or institutionally) in such a way as to *clarify and enhance* analysis of doctrine.

Just as Stanley Fish's critique of Dworkin[6] implies the need to examine sociologically the nature of the community of legal interpreters (primarily judges) and the forces at work promoting or disrupting conformity and consensus in it, Llewellyn's identification of the historical importance of specific period-styles among particular judiciaries points to the need for empirical inquiry into social, economic, political and professional conditions that make particular judicial styles pervasive.[7]

The institutional orientation of Llewellyn's study is further reinforced by his identifying, elsewhere in *The Common Law Tradition*, a range of 'steadying factors' which, together with the period-style of the time and place, promote consistency and predictability in appellate decision-making. These include the common training and experience of judges in a professional legal environment,

---

6   See Chapter 6, above, pp 172–173.

7   Llewellyn describes (1960: 24–25), for example, the 'single right answer' outlook (now strongly associated with Dworkin's legal philosophy: see above, p 165) as one such matter of judicial style to be considered sociologically.

the constraints of group decision-making and of the professional environment as a whole, shared judicial values, the public character of the judicial office, and a range of procedural factors limiting the variables to be considered in the decision-making process.

Thus, doctrine is to be understood, and can only be understood, in its institutional setting. Normative legal theory, insofar as it denies the need for systematic behavioural analysis, misrepresents the character of doctrine and prevents realistic understanding of the nature of law. In the light of all this, some analytical jurists' caricature of the realists as uniformly denying the fundamental significance of rules and other elements of legal doctrine is just a smokescreen obscuring the need to confront the important claims of constructive doctrinal realism.

The recapture of Grand Style

Llewellyn sought to make his version of realism a practical contribution to better, more predictable judicial practice. In his writings, Grand Style judging is advocated as far more conducive to certainty and predictability in law than Formal Style because, unlike the latter, it reveals the instrumental purposes of doctrine in judicial reasoning itself. The Grand Style invocation of principle and policy makes explicit what a particular newly formulated element of legal doctrine *is for*. By contrast, the air of 'single-line inevitability' conveyed by Formal Style deductive reasoning is likely to obscure reasons for doctrinal developments so that the real motivations behind judicial decisions remain hidden or ambiguous, and likely paths of judicial development of doctrine are harder to predict. Grand Style is more likely to produce 'rules which make sense on their face, and which can be understood and reasonably well applied even by mediocre men' (Llewellyn 1960: 38).

There is room for debate about the virtues of Grand Style. Behind these positions, however, lies Llewellyn's (1989: 80) conviction that doctrine cannot, and should not attempt to *control* judges, but should be framed to *guide* them. A creative, conscientious judge constrained by Formal Style expectations may well seek to escape the limitations of deductive logic by ingenious manipulation of the precedents, fine distinctions and covert reinterpretations of established rules. Judges hamstrung by rules that give no leeway to do justice are likely to behave unpredictably (Llewellyn 1940: 144). The vital point is that the effectively operating pressures for conformity in judging are not produced primarily by rules but by the whole institutional environment in which the job of judging is done. Doctrine, for Llewellyn, should guide judges in appropriate directions but give them creative freedom within the constraints inherent in their role as part of the judiciary as an institution.

Thus, Llewellyn's drafts in the 1940s for what became the American Uniform Commercial Code assumed that the Code would provide a framework of concepts and principles to allow for standardisation of law within the Code's scope. But its provisions should be 'purposive statements of principles based on facts of commercial transactions and designed to guide flexible decision-making' (Wiseman 1987: 497). The aim would be to provide doctrinal guidance easily intelligible in terms of the purposes it was intended to serve (Twining 1973: 305). Courts would be encouraged to develop the rules of the Code in the light of these purposes. Lengthy 'Official Comments' in the Code would elaborate its underlying reasons and policies as an aid to judicial interpretation and application. Judges could not be forced to reason in Grand Style but the means of doing so could be made available to them in statutory form (Wiseman 1987: 498–502; Twining 1973: 321–330).

At the same time, the Code, in Llewellyn's view, had to embody the realist insistence that doctrinal concepts and categories be made more functional by breaking them down into less abstract and generalised ideas that better represented the variety and complexities of practical conditions. Hence the Code would incorporate 'merchant rules' expressing the standards and practices, understandings and needs of merchants (trade usage could, for example, be assumed to provide the shared factual and normative assumptions underlying a merchant transaction). Equally, the Code would distinguish merchant from non-merchant contexts; and it would provide for issues of mercantile fact arising under the merchant provisions to be tried by a merchant tribunal possessing expert knowledge of the field (Wiseman 1987: 503–504, 505).

While important parts of Llewellyn's scheme did not survive the lengthy period of development of the Uniform Commercial Code, his proposals are a clear example of the effort to make constructive doctrinal realism serve practical professional needs for a rational system of legal doctrine.

The political context of American legal realism

Why has realism in this and other forms had little impact on normative legal theory in Britain, while it received, and still receives, much attention in the United States? It is important to note that the idea of realism's limited impact in Britain needs to be qualified by recognition that post-realist developments in legal theory, to be mentioned in the remaining sections of this chapter, are having an increasingly powerful influence on legal thought on both sides of the Atlantic. Is it merely a matter of a long delayed reception of realist ideas in Britain, rather than dismissal of them?

Orthodox contextual explanations of American legal realism encourage an image of it as a product of distinctive historical and political conditions in the United States. It is seen as a consequence of the extraordinary historical role of courts in American government (Hart 1977: 124), and especially of a constitutional framework allowing judicial review of the validity of legislation. This emphasis on courts reflects a more general view of political power as appropriately decentralised and dispersed: institutionally through the federal system and the doctrine of separation of powers, and geographically and culturally through the sheer practical impossibility of imposing uniform solutions to all governmental problems in a nation of such size and diversity.

More detailed analyses along the same lines seek to explain why the realist movement arose in the early decades of the twentieth century. It was a response to a crisis of 'overload' in legal doctrine and the resultant inability of courts to operate a system of judicial precedent on the traditional common law model: 'Toward the end of the nineteenth century the rate of acceleration in printed case reports became nightmarish. Digests of all reported cases decided from the institution of courts in the American colonies until 1896 – a period of over two hundred years – take up three shelves in the Law Library. Digests of cases decided since 1896 [and up to 1960] fill more than thirty shelves' (Gilmore 1961: 1041).

As Grant Gilmore explains, not only were many more cases being decided in the late nineteenth century and after, as both the population and the number of courts and state jurisdictions grew, but a higher proportion of cases was being reported, especially as a result of the establishment of the West National Reporter system in the 1870s. When the number of reported cases 'becomes like the number of grains of sand on the beach' a precedent system cannot work (Gilmore 1961: 1041). And the problem in the American context was exacerbated by the fact that most private law problems were left to the individual states, and were left by the states to courts.

This now familiar explanation of the crisis that produced the origins of American realism is usually supplemented, at least in modern American histories, with a more specific political explanation. Justice Oliver Wendell Holmes' famous dissenting opinions in the United States Supreme Court[8] are typically seen as a protest against the mindlessly mechanical legal logic of the majority of the court at a time (the beginning of the twentieth century) when American government was faced with immense problems of adapting to social and economic change.

---

8   Especially *Lochner v New York* 198 US 45, 75–76 (1905).

What Pound saw as 'mechanical jurisprudence' (see Chapter 6) to be remedied by legislative inspiration and a renewal of the traditional evolutionary practice of common law judging, Holmes saw as judicial frustration of the popular will for legal change by judges who imported their own prejudices into their decisions under cover of legal logic. But Holmes' view was not realist in the sense of those legal realists who adopted him as their mentor. While he claimed[9] that courts could operate objectively and leave policy convictions to be expressed by democratically elected legislators, the legal realists tended to see courts as inevitably involved in policy decision. The issue became what policies they promoted and how open they were in admitting value preferences.

So the orthodox story of legal realism sees its flowering as a dominant legal theory in the 1930s as an almost inevitable expression in legal thought of the political demands that gave rise to Franklin Roosevelt's 'New Deal' government in the same period. These demands were for clear policy uniting all government agencies to attack the social and economic crises of the Depression era beginning with the Wall Street stock market crash of 1929. Thus, for some writers, legal realism is essentially the jurisprudential analogue of the New Deal (White 1972; Murphy 1972: ch 4).

There is, undoubtedly, much truth in this. The urgent need for new approaches to legal scholarship that would provide guidance for 'social planning and perspective' to lift America from 'the social and economic debacle' was the theme of the 1932 presidential address to the Association of American Law Schools (Harno 1932). Equally, the shrill political criticisms that realism as a whole attracted from some extreme critics were exactly those applied to the Roosevelt New Deal: it was held to exhibit totalitarian or fascist tendencies and a contempt for the Rule of Law (Hull 1997: 234–239).

Many leading realists were fervent supporters of, and in several cases active participants in, the governmental activities of the New Deal (see eg Twining 1973: 58). In this regard, as so often, the most arresting statement is Jerome Frank's. In 1934 he described himself and other 'experimental jurisprudes' as 'humble servants to that master experimentalist, Franklin Roosevelt' (quoted in White 1988: 275). Thus, the problem of justice as the aim of judicial (and administrative) practice was solved for some realists by a belief in the inherent correctness of certain policies or of particular means of reaching them.

Two major conclusions follow if these kinds of explanations of American realism are treated as comprehensive. First, realism is essentially a parochial concern of American law and lawyers. Hence it has little, if any, wider

---

9   As, for example, in his *Lochner* dissent.

jurisprudential significance. Second, realism was a response to legal and political crises that have now passed. Gilmore (1961), for example, argues that various developments helped to defuse the American legal crisis of precedent 'overload'. Especially significant were: the American Law Institute's systematic Restatements of common law doctrine, which were widely relied upon by courts; certain changes in approaches to precedent, to judicial interpretation of legislation and to legislative drafting; the use of codification in important areas of American law; and the federalisation of private law.

These orthodox explanations of realism are not wrong. But they may not tell the whole story. First, the explanation in terms of the special role of courts in American government makes it hard to see why forms of legal realism developed independently in other countries having very different judicial systems. As mentioned earlier, a form of legal realism developed in the Scandinavian countries in the first half of the twentieth century. At the turn of the century in Germany a movement known as the 'Free Law' (*Freirechtslehre*) school, uniting legal practitioners and jurists, similarly stressed the indeterminacy of legal rules, taken alone, as predictions of judicial decisions. It emphasised the creative role of the judge, and the importance of explicitly recognising and responsibly developing this role (relatively free from doctrinal restraint) to meet the needs of the time.

A major impetus behind the Free Law movement seems to have been the perceived excessive abstraction of the German Civil Code which came into force in 1900 and was seen as hampering judicial resolution of problems arising from rapid social and economic change. In Scandinavia, also, legal realism was popularised in reaction to abstractions in legal reasoning and doctrine that seemed socially irrelevant or failed to address policy demands directly (Castberg 1955: 389–390).

Second, although Gilmore's tracing of American realism to the problem of precedent overload is plausible, it is doubtful whether the problem has been largely solved as he seems to suggest, or that it can be regarded as uniquely American. It is more likely that the seriousness of this problem in the United States at a certain time (together with the political and social crises of the Depression era) highlighted in a specially dramatic way a difficulty endemic to common law systems. This is the difficulty of interpreting and justifying judicial decision-making in a context of increasing governmental steering of social and economic life, a context in which courts' attitudes to policy-making and policy-implementation are increasingly crucial.

Finally, to describe American legal realism as the jurisprudential analogue of the New Deal ignores the fact that arguably its most important theorist, Karl Llewellyn, was not a New Deal supporter (Twining 1973: 125) and regarded the events and issues of the New Deal as largely irrelevant to realism's primary contributions to legal analysis. The New Deal era was an 'accident' which 'threw the whole emerging line of inquiry off-centre' and, if anything, hampered its development (Llewellyn 1960: 14). For Llewellyn, at least, realism was a response to dilemmas that long antedated the New Deal and in no way disappeared with the passing of the Roosevelt era.

What all of this suggests is that, while American legal realism did become a major movement at a certain time as a response to distinctively American legal, political and social circumstances, it can also be seen as a particularly explicit, unrestrained expression of more general problems in the development of Western law, which have remained unsolved in the forms of Anglo-American normative legal theory discussed earlier in this book. At the heart of those problems is the one which all attempts to portray law as an integrated system of ideas have failed to hide: that of the unrestrained power of the judge as a political actor. Various rationalisations have been offered but none has really resolved this issue.

Modern positivist analytical jurisprudence postulates a clear distinction between a 'core' and 'penumbra' of meaning of legal rules.[10] As long as the existence of a core of indisputable meaning of legal doctrine could be accepted, judicial decision-making could be seen to have at least *some* realm distinct from the expression of personal judicial values or preferences, or from policy-making judicial legislative activity. But it was noted in Chapter 4 that this claim could be maintained only through sociological inquiries into the nature of the judicial role which Hart's analytical jurisprudence was not prepared to undertake. Much other modern theory discussed in this book has tried to find the solution to the problem of explaining the judicial role in normative legal theory by postulating an overarching structure of legal values within which judicial decisions in hard cases are to be made. But, as has been argued in previous chapters, it may require a leap of faith to recognise these values and see them controlling actual judicial behaviour.

Legal realism has been marginalised in Britain partly because much of its literature does, indeed, reflect a distinctively American context and distinctively American problems while making little serious effort to address its arguments to wider issues and theoretical debates about Anglo-American law. Indeed, the very terms 'realism' and its often-identified opposite 'formalism' have little jurisprudential resonance in the British context. But realism's most rigorous

---

10 See Chapter 4, above, pp 99–100.

and least parochial writings have been very valuable in showing that normative legal theory cannot explain the character of law as doctrine without serious empirical examination of the social and political conditions in which that doctrine is developed and invoked.

Post-realist policy-science

Llewellyn's work offers perhaps the most instructive form of constructive doctrinal realism. The critique of normative legal theory that it implies (that conceptual analysis of law is pointless without a parallel analysis of the social contexts of legal interpretation) will be developed in the remaining chapters of this book. In this chapter it remains to consider briefly the way in which the other two types of realism – its policy-science and radical sceptical forms – have evolved in recent legal scholarship.

McDougal and Lasswell

As noted earlier, policy-science realism is compatible with various attitudes to legal doctrine. In the 1940s, the Yale law professor Myres McDougal and his political scientist colleague Harold Lasswell began a long-term collaboration founded in the conviction that the discipline of law should become a policy science: a technology for achieving social goals and realising democratic values in practice using legal doctrine and institutions.

In this way legal realism's critique of traditional legal analysis for failing to see doctrinal logic's subservience to considerations of policy could be made constructive. It could become a prescription for realistic legal education, scholarship and advocacy in which the rational elaboration of techniques of policy-formulation and implementation would be central (Lasswell and McDougal 1943).

The McDougal-Lasswell approach has been appropriately described by William Twining as 'a combination of utilitarianism and Freudian psychology, supplemented by some of the insights of American social science, and encased in an elaborate terminology' (Twining 1973: 385). Perhaps partly because of the last of these elements, it has had little enduring or widespread influence, except among some scholars of international law. Probably a more important reason for its limited impact is that it did not really address the practical problems of doctrinal rationality and predictability which realism had emphasised, but rather tried to persuade lawyers to avoid them by adopting new and unfamiliar modes of analysis.

Law and society

Much more important in its scale and influence is the now very lively 'law and society' movement which developed in the United States and other countries from the 1960s as a multidisciplinary movement committed to social scientific research on law.

In its broadest sense this is a modern phase in the continuing international development of sociology of law (sociologically informed empirical and theoretical research on law) which has a long history and a rich and varied theoretical tradition (see eg Cotterrell 1992). But, in the context of this chapter's concerns, an important unifying element in the early development of law and society researches was their (relatively atheoretical) concern with legal 'impact' or effectiveness: that is, with studies of the effects on behaviour of particular legal rules or other doctrine, or the effects of legal institutions in practice. This kind of impact study of law in action is a direct successor of the pioneer empirical researches of legal realists such as Underhill Moore, Charles Clark and William Douglas in the 1920s and 1930s (Schlegel 1995).

Law and society research in this form – not directly concerned with the nature of legal doctrine in general or with engaging with general theories of the nature of law – has little direct bearing on the concerns of normative legal theory. Thus, much law and society research has posed no challenge to this theory. It has restricted its concern to behaviour and left the theoretical analysis of the nature of legal doctrine to legal philosophers. Until relatively recently, the long tradition in the sociology of law of what I call empirical legal theory – concerned to explain theoretically the nature of law as doctrine and behaviour in historical and social context – has not been a central concern for law and society studies, at least in the homeland of American legal realism.

Economic analysis of law

Finally, among policy-science realism's successor movements it is important to mention the recent rapid development of economic analysis of law, a form of legal scholarship now very widely established and recognised in American law schools, though of less significance in Britain.

That the application to law of the theories and methods of economics has achieved a significant penetration in legal education and research is a tribute to the versatility of economic reasoning. Thus, techniques of positive (that is, essentially explanatory rather than prescriptive) economic analysis can be used in legal impact studies by considering how law can help to shape the behaviour choices that rational, self-interested individuals are likely to make in particular situations. For example, to the extent that crime is an option rationally chosen by the criminal, economic analysis can ask in what circumstances law can provide disincentives that make a choice in favour of criminal behaviour no longer rational (weighing up likely benefits and detriments) for the potential offender.

Beyond this kind of inquiry, normative (or welfare) economics assumes a goal of allocative efficiency – optimum allocation of resources for the maximum overall benefit of those amongst whom the allocation is to be made – and seeks to identify situations of inefficiency and prescribe means of correcting them. Thus, legal doctrine can be examined for its contribution to this kind of allocation. Much literature considers the allocative efficiency of liability rules in tort law and a variety of other doctrinal fields.

In this kind of writing, policy analysis from a social scientific field is being used to supplement established types of justifications in legal logic for existing doctrine. Thus, economic analysis appears exceptionally useful in doctrinal analysis. It does not undermine legal discourse. It offers a parallel commentary of justification or critique which seems to provide a powerful answer to realist claims about the inadequacy of doctrinal rationality. Economics is invoked to provide the rationality that realism found wanting.

The high point of this is probably found in the descriptive theory that the implicit goal of judicially developed common law doctrine is to promote an efficient allocation of resources in society. This is a kind of 'invisible hand' theory insofar as it claims that, whether or not the judges knew what they were doing in terms of economic rationality in developing common law rules, the case-by-case evolution of common law has in fact led to outcomes with a high degree of allocative efficiency (Posner 1972). Thus, a kind of unstated and often unrecognised economic rationality is claimed to lie beneath the rationality of legal logic. The invisible hand of economic reality is portrayed as guiding judicial development of common law rules.

This kind of analysis has some affinities with constructive doctrinal realism insofar as it seeks to supplement and enhance ordinary doctrinal analysis by reinterpreting it in a wider social scientific context. But economic analysis of law is probably, in general, better seen as a kind of modern policy-science approach insofar as much of it seems little concerned to illuminate through behavioural study the way doctrine is actually developed, interpreted and applied in legal contexts.[11] The logic of economic analysis is considered to explain important aspects of the way law is or should be, irrespective of

---

11 But cf Ellickson 1991 which provides an interesting example of economic analysis being used to structure an empirical study of disputing behaviour.

empirical study of the range of determinants of judicial behaviour in relation to doctrine.

Economic analysis of law has attracted strong criticism: for example, that its emphasis on cost-benefit efficiency is inappropriate or inadequate in explaining or evaluating legal policy; that its postulates of rational action are too unreal to provide the basis of explanatory models or theories; that its adherents claim far more significance for economic analysis than is justified by its narrow inquiries; that, while claiming to be empirical, it does not actually examine people's preferences but deduces them from premises of rationality that sometimes lead to tautologies; and that it is biased towards market solutions and unable to attach sufficient weight to non-market relationships. The matter is also complicated by the fact that several competing schools of economic analysis of law exist. But the merits of this burgeoning movement need not be considered here. What is important is to recognise that economic analysis of law has offered some legal scholars a means of confronting a post-realist world in which legal logic no longer seems sufficient.

Post-realist radical scepticism

Radical sceptical realism – wholly rejecting traditional forms of legal doctrinal analysis as pointless and mystificatory – can be seen as having two strongly contrasting post-realist successor movements, one in the law school environment and one almost entirely outside it in American political science.

Judicial behaviouralism

The latter is usually called judicial behaviouralism. In essence, it involves efforts to predict or explain the outcome of judicial decisions through systematic analysis of the behavioural characteristics of the judges involved. Computer analyses of the interrelations of such variables as judges' educational backgrounds, religious and political attitudes and a vast array of specific characteristics are used.

Legal doctrine provides variables for this kind of analysis insofar as published judgments, in previous cases decided by the judges being studied, may be thought to provide important sources of information on their personal values. But otherwise judicial behaviouralism is best seen as an effort to bypass doctrinal analysis and treat what judges do as all-important and what they say as a triviality to be left to lawyers for analysis. Since judicial behaviouralism does not at any point address any of the concerns of normative legal theory it is of little relevance here, except insofar as it holds doggedly to the view that law (as a socially significant phenomenon) is behaviour *and not* doctrine.

Critical legal studies

A much more significant form of radical scepticism in this context is represented by some of the work, since the 1970s, of the American Critical Legal Studies (CLS) movement. The first of the annual meetings of the Conference on Critical Legal Studies took place in 1977 as a result of a circular letter proposing 'a gathering of colleagues who are pursuing a critical approach toward the study of law in society' (Kelman 1987: 297). CLS writing reflects diverse influences from modern radical philosophy and social theory but is also 'in many ways ... a direct descendant' of legal realism (Tushnet 1986: 505).

It has taken to heart the realist idea that, as Holmes put it: 'General propositions [in legal doctrine] do not decide concrete cases'.[12] Just as Felix Cohen saw much of the general conceptual apparatus of legal doctrine as transcendental nonsense, CLS writers tend to see it as mystification. Arguments purporting to follow the logic of concepts could lead in diametrically opposed directions. In CLS jargon, concepts are 'flippable' equally in one direction or another.

Some CLS writers go further to argue that, because of the manipulability of concepts, legal texts are infinitely interpretable: there simply is no way of deciding that one reading is necessarily better than another (Tushnet 1983). Everything depends on how one wishes to string together doctrinal logic in arguments in which all the crucial concepts used are subject to a variety of possible interpretations. The interesting question is what determines 'possible' interpretations and for most CLS writers this is not something determined by doctrine itself but by the *political context* in which the interpretations are being offered.

To this extent CLS is consistent in its outlook with radical sceptical realism and shares with it an active interest in pouring scorn on lawyers' faith in legal logic (Kelman 1984). But this scepticism has not caused CLS writers to lose interest in doctrine. The general CLS position is that while orthodox legal reasoning often seems to produce radically indeterminate, even arbitrary, outcomes, legal doctrine is not as a result insignificant. Quite the opposite. It is one of the important means by which social life is constituted: that is, it provides categories of thought (for example, property, liability, binding agreement, good faith, crime, corporation, fiduciary relationship) by means of which we make sense of the social world and impose a kind of moral and intellectual order on

---

12 *Lochner v New York* 198 US 45, 76 (1905).

it. So legal doctrine has important ideological and legitimating effects, helping to 'teach' us how to think about society and convincing us of the 'naturalness' of social relationships which law defines.[13]

The legal historian Morton Horwitz has argued that the eventual triumph in the courts of particular conceptions of corporate personality – the abstract legal idea to which we have returned several times in discussions in this book – had special importance in legitimating the concentration of economic wealth and power in big business in the United States in the late nineteenth century. The 'natural entity' conception, which saw the corporation not as a legal creature of the state or as the agent of its members but as an autonomous abstract entity in law, made it possible, Horwitz argues, to justify freeing corporations from legal restraints, for example on their ability to own the stock of other corporations. In this manner doctrinal development (here the successful flipping of the meaning of a legal concept one way rather than another) cleared the way for corporate economic concentration, without lawyers or courts ever having to admit that this was what really lay behind the changes in legal ideas and the abstract arguments used to justify them (Horwitz 1992: ch 3).

Horwitz's study is a good example of the most productive kind of work that has arisen from the CLS movement, work aiming 'to uncover the specific historical possibilities of legal conceptions – to "decode" their true concrete meanings in real historical situations' (Horwitz 1992: 106–107). Doctrine and its development are taken very seriously, but the motor of doctrinal development is not considered to lie in legal logic, overarching values or traditions of the legal system (Pound, Dworkin) or mere judicial discretion as proposed by positivist analytical jurisprudence. The impetus for change in doctrine comes from outside the professional legal domain, especially in political struggle and the economic conditions, changes or crises of capitalist society. But these real forces are rarely revealed in doctrine itself or legal reasoning. Part of CLS's objective is to reveal 'hidden motives that the judges themselves would treat as illegitimate if forced to confront them'; it 'requires the analysis of the coherence of judicial explanations of outcomes ... But the goal is neither an alternative rationale nor a criticism of the outcome' (Kennedy 1979: 219, 220). Instead it is to show how a judge's formal rationale of the decision (presented as mere *legal* reasoning) obscures the real political significance of what is being decided.

Another example of this kind of analysis is found in Karl Klare's examination of American judges' interpretation of the 1935 National Labor Relations Act, 'perhaps the most radical piece of legislation ever enacted by the United States

---

13 See eg Gabel 1980 and Chapter 9, below, pp 250–252.

Congress' (Klare 1978: 265) and one that ostensibly gave major rights to employees against employers and greatly strengthened the role of collective bargaining in American labour law. Klare shows how, in a series of decisions widely regarded as employee victories, courts applied the Act to shape an institutional structure of collective bargaining that gave unions power at the expense of individual workers and helped shape 'the modern administered, and regulated system of class relations' (Klare 1978: 336). Again the essence of CLS method here is to show that what doctrine appears to say is not what it does: the narrow 'logic' of the cases is exploded by revealing in detail the economic and political context in which it is developed and how case outcomes relate to wider tendencies in American society and politics.

To the extent that this kind of inquiry is intended to increase understanding of the role and character of legal doctrine it can be seen as related to constructive doctrinal realism and certainly to the effort to develop empirical legal theory. But in much CLS work the analysis of doctrine is destructive rather than constructive. CLS is not concerned to make of doctrine a rational system or structure, or to make case outcomes more predictable, or even usually to develop any general theories about the nature of doctrine in its institutional contexts. Its broad aim is to expose the hollowness of claims for legal doctrinal rationality. This is seen as important because orthodox legal reasoning and the doctrine it produces hide the repressions, contradictions and alienating conditions of life of contemporary Western societies. At the heart of these problems is a 'fundamental contradiction' which Western 'liberalism' tries to obscure (Kennedy 1979: 211–213; but cf Gabel and Kennedy 1984: 14–18): the contradiction that individual freedom and autonomy are possible only under conditions of collective constraint and coercion.

The project of CLS is to demystify the legal ideas that obscure the contradictions of liberal capitalist society. Often, in CLS writing, these contradictions (as well as the concept of liberalism which is the focus of most CLS attack) remain frustratingly vague. It is significant that critical legal scholarship in Britain (which has developed contemporaneously with and for the most part independently of the American movement) generally avoids reliance on such concepts.[14] But at least it can be said that CLS gives legal doctrine (and presumably

---

14 The role of 'liberalism' for CLS seems in this respect exactly analogous to that of 'formalism' for legal realism. Both concepts indicate central objects of attack: formalism being associated by realists with too much abstraction and too little concreteness in legal reasoning, liberalism being associated by critical legal scholars with too much emphasis on law's social neutrality and too little on the politics of its practice. But the vagueness of both concepts seems virtually to ensure the unfocussed nature of the attack on them and the impossibility of judging its ultimate success.

the normative legal theory that helps to rationalise it) the backhanded compliment of asserting its great social importance – an importance that makes all the more necessary a concerted attack on its pretensions.

Legal professionalism and the legacy of realism

It would be pointless to try here to evaluate generally the whole range of 'sceptical' and 'realist' approaches to legal inquiry that have been discussed in this chapter. Their importance in the context of this book is, first, in their confrontations with normative legal theory and, secondly, in the insight they offer into relationships between normative legal theory and the political and professional environment of Anglo-American law. The politics of legal realism has been discussed throughout this chapter, but what of its professional ramifications?

It is often said in the American context that 'we are all realists now' (cf Schlegel 1995: 2). The most plausible meaning to give to this is that, whatever normative legal theory might suggest, many practising lawyers find no difficulty in accepting much of the substance of realism's scepticism about legal logic and general legal concepts, as well as its view that law as doctrine cannot be understood without seriously analysing the behavioural contexts in which doctrine is developed and applied.

Lawyers (in Britain no less than in the United States) cope with the indeterminacy of rules and they are well aware of 'human factors' in adjudication, the personality characteristics of judges, the importance of advocacy styles in affecting decisions, and the 'leeways of precedent'. For many lawyers, everyday experience of practice teaches that law in operation is much more a matter of behaviour (threat and compromise, negotiation and confrontation, bluff and counterbluff, timing and strategy) and economics (the relative cost to opposing parties of particular legal strategies) than of doctrinal logic.

But throughout this book it has been argued that law as a profession and as an intellectual discipline has often sought to present itself in quite different terms and normative legal theory has aided in the effort to portray law as an integrated structure of ideas, as a distinct body of esoteric knowledge. The flourishing of American legal realism seems like a moment when 'the dam broke' and the uncertainties over law's rational systematic structures of knowledge became a crisis of confidence in law as an intellectual field and a profession.

In the early 1930s there was already a relatively well-developed structure of university legal education in the United States, staffed by a substantial number of scholars ready and competent to think through the theoretical implications of this crisis. By contrast, in Britain, university legal education at that time was in a fledgling state. It held nervously to a vaguely Austinian conception of legal science (cf Dowdall 1926) and was presumably hardly ready to face the challenges of realism, even if they had presented themselves in the stark form in which they appeared in the United States. Only much later, from the 1960s, when a sizeable profession of full-time academic lawyers had been established in British universities, was a belated start made in addressing the challenges posed by American realism and its aftermath.

Where do matters stand now? On the one hand, the (sometimes unfair) charge that realism is unconcerned with legal values and with law's meaning (as opposed to its predictability and effectiveness as a governmental instrument) has been transformed into the sense that realism does not answer the most fundamental questions about the nature of law, which remain questions about its doctrinal structures (for example, about their bases of authority, moral integrity and social meaning). On the other hand, the realist idea that law's professional interpreters should be looked at critically in terms of the consequences and causes of their interpretations has taken many new forms. Normative legal theory's project of presenting law as, in some sense, an integrated or structured doctrinal whole has been overtaken by the expansion of this mood of critique.

One reason is that law's interpretive communities have themselves changed significantly, becoming less homogeneous and more varied. Some of their members have found themselves so much at odds with the dominant assumptions on which those communities are based that the very possibility of theoretical consensus about the nature of law as a ordered structure of doctrine has come to seem more remote. In these circumstances the impetus is towards a jurisprudence that stresses difference, rather than one that looks for a unity of legal meaning, form or experience. These critical developments are the concern of the next chapter.

Chapter 8

A jurisprudence of difference: class, gender and race

In 1848, sixteen years after publishing his *Province of Jurisprudence*, John Austin was living in Paris when revolution broke out. He heard 'communist and anarchical opinions' expressed everywhere and feared that France would 'fall into anarchy', with the 'heated mass' bursting into flames (quoted in Hamburger and Hamburger 1985: 169). A few months before, Karl Marx and Friedrich Engels had drafted their revolutionary *Communist Manifesto*. In it, they bluntly told the bourgeoisie, the capital-owning middle classes, 'Your jurisprudence is but the will of your class made into a law for all' (Marx and Engels 1888: 21).

Thus they made clear what may have been implied in Austin's work[1] but would remain unmentioned after his time in almost all the contributions to normative legal theory so far discussed in this book: the idea that law expresses the outlook of particular social groups but claims authority as the law of society as a whole – the law of some, imposed and legitimated as 'law for all'.

This idea was surely not strange or unattractive to Austin. His fear of the masses and distrust of democracy were much encouraged by the events of 1848 but had long predated them. As noted earlier, Maine and Pound too warned about the risks of pandering to the broadest popular will in legal matters. More recent jurists have usually assumed or affirmed the value of democracy without troubling to examine how far democratic processes actually produce a law *of all* as well as a law for all.

---

1 Because of the awkwardness, though not impossibility (see p 66, above), of thinking of sovereign and subjects as the same people.

These questions could be avoided in normative legal theory subject to a key condition being met: that law's interpretative communities remain relatively homogeneous and not subject to uncontrolled infiltration from sections of society likely to be deeply disaffected with law's fundamental practices or doctrine. With this condition satisfied, normative legal theory could avoid engaging with questions about 'the social' – the social environment in which law is created, interpreted and enforced.

So Bentham's and Austin's normative legal theory refers to law's regulated population only to check that the bulk of it is habitually obeying lawful authority. If so, the theory need ask no further questions about the social (cf Conklin 2002). The social composition of the sovereign, for example, is not a theoretical issue. Again, in Hart's theory of law, 'officials' of the legal system are made central but their nature is not discussed.

As we have noted, it is only with the emergence of legal realism that serious questions begin to be asked in Anglo-American jurisprudence about the social character of those who make and interpret law. But even here the inquiry is not 'In whose name do they do so?' and 'What are their social allegiances?', but rather 'How can lawyers know with certainty what legal officials will decide?' and 'How do judges go about their job?'. The issues are legal professional: 'How does the interpretive community function?', not: 'What is its social character?'.

In types of normative legal theory that see law as an expression of community in some sense, the social cannot be easily ignored. As has been seen, classical common law thought implied romantic, fictionalised images of community. Maine's theory tried to clarify some of this imagery through serious historical study. More recently, Ronald Dworkin has made the notion of an interpretive community central to his theory. For him, the personified community makes law. While his concern (no less than that of the legal realists) is to ask, 'How does this community function?', the very fact that his answers depend on a strong conception of community (while realism's do not) suggests that the nature of law's interpretive community ought to be studied. How integrated is any such community? What divisions or conflicts exist in it? Is it a single community or many? Who is included in it and who excluded? How does its nature shape practices of legal interpretation?

We have seen, however, that Dworkin is uninterested in these questions as issues for normative legal theory because, while law must be understood as an interpretive practice, questions as to who engages in the practice do not, for him, affect its essential nature as a practice. So normative legal theory still seems not to need to address the nature of the social.

This chapter is concerned with the breakdown of conditions that made it seem acceptable for normative legal theory to ignore systematic knowledge of the social. Theory discussed earlier foreshadows this breakdown and, in this context, it is useful to divide this earlier literature into two broad categories.

On one side are theories that see law in a 'top-down' manner, as the sovereign's commands to subjects, as a hierarchy of norms or rules (Kelsen and Hart), or as the imperative decisions of judges (realism). These theories are much more concerned with who or what rules (the sovereign, the judge, the abstract and self-renewing authority of law itself) than with law's social sources. Their hierarchical image of law addressing individuals as subjects or citizens is an image of *imperium*.

On the other side are *community*-oriented theories. Classical common law thought as well as Dworkin's, Pound's, Finnis' and Fuller's theories emphasise (in various ways) an image of law's regulated population as in some sense collective moral authors of it (or morally responsible for it) rather than merely passive regulatees. Community (its identity, values or well-being) is portrayed as the *raison d'être* or source of law. Not surprisingly, these *community-oriented* approaches typically stress the interdependence of law and morality, whereas *imperium-oriented* approaches emphasise the importance of keeping law and morals analytically distinct.

The distinction between these two types of legal theory (Cotterrell 1995: ch 11) helps in understanding the emergence of recent critical approaches which will be considered in this chapter and the next. The imperium route in legal theory might encourage questions about the politics of law and the bases of its political authority. Thus, as has been seen, realist questions about judges inspired, in critical legal studies and 'law and society' research, questions about who exercises power through law and the consequences of that exercise. Correspondingly, a community-orientation in legal theory might encourage questions about the nature of communal identity and social difference, who law speaks for and whose voices and experiences are excluded from legal expression. What does community mean in reality? What is the nature of the social? What moral foundations can (and must) law rely on when its social environment ('the realm', 'the community' or 'society') seems radically diverse rather than a morally-integrated whole?

These questions could become pressing in the context of normative legal theory only when conditions were right: only after templates for radical critique of law had been supplied (especially by Marx's work) and only after law's interpretive communities had expanded to include dissidents with the incentive to speak and the eloquence and authority to be heard.

The ghost of Marx

In Karl Marx's view, law and the state serve the interests of the dominant classes of society by holding in place a system of class exploitation. For Marx, the history of all societies up to the present day has been one of class conflict and of the subjection of some classes by others.

In capitalist society those who own factories, machinery, raw materials, land and technical processes needed to produce industrial and commercial wealth dominate all who lack such productive means of their own. These latter can earn a livelihood only by working for wages from the owners of the means of production. Capitalist society is thus divided primarily into two great classes, the owners and the non-owners of productive means, whose interests are irreconcilably opposed. The interest of the bourgeoisie who own productive enterprises is to maximise profit and enhance their capital, purchasing as cheaply as possible (by paying minimum wages) the labour power of the working class or proletariat. The interest of this subordinate class is to achieve full recompense for the use of its labour power and ultimately to free itself from exploitation. Around these classes others are arranged, but the structural opposition of the interests of bourgeois and proletarian is the essence of capitalism.

Law, in the Marxist view, acts where necessary as a coercive instrument (especially through criminal law and public order law) to repress dissent by the exploited. More routinely, however, law serves as a normal framework of capitalist social relations. Thus, contract and property law, in particular, provide the everyday basis of transactions, guaranteeing capitalists' security in their acquired profit and freedom to trade, and supplying the formal structure of employment relations by which employees 'freely' contract with employers to receive wages in return for work.

But law has another fundamental function: it helps to teach people how to think. It teaches, for example, about the 'sanctity' of property, the 'freedom' of contract and the 'equality' of citizens before law. So property is legally sacred, however much the capitalist accumulates. The propertyless must respect to the fullest extent the property rights of the wealthy, however arrogantly or coercively those rights are used. Again, legally, a contract is binding even if made by persons of unequal economic power, knowledge or opportunities. Contracts must be honoured, however arduous, unfair or unwanted: *Pacta sunt servanda*, as the legal maxim has it. Above all, law teaches that citizens are equal, even if some have no financial resources to assert legal rights while others can call on the best lawyers and pay for as much litigation as necessary to secure the aid of courts.

Modern law contains rules and procedures to address some of these actual inequalities but Marxists argue that law's broad messages remain unchanged: it shapes all classes' ideas about, for example, property, contract and responsibility, emphasising formal equality and diverting attention from inequality. So it helps to constitute the way people think of social relationships in general and the place of rights and duties in them.

Law, in this way, shapes the society in which we live because it shapes our social practice and social thought. In other words, it has an *ideological* function: it helps to make the social structures of capitalism seem normal and natural so that it is almost impossible to contemplate other ways of organising society. In response to this, Marxist theory advocates 'consciousness-raising': teaching subordinate classes how to escape from ideological thinking so as to see the reality of their position and recognise conditions under which it could be changed.

What would happen if proletarians permanently convinced by Marx's ideas actually became powerful members of law's interpretive communities? Normative legal theory might be burst asunder because, if law's interpreters disagree about the very nature and legitimacy of the existing social order, it would be hard to talk calmly, like Pound, of balancing interests and orderly adjustment through law to changing patterns of human demands. It would be hard to give meaning to the idea of community or to avoid asking why or when the bulk of the population would obey an Austinian sovereign.

In 1917 in Russia, revolution did bring Marxist proletarians into law's interpretive communities and soon produced polarised opinions among them. According to one (radical) view, law, being inherently the coercive agent of class domination or the framework of capitalist property-relations, would gradually disappear and be replaced with administrative measures untainted with bourgeois ideas of rights (Pashukanis 1978: 130–133). On the other (conservative) view, law should be retained, strengthened and turned to new purposes to serve proletarian interests and restructure society to create socialism: even bourgeois normative legal theory, part of 'the scientific inheritance of old society', could be used in this project (Vyshinsky 1951: 318–319). Ultimately the conservatives won in Russia and Marxism in legal practice in Soviet states embodied an eclectic, imperium-oriented legal theory, treating law as an instrument of power and policy. Available in theory for any purpose, law was now to be directed to the ultimate good of constructing socialist societies (Sypnowich 1990: 24–26).

Marxist legal theory has been just a curiosity for most Western jurists. Austin may have feared revolution, but Anglo-American normative legal theory has never been significantly threatened by Marxism which 'failed to make any serious inroads on the jurisprudential orthodoxy' (Douzinas and Warrington 1991: 144). One reason is that Marx's writings speak to those without property or power, thus to categories of people hardly represented in the inner circles of law's interpretive communities of judges, lawyers and jurists. Beyond this, Marx's legal thought is disabled by its lack of clear guides as to what might replace existing law. Hence the dilemma for legal theorists seeking to build on his ideas.

On one view, if law can serve socialism as well as capitalism, what is needed is not new normative legal theory (legal positivism in some form might serve well enough) so much as a radical shift in legal policies (cf Sypnowych 1990: 36). On the other, if law is tied by its very nature to commodity-relationships that reach full development only in capitalism, this has important implications for legal theory, as the Russian jurist Evgeny Pashukanis showed.

On this latter view, the essence of law is not the norms or rules that, according to most normative legal theory, create rights, duties and legal relationships. Rather law's basis is in *social relationships*, which make norms or rules meaningful and without which these would be 'lifeless, formal constructs' (Pashukanis 1978: 93, 106). In capitalist society, the form of law (as rights and duties linking autonomous persons in legal relationships) is 'rooted in the material conditions of production' (Pashukanis 1978: 94). So law's nature is governed by the nature of the social: in capitalism, by the essentially economic relationships that take the legal form of relations between property owners.

Thus, the social relations that law regulates are the skeleton around which all legal procedures and concepts are built. Legal analysis presupposes these relations, reformulating them as relations of formal equality (that is, relations between persons equal before the law). So, for Marxists, it is wholly unsurprising that orthodox jurisprudence – looking at the social world through a legal prism – treats the structures of capitalist society as utterly natural. Few jurists, according to Marx's understanding of the main class allegiances of lawyers, will have any incentive to see matters differently.

Yet the ghost of Marx haunts much of the contemporary critical legal thought to be discussed in the following pages. Marxism is the first important body of modern theory that denies any moral and political unity of the social and portrays it as a field of irreconcilably conflicting interests and radically divergent social understandings. Marxism clears the way and provides a critical vocabulary for other approaches.

If normative legal theory has been able to avoid confronting Marxist views of the social, the reasons have been political and professional rather than intellectual. Marxist legal theory has not persuasively answered political problems in modern Western societies: it has held out as a practical model nothing more attractive than the legal experience of Soviet states. Additionally,

Marxism contributes little to any sense of legal professionalism, seeing lawyers mainly as servants of capital and enemies of social progress and indicating no professional role that can free them from this pariah status conferred by the judgment of history. Marxist legal theory has had neither professional nor political applications sufficiently attractive to support its intellectual challenges.

Equality, difference and liberal feminism

If Marxism has not made Anglo-American legal theory recognise fundamental divisions of the social, other movements have been more successful in developing a jurisprudence focussed on social difference. This is because law's interpretive communities have in recent times been entered by members of previously marginalised sections of society who have refused to be co-opted to support the dominant outlooks of legal theory.

Without doubt the most powerfully influential of these new movements has been *feminism*. Why has feminism succeeded in challenging Anglo-American legal theory while Marxism failed? One reason is that it initially confronted normative legal theory not with a radical critique of that theory's conceptual frameworks but by accepting them while demanding that they should be applied conscientiously in legal practice.

'To be a feminist ... is to believe that we belong to a society, or even civilization, in which women are and have been subordinated by and to men, and that life would be better, certainly for women, possibly for everybody, if that were not the case' (Dalton 1988: 2). Feminists set about achieving this change initially without challenging any frameworks of established normative legal theory. But, starting from an insider position compatible with the theoretical outlook of many jurists, they gradually developed increasingly radical critiques of the whole enterprise of legal theory.

At first, feminists concentrated on practical demands for new legal policies to promote equality, for example to attack sex discrimination at work, to guarantee equal pay for equal work of men and women, and to ensure women's fair treatment in the criminal justice system. These demands could be made while affirming ideas underpinning much normative legal theory: the central importance of rules, interpretation and discretion, the Rule of Law and equality before the law; or that the political community is the moral author of law. Accepting these notions, at least for the purposes of argument, liberal feminists asked merely that law in practice conform to its self-images: as rationally interpreted, rule-governed, equally applied to all and morally responsive to the whole community as regards its aims and principles. They influenced law reform and insisted that legal analysis pay consistent attention to the (gendered) nature of the social.

But liberal feminism merely requires law to act in line with its usual practices of channelling power and making power's exercise more tolerably predictable. It treats law as a theoretical given. Just as, for example, criminal, fiduciary or consumer protection law acts to prevent or limit arbitrary coercion or victimisation of individuals, so should anti-discrimination law confront other kinds of victimisations as 'individual aberrations' (cf Beger 2002: 176). And, just as law is used to mitigate imbalances in resources (for example, through redistributive taxation and social welfare law), so it should authorise affirmative action to enhance opportunities for women where these have been greatly unequal to those of men. Thus, for all its great practical significance, liberal feminism essentially says nothing about the conceptual foundations of normative legal theory.

Very quickly, however, modern feminist thought moved beyond these positions. The stress on achieving legal equality seemed counterproductive in 'areas of law encompassing precisely the areas of women's lives in which they seemed most inescapably and concretely unlike men – sexuality and reproduction'. Judges' 'equality analysis proved unable to wrap itself around these intractably female issues' (Dalton 1988: 5), for example in cases dealing with employment rights surrounding pregnancy and maternity leave. Law in practice only mirrored normative legal theory's blindness to any patterned differentiation of the social. As a consequence, the recognition of difference could appear as 'special treatment' impossible to justify in terms of the idea of equality before the law.

From another point of view this concern with difference raises many questions as to how far law can recognise women's outlook and experiences and whether it can be made to do anything other than measure women's position against pre-established male standards and viewpoints. Much feminist writing has thus hovered around equality-difference issues. On the one hand, some seemingly natural differences between men and women are recognised: 'Unlike economic class, sex class sprang directly from a biological reality; men and women were created different ... The biological family is an inherently unequal power distribution'; men's 'structural capacity to rape and woman's corresponding structural vulnerability are as basic to the physiology of both our sexes as the primal act of sex itself'.[2] Recently Robin West (1992: 823) has written that

---

2   The first statement is by Shulamith Firestone, the second by Susan Brownmiller, both quoted in MacKinnon 1989: 55–56.

'because of ... [their] biological, reproductive role' women's lives are not autonomous but 'profoundly relational' in a way that men's are not.

Feminists most strongly emphasise, however, social conditions, institutions and attitudes that reinforce patriarchy: that is, the organisation and patterning of society in terms of male power, prerogatives and perceptions. So, beyond whatever differences in circumstances might be implied from sexual division itself, gender differences are seen as socially constructed. In other words, they exist as systematic patterns of domination expressed in, for example, work conditions and opportunities, domestic institutions, education, culture, politics and law.

How difference is to be conceptualised and what conclusions are to be drawn from its existence remain the most basic questions for feminism in legal thought. What are the main components of gender difference? In what respects is difference to be condemned (as gender discrimination and its consequences) and in what respects celebrated? How should law respond to gender difference?

These questions suggest the need for empirical legal theory – to look at history and social conditions systematically to see how the nature of law has been shaped in particular times and places. But they bear on normative legal theory too if the focus of inquiry is on the integrity of law's doctrinal structures, the authority that underpins them, their sources of meaning or the nature of the interpretive practices that produce them. One might ask as a sociologist: how in a particular society has law been shaped by patriarchy and served to reinforce it? And one might ask as a legal philosopher: when one participates in interpreting law and is addressed by law is this as a man or a woman, or irrespective of gender? In what ways do law's doctrinal structures reflect or deny one's experience and outlook as a man or as a woman? Is law in its very nature gendered?

Different moral voices in law

In her book *In a Different Voice* (1982), the social psychologist Carol Gilligan discusses a hypothetical problem she calls 'the Heinz dilemma':[3] Heinz knows that a particular drug, which he cannot afford, is necessary to save his wife's life; should he steal it from the chemist who stocks it? Gilligan reports the answers of two eleven-year-old children, Jake and Amy, to this question.

---

3   Quotations in this and the following three paragraphs are from Gilligan 1982: 25–31.

Jake is convinced that Heinz should steal the drug: 'a human life is worth more than money'. He thinks a judge would agree and would give Heinz a light sentence if caught: laws can make mistakes 'and you can't go writing up a law for everything that you can imagine'. He calls the moral dilemma 'sort of like a math problem with humans'. Gilligan comments: 'Since his solution is rationally derived, he assumes that anyone following reason would arrive at the same conclusion.' At 'the juncture of childhood and adolescence,' Jake's 'emergent capacity for formal thought, his ability to think about thinking and to reason things out in a logical way, frees him from dependence on authority and allows him to find solutions to problems by himself'. His 'ability to bring deductive logic to bear on the solution of moral dilemmas, to differentiate morality from law, and to see how laws can be considered to have mistakes' points to what is often seen as moral maturity.

Amy's response to the problem is, by contrast, 'evasive and unsure'. Should Heinz steal? She says: 'Well, I don't think so ... there might be other ways besides stealing it, like if he could borrow the money or make a loan or something, but he shouldn't really steal the drug – but his wife shouldn't die either ... If he stole the drug he might save his wife then, but if he did, he might have to go to jail, and then his wife might get sicker again, and he couldn't get more of the drug ... So, they should really just talk it out and find some other way to make the money.'

Gilligan comments that Amy sees the dilemma 'not as a math problem with humans but a narrative of relationships that extends over time'. The issue is not the chemist's assertion of his rights but his failure to respond to need. Amy tries to consider everyone involved in the situation. Rather than a well-defined problem of moral logic, she sees a problem of sustaining the whole network of relationships (here involving not just the chemist and Heinz and his wife, but also imagined others who might be involved with or dependent on these) and making it somehow respond to the needs of all. Communication is the key. But this is an ongoing, open, indeterminate process that does not lend itself to codified solutions: hence Amy's hesitant, exploratory discussion.

Jake's method, by contrast, stresses objectivity and strictly limits the context of the problem to make it manageable. His solution involves a hierarchical ordering of rights, involving an 'imagery of winning and losing and the potential for violence' (Gilligan 1982: 32), because a solution must be imposed for the benefit of one side at a cost to the other.

Influential criteria of moral development would treat Amy's responses as less mature than Jake's. In a follow-up study four years later, Gilligan found that Amy had apparently changed her mind. The solution to Heinz's dilemma which she now offered was the same as Jake's. But, crucially, her feelings about the issues remained unchanged. She had, as Gilligan puts it, learned to speak in another moral 'voice' – one more highly favoured and socially respected than that which she had earlier adopted. Yet the new approach she had now adopted remained, for her, ultimately unreal and problematic, rendering her 'more deeply uncertain, more susceptible to the tension between what she thinks and what she really thinks, less convinced that her voice will be heard' (Gilligan 1985: 40, 41). Jake, by contrast, had become more certain of the solution he had arrived at four years before.

Ethic of care and ethic of justice

This story illustrates the central theme of Gilligan's famous work on moral development: the nature and significance of two sharply contrasting *moral voices* (Gilligan 1985: 44) that have a direct bearing on legal thought. One voice (which Jake is developing) is that of justice, fairness, reciprocity and rights. Its tone is abstract, detached and formal. It values equal treatment according to rules but its imagery is of hierarchy: winners and losers as those rules are applied. In contrast, the other voice (which Amy wants to articulate but eventually suppresses) emphasises commitment, care and response to need. Its tone is of engagement, particularity, adaptability and sensitivity to contexts and its imagery is of a web or network of relationships.

Gilligan is careful to say that this different voice is not necessarily woman's voice contrasted with man's (1985: 38). Her claim is that, for whatever reasons, women more often than men find this voice (which she terms the *ethic of care* or *responsibility*) congenial or natural, whereas the reverse is true for the other voice, the *ethic of justice* or *rights*. The ethic of justice 'may appear frightening to women in its potential justification of indifference and unconcern' while 'from a male perspective' the ethic of care 'appears inconclusive and diffuse' (Gilligan 1982: 22).

Though Gilligan is not a jurist, her ideas have greatly influenced feminist legal theory. They are said to explain 'the alienation that many women feel while in law school and in legal practice, while suggesting that an alternative jurisprudence could be built around themes of caring, relationships and responsibility' (Whitman 1991: 499). Gilligan's identification of an alternative ethics suggests new possibilities for legal practice, which otherwise seems to respond overwhelmingly to the ethic of justice. It has inspired advocacy of mediation in contrast to win-lose rights adjudication (Menkel-Meadow 1985b) and suggests 'a whole different sort of process: dialogue between the parties' (Menkel-Meadow 1985a: 52) and perhaps a fundamental challenge to adversary legal culture. Legal argument might become 'a quiet conversation' in the courtroom (Menkel-Meadow 1985a: 57), a pooling rather than a battle of ideas. The image of law holding the ring for litigation tournaments might give way to an idea of law as a framework for co-operation designed to remove sources of friction.

Perhaps the ethic of care suggests also what equity in practice ought to be: the sensitive adaptation of legal rules to circumstances, as opposed to the sclerotic formality that some nineteenth century Chancery judges developed. And, while judicial processes have been declared poorly suited (Fuller 1978) to resolving polycentric problems (those with many ramifications and components rather than a few central issues that can be closely defined), perhaps this should not be complacently accepted (cf Allison 1999). Law might be made more receptive to the multiple perspectives of the ethic of care, for example through wide-ranging, imaginatively organised inquisitorial processes.

For normative legal theory the ramifications are very wide. If the ethic of justice is expressible in rules and rights, could the ethic of care be expressed in legal forms and processes concerned with the quality of social relationships in all their flexibility and fluidity? Could law promote 'inclusive' as contrasted with 'fair' solutions to interpersonal problems (Gilligan 1985: 45), solutions not involving one side winning and the other losing but transforming the position of both to make a more satisfactory relationship respecting each party's needs?

Undoubtedly, legal thought along these lines moves into unknown, even utopian territory, but feminist perspectives clearly have the potential to challenge any assumption in legal theory that a model of law in terms of rules or norms alone is self-evidently satisfactory or that a focus on rights must be central to interpretive practice in law. A more pessimistic view would be that the ethic of care cannot find a significant place in law's practices of interpretation or structures of understanding. Then we should have to say that law speaks always from a certain, distinctive but strictly limited ethical standpoint. This is very different from the law-morality connections that positivists and natural lawyers argue over. The point would be rather that law understands the social in a permanently skewed way: as a moral environment very different from that which large sections of law's regulated population actually seek to inhabit.

Gilligan has been accused of *essentialism*: that is, of postulating an essential quality of women, or of women's dominant moral outlook. The criticism is unfair insofar as she insists not only that the ethic of care can be appreciated and adhered to by both women and men but also that individuals often clearly understand and value both ethical outlooks. But her thesis has been influential in feminism largely because it claims that men's and women's frameworks of moral interpretation are significantly different.

The American lawyer Catharine MacKinnon, another influential contributor to feminist legal theory, calls Gilligan's thesis 'infuriating' because 'it neglects the explanatory level' (MacKinnon 1985: 73–74). The issue for MacKinnon is *why* women's outlook is often as Gilligan describes it. Her answer is that the situation of women in society, their domination by men, produces this outlook as an adaptation to circumstances. MacKinnon demands, in effect, a proper recognition of patterned divisions in the social: the ethic of care is a product of gender oppression, an adaptive response to relative powerlessness (MacKinnon 1985: 27–28). 'Women value care because men have valued us according to the care we give them ... Further, when you are powerless, you don't just speak differently. A lot you don't speak. Your speech is not just differently articulated, it is silenced' (MacKinnon 1987: 39; cf 1989: 51–52).

Recent research might suggest some mechanisms of this adaptation. In England, Belinda Fehlberg studied cases of women who, having charged their assets with their spouse's or partner's business liabilities, were later saddled with huge debts. She found that they had decided to act as a surety mainly with little attention to the rights involved but to protect relationships, demonstrate loyalty or avoid conflict – including, in some cases, violence or the threat of it. So, behind moral choices that emphasise care and responsibility may lie subtle or not-so-subtle pressures arising from a sense of actual or potential dependence, either in one's personal circumstances or more generally in circumstances that typically affect women (Fehlberg 1997: ch 6; and see Auchmuty 2001).

Systematic study of the social might, indeed, explain much about the ethic of care, but the legal significance of this ethic would not be thereby undermined, any more than the primary conceptual questions of normative legal theory are made redundant by empirical inquiries in the history or sociology of law.

Radical feminism and the gender of law

MacKinnon's own theoretical ideas are entirely different in orientation from Gilligan's. Her feminism is, in important respects, modelled on Marxism. Just as Marx focusses on domination and exploitation between classes, MacKinnon emphasises these phenomena between the sexes. While Marx sees capitalists expropriating workers' labour power, MacKinnon sees men expropriating women's sexuality: 'that which is most one's own, yet most taken away' (1989: 3), packaged, displayed, exploited, abused, distorted and violated. For Marx, ideology disguises economic inequality behind forms of legal equality, freedom of contract and sanctity of property. Similarly for MacKinnon, male domination is obscured by dominant social ideas of the nature of consent (especially to sexual activity), normal heterosexual relations, the family and femininity.

For Marx and MacKinnon, political strategies are also similar up to a point, emphasising a fusion of practice and theory, and a need to attack ideology which blinds the subordinated to possibilities for their liberation. Both Marxism and MacKinnon's feminism put much emphasis on consciousness-raising, creating awareness of the reality of social conditions to show how to act against them. But consciousness-raising, for Marx, is only a prelude to action. Changing understandings and attitudes in relation to gender can be, in MacKinnon's view, social change in itself (MacKinnon 1989: 7–8).

All this theory is directed to political action. The personal realm of sexual relations and the (socially constructed) gender roles arranged around it are the focus of a politics aimed at radical change: as the feminist slogan has it, the personal is political. But Marxism's ambivalence about law (whether it is part of the problem or part of the solution when practical political strategies are being devised) is replicated in MacKinnon's work, as in that of other feminists, many of whom consider that to appeal to law may be to rely on practices and ideas fundamentally at odds, at least in some respects, with feminism's projects (Smart 1989; Lacey 1993: 109–111).

MacKinnon's own practice as a lawyer, however, emphasises law's possibilities. Collaborating with the feminist campaigner Andrea Dworkin, she drafted anti-pornography ordinances for two American cities, aiming to facilitate private legal actions against what the drafters saw as a primary exemplification of women's subordination and degradation.

A broader object of this particular legal initiative was clearly to use law to help reshape popular understandings of the nature of pornography (MacKinnon 1985: 34–35) and so to contribute to consciousness-raising. The model anti-pornography ordinance defines pornography as 'the graphic, sexually explicit subordination of women' in words and/or pictures that portray women in any of a range of situations of dehumanisation, humiliation, violence and degradation described in a long list set out in the ordinance.[4]

The provisions directly apply MacKinnon's theoretical ideas: pornography exemplifies sexual expropriation, and women's subordination (especially violent subordination) is centred on the expropriation of their sexuality. Because the ordinance goes on to provide that the use of men, children or transsexuals in the portrayals of subordination referred to in the definition also constitutes

---

4   The MacKinnon–Dworkin ordinance, as instituted in Indianapolis, was later declared unconstitutional as infringing the US Constitution's free speech provisions: see *American Booksellers v Hudnut* 771 F 2d 323 (7th Cir 1985), affirmed 106 S Ct 1664 (1986). The terms of the model ordinance are reproduced in Dworkin [A] 1985: 24–28.

pornography, it emphasises the centrality of sexual subordination (rather than the social position of women as such) as the evil that feminism must attack.

How do these practical interventions relate to normative legal theory? Like Marxism, MacKinnon's feminism sees a fundamental, conflictual division of the social, despite appearances of practical co-operation and even harmonious co-existence. What happens when that division is reproduced in law's professional interpretive communities? Feminist lawyers, especially since the 1980s, have gradually become a significant part of the membership of these communities in Britain, the United States and other Western countries. In this situation, given MacKinnon's theses, it becomes hard to understand how legal interpretation can be a search for 'right answers' when the fundamental nature of law may be disputed. Again, it is hard to know how legal ideas are to be interpreted 'in the best light' (Ronald Dworkin's other formulation) when that depends on appealing to basic legal principles or values on which consensus is non-existent, or represents only what people (like Gilligan's Amy) 'think', but not 'really think' (cf Gilligan 1985: 49).

So, radical feminism (that is, for MacKinnon, feminism unmodified by liberal presuppositions) declares that *law itself is gendered*: all its concepts, ways of reasoning, practices and procedures embody what she calls 'the male point of view', 'the male experience' and 'there is no ungendered reality or ungendered perspective' (MacKinnon 1989: 114, 169). For example, in rape law's treatment of the idea of 'consent', criminal law's view of reasonable responses to provocation, and property law's view of rights in the home, a particular view of women's situation is maintained in legal doctrine. The relevant concepts often routinely fail to recognise women's experiences and reflect widespread male assumptions about the nature of the situations involved.

The essence of the problem from a feminist standpoint, in these cases and many others, is that legal norms presuppose and acquire meaning from social relations typically understood in a partial, limited way. Understandings of the meaning of consent or force in rape law or in sexual harassment cases presuppose a particular view of what is normal in sexual relationships (MacKinnon 1989: 111–113, 172–183). Criminal law's view of reasonable retaliation against attack (eg Edwards 1996: ch 6) depends on a view of normal social interaction and what might be threatening in it. Again, tendencies in English law to insist that beneficial property rights in a home depend on contributions to obtaining rather than maintaining it[5] suggest a view of ordinary domestic relations of mutual support as having no bearing on the law of property.

---

5   See especially *Lloyds Bank v Rosset* [1991] 1 AC 107.

Beyond such specific instances, radical feminism charges legal thought in general with making unsustainable claims to objectivity and universality. Since there is no gender-neutral viewpoint on social life and hence on law's relation to it, 'objectivity' means, in practice, a male view, and 'universality' means the particularity of male experience (MacKinnon 1989: 162–163). Thus, for MacKinnon, normative legal theory's abstractions and claims to be a 'science of law' disguise the contingency of all its viewpoints. And, as she makes clear, feminism itself can make no higher claim than to present just *other* viewpoints. 'Women's situation offers no outside to stand on or gaze at, no inside to escape to' (1989: 117). Feminism teaches, therefore, that the most to be hoped for is provisional, practical knowledge based on particular experience. Legal interpretation is an ongoing conflict between different reports from experience, not an orderly refinement of reasoning in a professional community.

The idea that existing law is gendered in all its practices and doctrine and that no interpretation or application of it can be objective or neutral in gender terms has been feminism's most important contribution to legal theory. But MacKinnon's version of this theory has been much criticised. It has been portrayed, like Marxism, as rooted in forms of social analysis out of touch with contemporary conditions in advanced Western societies. Just as class, Marxism's central concept, no longer seems to grasp analytically the range and fluidity of social diversity, MacKinnon's view of the subordinate situation of women may not grasp the complexity and variety of the situations of both men and women and the difficulty (perhaps the offensiveness) of broadly categorising individuals and their experience, giving them a fixed identity in theoretical terms that they might want to reject.

The danger here, like that discussed above in relation to Gilligan, is of essentialism: treating 'women' as a category with essential characteristics. MacKinnon writes that feminism's 'claim to women's perspective is its claim to truth' (MacKinnon 1989: 121). But what if there is no single perspective and some women see gender relations differently from the way MacKinnon's theory portrays them? Like Marxism, her radical feminism claims a higher truth beyond the variety of individuals' experiences. Opposing perspectives are to be addressed through consciousness-raising. But MacKinnon's and Andrea Dworkin's powerful focus on violence, for example, while surely justified, might divert attention from or distort many other less obvious and direct contexts of gender inequality. Moreover, for individual women who do not see themselves as victims or subordinates at all and seek to learn from and build constructively on their experience rather than relating to some universalised experience of 'women', MacKinnon's message of a general condition of subordination may seem depressingly rigid and unreal (Abrams 1990), even though its expressed purpose is liberatory.

It is unsurprising that mainstream normative legal theory has tried hard to ignore both Marxism and the most radical versions of feminism. Both of these intellectual movements derive, from their speculation on the social, definite conclusions about law's essential nature. They may see normative legal theory's interests in law's interpretive practices, doctrinal structures or bases of authority as trivial insofar as the nature of these things is conclusively determined by the nature of the social itself (seen, for example, in terms of class conflict based on economic conditions, or gender relations based on patriarchy). For its part, normative legal theory rightly sees these radical theories as largely uninvolved with its own analytical projects (except to declare those projects redundant). So no points of contact exist.

But when feminism adopts a more nuanced view of law – seeing law's gendered doctrinal characteristics as neither inevitable nor exhausting all law's important aspects – it properly demands a hearing in normative legal theory's debates. It requires that normative legal theory examine how its conceptual inquiries about law are coloured by its assumptions about the social. To the extent that these demands are ignored, normative legal theory merely shows its analytical inadequacy in current conditions.

Postmodern feminism

Claims about the impossibility of objectivity, coupled with criticisms of tendencies to essentialism in theories such as MacKinnon's, lead many contemporary feminists to conclude that feminist theory can only displace (not replace) 'masculinist narratives' in law and that no theory 'can speak univocally for all women' (Dalton 1988: 7). So a viable contemporary feminism must recognise contingency and variability in women's situations. Differences between the experience of women of different classes, races, religions or ethnic groups are only a starting point. The key question is: Is there any unity to women's experience, or men's? If not, how can feminism do what it has always sought to do: speak to and for women and represent their situation? Gender difference must be recognised, but 'its meanings are always relative to particular constructions in specified contexts' (Scott 1988: 47).

The implications of this are radical for the very idea of explanatory theory. Suppose that all legal thinking represents views from particular standpoints reflecting particular experiences or assumptions about the nature of the social. Suppose that the social is itself contingent, changeable and full of diversity and that there are no agreed criteria for understanding it. Then the range of potential standpoints in interpreting or explaining law is also bewilderingly diverse and there is no way to compare or evaluate these interpretations and explanations.

Modern thought sees in this situation the dangers of relativism or nihilism, the impossibility of saying anything because there are no bases for agreement about the significance of what is said, no secure foundations of knowledge, no universally approved criteria of judgment. This is a recipe for cynicism, an invitation to give up on rationality, on any search for coherent principle, scientific rigour or moral meaning (cf Carrington 1984).

A postmodern view might, by contrast, merely accept this situation of unending contingency and make the best of it or even welcome its liberating potential: since theory cannot have foundations, its use is more clearly seen simply in terms of the practical results it can achieve, without preconceptions, with infinite sensitivity to context, free of old philosophical baggage relating to epistemology (questions about what counts as knowledge) and ontology (questions about what we can seek knowledge about).

Thus, the American postmodern feminist lawyer Mary Joe Frug writes: 'I am in favour of localised disruptions. I am against totalising theory' (Frug 1992: 125). In her view, legal discourse is a setting for political struggle over sex differences: 'legal rules – like other cultural mechanisms – encode the female body with meanings' (1992: 129). For Frug, sex differences are semiotic – that is, 'constituted by a system of signs that we produce and interpret' (1992: 126) and law is a very important part of this system of signs. In contrast to MacKinnon's focus on 'women's perspective', Frug sees no need to postulate 'a singular feminine identity' but only a 'decentred, polymorphous, contingent under-standing of the subject' (1992: 126, 129). Women's standpoints are extremely varied but law helps to create 'a common residue of meaning that seems affixed, as if by nature, to the female body' (1992: 129). And law reinforces the culture of male/female relationships as much by what it does not say as by what it does, as much by what is not legally enforced as by what is.

According to Frug, law helps to 'terrorise', 'maternalise' and 'sexualise' the female body. Law terrorises by inadequately protecting women and encourag-ing them to seek refuge against insecurity (and, by a tragic irony, Frug herself met a violent death in 1991, killed near her home by an unknown assailant in a quiet suburban street where she might reasonably have expected to be safe).[6] Law maternalises by rewarding motherhood in many ways while penalising female conduct considered inconsistent with this (child custody, employment,

---

6 At the time of her murder she was a professor at the New England School of Law in Boston, Massachusetts. She lived in the wealthy suburbs of the nearby town of Cambridge.

birth control and abortion laws are all relevant here). And law sexualises the female body (towards monogamy, heterosexuality and passivity, but also indirectly towards commercialised forms of sex) through complex mixes of enforcement and non-enforcement of legal rules on, for example marriage, divorce, prostitution, pornography, advertising, entertainment, rape and sexual harassment. Law shapes what are considered to be acceptable social roles for women, but always in particular contexts.

Frug's thoughtful approach, sketched in posthumously published fragments of her work, focusses clearly on women's control by law but tries not to essentialise women's experience or perspectives. The way law and culture impact on women varies greatly with circumstances. Nevertheless, they define what it is to be a woman in those circumstances. Frug examines how legal doctrine enshrines control but she also stresses how enforcement varies, so she implies the importance of sociolegal research on the use or non-use of law in patterning social relationships and shaping social identities.

Frug thinks that feminism, even if it challenges the general category of 'woman' in the way she suggests, will not quickly discard it (1992: 130–131) and many writers have argued that feminism must face the political necessity as well as the theoretical difficulty of working with this category (Minow 1988). The concept of 'women's experience' may also be unavoidable despite its problems. The question is: 'How can we write about identity without essentialising it?' (Scott 1992: 33). An answer is surely to see 'experience' as being always the experience of particular historical and social contexts.

Some feminists have, however, wanted to make much more extensive claims about the social construction of difference: claims that seemingly clear natural dichotomies are produced (constructed) by particular social practices (including those of law).

Most modern feminists have distinguished between sex as something biologically determined and gender as something socially constructed (in the form of expectations about feminine roles, capacities, attributes and entitlements). But some recent writers have challenged this distinction and suggested that sexuality is no less constructed: in the sense that society imposes a 'system of compulsory heterosexuality' (Butler 1990: 18), especially by marginalising and penalising the expression of gay and lesbian sexuality. Society defines not just 'normal' femininity or masculinity, but also what 'normal' sexual preferences are. On this view, the problem of essentialism is not adequately addressed by filling in the 'category of "women" ... with various components of race, class, age, ethnicity and sexuality' to make it complete. What is needed is to transform 'existing identity concepts' that presuppose an absolute sexual dichotomy between men and women as immutable (Butler 1990: 15; and see Beger 2002).

These issues need not be further explored here. Their importance for legal theory is to suggest that when the social is viewed speculatively in terms of experience (for example the experience of a particular interpreter or observer of law) it seems to disintegrate readily into a condition that defies any fixed categorisation, since no category can encapsulate the entirety of any individual's experience.

One extreme, almost paradoxical conclusion might be that equality returns in the form of *infinite difference*. In other words, because the social is composed of innumerable different circumstances, identities and relationships, it can be generalised about only in terms of the equal uniqueness of all individual lives. So it is, indeed, appropriate for law to address the social in terms of the formal equality of subjects or citizens (ignoring actual substantive differences between human beings). Perhaps law can do no more than this. What this returns us to, then, having come full circle through the range of feminist arguments bearing on legal theory, is only liberal feminism's basic claim that law should live up to its pretensions to formal equality.

This seemingly bizarre conclusion from so much radical critique is not inevitable, however. Law's abstract formality might be re-evaluated and even treated with new respect as a result of these feminist analyses, but it can no longer be viewed as embodying objectivity or a neutral approach to the social. When Austin's writings speak of subjects of the sovereign, or Hart's speak of citizens and officials who view legal rules from internal or external standpoints, it is no longer possible to imagine that these abstract persons conceptualised in normative legal theory can also be thought of in any simple way as representing real human beings engaging in actual social practices. Hart's assumption that the study of legal language and ideas alone can be a descriptive sociology, the opening of a window on the social, cannot be taken seriously once the gulf between juristic thought and the diversity of social experience has been revealed.

For example, Hart (1960: 82–83) sees a sharp distinction in ordinary linguistic usage between 'having an obligation' (recognising a normative commitment) and 'being obliged' (merely feeling pressured to comply). How does this distinction operate if the very foundations of law's structure of obligations seem alien? One might 'think' oneself under an obligation, but in the manner of Carol Gilligan's Amy, 'really think' oneself merely obliged to comply. Hart's ordinary language distinction presupposes a world of clearly differentiated insiders and outsiders, but feminism's jurisprudence of difference suggests that law and society are not like this: there is no inside and outside, but only a host of conflicting interpretations and judgments of law and a vast range of standpoints from which they are offered. None of this makes the concepts of normative legal theory necessarily redundant for their particular analytical purposes. But it emphasises how narrow those purposes often are and how little they may relate to any serious project of understanding law's relation to the social.

Critical race theory

The far-reaching implications of this view of normative legal theory and of law's conceptual structures have been made clearer by writings that explore law's relations not just to gender but also to race. If feminist lawyers have often felt alienated from or ambivalent towards law, this has certainly been no less the case for black and ethnic minority legal scholars and activists who have noted law's casual racism in many contexts.

They have pointed to long experience of discriminatory policing and of the inability of members of ethnic and racial minorities effectively to claim or enforce rights supposedly conferred equally on all citizens. Directly or indirectly, they have asked whether for these minorities the experience of having a legal obligation is significantly different (whatever Hart's concept of law might suggest) from that of being obliged (coerced) by law – when law's alien character, the sense that it is not *their* law, is so clearly revealed to them.

Feminism has confronted women's circumscribed place in society. But what is now called critical race theory (CRT) has faced legal and social traditions that, at the extreme, have not just assumed a circumscribed social place for some minorities, but sometimes even denied *any place* in the social for them.[7] These far extremes are associated historically with slavery, genocide and colonialism. In the British Empire, the slave trade was outlawed in 1807 and slavery itself in 1833.[8] In the United States, slavery was finally abolished during the 1860s through constitutional amendments. Apart from that, the experiences of colonisation and genocide are intertwined in complex ways in Anglo-American history in the subjugation of native populations whether as part of nation-building or imperial conquest.

Such stains on *legal* history (most of these actions having been authorised or excused by law) have not been fully erased. The prominent critical race theorist Patricia Williams, a black American law professor, writes of her feelings when

---

7   The history of gender relations shows that women have often been excluded by law from the social in almost every respect: see eg Goodrich 1995: ch 5. But the history of racism reveals, not infrequently, a further extension of the exclusion of the other in some situations even to the horrific extreme of annihilation.

8   Stat 47 Geo III, c 36; Stat 3 & 4 Will IV, c 73, s 12.

examining a document 'that could have been the contract of sale of my great-great-grandmother' Sophie, a slave (Williams 1991: 157). As Williams points out, from the slave's viewpoint there is no such thing as slave law governing dealings with slaves and their position. Law is not visible to the slave. Sophie was an object of property, not a subject before law. The extremity, therefore, is to be entirely outside the social, not recognised as having even a subordinate position in it.[9]

The legacy of this situation, long after slavery, is a need to have clearly affirmed that one is fully within the social and within law's purview as subject or citizen. Williams describes how she looked for a flat to rent on moving to New York. Her law professor colleague Peter Gabel had moved to the city at the same time. Gabel was happy to make a provisional agreement to rent his flat on the basis of a handshake and good feelings about his prospective lessor, but Williams notes that in 'my rush to show good faith and trustworthiness, I signed a detailed, lengthily negotiated, finely printed lease establishing me as the ideal arm's-length transactor' (1991: 147). For Gabel – a white, middle-class, critical legal scholar, reluctant to alienate others by standing on his rights, willing to assume a sense of community and comfortable with informality – the formal lease was secondary. But, to Williams, the formality of reliable legal relations symbolised hard-won racial victories: a sense of security based on being clearly recognised in the framework of legal protections, entitlements and obligations governing the social.

Critical race theory developed as an explicit movement in American legal scholarship from the mid-1980s when a new 'strange, bright writing popped up in the law reviews' (Matsuda 1996: 48). Whereas feminist legal theory was inspired by a wealth of feminist writing in other fields beyond legal scholarship, CRT positioned itself initially mainly in relation to other critical movements in legal scholarship, arguing primarily that white critical legal scholars' typical distrust of rights 'failed to account for the understanding of rights and racism emanating from subordinated communities' (Matsuda 1996: 50).

As Williams puts the matter (1991: 148): 'One's sense of empowerment [or lack of it] defines one's relation to the law.' CRT's typical attitude to rights is not based on a liberal belief in law's capacity to provide a neutral framework of social interaction, and so the possibility of colour-blind fairness in the Rule of Law. CRT seems rather to assume that law is a substitute (inadequate but all that exists) for relations of community that can genuinely bridge all social groups.

---

9   Cf Taney CJ's adoption in the US Supreme Court in *Dred Scott v Sandford* 60 US 691, 701 (1857) of what he held to be a then-established legal understanding in American states that a black person 'had no rights which the white man was bound to respect'.

The approach is less one of belief in rights than pragmatic use of them as weapons to achieve gains and security in an uncertain world.

At any time the liberal promise of rights might be frustrated: the claimed right might turn out to be non-existent when filtered through racist interpretive practice. Securing it might be a Pyrrhic victory when mechanisms for its enforcement are found not to work for minority claimants. Yet, despite everything, when all illusions have been dispelled, 'rights rhetoric has been and continues to be an effective form of discourse for blacks' (Williams 1991: 149; and see Matsuda 1996: 6–7).

For normative legal theory the importance of these views is to affirm that law's conceptual structures are important but not in the way many theorists assume. Rules and rights matter because there is a strain in legal interpretation towards rational consistency rather than arbitrariness (and the epitome of arbitrariness is surely to distinguish legal situations on such a basis as skin colour). This strain towards consistency is represented in legal theory by recurring concerns to seek unity, system and principle in legal doctrine, and to characterise legality in terms of predictability and fidelity to rule or (in modern natural law theory) as a moral virtue founded in universal or self-evident human needs.

CRT is bound to find these kinds of tendencies in legal thought helpful. But other preoccupations of normative legal theory may be less so. Can, for example, the nature of rules and rights be meaningfully judged in terms of the authoritative (political or official) sources from which they arise? A command of the sovereign, a norm authorised by a Kelsenian basic norm, or a rule validated by reference to a rule of recognition: the significance of all of these might need to be judged by considering how they interrelate with (and are transformed by) other kinds of authority, and other commands, norms or rules that have their sources in culture: that is, in a general climate of values, understandings and beliefs in which racism can exist. The promise of law is radically scaled down in these circumstances. It becomes only the chance of protection 'in a morass of unbounded irresponsibility' (Williams 1991: 158).

Extreme ambivalence towards law – perhaps a kind of 'cynical hopefulness' (cf Matsuda 1996: 49) – is more prominent in CRT even than in feminism. This undermines all of normative legal theory's assumptions about the viability of some kind of insider/outsider distinction in relation to legal thought or legal experience. CRT is clearly inside and outside the law at all times, simultaneously observing its injustices and participating in its interpretive projects, seeing law from the standpoint of subjects who can also very easily feel the pain of being merely law's objects.

CRT represents, more powerfully in some respects than feminism, the ultimate breaking open of law's interpretive communities so that, far from law's being able to ignore the patterned diversity of the social, the social in all its diversity has entered legal interpretive practice.[10]

In a sense, the social also now refuses to allow its boundaries to be delimited by law. Those whom law claims authority to put beyond those boundaries (for example, aliens, immigrants, asylum-seekers, prisoners) demand a voice in interpreting law's moral meanings, often invoking human rights. So too do those whose lifestyles and sexual preferences defy law's traditional assumptions about 'the family', often seen as the irreducible atom or microcosm of the social. We might say that the social now demands that all of its often contradictory self-understandings should become law's understandings. For legal theory, the implication is that assumptions about the social that remain unstated in this theory must now be brought to light to reveal how they have influenced its viewpoints.

In many respects, CRT's specific findings have mirrored those of feminist legal theory. Its liberal, civil rights antecedents promoted anti-discrimination, equal opportunities and affirmative action initiatives in law, just as liberal feminism demanded that the Rule of Law's promises of equality of citizenship should be kept. Criticisms of liberal legalism's inadequacies led CRT, like feminism, directly to various kinds of radicalisation (Minda 1995: 169–171). CRT writings have noted the difficulty of articulating the 'different voices' of minorities and the way that those voices are easily silenced, often by adaptive self-censorship. In this context, as in the context of gender difference, there may be a gulf between what a person thinks and 'really thinks'. By 'setting up regions of conversational taboo and fences of rigidified politeness, the unintentional exile of individuals as well as races may be quietly accomplished' (Williams 1991: 65). One can learn how 'to accommodate a race-neutral world view ... to become an invisible black, a phantom black', rather than to 'insist on your right to name what your senses well know' (Williams 1991: 108, 119).

Again, like radical feminism, CRT attacks illusions of neutrality and objectivity created by abstract, detached styles of reasoning in law and elsewhere (Matsuda 1996: 8–9; Williams 1991: 47–48). Partly for this reason, some CRT writing has adopted a striking narrative style that emphasises personal accounts, story-

---

10　One indication of this is that legal issues are often hard to separate from more general social issues in CRT literature. Another is the insistence in much theory considered in this chapter that social relations are conceptually more fundamental than rules or rights for legal analysis, whether these social relations are seen as primarily property relations (Pashukanis); relations of sexual domination and submission (MacKinnon); race or ethnic relations (CRT); or a focus of competing ethical interpretations (Gilligan).

telling, autobiography and even the recounting of dreams. The aim is to make arguments vivid, to bring the raw experience of life as forcefully as possible into conceptual debates around law. The final trajectory, to date, of CRT may be to recognise, like postmodern feminism, that all categories of identity are potentially disabling in their rigidity. Ethnic and racial categories as markers of identity and interest may actually be experienced as fluid or indeterminate. For some people these categories may seem as deeply problematic or oppressive as the universal category of 'women' is for many postmodern feminists.

Politics, professionalism, difference

Feminism and CRT affect, at least potentially, both the politics of law and the structure of law's professional communities more fundamentally than do any of the contributions to legal theory considered in earlier chapters. By bringing the idea of the differentiation of the social explicitly into the practice of legal interpretation, feminist legal theory and CRT have opened the way for a range of other kinds of analysis of law focusing on difference, such as those reflecting gay, lesbian and transsexual experience, or highlighting religious or cultural differences. We might refer to all of these theoretical approaches taken together as a new *jurisprudence of difference*.[11]

Within this jurisprudence, feminism in particular has shown that many legal issues that were once considered to be entirely removed from politics (for example those related to the organisation of family and domestic life and the governance of sexual relations) are in fact a frontline for new types of politics. In this perspective the key to the realignment of law's relations with politics is feminism's attack on liberal understandings of the boundaries between *public* and *private* realms of life (see eg O'Donovan 1985; Lacey 1993).

From a common liberal standpoint, law marks the boundaries between two entirely separate regulatory regions: on the one hand, a public realm in which politics determines policy which is then translated, in part, into publicly enforced legal rules; on the other, a private realm of freedom from which public regulation is excluded and which is symbolised by the intimacy of home and family. Feminism has done much to destroy myths about both the regulation-free character of domestic relations and the nature of the 'freedom' protected in this realm (eg Olsen 1983).

---

11 This term is used throughout the remainder of this book to encompass all kinds of legal philosophy treating, as fundamental to their view of the nature of law, what they see as the patterned differentiation of the social.

Insofar as feminism and CRT have challenged normative legal theory's complacency about the nature of the social, they have invited it to confront political issues far more extensively than before. A current challenge to normative legal theory is that it will not be able to maintain old claims to protect the integrity of the legal realm in the face of political conflict unless law's conceptual structures (including those underpinning the idea of the Rule of Law) can be made sufficiently sensitive to legal interpreters' own experience of the differentiation of the social.

What has been the relation of the new jurisprudence of difference to lawyers' professionalism, the self-identity of lawyers as a professional group? In an important sense the effects have been largely negative. The aim of these new movements in thought about law has been, in part, to undermine lawyers' satisfaction with their familiar practices and to declare the unacceptable moral arbitrariness of these practices.

The jurisprudence of difference advocates new legal methods of interpretation, persuasion and evaluation to counter the power of established professional methods. Thus, if the different ethical voice which Carol Gilligan identifies is heard in law, it questions radically what 'thinking like a lawyer' should mean. Gilligan's insights suggest that lawyers' traditional structures of argument and analysis are flawed because they fail to recognise and reflect widespread moral expectations and understandings. And it is unclear whether the flaw can be corrected. On the other hand, calls for law to combine the ethic of justice and the ethic of care imply an optimism that legal practice may become genuinely responsive to the diversity of moral understandings pervading the social, and hence that the lawyer can become a true moral agent of social integration.

Some other strands in the jurisprudence of difference bluntly challenge the lawyer with a question: whose side are you on? Marxism posed this question most clearly, portraying lawyers' normal situation in capitalist society as that of servants of the propertied classes. So the first rites of passage for a Marxist jurist are: (i) to understand clearly that legal practice is necessarily partisan in class terms; and (ii) to identify unambiguously with the interests of the propertyless. Some radical feminism and critical race scholarship seems to move along similar lines.

Legal practice, on this view, is a form of political practice: a conclusion that critical legal studies (CLS) and, earlier, some legal realists had already reached. But unlike the situation with CLS, whose ultimate political aims are usually ambiguous, vague or contested, the politics of legal practice informed by a radical jurisprudence of difference are relatively straightforward. The aim is to use law pragmatically, as an instrument of persuasion and coercion to advance the cause of a specific constituency: for example, women in general, or some racial, ethnic, religious or sexual minority, or any broader or more specific groupings.

To put the matter polemically, legal practice in this radical understanding conforms to a stereotype of the lawyer as a 'hired gun' available to enforce the interests of the hirer. But the hirer is not, as so often in negative images of lawyers, some rich property owner or powerful corporation. Nor is it society at large, hiring lawyers as public-spirited professionals to serve its common welfare. Instead, the radical lawyer is hired to serve (and usually willingly serves, through personal commitment) the interests of particular subordinate groups, setting out to redress specific *sectional* injustices arising from prejudice, ignorance or structured inequalities.

The lawyer of this persuasion needs no belief in law's overall moral integrity, nor any strong positive valuation of it as a rational system, and may typically act without any commitment to an idea of legal professional unity focused on these characteristics of law. The radical lawyer's wide-open eyes typically see law not as a normative framework but as a battleground on which to fight with the weapons of legal training and experience, on behalf of a particular constituency, for access to state power.

For lawyers such as these, whose focus is firmly on the differentiated social rather than on the task of interpreting legal doctrine as such, normative legal theory's concern to elaborate law's conceptual unity or structure may seem dislocated and unreal: rather like asking what time it is on the moon. In other words, although the theorist's conceptual questions remain intelligible in form (and it might be useful sometimes to respect that form for particular practical or strategic purposes), they presuppose a set of reference points that in the radical lawyer's experience simply do not exist.

In a sense then, normative legal theory has reaped its reward for substantially ignoring the patterned differentiation of the social as a field of meaning and experience. The differentiated social, represented to law by various kinds of radical legal practice, now substantially ignores normative legal theory! But it might not be a welcome development to discard aspirations to doctrinal integrity, unity and system in law and to reject entirely normative legal theory's project of constructing law's underlying rationality, moral meaning and principled structure.

A radical politics of law can easily become a narrow appropriation of law in pursuit of private interests (even if these are interests of substantial social groups). Perhaps the idea that law exists to regulate, in some systematic way, the social as a unified whole ought to be maintained. As noted earlier, this is possible only if normative legal theory recognises the patterned differentiation of the social even as it attempts to show the theoretical unity of law.

Beyond that, a new sensitivity is surely also required to the shifting boundaries of the social itself, to changes in its scope and nature, and hence to changes in the range and character of law's regulatory responsibilities. These matters, which pose the greatest current challenges for normative legal theory, are addressed in the final chapter.

Chapter 9

The deconstruction and reconstruction of law

On one interpretation of the lessons of the jurisprudence of difference, a serious crisis looms for legal theory. Law, confronted by the differentiation of the social, might seem little more than a set of tools or strategies for achieving or frustrating the interests of particular groups. If legal doctrine is just a rationalisation of *ad hoc* political decisions or a rhetoric of persuasion one might ask: what is left of law for normative legal theory to analyse as a structure of doctrine, a conceptual system, a body of principles or a practice of interpretation?

It is hard to talk of objectivity in law if all legal thought is produced from particular social standpoints. Equally, legal interpretation can hardly be considered the collective project of a single interpretive community when the interpreters are divided into many *competing* communities (reflecting different experiences and interests of, for example, ethnicity, race, religion, gender, sexual orientation and economic class, in all kinds of combinations). If interpretive communities understand the very nature of law and the social in contrasting ways they surely have little prospect of agreeing on, or even constructively debating, the 'best' readings of the meaning of legal doctrine.

So the patterned differentiation of the social seems to fracture law as a system of meanings (cf Schlag 1991). How can normative legal theory make sense of law as a theoretical unity – a coherent, principled practice or rational system of ideas – when the diversity of the social has, in a sense, invaded law and challenged the projects of conceptual analysis on which legal theory has traditionally focussed?

It is not necessary to conclude that radical disagreement actually pervades all aspects of legal thought. It is rather that potentially *anything* about law might become contested because law lacks secure foundations to put at least some matters beyond the possibility of disagreement. No objective criteria of truth or value provide an unchallengeable basis of legal or social knowledge.

This, in essence, is the main problem posed for legal theory by what is widely called the 'postmodern condition' (cf Lyotard 1984), a condition in which all certainties underpinning modern thought have been challenged. The primary challenge is to *foundationalism,* 'the idea that claims of a certain category – knowledge claims, moral claims, political claims – rest on or require foundations that must be unearthed by philosophical inquiry' (Luban 1994: 134). Normative legal theory has always sought these kinds of ultimate foundations for law. Ideas of science and moral progress, as well as political ideologies, have relied on the modern faith in bases of understanding that could be philosophically demonstrated and defended.

To challenge this faith – that is, to espouse *antifoundationalism* – is, as noted in the previous chapter, to raise spectres of relativism and even nihilism for modern thought, the prospect of hopeless uncertainty and helplessness. If our ways of thinking have no secure foundations, what can we know? How can we be sure of anything? Why is any view better than another? Are there no unassailable truths?

This seemingly stark crisis for modern thought becomes a taken-for-granted starting point and perhaps even an opportunity, a liberating prospect or 'an exhilarating moment of rapture' (Douzinas and Warrington 1991: 15) for postmodernist thinkers. It opens up the possibility of 'deconstructing' false certainties of modernity so as to remove unnecessary barriers to new ways of thinking, new interpretations and evaluations, new visions of law and society. The implications of this development for normative legal theory are the concern of this chapter. But it will be important also to ask how, after law's deconstruction in the light of postmodern understandings, its *reconstruction* in new forms may be possible and vital new tasks may emerge for legal theory.

Postmodernism and deconstruction

'Postmodernity' is the term often used to refer generally to contemporary cultural conditions in Western societies which are characterised by a loss of faith in absolutes of all kinds. 'Postmodernism' sometimes designates a style that reflects those conditions, one of 'flip, condescending and mocking tones' (Frug 1992: 127) that 'celebrates surfaces, irony and pastiche and eschews master narratives' (Balkin 1992: 1973).

Narratives are stories told or accounts given from particular viewpoints, with particular interests in view. So the term 'master narrative' (or 'grand narrative'), used by postmodernist writers, suggests an account presented as a fundamental key to understanding, a set of truths, a way to orient thought and interpret experience. Master narratives are general theories or philosophies of all kinds, now said to be discredited by antifoundationalism. As part of the modern project of the Enlightenment to pursue rational knowledge, the master narratives of progress, science, reason, nature, religion, ethics and history took the form of abstract theories or philosophies claiming objective validity.

So postmodernism is also often taken to mean 'a set of general perspectives for interpreting and evaluating culture and the products of culture' (Balkin 1992: 1971), including all the master narratives characteristic of modernity. In the particular context of legal theory it opposes all general theories of law and society, seeking to show the repressed contradictions and unnoticed contingencies hidden by their logic. Sometimes this leads to doubt about the 'possibilities' of theory at all (Gabel and Kennedy 1984: 47–48; Hunt 1990: 521–522), but, more often, to a search for a different kind of theoretical analysis that can fully recognise contingency, variability and contradiction. In that way, it is suggested, theory in some modest, provisional form might reflect the fluid, open, ungrounded, insecure, undetermined, contested character of contemporary social experience.

One key to all this (a key that has been particularly important in recent Anglo-American legal scholarship) is the idea of *deconstruction* associated with the French philosopher Jacques Derrida. Deconstruction is, strictly speaking, neither a method nor a technique but an event, a transcending of the limited understandings of modern thought in various ways, though without the possibility of reaching any complete knowledge or understanding. But the term is often used to refer generally to approaches that aim at this transcending by critically interpreting texts or ideas.

Derrida notes that conventional thinking is arranged around oppositions such as normal/abnormal, simple/complex, central/peripheral, present/absent, same/different or independent/parasitic. In each case the first term seems dominant, the second defined in opposition to it. Actually, however, each term is intelligible only in relation to the other. Neither provides a self-sufficient foundation for the other. For example, centrality only makes sense if we have an idea of what it is to be peripheral but the peripheral can only be judged by reference to what is central. There is a 'chicken-and-egg quality of mutual dependence and difference' (Balkin 1987: 752), which Derrida terms *différance*.

As Jack Balkin puts the matter in a useful interpretation of Derrida's early ideas in their relation to law, Derrida 'means to deny that there is any self-sufficient, originary foundation for a system of thought ... When we hold an idea in our minds, we hold both the idea *and its opposite*' (Balkin 1987: 753, emphasis in original). This is necessary to make sense of each of them, but one of the pair of ideas is usually privileged, so that there is a tendency to think of it as though it exists independently as foundational and can dispense with its opposite, which is in fact needed to give it meaning. Thus speech is often considered more fundamental than writing, the latter being a derivation or expression of the former, but Derrida shows that the qualities that are assumed to make writing less immediate than speech actually apply to speech too, and it is possible to reverse all the arguments to show, if we wish, that writing is more fundamental than speech.

The point is that what is treated as fundamental always depends on what seems less so, and the characterisation of fundamental or not fundamental can always be reversed because ultimately there is no unassailable foundation point of thought by reference to which other matters can be judged subordinate, derivative, peripheral or parasitic.

Deconstruction, Balkin suggests, is important to legal theory because although law is more pragmatic than philosophy its 'doctrines are based upon a group of foundational concepts and principles' and, using Derrida's methods, 'we discover that each legal concept is actually a privileging, in disguise, of one concept over another' (Balkin 1987: 754). At one level, this is no more than critical legal scholars have always claimed: what seems natural, solid and secure in law is the result of forgotten, controversial political choices; matters could have been different, and legal ideas are much more contingent than they sometimes seem.

Deconstruction adds, however, the important idea that the traces of the other opposing concept always remain in the now privileged one. The politics of deconstruction involves bringing to light the hidden history of the (incomplete) suppression of the opposite or other. The other remains what Derrida calls a 'dangerous supplement' – dangerous because it always remains as a trace in the privileged concept or text. Brought to light, the supplement serves as a subversive reminder of what has been partly suppressed but ultimately cannot be excluded if the privileged concept or text is to remain intelligible. And the process of unearthing these subversive reminders is endless because every supplement is itself supplemented in an endless sequence. Deconstruction implies a 'reaching towards an unmediated, complete, self-sufficient presence' which can never be grasped (Balkin 1987: 760). So it points not towards the possibility of some 'finished' or adequate understanding but only towards endless critique of what modern thought has mistakenly taken to be foundations of knowledge, especially as expressed in its grand narratives.

Although deconstruction has been most influential as an approach to the interpretation of literary and other texts, 'the "text" [to be deconstructed] of which Derrida speaks is not merely words, but life itself' (Balkin 1987: 760). Thus, deconstruction applied to law is a call 'to remember aspects of human life that were pushed into the background by the necessities of the dominant legal conception we call into question' (Balkin 1987: 763).

This remembering is claimed to be deconstruction's subversive and liberating potential for legal study. It offers a different way to view law, one that may deliberately elevate 'trivialities' to show what has been sacrificed by their being successfully rendered trivial. Or it may deliberately 'misread' legal doctrine to draw out meanings that have been firmly excluded by the dominant readings of it. In this way dominant concepts are confronted with their repressed opposites or 'others'.

For critics of deconstruction, the results seem often perverse, wilful exercises in obscurantism, mystification or irrelevance – indeed, just misreadings or exercises in the pursuit of triviality. For sympathisers, however, deconstruction can bring to light matters that have become almost impossible to talk about because of their suppression in modern thought. It is a way of recovering ideas, traditions, aspirations and sentiments lost from, yet somehow haunting, modern legal sensibilities.

Recovering minor jurisprudences

Interesting examples of this approach in legal analysis are found in the work of Peter Goodrich. Derrida is one influence on Goodrich, another being Lacanian psychoanalysis (Goodrich 1990: ch 8; 1997). But Goodrich's aims are often those of Derridean deconstruction, sometimes expressed psychoanalytically as being to bring to light 'the unconscious of law' or to glimpse and try to reconstruct repressed traces of ideas or experiences no longer recognised explicitly in modern legal consciousness (Goodrich 1994: 127).

Goodrich frequently returns in his writings to the interpretation of a puzzling detail of Anglo-American contract law. This is the 'postal rule' according to which acceptance of a contractual offer is completed when the acceptor posts a letter of acceptance, not when the offeror receives it and, indeed, even if it is never received.[1] 'Such an arbitrary drawing of the line [on the question of what is needed to complete the contract] ... has been viewed by most commentators at best as an ill-conceived concession to the needs of business certainty and at

---

1 *Adams v Lindsell* [1818] 1 B & Ald 681; *Eliason v Henshaw* 4 Wheat 225 (1819) and American authorities cited in the note to that case, as reported in 4 Law Ed 556. See Goodrich 1990: 149–153; 1994: 120–126; 1995: 198–210.

worst as irrational by virtue of being inconsistent with the consensual principles of contract formation' (Goodrich 1995: 198). Goodrich insists on the exceptional nature of the rule judged against requirements for full communication and voluntary assumption of obligations in creating contracts.

Thus, the postal rule is the 'other' of general contract principle but, seen from another standpoint, 'the postal exception may well be more significant than the standard rule' (1995: 202). Historically, it was established before the standard rules on offer and acceptance. More importantly, while the idea of 'full communication suggests a linguistically unrealistic ideology of consensus, the postal rule ... faces the consequences of ... failure of delivery or noncommunication which constantly threatens to undermine the subjective theory of contracts' (1995: 202). In other words, the postal rule preserves a trace of a reality that the rule of full communication, 'part of the blindness of the law' (1995: 202), ignores: that it may not be important for a contract to be 'adequately consensual', that it may not need to be an *agreement* in any significant sense.

In Derridean terms, contract law operates with a 'metaphysics of presence': the image of people meeting, speaking and agreeing. But the repressed other of contract, which remains very much its reality, is that writing is more fundamental than speech, and the mechanism (here the postal service) is more fundamental than the intention it carries. Perhaps the postal rule also symbolises the fact that the idea of the freedom of the parties in contract always depends on legal and social institutions which the parties cannot control. Freedom relies on its other or opposite, constraint. Ultimately what is fundamental and what derivative or exceptional depends on how we look at it.

Goodrich offers no proof or even convincing rational justification of any of this. No grand narratives of science, logic or historical causation are prayed in aid. The discussion is rich in rhetoric, a lost art with whose fate he is much concerned. The reader cannot rationally argue around these interpretations but only accept or reject their suggestiveness. The aim is not to pursue 'the classical but intrinsically uninteresting' question of 'what law in general is' but to explore 'how law is lived', focussing on its 'rituals, its repetitions, its texts, its symbols, its icons' (Goodrich 1990: 2–3), on what it denies and represses (and so, by negatively recognising, affirms).

Like many postmodernist legal scholars, Goodrich is concerned with the 'other' that law excludes and so implicitly recognises. This other may include *phenomena* such as kinds of judgment, evaluation, experience and expression that perhaps once related to law but are now considered entirely alien to it: a spirituality or poetics now excluded from law but that may reflect something important it has lost in its 'soulless modernity' (Goodrich 1995: 247). Equally, the other may refer to categories of *people* that law has treated as not its subjects, or not fully so – such as women (Goodrich 1995: chs 5 and 6) or aliens in its jurisdiction (Douzinas and Warrington 1994: ch 6); or to human *characteristics* law ignores in its view of the subjects it regulates.

Consider a further example of the profound or the trivial, depending on how one wishes to read the analysis. Goodrich describes a case unlike any that might be met in the law reports. A man's advances are emphatically rejected by a woman with whom he is sexually obsessed. He offers her a large sum of money if she will sleep with him just once to cool his erotic madness. She agrees. But the night before the contract is to be fulfilled, he dreams he is making love to her and next morning he discovers that his vivid, exciting dream has cured his mania. The woman, however, demands payment on the grounds that her image has cured him and so she has fulfilled the contract, even if by means different from those envisaged. A judge charged with resolving the dispute commands the man to bring the promised money to court. Before both parties, the judge takes the coins and pours them into a brass bowl. Judgment is given for the woman but the coins are returned to the man because, just as he has been satisfied by the woman's image and an imaginary pleasure, so the woman has been paid by the sight and sound of the gold (Goodrich 1996: 38–39).

In another case a suitor seeks the love of a woman who already has a lover. She promises that if she were to lose her present lover she would take the new suitor in his place. Later she marries her lover but the suitor demands that she keep her promise because now she no longer has a lover but merely a husband. The woman denies that she has lost her lover by marrying him. The Court of Queen Eleanor of France finds in favour of the suitor on the grounds that the relations of lovers and married couples are fundamentally different and the husband has necessarily ceased to be a lover of the woman who is now his wife (Goodrich 1996: 29).

These 'cases' are trials before 'courts of love'. The existence of such courts in medieval times is recorded in literature but they are widely regarded as 'products of romantic fiction, and as such ... trivial affectations, ironic and theatrical diversions from truth' (Goodrich 1996: 37). From a modern perspective they have no jurisprudential importance. Yet, as vehicles of a subversive, repressed or, indeed, merely playful and unserious 'minor jurisprudence' they might suggest how people (women) and things (the play of emotions, the poetry of relationships), excluded from the real business of law, try to take on its forms, looking for a place in them.

The courts of love bring into a kind of legal discourse matters that have no place in law and seem absurd in it because legal analysis itself is so alien to the facets of life presented to it in this way. Goodrich suggests there are many such minor jurisprudences, cast off from or never recognised in modern law, yet somehow related to it. Thus, the aristocratic women who may have amused themselves as witty judges in courts of love (and had no possibility of being judges in any other court) present instructive models of a law that could never be: a legal fantasy that casts a different, perhaps melancholy gaze on the law that actually exists.

While the jurisprudence of difference stresses relationships rather than rules as basic to law, postmodernist jurisprudence argues for 'a right to a life – to a literature, a poetry, an ethics, an intimacy or imagination – within law' (Goodrich 1996: vii): something that can give vitality to its barren, life-drained forms. Law is thus seen as much more than the abstract concepts that normative legal theory has taken as its basis. But what exactly that 'much more' amounts to cannot be conclusively defined, just as deconstruction cannot postulate any endpoint for its analyses.

Law without foundations

Postmodernist thought takes to its ultimate conclusions an insight of normative legal theory noted earlier in this book: that law regulates its own creation.[2] Normative legal theory always avoids the radical implication of this notion (the conclusion that legal reasoning is ultimately *circular*) by seeking foundations of law in concepts such as a habit of obedience grounding sovereignty (Bentham, Austin), the acceptance by officials of a rule of recognition (Hart), or the effectiveness of a basic norm (Kelsen). The search is for law's 'own particular origin, some paternity which distinguishes it from any other institution, and from any other structure of norms' (Davies 1996: 65).

Law's foundations, if they can be specified, are assumed to give it identity and unity, fix its scope and limits and indicate the source of its authority. So the search for foundations has been unavoidable as the key to answering the central questions of normative legal theory. But postmodern antifoundationalism denies the very possibility of ultimate foundations of law and legal authority. So postmodernist thought stands astride the path of normative legal theory's researches, challenging them even more uncompromisingly than does the jurisprudence of difference considered in the previous chapter.

According to postmodernists, the circularity of normative legal theory's most familiar ideas is easily shown. For example, in Hart's thesis 'the officials recognise the rule [of recognition] which recognises them as officials' (Davies

2   See Chapter 4, above, p 104.

1996: 27). In other words, although the view of rules held by those people whom Hart calls officials is crucial in determining the minimum conditions of existence of a legal system,[3] officials of a legal system are only recognisable as such if the legal system already exists. The analysis is circular. Similarly in Kelsen's theory the effective presence of a basic norm indicates the existence and identity of a legal system but, after a revolution, the basic norm can only be conclusively identified once law is functioning in a stable manner (Davies 1996: 82–83). Which comes first? Legal system or basic norm? Again, natural lawyers see a higher law as providing ultimate authority for human (positive) law. But nature 'refuses to reveal its commands to us clearly' and 'some human institution or individual' needs authority conferred on it (By whom? From where?) 'to clarify the content of natural law'. So 'human contingencies' remain necessary to a theory designed to transcend them (Davies 1996: 29).

A different kind of problem can be raised in relation to Austin or Bentham's theories of sovereignty. Why should it be assumed that the existence of a habit of obedience confers authority on a sovereign to make law? The habit of obedience cannot be analysed in legal terms (Conklin 2002). The fact that someone is regularly obeyed does not *logically* produce any reason to recognise that person as authorised to create law.

A parallel argument can be raised in relation to Ronald Dworkin's legal theory. For him, the key to law lies in its interpretive character. But why are struggles around the use of governmental power to be thought of as deliberations of an interpretive community, as though that, in itself, validated them as law? What is presented is less a basis for law than 'an idealised and ... limited integration of conventional social values' (Davies 1996: 99); the 'grand narrative of law ends up having a rather lame hero: a functional judicial superman [Hercules] standing in for (the friends of) the professor of jurisprudence' (Douzinas and Warrington 1991: 24). How does interpretive practice create something entitled to recognition as law, with foundations making it more than just words uttered in debate? A focus on interpretation does not explain the act of decision or judgment which is 'a non-logical move' and an ultimately coercive ending of debate (Davies 1996: 34, 91–100), dependent on structures of power that interpretive theory lacks the resources to analyse.

Problems such as these underpin postmodernists' claims that law's authority is founded on myths and hence that much else in its doctrinal structures has similarly (rationally) shaky foundations (cf Fitzpatrick 1992; 2001).

The claims are undoubtedly striking but something important seems missing from them because of the limited, perhaps ungenerous way, in which they read

---

3 See Chapter 4, above, p 95.

normative legal theory. The attack is essentially on legal theory's conceptual analyses and the method of attack is to show that all such analyses are circular or based on arbitrary postulates that cannot be rationally justified. But what if a normative legal theorist were to admit all this? Would that be to admit the redundancy of normative legal theory? Surely not, if the theorist were to admit also that conceptual analysis of law always presupposes social conditions that must be examined empirically. If law is analysed conceptually in isolation from its specific social contexts it does, indeed, seem circular (and, one might add, arid and scholastic). But the point is that it cannot properly be so analysed and much legal theory implicitly recognises this.

For example, Austin's 'habit of obedience' is a shorthand reference to social conditions in which law can exist, which he assumes to be those of peace and popular acceptance of government. Once these conditions are actually in place in a given territory, lawyers and legal theorists can observe the recognition of authority as a factual state of affairs. Then the task for normative legal theory is to make sense conceptually of the structure of legal authority and the rational character of law that can exist in such conditions of political and social stability.

Similarly, the recognition of Hart's officials is essentially an empirical matter (consistently with the methods of linguistic philosophy, Hart would probably advocate studying it in terms of language use). A sociologist would point to the historical emergence of professional classes of advisers, advocates, adjudicators and rule enforcers as a social process occurring perhaps at recognisable stages in the development of societies (Schwartz and Miller 1964). Conceptual analysis of officials' internal views of legal rules becomes feasible and realistic as social development produces the conditions for this. To consider the matter solely in terms of conceptual analysis as though these conditions were not relevant makes it obviously circular: conceptual inquiries must be viewed in social context and the social context needs empirical (sociological and historical) analysis.

Again, to theorise law as an interpretive process is inadequate if done without examining empirically the social structure of interpretive communities: how they come about, what their composition is, how power is exercised in them, how they relate to each other and what their objectives are. But, if systematically related to these matters, the idea of law as an interpretive practice can be enlightening.

Similar responses can be made to most of postmodernism's criticisms of circularity in legal theory. Postmodernist criticisms are powerful but they do not destroy normative legal theory's projects. They merely show that those projects (often too narrow as their authors frame them) must be reinterpreted in a sociological context. Merely? The extent of the reorientation of thinking required here must not be under-emphasised. Some legal philosophers might find it no less painful to hear that their conceptual analyses depend entirely on sociological validation than to be told (by postmodernists) that their project is pointless because of its circularities. The choice is between postmodern deconstruction or sociological reconstruction of legal theory. In fact, the former should lead to the latter.

Postmodernist analyses themselves, however, usually avoid systematic empirical inquiries because many of social science's theories and methods import the kind of master narratives that postmodernism rejects. But this lack of interest is ultimately disabling. For example, when postmodernists ask how law, with all its circularity, initially comes into being and is developed, they typically speak of 'violence' (coercive acts, decisions backed by force) as the answer (eg Derrida 1992: 13–14, 31). But this concept remains opaque, generalised, indeterminate and usually unconnected with any detailed historical or social inquiries. The postmodernist challenge should not go so far as to undermine support for systematic empirical inquiries about law. I shall suggest later that normative legal theory must ally itself with these inquiries if it is to retain relevance in contemporary legal conditions.

Derrida, justice, autopoiesis

How might postmodern antifoundationalism be developed into new legal theory? Two different directions are signalled in recent literature.

Derrida and justice

One is shown by Derrida's (1992) essay 'Force of Law' which has been much discussed by Anglo-American legal scholars. His purpose here is to make clear that deconstruction (and by implication postmodernism) is not merely a matter of endless critique 'enclosed in purely speculative, theoretical, academic discourses' but aspires 'to something more consequential, to *change* things' (Derrida 1992: 8, emphasis in original). And Derrida sees law schools, rather than university departments of literature or philosophy (where his work has had most influence) as the proper home of ideas that can potentially make such an impact.

The ideal to which law aspires is clearly justice. Thus, deconstruction of law (the endless confrontation of legal concepts with their 'dangerous supplements' and the demonstration of their always insecure foundations) aims always at finding justice, yet can never do so because, just as deconstruction has no limits, justice cannot be conceptualised as a finite quality. Derrida even suggests that deconstruction (of law) *is* justice, by which, presumably, he means that justice is the transcendent state of affairs that law can never reach yet must always be driven towards by deconstructive questioning. Justice is 'infinite, incalculable, rebellious to rule and foreign to symmetry'. Law, by contrast, is 'stabilisable and statutory, calculable, a system of regulated and coded prescriptions' (1992: 22).

At one level, this is hardly news for legal theory or for practising lawyers who are entirely familiar with the idea that the juxtaposing of concepts of law and equity in legal systems is ideally always a recognition of the timeless problem of adapting rules to the requirements of justice in individual cases. Restated in Derrida's terms, however, these commonplace ideas take on some new aspects. He suggests that any modern science of law is aimed at an impossible but vital task: pursuing justice, which cannot even be defined, let alone achieved.

So law and equity (individualised, particularised justice) do not merely confront each other as Anglo-American lawyers might think. Rather, law's *reason for existence* is to achieve justice, and justice cannot be pursued effectively *except* by means of law. Thus, to say that law lacks foundations is not necessarily to belittle it as a form of knowledge and practice. Perhaps legal theory should be wholly unconcerned with the ungrounded character of its knowledge and reasoning and concentrate instead on clarifying what the pursuit of justice entails. Since deconstruction is the endless effort to recognise the other (the suppressed opposite or excluded) it follows that justice is, for Derrida, limitless recognition of responsibility to the other.

The aim becomes that of finding an ethics to guide law and give it meaning in postmodern conditions where faith in grand narratives has disappeared. But, as Jack Balkin points out, a limitless recognition of responsibility, in the sense of an infinite concern for the other, is not practical and is likely to remove all those criteria that make legal and moral evaluations possible (Balkin 1994: 1149–1154). An 'ethics of alterity' can only operate when contexts in which that ethics is to operate (that is, in which justice is to be sought) can be categorised so that cases can be distinguished. Justice depends on categories, usually legal ones, and categories can be established only in relation to specific *contexts*.

Consequently, it follows again that postmodern efforts to confront legal theory can only lead to constructive outcomes if they recognise the need to study empirically the social contexts of law. Without that, postmodernist thought produces only demonstrations of circular reasoning or abstractions impossible to operationalise in practical legal contexts. But Derrida shows no interest in empirical studies of law's social contexts (cf Teubner 1997).

Autopoietic law

A very different response to antifoundationalism is found in Niklas Luhmann's *autopoietic* theory of law, developed in the Anglo-American context especially by the comparatist and private lawyer Gunther Teubner. Autopoietic legal theory starts by explicitly recognising law's unfounded character. The fact that law regulates its own creation is, for autopoieticists, the most important thing about it and, far from a weakness, makes law effective to fulfil its modern functions. To say that modern law is autopoietic is to say that it is, in particular ways, self-producing, self-maintaining and self-describing (Teubner 1993: 24).

Certainly, law is continually stimulated in its operations by 'external' develop-ments such as economic interests, scientific information and policy demands, but it processes information from these sources always in its own way, 'internally' to the legal system, which is thought of here not as a set of institutions but as a discourse or system of communication of which the essential, defining characteristic is that all its communications centre on the opposition 'legal/illegal' (see Přibáň and Nelken 2001). All information that the legal system chooses to notice is processed in specifically legal terms, in terms of the need continually to distinguish legal from illegal, or legally right from wrong. All law's communications focus on this binary coding.

Considered solely in relation to normative legal theory, autopoiesis theory might be seen as a response to postmodernist criticisms of this theory. In answer to the charge that normative legal theory's analyses are circular or based on arbitrary postulates that cannot be rationally justified, theorists of autopoie-sis simply answer: 'True! But so what? This is how law is and it works; it does its job.' Autopoiesis theory sees law as a discourse in which legal ideas are always produced from other legal ideas, legal justifications are always justifications in terms of other law, and the nature of law is ultimately described in circular ways. None of these features impedes law in fulfilling its specific function of producing decisions as to what is legal or illegal. And those decisions then provide information which other systems can read in their own way, according to *their* own criteria.

So law is just one among many systems in a modern complex society. Science, the economy and the political system, for example, may also be autopoietic systems – each functioning independently in terms of their distinctive binary coding (for example, 'truth/falsity' in science, 'efficient/inefficient' in the economy). The separation and reintegration of systems, and their emergence as autopoietic, is in Luhmann's analysis an evolutionary response to complexity in modern societies. Distinct discourses eventually arise to deal with the different aspects of modern social life.

The implications of autopoiesis theory extend far beyond normative legal theory's concerns. But, viewed solely in relation to them, it gives exactly the answer that, I suggested earlier, should be addressed to postmodernist claims about law's ungrounded character: the significance of the circularity of legal thought must be understood *in social and historical context*. So Luhmann and Teubner are concerned with social developments (essentially increasing social complexity) that have made it necessary (though not inevitable) that law should become self-referential in the way autopoiesis theory describes.

The most important problem with the theory is that although it claims to be sociological it is not sociological enough. It focuses on the abstraction 'law' (as a discourse or communication system) rather than on professional, political, organisational and ideological conditions that have made possible law's presentation as an autonomous system (Cotterrell 2001). In the autopoieticists' view, law acts, 'thinks' (Teubner 1989) and develops as an abstract system. But this book has suggested that normative legal theory's abstractions should be seen, in part, as a response to professional and political needs of people (especially lawyers) with specific interests and concerns.

Autopoiesis theory offers a pure sociology of law's abstraction. It treats human individuals as agents of this abstract legal system, but the system is portrayed as having a life of its own in some sense. The social context that gives it that apparent life remains only very faintly sketched. The particular forces and interests that give rise to law's development, inspire its interpretations and guarantee its authority remain vague in autopoiesis theory. The autopoieticists' prevailing image of law is of self-sufficient abstraction.

Law's empty shell

An idea of contemporary law's self-sufficiency pervades much postmodernist legal theory and, despite the general failure to explain the social context that makes this idea seem plausible, the idea in itself is postmodernism's most important contribution to legal theory. The implication is that law is unaffected by the collapse of faith in grand narratives and may even be more powerful as a consequence of it. Contemporary law might even be the perfect postmodern form of knowledge: transient and disposable, rooted in nothing more than decisions (of courts or political authorities) that could go one way or another, ethically uncommitted or ambivalent, a technique available for any purpose, a purely instrumental or pragmatic knowledge, and a knowledge concerned only with surfaces and masks (treating persons before it mainly as interchangeable subjects, with little concern for the characteristics that make each human being unique).

Seeing contemporary law in this way, many postmodernist scholars emphasise its ethical emptiness – its unconcern with the ultimate worth of human relationships. They note its 'sepulchral quality' and 'something decayed or rotten' in it 'which condemns it or ruins it in advance' (Derrida 1992: 39; Douzinas and Warrington 1994: 51, 194). Yet the collapse of grand narratives and the fragmentation of meaning might make law 'the last universal, the emblem of the same in an era of encroaching difference, the symbolisation of a formal unity in the face of substantive fragmentation' (Goodrich 1995: 242).

Consequently, and with appropriate postmodern irony, ethically-empty law is seen by some writers as taking on moral authority as the only universal regulation in contemporary societies in which all other authority is open to challenge. Legal 'form acquires moral value in itself and the law becomes the modern repository of a downgraded virtue' (Douzinas and Warrington 1994: 157).

Thus, another major theme of postmodernist legal theory is that law itself creates meaning in a postmodern world where other sources of stable meaning have become contested and unreliable. Law, in this sense, is constitutive of society (Davies 1996: 51–56), producing the relatively stable understandings on which social life depends in conditions where there are few other sources of certainty. So law supports stable ideas of responsibility, subjectivity, obligation, entitlement, fault, property, contract and authority, and a whole range of parameters of individual life (cf Goodrich 1990: 281–283).

It should be clear that if postmodernists avoid normative legal theory's 'intrinsically uninteresting' question of the nature of law, they nevertheless often have much to say both about the nature of law's conceptual structures (riddled with circularity and founded on arbitrariness) and its moral meanings (ultimately empty yet practically powerful). For this reason, legal theory cannot avoid confronting postmodernist critiques.

But the often rhetorical style of postmodernist writing on law, coupled with its lack of concern for systematic empirical examination of law's social contexts, threatens to undermine much of its critical power. For example, when Goodrich disclaims interest in general questions about the nature of law he leaves himself open to the criticism that it is unclear what law he is interested in and what law is outside the scope of his discussions. Like most other postmodernist jurists he focusses mainly on legal traditions of his own nation: in his case, English common law. But, in the absence of any strong concern with historical development (analysis of which might admit grand narratives of historical causation or progress), illustrations are taken as readily from the seventeenth century as the present day, as though chronology were irrelevant.

Critique is disembodied and suggestive, conforming to postmodern not modern criteria of discourse.

Ultimately this poses a serious dilemma, apparent also in claims about law as constitutive of society. What, if any, are the contextual limits of postmodernist (and other critical) claims? Many writers, of various theoretical persuasions, now stress the idea of law's constitutive power. This emphasis is present, for example, in Mary Joe Frug's feminist claims that law encodes the female body with meanings and plays a major role in constructing sex differences.[4] Other writers argue that law has a powerful effect in constructing racial difference and identity (Lopez 1996). On one view, law 'is a discourse that mediates among virtually all the discourses of our world, all ways of talking' (White 1990: 261).

Perhaps law does have this great power in some societies and cultures. But in others the claim can seem absurd. Law must be analysed in context. In the United States, where law has remarkable cultural centrality, the idea of its overwhelming constitutive power may seem superficially plausible, especially as modernity's grand narratives are challenged. But, elsewhere, the idea of law having an almost autonomous power to establish understandings and values is much less persuasive (Douzinas and Warrington 1991: 120; 1994: 172). This idea may merely provide an excuse to forget that law is shaped by its cultural contexts as much as it influences them – even if, in postmodern conditions, cultural context shapes law into the forms postmodernist writers describe.

Pragmatism

In the Anglo-American context, perhaps these contextual considerations help to explain a significant difference between some recent orientations in American legal theory, on the one hand, and British and some other non-American anglophone theory, on the other.

In American legal thought pragmatism has enjoyed a strong recent renaissance. Pragmatism's significance as a philosophical underpinning of American legal realism was noted earlier.[5] In a contemporary postmodern climate in which all philosophical foundations of knowledge are challenged, pragmatism adopts a reassuring, practical, business-like position. 'Whatever works in context becomes the standard for ... theoretical investigation and judgment' (Minda 1995: 230): what we know is what produces results, knowledge that can be put to use. No deeper foundations of understanding are necessary:

---

4   See Chapter 8, above, pp 226–227.
5   See Chapter 7, above, p 178.

'In its rejection of speculative distinctions and possibilities detached from practice and its insistence that workaday concepts do not require theoretical foundations, pragmatism offers a liberating prospect to legal theorists: the prospect of proceeding directly to the ordering of practical affairs without becoming enmired in the scholastic swamps of philosophy' (Luban 1994: 127).

Pragmatism at its most optimistic suggests that 'human nature is not fixed within its present depressing parameters' (Luban 1994: 127). This is because pragmatist antifoundationalism proclaims a new freedom from deterministic, constraining, fixed ideas about history, society and law. The traditional speculations of philosophy can be discarded. Knowledge, scaled down to no more than practical ideas that work in context, sets out to solve the problems of the future unconstrained by the intellectual baggage of the past.

As an instrumental approach to knowledge, pragmatism coexists easily with instrumental views of law (such as legal realism). Its temper is very different from that suggested by the melancholy view of morally-empty but powerful law that, for example, Goodrich's work offers. Pragmatist legal theory requires that law's capabilities and limits be judged in the specific contexts of its use. In that sense, it suggests a need for the modifications of normative legal theory (to make it more sensitive to social context) suggested earlier in this chapter. But its resolutely instrumental approach misses much of the moral force of postmodernist legal theory's critique of law that this chapter has emphasised. American pragmatist legal theory tends to portray law as an empty vessel that can be filled with any content, no longer needing the moral underpinnings that philosophy might once have been asked to provide (Luban 1994: 136): for pragmatists, law's moral and philosophical emptiness opens possibilities to seize.

By contrast, much recent postmodernist legal theory in Britain, at least, sees this emptiness as a moral challenge and a cause for apprehension. Pragmatism seems generally unattractive in this context because it usually fails to engage theoretically with profound moral issues about the nature of contemporary law. It appears complacent in the face of what postmodernists see as the 'estrangement' (Goodrich 1996: vii) of law's clever technicalities from meaningful life. The advent of purely instrumental views of law is not, on this view, a liberation to be celebrated but a loss to be mourned.

It would be easy to speculate about links between the more optimistic aspects of resurgent American pragmatism with its 'experimental, try-it-and-see approach to life' (Luban 1994: 140), and some wider American outlooks, especially in a period of confidence while the United States enjoys sole super-power status. The pragmatist view that knowledge is validated by successful practice assumes that adequate criteria exist for judging success or failure, that these terms have reliable meaning when applied to life's complexities, ambiguities and ironies. In any case, much postmodernist legal theory outside the United States (certainly in Britain) suggests a different outlook from that of pragmatism: a deep uncertainty as to what ethical underpinnings of contemporary law (and perhaps of the social in general) are now possible, but a strong sense that such underpinnings must be rebuilt and that law without them is indeed an empty shell, powerful but dangerous, because ethically unguided or morally incoherent.

Reorienting legal theory

The currents of criticism that now surround normative legal theory do not necessarily sweep it into irrelevance. These critiques, valuable as many of them are, do not destroy the worth of normative legal theory as an enterprise. It is still necessary to try to draw conceptual maps of law, to examine the bases of legal authority, to consider the unity or structure of legal doctrine, to explain the characteristics of legal interpretation and to ask how far law can usefully be analysed independently of morality or ethical debate. However, contemporary critiques considered in this and the previous chapter show that all of these matters must be considered differently from the ways in which the classic normative legal theorists usually considered them.

First, legal theory cannot aim to draw a single universally correct conceptual map of law; many can be drawn and they may serve different purposes related to the different standpoints of the mapmakers. But we might still hope to integrate to some extent, or productively compare, these different views of law, broadening understanding by treating each of them as a valid, partial perspective on legal experience.

Second, the bases of legal authority for which normative legal theory has searched have to be seen as many and inherently controversial: they are, from one viewpoint, mythical; from another, they lie beyond law as jurists understand it, in social conditions which juristic thought can only presuppose.

Third, questions about law's systemic unity and structure need to be rethought. It remains important to lawyers that legal doctrine should have some structure and unity, and normative legal theory has plotted and rationalised their efforts to find this. But portraying the unity and structure of law has to be recognised now as also an attempt to represent a unity and structure of the social. And it is necessary to ask what kind of unity and structure that can be.

Fourth, as regards legal interpretation, far more needs to be known about interpretive communities: how they work and where the power or authority lies to make interpretations binding as law.

Finally, while morality haunts law the relationship between law and morality remains unclear. Contemporary law, as postmodernism portrays it, is ethically barren, yet morality of a sort may be fabricated by this law. Law's moral meaning seems deeply problematic today. Yet it seems vital to clarify what this meaning can be in the context of the ethical issues that arise in human relationships and the moral frameworks available to organise contemporary social life.

How is it possible to reconstruct normative legal theory in the light of contemporary critiques? Postmodern antifoundationalism has challenged standard claims about law's bases of authority. As has been seen, this can encourage a view of law as self-founding (as in autopoiesis theory) but the significance to be attached to the claimed circularity of law's ways of reasoning can only be judged by studying law in social context. Normative legal theory's conceptual inquiries need to be related to specific historical settings and social conditions. It is necessary to ask what social tasks legal reasoning has to fulfil in particular contexts. So the postmodernist critique ought to point legal theory towards *systematic study of the social.*

At the same time, this critique casts doubt on familiar ways of picturing law's limits by means of such concepts as sovereignty, rule of recognition or basic norm. If these concepts are not foundational guides to what must be recognised as law, the province of jurisprudence may be less determinate than jurists have usually assumed; it may be harder to state clearly what is or is not within the scope of law so as to exclude 'the non-legal, the extraneous, law's other' (Douzinas and Warrington 1991: 25). Jurists' typical confidence in separating law from non-law, legal insiders from outsiders, and internal from external views of law, may be unwarranted (Cotterrell 1998). A broader, *more pluralistic view of law* may be needed if the idea is accepted that any juristic (lawyers') conception of law will necessarily contain (and depend on) the trace of its suppressed 'others' – that is, forms of regulation not recognised officially by courts or other state agencies but significant in the experience of citizens (Tie 1999).

The jurisprudence of difference, considered in Chapter 8, adds other insights. It challenges normative legal theory's relative unconcern with the nature of the social as a field of diverse understandings and experience. In particular, it challenges the assumption that portraying law as a conceptual unity accurately represents the character of the social as a unity. The jurisprudence of difference asks whether society is unified in a legally significant sense and whether law can ever have the same meanings for all parts of the social. It suggests that law must recognise patterned differences in social experience and understanding at the same time as it insists on the formal legal equality of persons. Thus, this theory implies that law is concerned with regulating *differentiated communities and relationships between these communities*, which represent the differentiated character of social experience. But the jurisprudence of difference does not adequately indicate how communities should be conceptualised, what their boundaries are or how law should treat them and address relations between them. Clarifying these matters is a vital task for legal theory.

As has been seen, the jurisprudence of difference suggests a further reorientation of normative legal theory: towards treating *social relationships as a basic focus of legal thinking*, perhaps more basic than other foci such as rules, norms and rights. All of these latter concepts are important but, as portrayed in critical literature, they often appear derivative rather than central. Rules are a basic currency of law, but they exist to support social relations, whether just or unjust. Similarly, asserting rights is often seen by the jurisprudence of difference as a tactic (necessary but unreliable and not to be overestimated) to secure satisfactory social relations.

How should these ideas be mapped on to existing approaches in normative legal theory? In Chapter 8, a distinction was drawn between imperium-oriented and community-oriented theories of law.[6] The former emphasise law's hierarchical structure and its power of command and control. They stress the need to trace law's authority to some single point of origin (such as sovereign, rule of recognition or basic norm) which can then provide a key to law's unity as a system. If, as has been seen, postmodernist critiques question law's authority portrayed in this way, the issue is not that law lacks authority but that the basis of this authority is revealed as mysterious, mythical or illusory – that is, irrational. So foundationless law must be supported by a kind of faith (Goodrich 1990: 283–284) and questions need to be asked about the nature of the faith and the conditions necessary for it to be sustained. Unsurprisingly, there has been some revival of interest recently in studying law's links with religion (eg Oliver, Douglas-Scott and Tadros (eds) 2000; Ahdar (ed) 2000).

Images of law as a commanding structure ruling citizens or subjects and controlling the social remain strong in Western societies today, even if postmodern worries about the moral emptiness or uncertainty of law's dictates proliferate. But because normative legal theory's explanations of the bases of law's authority seem circular, imperium-oriented legal theories have a void at the heart of their conceptual analyses. They need to be supplemented by inquiries about the social that can clarify, explain and even justify the *basis of faith* on which law's authority ultimately depends.

---

6   See, above, p 211.

Community-oriented legal theories face parallel challenges. What does community mean? Is it meaningful to think of contemporary political societies (that is, societies that correspond in extent to the jurisdictional reach of nation state legal systems) as communities? Can a society in this sense realistically be considered the moral author of its law? Or must it be said that only some sectors of any such society can be thought of in that way? How far must class, gender, race and other differentials be taken into account in considering who makes law and for whom?

Ronald Dworkin's liberal legal theory personifies communities as moral agents and treats states or nations as political communities (Dworkin 1986: 171–175; 1989: 494, 496ff). But this assumes a moral unity of state law as communal law at the price of some sociological distortion. The jurisprudence of difference reveals law's interpreters as, at best, a profoundly disunified community. It implies further that, in significant ways, the social is not unified and that law imposed for all in a nation state is often not experienced as a law of all.

The matter is complex. There seems no future for a legal theory that merely divides the social into fixed categories (or even communities) of, for example, economic class, race, ethnicity, gender, religious affiliation or sexual orientation. Postmodernist writings in feminism and other areas of the jurisprudence of difference recognise this in their rejection of all forms of essentialism. Clearly much law represents interests, experiences and aspirations that cut across all rigid categorisations. Any concept of community useful to legal theory will have to represent adequately the *social complexity* that postmodernists emphasise.

Theorising legal communities

Normative legal theory must recognise social diversity by explaining law in terms of the regulatory requirements of different communities. These, in turn, are to be seen both subjectively and objectively: people living in a particular community experience their membership in it subjectively, as their own experience, different from that of non-members; non-members look at relations of community from the outside. This is reminiscent of the distinction that Hart draws between internal and external views of law. But critical legal theory (especially the jurisprudence of difference) teaches that *there is no single inside and outside of law*. The meaning of law depends on one's standpoint in various communities of interpretation.

From a Hartian standpoint, legal officials are pre-eminently insiders and, by contrast, 'ordinary citizens' (Hart 1961: 39, 60, 117) may often be outsiders who adopt only an external view of legal rules. From a Dworkinian standpoint, citizens in a political society may all be potential insiders able to interpret law and make judgments about it which might even challenge the judgments of the highest court in the land (Dworkin 1977: ch 8; 1985: ch 4). But these theoretical positions do not exhaust the possibilities. Even among legal officials there are different interpretive communities seeing law differently (for example, there may be conflicts between interpretations of law made by lower and higher courts, or judges and administrators, or lawyers and law enforcers). And, as has been seen, there may be many different interpretations as between different social groups, and between legal scholars who see themselves as representative of those groups.

So it is necessary to discard any simple distinction between legal insiders and outsiders, or between participants in and observers of law. One can be inside or outside many different legally-relevant social groupings. Also, the distinction between 'internal' participation and 'external' observation is not fixed. People observe law as they participate in it in different ways and contexts. And they participate in law by observing its processes, judging the meaning of the practices they associate with law, using their observations to inform their involvement with it.

Legal communities cannot necessarily be thought of as having fixed boundaries, like walled villages or nation states with policed territorial borders.[7] Neither, despite some claims of feminism and critical race theory, are they communities of gender, race or ethnicity, because these categorisations are too rigid to reflect the complexity of social experiences, aspirations and interests. Nor can community be equated now with the nostalgic idea of local community with its strong ties of neighbourliness and its association with static, unchanging ways of life.

If community is to be a useful category for describing the components of the social – law's social environment – today, it has to mean fluid, flexible, changing, overlapping patterns of social relationships. So community is an abstract idea that can be used to conceptualise these shifting patterns. Since normative legal theory has always used abstractions such as sovereignty, norm or rule, community is one more to add among its key concepts.

---

7   Dworkin's idea of liberal community shows how problematic the idea of treating nation states as political communities is, unless the word community is drained of all sociological significance. He sees membership in a national political community as implying actual or potential public participation in the nation state's institutions (Dworkin 1989: 496). But for many people that participation is minimal or non-existent. Perhaps in recognition of this problem he adds that being 'particularly affected' by a political community's collective acts also makes someone a part of it. But this would make a slave a member of the community that enslaves him. The idea of community is rendered meaningless.

The term 'community' most usefully refers to ideal *types of social relationships*. An ideal type is a conceptualisation of a social phenomenon (for example, 'capitalism', 'the family', 'economic activity') that deliberately does not take into account all the complex variations of the phenomenon in reality, but presents it in a pure, simplified way that allows it to be logically examined. An ideal type is 'ideal' only in the sense of being a pure idea, an abstraction. It is a deliberately created device, a framework for examining the actual phenomena to which it is intended to relate, a means of organising or making sense of the complexity of social or historical experience.

Max Weber developed this notion of ideal types and used it to characterise all social action in terms of just four types (Weber 1978: 24–25). Building on Weber's thinking, it is possible to suggest four basic types of community that can combine in an infinity of ways in the actual relationships between people that make up the social (Cotterrell 1997). One type is *instrumental community*: social relationships centred on the pursuit of common or convergent purposes, which are often but not necessarily economic. A second type is *community of belief or values*: here social relations are based on shared ultimate beliefs or values held for their own sake and not to achieve some ulterior purpose. Third, *affective community* refers to social relations based on emotional attachment between people. Finally, *traditional community* is based on shared customs, traditions, experiences or history, or just living in the same environment or speaking the same language.

These types of community often interrelate and overlap in reality. Individuals inhabit many different social relations of community that combine these four types and the combinations that actually exist to form the social can be called networks of community. Significantly, the regulatory problems that each type of community suggests differ. Identifying those differences helps in addressing issues that the jurisprudence of difference and postmodernist legal theory raise for normative legal theory.

Affective community, for example, is notoriously difficult to regulate. Law, as postmodernists have noted, avoids concern with emotions. Weber (1978: 24–26) saw emotionally-based social action as ultimately irrational, because it is not subject to control by rational rules. Yet affective relations, governed by love or hatred, are often intense and certainly provoke regulatory problems. Law is often confronted by them. Such matters are not fictions or fantasies, found only in medieval courts of love. They can arise in any context of human interaction but are most often recognised as presenting regulatory problems for law in connection with sexual, domestic and family relations.

Traditional community – social relations based on ties of locality, custom or familiar environment – may be becoming weaker in contemporary complex societies. People are increasingly mobile and ties to place often seem to matter less than in earlier times. But regulation of these relations is one of law's most familiar tasks: for example, by providing basic conditions of neighbourly coexistence through rules of criminal and tort law.

In some respects, the force of traditional community weakens with globalisation and the proliferation of relationships having no strong tie to any specific geographical location. But new transnational relationships focussed on the need to protect endangered natural environments are also developing and demanding new forms of legal regulation not bounded by the frontiers of nation states. These are new expressions of traditional community. Also, ties of common history, tradition and custom remain very important to some social groups that are minorities within nation states or extend beyond the borders of states. While normative legal theory has often paid little attention to law's modern relationship to custom and tradition (cf Krygier 1986; Luban 1994: ch 2), a theoretical focus on law and community provides a reminder that these phenomena remain, in some parts of the social, very important bases of communal relations.

By contrast again, community of belief or values can often be a strong social bond. A theory such as Ronald Dworkin's presupposes that law's interpreters try to portray their legal system as expressing a coherent set of values. At the same time, critical legal scholarship often doubts whether legal interpretation has any common ground. So what, if any, set of values can provide a coherent overall framework of the social in complex contemporary conditions?

A belief in the worth of individual human autonomy and dignity might be proposed as the foundation of such a value system,[8] its most obvious, direct legal expression being human rights law. But this kind of community of values is not specific to any nation state. It is often extended to proclaim a 'bond of humanity' unlimited by state frontiers, or a transnational value system centred on the idea of the worth of each human being irrespective of race, class, gender or creed. Beyond this, many different, competing expressions of community of values exist, uniting people in social networks within and beyond nation states through shared religious or other beliefs and commitments.

These commitments of belief divide citizens too, as exemplified by fierce controversies around issues such as abortion. Values are often open to diverse interpretations. Law that explicitly justifies itself as an expression of them is

---

8   On sociological arguments that this is the *only* value system that can unite complex contemporary Western societies and provide a general moral foundation of their law, see Cotterrell 1999, especially ch 7.

often weak law, because controversial. But law's relation to ultimate beliefs or values is a only one aspect of the moral life of law, not the whole of it. Law addresses many moral matters as a matter of routine, but controversies around natural law theory, for example, express in normative legal theory the particular problems that arise for law in defining and regulating relations of community based on ultimate values or beliefs.

Finally, instrumental community seems to present fewer legal problems theoretically than does any of the other three types of community. Instrumental relations are limited by the common project in hand and they end when that project is completed or abandoned. They are limited by its scope. So instrumental community is often a relatively weak form of community, easy to establish and to terminate. But the law that regulates it (most obviously contract, corporate and commercial law) may often be strong and effective because of its generally well-defined scope and limited objectives. Pragmatist legal theory is perhaps most at ease with law thought of in this way and addressed to this type of community. Law is readily seen as a mere technique or instrument when it frames social relationships that are themselves instrumental. Law's link to them often seems simple and efficient. Both law and the social relations it regulates look like means to an end: instruments of economic or other goals.

The differentiation of types of community, sketched above, provides a way of thinking theoretically about the nature of social relations in terms of their general regulatory problems. A law-and-community approach addresses normative legal theory's need to recognise the diversity of meanings, understandings and experiences of law produced by the differentiation of the social. For example, law's relation to morality appears in a new light in this perspective because different types of community have different moral requirements. As law regulates networks of community it has the task of interrelating their moral aspects. Conversely law gets moral authority from its nature as a regulation of networks of community. This will be a complex moral basis, given the complexity of the interaction of types of community with which law is concerned.

Legal theory beyond the nation state

This law-and-community approach presupposes that law eventually has to be seen by normative legal theory as not limited by the jurisdictional reach of nation states. For Austin, international law was not law since it lacked a source in a determinate, indivisible sovereign power. Kelsen and Hart, by contrast, found no difficulty with international law's juridical status.[9] In the contemporary world it would be strange, indeed, to refuse international law recognition as law, though its authoritative force remains still insecure in various respects. Now, law regulates relations not just between states, or between individuals within a state, but across state frontiers or irrespective of them. The growth of transnational regulatory regimes is impossible to ignore in the fields of human rights, criminal justice, finance, commerce, environmental control, intellectual property and information technology, among others.

The status of many of these regulatory regimes is, in some respects, uncertain. They are developed often by international agencies and institutions such as courts and rulemaking authorities ultimately given legitimacy by the consent of states. The political authority that supports them and the regulation they produce is ultimately parasitic on the established structures of political authority that create law in nation states: the kind of authority that normative legal theory has long been concerned to analyse. Yet it seems clear that transnational regulation (as well as more localised forms of regulation in nation states) seeks and requires other, stronger authority if it is to flourish and become powerful and normatively stable: if, that is, the Rule of Law in something like the form that normative legal theory has analysed or presupposed it is to be extended to arenas other than nation state jurisdictions.

We might return to the dichotomy between imperium-oriented and community-oriented legal theories in trying to predict the possibilities for legal development here. Could the simplest and most criticised of Anglo-American imperium-oriented theories assist? Is it possible to foresee a new kind of Austinianism, in which the sovereign-subject relationship, fixed by the sovereign's commands and the subjects' habit of obedience, again becomes a persuasive representation of legal reality? The discussion of Austin's thought in Chapter 3 emphasised his stark portrayal of law as an expression of power: an idea carried through to legal realism and ultimately to some modern pragmatist views of instrumental law. Could a new *international* Austinian sovereign be in the process of forming? Is a habit of obedience by states developing which may make their primary law-making agencies ultimately the delegates of this new sovereign?

I argued earlier that Austin's failure was not so much a logical one as a failure to make central in his theory questions which later writers in the context of their own times have found pressing.[10] For Austin, utility, not liberty or the Rule of Law, is the *leitmotiv* of the sovereign's regulation: law is an instrument of

---

9   See Hart 1961: ch 10 and, on Kelsen, pp 109–110, above.
10 See above, pp 76–77, 111–112.

subjection and a means of producing order in the social, an environment in which chaos, irrationality and violence always threaten. The Austinian ideal is rational acceptance of a subjection guided by the sovereign's understanding of what is necessary for the general welfare. In a new era, could a world legal order based on some such sovereignty arise? Austin's emphases (and his silences) might then again seem relevant.

The world is far from having reached a position where Austin's kind of normative legal theory, dressed in new international garb, could again be a theory for the times. Nevertheless, legal thought emphasising hierarchies of authority and the imposition of law as rule, norm or command seems appropriate to a world characterised by vast imbalances of power between states and the creation of transnational rule-systems significantly reflecting those power relations.

A different set of issues is posed by the tradition of community-oriented legal theories. As has been seen, these treat a community (however defined or assumed) as the moral agent or guarantor of law and suggest that law's authority, meaning and authority derive from sources in that community. So they imply a need to ask what this community can be when law is thought of as transnational regulation.

One route to an answer is suggested by the earlier discussion of ideal types of community. There can be no single transnational community of law, any more than (as the jurisprudence of difference makes clear) there can be a single national community of law for all regulatory purposes. Transnational law, like national law, must seek its moral authority in its ties to many networks of community. These express in various combinations the radically different types of community already discussed.

Normative legal theory is faced with the daunting but urgent task of making theoretical sense of the many new kinds of transnational (and intranational) regulation now developing. In pursuing these conceptual analyses it surely has no option but to try to understand theoretically the nature of the different networks of community that exist and are developing irrespective of national state jurisdictional boundaries. Ultimately then, the conclusion must be that normative legal theory and empirical legal theory need to become a single enterprise. But this is not to deny or belittle the worth of normative legal theory's traditional projects of conceptual analysis. It is to insist that in the context of a rapidly changing legal environment the tasks of legal theory cannot remain static. To understand how those tasks are changing and how they can be addressed the environment itself has to be understood systematically.

Legal theory and legal professions

Throughout, this book has attempted to relate trends in normative legal theory to the concerns of Anglo-American legal professions. How, finally, should the relationship between legal theory and legal professionalism be understood today? Some contemporary postmodern juristic analyses might seem entirely unconnected with legal professional concerns. For example, Balkin (1992: 1985–1986) has noted a remarkable and perhaps disturbing divorce between theoretically-informed academic constitutional law scholarship in the United States and the very prosaic practice of constitutional law in American courts. In law, theory is said to have become radically divorced from practice (Luban 1994: 3).

This is something more than the perennially different outlooks of theorists and practitioners on their common intellectual field: there may no longer be a common field! Academic studies of law themselves have become fragmented: 'The idea of a common language and a common vocabulary among legal academics, and indeed, a common canon of legal materials, has increasingly become a fiction' (Levinson and Balkin 1991: 1653). Is it possible to talk seriously of any sense of unity or large-scale principle or integrity in law in this situation?

Academic lawyers have become increasingly interested in legal theory but, as has been seen, they hardly form a cohesive interpretive community. In these circumstances they seem to have little prospect of speaking with one voice on politics or on issues relating to lawyers' professionalism. Instead, politics as a field of struggle tends in some circumstances to become situated in law schools themselves – at least, this has been the experience in some United States law schools as critical and postmodernist legal studies have proliferated. The focus of political action has often been identified by critical and postmodernist legal scholars as lawyers themselves: influencing the way lawyers practise law or students learn it has become almost the whole of politics for some legal scholars. Thus, politics and issues about professionalism are fused in this understanding far more completely than at any previous time in the modern history of Anglo-American legal scholarship.

Some postmodernists rightly see this fusion as self-defeating: the 'American law professor', writes Goodrich, 'is too well paid to be politically committed, too status conscious ... and too insular ... law is the least threatened and one of the best paid of academic disciplines' (Goodrich 1996: 194, 218). A politics focused only on law schools might seem, as Goodrich suggests, little more than narcissism and ineffectual posturing. And the problem is in no way restricted to American contexts.

Postmodernism in general is often said to be politically ineffectual, however fierce its critiques of law's pretensions or modernity's self-deceptions. Postmodern politics focusses on the local and the specific, rather than on grand themes and ideologies. In this respect it very properly recognises the fragmented character of social life and the lack of appeal that grand narratives of political emancipation have in postmodern conditions. But a more vibrant politics could be one informed by empirical study of the variety of networks of community and detailed consideration of contemporary challenges posed for (and by) law in regulating these networks and conflicts that arise between them.

The fragmentation of experience that contemporary critical theory recognises is surely affecting legal professions. They are becoming more varied in outlook, more obviously affected by the jurisprudence of difference and, in some respects, less able to maintain collective solidarity and identity and the settled norms of practice that stable professionalism (as opposed to *ad hoc* entrepreneurial activity) relies on or aspires to. In this context it is unsurprising that lawyers feel a more pressing need to look outwards to law's rapidly changing social environment rather than inwards towards established professional traditions. They increasingly observe, and are fitting themselves to relate to, a world of transnational (and intranational) communities that require morally meaningful regulation.

Legal theory can ally itself with this outlook by theorising the development of forms of legal regulation that escape the limits of nation state jurisdictions and by examining the interaction of these regulatory forms with state law. It can ask how regulation needs to be rooted in the moral conditions of existence of social relationships of community. Certainly, legal practice does not depend on normative legal theory in any direct way. But, as this book has argued, legal theory often develops and rationalises notions about law that underpin and inform legal practice. Ultimately, a sense of legal professionalism presupposes basic shared ideas among legal practitioners about the nature of law. One of normative legal theory's practical tasks has been to make these ideas explicit and coherent.

Contemporary critiques of normative legal theory mirror, to some degree, the apparently increasing difficulty of maintaining a strong sense of legal professionalism in current Anglo-American conditions. These critiques show that legal theory must add to its concern with rules and norms, a more systematic concern with the nature of social relations. They warn, rightly in my view, that normative legal theory will become increasingly remote from the changing situation of law unless it looks beyond its familiar ways of conceptualising legal doctrine to develop a systematic understanding of changes in the social. Normative legal theory must ally itself with empirical legal theory to make sense of law's changing circumstances. And this outward gaze beyond the traditional concerns of normative legal theory mirrors the new horizons that legal practitioners increasingly find a need to survey today.

But, of course, law is not just a professional preserve. The value of normative legal theory extends beyond the contributions it might make (or has, in the past, made) to legal professionalism. Its intellectual strength and enduring fascination have come from its commitment to make legal knowledge a system of reason, a structure of thought that does justice as an intellectual creation to the efforts of all the legal minds that have sought solutions to practical problems of social regulation through the ages. The main purpose of this book has been to introduce, critically and constructively, some of the most valuable products of that commitment.

Notes and further reading

In the following notes, some subtitles of works are omitted where the main title provides sufficiently clear identification. Sources also included in the list of text references are cited by author and date only.

Chapter 1 – Legal philosophy in context

Jurisprudence, legal philosophy and legal theory: The designations 'normative legal theory' and 'empirical legal theory', used in the text, roughly parallel Kelsen's designations of normative and sociological jurisprudence (Kelsen 1941b) but, unlike Kelsen, I see these not as different sciences with different subject-matter but as elaborations of different kinds of perspectives on law as a field of experience. Both are concerned with the nature of law as a normative and empirical phenomenon. Typically, however, they conceptualise this phenomenon differently, seek knowledge of it in different ways and use this knowledge for different purposes. Empirical legal theory generalises from studies of historical and social experience of law. Normative legal theory generalises from typical juristic understandings of legal doctrine and reasoning.

Legal philosophy and legal practice: On legal philosophy and legal practice see also R H S Tur, 'Jurisprudence and Practice' (1976) 14 Journal of the Society of Public Teachers of Law (ns) 38; R Cotterrell, 'Pandora's Box: Jurisprudence in Legal Education' (2000) 7 International Journal of the Legal Profession 179. On the uses of legal philosophy in clarifying essential concepts used in legal practice see eg A L Goodhart, 'An Apology for Jurisprudence' in P Sayre (ed) *Interpretations of Modern Legal Philosophies* 1947. P W Kahn, *The Cultural Study of*

Law 1999, ch 1 criticises what he sees as the orientation of legal philosophy and legal scholarship towards serving the needs of legal practice.

Justifying normative legal theory: On the functions of legal philosophy see also W Twining, 'Some Jobs for Jurisprudence' (1974) 1 British Journal of Law and Society 149; P Soper, 'Making Sense of Modern Jurisprudence' (1988) 22 Creighton Law Review 67. On lawyers as legal philosophers see W Friedmann, *Legal Theory* 5th edn 1967, pp 3–4, noting that the dominance of lawyers in this enterprise has occurred since the nineteenth century: 'The decisive shift from the philosopher's or politician's to the lawyer's legal philosophy is of fairly recent date. It follows a period of great developments in juristic research, technique and professional training. The new era of legal philosophy arises mainly from the confrontation of the professional lawyer, in his legal work, with problems of social justice.' I would modify this only to suggest (i) that legal philosophy may have aided as well as reflected developments Friedmann refers to and (ii) that problems of explaining the integrity of law as an intellectual field and a learned professional practice may have been as important as those of social justice in determining the shape and influence of modern Anglo-American legal philosophy.

Legal philosophy in social and political context: A contextual view provides its own special criteria of relevance. Since the context with which this book is concerned is Anglo-American, discussion in it is confined to theory that has had most prominence in this legal professional and political context. The fact that intellectual quality does not guarantee wide political and professional influence is amply shown by the fate of the jurisprudential teachings of Adam Smith and other advanced, legally-relevant literature of the Scottish Enlightenment (for example, writings by Adam Ferguson and John Millar). Smith's Glasgow lectures in the 1760s (published as *Lectures on Jurisprudence* 1978) remain relatively neglected in juristic discussion in Britain. But see K Haakonssen, *The Science of a Legislator* 1981; D N MacCormick, *Legal Right and Social Democracy* 1982, ch 6.

How should legal philosophy be interpreted contextually?: On related 'contextual' approaches in other intellectual fields, see eg J Tully (ed) *Meaning and Context* 1988. Karl Mannheim's writings on the sociology of knowledge also contain valuable guides to interpreting currents of ideas in social context: see eg *Ideology and Utopia* 1936; *Essays on the Sociology of Knowledge* 1952; Mannheim 1956; *Structures of Thinking* 1982. Properly used, the sociology of knowledge should not require that ideas be reduced to, or explained away in terms of, social conditions. It should force us to keep in mind the dialectic between intellectual imagination and the conditions that allow it to flourish. The possible relevance of approaches such as Quentin Skinner's for the study of legal philosophy is noted in W Twining, 'Talk About Realism' (1985) 60 New York University Law Review 329, at p 336.

Chapter 2 – The theory of common law

The character of common law thought: One of the best discussions of classical common law thought is in Postema 1986, which emphasises the importance in common law thinking of the idea of community as the foundation of law. Postema suggests a relatively explicit appeal to community as characteristic of common law reasoning but I think that this appeal is usually implicit and many terms (for example, realm, commonwealth, subjects, people, nation) are used to indicate the social entity from which law gains its authority and meaning. Postema also tends to imply a more developed conception of the nature of community and of the relationship between law and community than the limited theoretical vision of common law thought in general might warrant. Common law thought does not present a theory of law. It merely provides the elements from which a rudimentary theory can be constructed. See also Lobban 1991, arguing that common law's 'essential theory' treated law as 'a system of remedies' drawing 'on a multiplicity of sources to arrive at its solutions' (p 14). H J Berman, 'The Origins of Historical Jurisprudence' (1994) 103 Yale Law Journal 1651 argues that it was not until the seventeenth century that the 'strong conviction that the primary source of the validity of law ... is its historical character, its source in the customs and traditions of the community' (p 1655) arose among common lawyers, especially through the influence of Edward Coke, John Selden and Matthew Hale. On Blackstone's view of common law see D Boorstein, *The Mysterious Science of the Law* 1941; D Lieberman, *The Province of Legislation Determined* 1989, Part 1; Lobban 1991, ch 2.

The common law judge: See generally Levy-Ullmann 1935, Part 1 ch 3; Lieberman, *Province of Legislation*, op cit, Part 2. For Blackstone's views on precedent and the judge's role see especially Blackstone 1809 I, pp 69–71.

Can common law thought explain legal development?: On common law as custom see Simpson 1973; Postema 1986, pp 4–13. On records and reporting of common law see F Pollock, *Essays in the Law* 1922, chs 9 and 10; Levy-Ullmann 1935, Part 1, ch 4.

Common law and legislation: See Levy-Ullmann 1935, Part 2; Postema 1986, pp 15–19; C K Allen, *Law in the Making* 7th edn 1964, pp 444–469; Sommerville 1999, pp 91–96; McIlwain 1910, ch 4; T F T Plucknett, *Statutes and Their Interpretation in the First Half of the Fourteenth Century* 1922; Lieberman, *Province of Legislation*, op cit. On controversies around the role of legislation in the context of custom and common law see J Waldron, *The Dignity of Legislation*, 1999; Waldron, 'Custom Redeemed by Statute' (1998) 51 Current Legal Problems 93.

The political and social environment: Sommerville 1999 summarises the typical outlook of common lawyers in the crucial years of the early seventeenth century when modern conceptions of the sovereignty of Parliament began to establish themselves firmly in legal theory. Also valuable on the political significance of common law ideas of immemorial custom are Pocock 1957; G Burgess, *The Politics of the Ancient Constitution* 1992. See also J U Lewis, 'Coke's Theory of Artificial Reason' (1968) 84 Law Quarterly Review 330. Gough 1955 is the standard modern account of the use of natural law ideas in English legal history. J Goldsworthy, *The Sovereignty of Parliament* 1999 surveys the development of English ideas of parliamentary sovereignty in relation to common law thought through seven centuries. An important discussion of political authority from within the tradition of classical common law thought is Matthew Hale's mid-seventeenth century critical analysis of Hobbes' ideas on sovereignty and legal authority: see Yale 1972.

Savigny: a theory for common law?: On historical jurisprudence generally see Stein 1980. On Savigny see Symposium on 'Savigny in Modern Comparative Perspective' (1989) 37 American Journal of Comparative Law, no 1; S Gale, 'A Very German Legal Science: Savigny and the Historical School' (1982) 18 Stanford Journal of International Law 123. Among older literature see especially H Kantorowicz, 'Savigny and the Historical School of Law' (1937) 53 Law Quarterly Review 326. On Savigny's influence in England, see Stein 1980, pp 72ff. Among American literature, Carter 1907 reflects Savigny's thinking throughout; see also H G Reuschlein, *Jurisprudence: Its American Prophets* 1951, pp 58–63 on the influential American Savignian legal scholar T M Cooley. R Zimmermann, 'Savigny's Legacy' (1996) 112 Law Quarterly Review 576, argues that Savigny's thinking is significant for the development of contemporary European legal thought. On difficulties in using the concept of 'culture' in legal studies see R Cotterrell, 'The Concept of Legal Culture' in D Nelken (ed) *Comparing Legal Cultures* 1997.

For the background and consequences of the codification controversy in Germany see J P Dawson, *The Oracles of the Law* 1968, ch 6. In England, Bentham advocated codification to banish what he saw as irrational common law methods: see below, Chapter 3. The German controversy was replayed in the United States but with different results (codification arguments made little headway, whereas the major German codification of civil law occurred, despite Savigny's delaying influence, with effect from 1900). See Reuschlein, *Jurisprudence*, op cit, pp 63–71, noting: 'No more significant warfare has ever been waged in the history of American juristic thought than the bitter warfare between codification and custom which ranged over the second half of the nineteenth century' (p 69). See also P J King, *Utilitarian Jurisprudence in America* 1986, ch 5.

Maine's historical jurisprudence: The best modern general source on Maine's ideas in the context of his times is Cocks 1988. See also eg Stone 1966, pp 119–147. Feaver 1969 is an excellent biography. Diamond (ed) 1991 contains commentaries on most aspects of Maine's work.

Maine on politics and society: See eg Collini, Winch and Burrow 1983, ch 7; Burrow 1966, ch 5; Diamond (ed) 1991, Part 1; G A Feaver, 'The Political Attitudes of Sir Henry Maine' (1965) 27 Journal of Politics 290; B Smith, 'Maine's Concept of Progress' (1963) 24 Journal of the History of Ideas 407; Barker 1928, ch 6. Maine's 'administrative' view of legal problems was surely influenced by his experience in colonial government in India from 1862–1869 as legal member of the Governor-General's Council: see Diamond (ed) 1991, Part 4. One consequence of it was his clear appreciation of the value of codification of law as an instrument of modernisation in the Indian context: see Feaver 1969, pp 76–77; Cocks 1988, pp 82–84. On Maine's *Popular Government* see Cocks 1988, pp 131–140.

Historical jurisprudence and the legal profession: Professionalisation: some writers assert that by the seventeenth century 'the English bench and bar had become professionalised': White 1976, p 19. What seems to be meant is that specialised legal tasks of barristers, attorneys and solicitors had become established. My concern with professionalisation, however, centres on the self-conscious development of modern professional organisation entailing the claim to esoteric but scientific knowledge, associated training and well defined qualifications for entry into the professional group. Cocks 1988 emphasises the tensions between Maine's ideas and aspirations and the attitudes of legal practitioners in his time. On Maine and legal education see Feaver 1969, ch 3; papers by Stein and Twining in Diamond (ed) 1991; and R C Cocks, '"That Exalted Science of Jurisprudence"' (1999) 20 Journal of Legal History 62.

The fate of Maine's new science: On Maine's unreliable use of evidence ('polemical rather than scholarly') see Kuper 1991, p 103. On his influence generally see Cocks 1988, ch 6. For his place in the development of the social sciences see papers by Shils, Macfarlane, Peel and Abrahams in Diamond (ed) 1991, Part 2 and G Stocking, *Victorian Anthropology* 1988. On Maine's late disillusionment with legal education and the legal profession, which he saw as wedded to technicality and unconcerned with the broad cultural approach to legal studies that he advocated, see Cocks 1988, pp 93–99. William Robson wrote perceptively ('Sir Henry Maine Today' in W I Jennings (ed) *Modern*

Theories of Law 1933, pp 178–179) that Maine was 'not only original, he was unique. That fact is to our grave discredit as lawyers. He blazed a great trail and opened up the heavens ... But who, one may ask, has followed him? ... we lawyers have remained cloistered in our narrow walls, treading complacently the old paths'.

Chapter 3 – Sovereign and subject: Bentham and Austin

Bentham's main work of normative legal theory is Bentham 1970. The manuscript, substantially completed by 1782 but put aside by its author, lay buried among the mass of Bentham's papers for one and a half centuries until rediscovered by Charles Everett in 1939. Everett edited the work and published it as *The Limits of Jurisprudence Defined* in 1945. The story of the origins of Bentham's manuscript and the scholarly detective work which led to its identification and publication is told in Everett's preface to the 1945 edition and H L A Hart's introduction to the revised and expanded 1970 version, published as *Of Laws in General.*

Austin was a member of Bentham's circle, although the personal relationship between the two seems to have cooled by the time Austin gave his London University lectures between 1829 and 1833 (cf Rumble 1985, pp 15–18, 34–35). The first few lectures of Austin's course were published in expanded form as *The Province of Jurisprudence Determined* in 1832. The rest remained unpublished until after his death in 1859. Sarah Austin published a second edition of *The Province* in 1861, and the remaining lectures in 1863 insofar as they could be reconstructed from Austin's notes. *The Province* is currently available in several imprints. The Cambridge edition cited in the text clearly indicates later editorial additions to Austin's original text. There are three contrasting full-length modern studies of Austin's work. Rumble 1985 deals with Austin's career as a whole and contains profound discussions of many aspects of his thought. Hamburger and Hamburger 1985 is a more conventional biography, providing a valuable portrait of both John and Sarah Austin. Morison 1982 is particularly geared to the interests of students of normative legal theory but tends to interpret Austin's aims and methods somewhat narrowly.

The empire of darkness and the region of light: On Bentham's critique of common law and his views on codification see Postema 1986, chs 8 and 12; Lobban 1991, chs 5 and 6. For Austin on codification see Austin 1885, pp 660–681, 1098–1100. On German influences on Austin, see M Lobban, 'Was there a Nineteenth Century "English School of Jurisprudence"?' (1995) 16 Legal History 34; Lobban 1991, pp 227–232; Morison 1982, pp 60–63; Rumble

1985, pp 31–34. Despite Austin's dismissal of most of Savigny's criticisms of codification as absurd and irrational (Austin 1885, pp 675–680), he regarded highly some of Savigny's writings, especially his influential book on the concept of possession. For Austin, this exemplified the best kind of German Romanist juristic scholarship: rational, systematic and distilling succinct logical principles from historically developed doctrine. Austin saw Savigny's *Of the Vocation* as an unfortunate, emotionally inspired aberration. Bentham's principle of utility is expounded in his *An Introduction to the Principles of Morals and Legislation* 1789 (Athlone edn 1970).

Positive law and positive morality: The insistence on treating positive law as the sole or distinct object of study for legal scholarship is characteristic of the approach to legal thought known as legal positivism. See below, Chapter 4.

The coercive structure of a law: The classic critique of Austin's command theory of law is Hart 1961, chs 2–4. On Austin's discussion of sanctions see C Tapper, 'Austin on Sanctions' [1965] Cambridge Law Journal 271.

Sanctions and power-conferring rules: Hart 1961 provides the most influential modern critique of Austin's treatment of power-conferring rules. See also the thoughtful discussion of the nature of these rules in MacCormick 1981, ch 6. For an attempt to defend Austin see Moles 1987, pp 65–70. While Moles' approach seems, in this respect, broadly along the right lines it does not address major criticisms which Hart and others raise and fails to make clear the crucial difference of aims (reflecting different political philosophies) as between Austin and Hart which is emphasised in the text of this chapter and the next.

Sovereignty: Hinsley 1986 and J Hoffman, *Sovereignty* 1998 give useful accounts of the development of the concept of sovereignty. See also M Francis, 'The Nineteenth Century Theory of Sovereignty and Thomas Hobbes' (1980) 1 History of Political Thought 517. On the abstract character of Austin's sovereign see Manning 1933, p 207; Moles 1987, p 71; and cf Fuller 1940, p 46 insisting on Austin's ambiguity. Lobban (1991, pp 245ff) adopts a view close to that in the text, stressing that Austin's sovereign is an 'abstract concept', but he suggests that Austin's tendency (unnecessarily) to confuse government and sovereignty in his writings encouraged criticisms such as Hart's. On Bentham's ideas see also J H Burns, 'Bentham on Sovereignty' in M H James (ed) *Bentham and Legal Theory* 1973.

Some characteristics of Austin's sovereign: For a sample of commentary and criticism see eg Buckland 1949, ch 9; Maine 1875a, chs 12 and 13. Lobban 1991, pp 245–253 argues, consistently with the text, that Austin's sovereign must be understood as 'a theoretical postulate to stand at the head of his series of definitions' and 'an abstract source of laws', to be distinguished from the actual person or persons exercising sovereignty. Despite the apparent problems stressed by many critics in applying Austin's theory of sovereignty to the case of the United States, American Austinians of the nineteenth century seemed to find no great difficulty in doing so: see King, *Utilitarian Jurisprudence in America*, op cit, ch 7. For critiques see *ibid* ch 8; and J Dewey, 'Austin's Theory of Sovereignty' (1894) 9 Political Science Quarterly 31 (incoherences in Austin's analysis point to the need for a conception of popular sovereignty). See also S M Woody, 'The Theory of Sovereignty: Dewey versus Austin' (1967–1968) 78 Ethics 313 (defending Austin in part against Dewey's critique).

Must the sovereign be legally illimitable?: On Bentham's views see Postema 1986, pp 237–256; Hart 1982, ch 9; O Ben-Dor, *Constitutional Limits and the Public Sphere* 2000 (a study of Bentham's conception of constitutional limits: chs 2 and 3, in particular, focus on Bentham's understanding of sovereignty).

The judge as delegate of the sovereign: For Austin's views on 'judiciary law' see Austin 1885, pp 641–660. See also the detailed, sympathetic examination in Rumble 1985, ch 4. For Bentham's views see Postema 1986, chs 10–13.

Austin's theory of the centralised state: Austin's views on centralised state organisation and delegation, which he saw as its correlate, are expressed in his essay 'Centralization' (1847) 85 Edinburgh Review 221. For a thoughtful discussion of his later political ideas see Rumble 1985, ch 6. On the relevance of changes in Austin's political outlook for the ideas expressed in his lectures see Hamburger and Hamburger 1985, ch 9.

Austin and the legal profession: For general background see the excellent discussion of relationships between trends in jurisprudence and legal professionalism in England in Sugarman 1986. Also of interest is W Twining, '1836 And All That: Laws in the University of London 1836–1986' (1987) 40 Current Legal Problems 261. For illustration of Austin's influence on legal scholarship see R A Cosgrove, *The Rule of Law: Albert Venn Dicey, Victorian Jurist* 1980, pp 23–28.

Chapter 4 – Analytical jurisprudence and liberal democracy: Hart and Kelsen

Empiricism and conceptualism: For Kelsen's own comparison of his work with Anglo-American analytical jurisprudence see Kelsen 1941b. For the methods-debate around Austin's work see Morison 1958 and 1982; Hart 1958, p 65 (broadly empiricist interpretations); Manning 1933; Stone 1964, ch 2;

Moles 1987, ch 1; Lobban 1991, ch 8 (broadly conceptualist interpretations). Rumble 1985 wisely equivocates: while Austin would have tended to adopt the empirically oriented view typical of the utilitarians, 'his actual approach to the problems of jurisprudence is not nearly as empirical as Morison suggests' (p 96); but cf W Rumble, 'John Austin and his Nineteenth Century Critics: the Case of Sir Henry Sumner Maine' (1988) 39 Northern Ireland Legal Quarterly 119 (emphasising Austin's empirical concerns and important similarities between his outlook and Maine's). Often the antagonists in this debate are talking of a variety of ambiguities in Austin's methods and not necessarily of the specific methodological distinction around which this chapter is organised.

Hart's linguistic empiricism: Hohfeld's major work is *Fundamental Legal Conceptions as Applied in Judicial Reasoning* 1923. On Hohfeld see Stone 1964, ch 4, in which Kocourek's ideas are also discussed. For general studies of Hart's work see MacCormick 1981; M Martin, *The Legal Philosophy of H L A Hart* 1987; M D Bayles, *Hart's Legal Philosophy* 1992; and J Coleman (ed) *Hart's Postscript* 2001. Many of the essays in Leith and Ingram (eds) *The Jurisprudence of Orthodoxy* 1988 are highly critical of Hart's ideas, as is Moles 1987. See also M H Kramer, *Legal Theory, Political Theory and Deconstruction* 1991, ch 3.

The character of rules: See Hart 1961, pp 55–61 on the nature of rules, and pp 82–91 on obligation; M Gilbert, 'Social Rules: Some Problems for Hart's Account and an Alternative Proposal' (1999) 18 Law & Philosophy 141. On the internal aspect of rules see also D N MacCormick, *Legal Reasoning and Legal Theory* 1978, pp 275–292; R Holton, 'Positivism and the Internal Point of View' (1998) 17 Law and Philosophy 597–625. Hart eventually recognised that the 'practice theory' of rules (ie that they are constituted by the combination of observable regularities of behaviour and an 'internal' acceptance of them as guides to conduct and standards of criticism) cannot apply to legislative rules existing as law from the moment of enactment and before any occasion has arisen for their practice: see Hart 1994: 255–256.

Sociological drift: For critiques attacking the insensitivity of Hart's legal philosophy to sociological questions see eg G Hughes, 'Professor Hart's Concept of Law' (1962) 25 Modern Law Review 319; J P Gibbs, 'Definitions of Law and Empirical Questions' (1968) 2 Law and Society Review 429; S Roberts, *Order and Dispute* 1979, pp 24–25; M Krygier, 'The Concept of Law and Social Theory' (1982) 2 Oxford Journal of Legal Studies 155; B Edgeworth, 'Legal Positivism and the Philosophy of Language' (1986) 6 Legal Studies 115; P Fitzpatrick, *Modernism and the Grounds of Law* 2001, pp 97–99. A serious attempt to meet these reiterated criticisms would lead Hart's normative legal theory to become integrated (productively in my view) with empirical legal theory associated with sociology of law. See also E Colvin, 'The Sociology of

Secondary Rules' (1978) 28 University of Toronto Law Journal 195; and especially H Ross, *Law as a Social Institution* 2001, developing a detailed argument that Hart's work could be considered 'an inchoate essay in interpretive sociology' (p ix).

Hart acknowledged in a private conversation with the present author (30 June 1988) that he regretted having referred to *The Concept of Law* as an essay in descriptive sociology and that it could have been better called an examination of concepts necessary for a descriptive sociology. If the word 'useful' is substituted for 'necessary', such a formulation defuses many criticisms in the text. On the other hand, it is not clear how far such a reformulation would be consistent with Hart's empiricist method.

The structure of a legal system: See Hart 1961, pp 91–110. Doubts about the viability or utility of the distinction between primary and secondary rules as Hart describes them have long been expressed. See eg L J Cohen, Book Review (1962) 71 Mind 395; C Tapper, 'Powers and Secondary Rules of Change' in A W B Simpson (ed) *Oxford Essays in Jurisprudence* 2nd ser, 1973; Fuller 1969a, pp 134–137. J W Harris, *Law and Legal Science* 1979, pp 92–106, argues that law should be understood in terms of duty-imposing and duty-excepting rules. Despite Hart's original claim (1961, pp 94–95) that the rule of recognition's very reason for existence is to remedy legal uncertainty his last writings assert that its function is 'to determine only the general conditions which correct legal decisions must satisfy' and that it does not and should not necessarily remove uncertainty (1994: 251, 258). This seems a defensive response to Dworkin's claim (see Chapter 6) that seeking conclusive criteria of legality by appeal to a rule of recognition is misguided.

Hart's hermeneutics: See also J Jackson, 'The Concept of Fact' in Leith and Ingram (eds) *Jurisprudence of Orthodoxy*, op cit. On Hart's project of a descriptive legal theory, now faced by Dworkin's challenge, see papers by S R Perry and L Murphy in Coleman, *Hart's Postscript*, op cit.

Judicial decisions and the 'open texture' of rules: See Hart 1961, ch 7; Hart 1977; MacCormick 1981, ch 10. See also B Bix, 'H L A Hart and the "Open Texture" of Language' (1991) 10 Law and Philosophy 51; D Lyons, 'Open Texture and the Possibility of Legal Interpretation' (1999) 18 Law and Philosophy 297; K E Himma, 'Judicial Discretion and the Concept of Law' (1999) 19 Oxford Journal of Legal Studies 7. A C Hutchinson, 'A Postmodern's Hart' (1995) 58 Modern Law Review 788 argues, like the text, that Hart's approach implies that certainty in the meaning of legal rules does not depend on the general nature of rules (as possessing a core and a penumbra) but on the social practices of their use. For Hart's final restatement of his views on judicial discretion see Hart 1994: 272–276.

Kelsen's conceptualism: The lack of a biography of Kelsen in English remains a regrettable gap in the literature. A brief introduction to his life, career and milieu and the influences on his work is contained in A Calsamiglia, 'For Kelsen' (2000) 13 Ratio Juris 196. Internationally, Kelsen is probably the most discussed of all twentieth century jurists. Among general studies in English see W Ebenstein, *The Pure Theory of Law* 1945; R Moore, *Legal Norms and Legal Science* 1978; R Tur and W Twining (eds) *Essays on Kelsen* 1986; S L Paulson and B L Paulson (eds) *Normativity and Norms* 1998. On neo-Kantian aspects of Kelsen's pure theory see Paulson and Paulson, op cit, Part 3; Tur and Twining, op cit, Part 1. Hart's difference with Kelsen over conceptualism is explicit in 'Kelsen Visited' in Hart (ed) 1983.

'The machine now runs by itself': On the concept of the basic norm (*Grundnorm*) see Kelsen 1945, pp 115–122; Kelsen 1967, ch 34; and the changed formulation in Kelsen 1991a, ch 59; For commentary see Paulson and Paulson, *Normativity and Norms*, op cit (papers by J Raz, T Honoré, G Edel and G Luf); S L Paulson, 'On the Puzzle Surrounding Hans Kelsen's Basic Norm' (2000) 13 Ratio Juris 279; U U Bindreiter, 'Presupposing the Basic Norm (2001) 14 Ratio Juris 143. The serious problem which Kelsen eventually found in specifying theoretically the nature of the basic norm can be considered, in relation to the themes developed in the text, a direct result of his conceptualism which requires legal philosophy to construct an epistemology of legal knowledge. Hart's empiricism (whatever its other problems) avoids these difficulties by treating the question of the existence of the rule of recognition simply as a matter of the actual social practices of officials. On changes in Kelsen's theory over time see L Gianformaggio (ed) *Hans Kelsen's Legal Theory: A Diachronic Point of View* 1990; and S L Paulson's introduction to *Normativity and Norms*.

Democracy and the Rule of Law: For Kelsen's ideas on democracy see Kelsen 1945, pp 284–300; and the brilliant discussion in Kelsen 1955, a remarkable and unjustly neglected essay. The link between philosophical and political relativism is elaborated also in 'Absolutism and Relativism in Philosophy and Politics' in Kelsen 1957. For Kelsen's conception of the identity of state and legal order see Kelsen 1967, pp 284–319; and Kelsen 1945, pp 181–192: 'The result of our analysis is that there is no sociological concept of the state different from the concept of the legal order' (1945, p 192). Kelsen's rejection of God as well as the state as transcendent entities suggests a straightforward atheism but issues raised in theological literature are frequent concerns of his writings. Kelsen's insistence seems to be that the responsibility for actions and the consequences of beliefs, including issues of conscience and faith, should be borne directly and personally by individuals, not assigned elsewhere.

On continuing concerns about the legal frameworks of modern state intervention in Western societies see eg T Lowi, 'The Welfare State, the New Regulation and the Rule of Law' in A C Hutchinson and P Monahan (eds) *The Rule of Law* 1987; W E Scheuerman, 'The Rule of Law and the Welfare State' (1994) 22 Politics and Society 195; G Lawson, 'The Rise and Rise of the Administrative State' (1994) 107 Harvard Law Review 1231; R Cotterrell, 'The Rule of Law in Transition' (1996) 5 Social and Legal Studies 451. B Kriegel, *The State and the Rule of Law* 1995 (defending the state founded on the Rule of Law by comparison with other historical conceptions of the state). For an argument that Hobbes' legal theory prefigures notions of the Rule of Law see D Dyzenhaus, 'Hobbes and the Legitimacy of Law' (2001) 21 Law and Philosophy 461.

Chapter 5 – The appeal of natural law

Legal positivism and natural law: The best-known concise summation of legal positivism is Hart 1958. Austin's views on natural law are in Austin 1885, lecture 32. For the history of natural law theory see eg H McCoubrey, *The Development of Naturalist Legal Theory* 1987; Weinreb 1987; H A Rommen, *The Natural Law* 1948. For general sources on current debates around natural law theory see J Finnis (ed) *Natural Law* (2 vols) 1991; R P George (ed) *Natural Law Theory* 1992. For a helpful brief survey see A J Lisska, 'Bentham and Recent Work on Natural Law' (1998) 51 Current Legal Problems 299. On natural law and common law see Gough 1955.

Natural law and legal authority: Among recent discussions of Aquinas' legal theory see especially A J Lisska, *Aquinas' Theory of Natural Law* 1996; Finnis (ed) *Natural Law*, op cit, Vol 1, Part 2; J Finnis, *Aquinas* 1998, chs 7 and 8; N Kretzmann, 'Lex Iniusta Non Est Lex' (1988) 33 American Journal of Jurisprudence 99; and the valuable discussions in Finnis 1980.

The 'rebirth' of natural law: See generally J Stone, *Human Law and Human Justice* 1965, ch 7; Haines 1930, especially Parts 2 to 5; Rommen, *Natural Law*, op cit, chs 6 and 7.

Anglo-American lessons from the Nazi era: On the Hart–Fuller debate see eg P Soper, 'Choosing a Legal Theory on Moral Grounds' in J Coleman and E F Paul (eds) *Philosophy and Law* 1987. Fuller's opposition to Nazism was deep and consistent: see eg Summers 1984, pp 7, 152. The claim (in M H Kramer, *In Defense of Legal Positivism* 1999, p 114) that Fuller had a 'flirtation with Nazism' seems entirely unfounded. Fuller's interest in Nazi legal mentality (Hull 1997, pp 244–245) in no way justifies this slur. On post-war legal problems arising from the legacy of the Nazi regime see H O Pappe, 'On the Validity of Judicial Decisions in the Nazi Era' (1960) 23 Modern Law Review 260; McCoubrey, op cit, ch 7. On the Nazi legal order see, among convenient sources in English,

Müller 1991; Neumann 1986, ch 16; Neumann 1944, pp 440–458; W E Scheuerman (ed) *The Rule of Law Under Seige* 1996, chs 5 and 6 (essays by Otto Kirchheimer). E Fraenkel, *The Dual State* 1941 argues that a regime of legality existed as a cloak for the parallel regime of arbitrariness. M Stolleis, *The Law under the Swastika* 1998 stresses the combination of terror and normal legal practice under the Nazi regime.

On legal positivism in Nazi Germany see also I England, 'Nazi Criticism against the Normative Theory of Hans Kelsen' (1998) 32 Israel Law Rev 183 (Nazi legal theory reflected a more general antagonism to values of reason and scientific objectivity); W Ott and F Buob, 'Did Legal Positivism Render German Jurists Defenceless during the Third Reich?' (1993) 2 Social and Legal Studies 91 (absolving positivism from blame); A Kaufmann, 'National Socialism and German Jurisprudence from 1933 to 1945' (1988) 9 Cardozo Law Review 1629 (a positivist attitude to Nazi law was pragmatically combined with an anti-positivist view of the surviving remnants of pre-Nazi law). Kaufmann also shows the widespread prostitution of legal philosophy to support the aims of the regime. See also P Caldwell, 'Legal Positivism and Weimar Democracy' (1994) 39 American Journal of Jurisprudence 273 (in relation to public law, the politics of legal positivism depends on historical context).

The ideal of legality and the existence of law: Franz Neumann's major work on the Rule of Law (Neumann 1986) was written as a London University PhD thesis soon after he left Germany in 1933. A German translation was published in 1980, but the original English version appeared in book form only in 1986. The major themes of the thesis are reiterated in Neumann 1944 and his 1937 essay 'The Change in the Function of Law in Modern Society' reprinted in Scheuerman (ed) *The Rule of Law Under Siege*, op cit (a collection of essays by Neumann and Kirchheimer). On Neumann and Kirchheimer see W E Scheuerman, *Between the Norm and the Exception: The Frankfurt School and the Rule of Law* 1997; Cotterrell 1995, ch 8.

A purposive view of law: Summers 1984 is a useful study of Fuller's work as a whole. The posthumously published *The Principles of Social Order* (K Winston, ed) rev edn 2001, collates many of Fuller's important later papers. Witteveen and Van der Burg (eds) 1999 contains valuable essays on most aspects of his work. For other recent discussions of Fuller see eg C Covell, *The Defence of Natural Law* 1992, ch 2; Special issue on Fuller (1994) 13 Law and Philosophy No 3; Kramer, *In Defense of Legal Positivism*, op cit, ch 3. P R Teachout, 'The Soul of the Fugue' (1986) 70 Minnesota Law Review 1073 argues that Fuller should be understood not as a system-building theorist but as an ethical critic.

Fuller and the common law tradition: For Fuller's conception of the varieties of social ordering see also eg his 'Some Unexplored Social Dimensions of the Law' in A E Sutherland (ed), *The Path of the Law from 1967* 1968; 'Two Principles of Human Association' in J R Pennock and J W Chapman (eds) *Voluntary Associations* 1969; 'The Law's Precarious Hold on Life' (1969) 3 Georgia Law Review 530; 'Law as an Instrument of Social Control and Law as a Facilitation of Human Interaction' [1975] Brigham Young University Law Review 89; 'Mediation: Its Forms and Functions' in *Principles of Social Order*, op cit; 'Some Presuppositions Shaping the Concept of "Socialization"' in J L Tapp and F J Levine (eds), *Law, Justice and the Individual in Society* 1977. See also J Boyle, 'Legal Realism and the Social Contract' (1993) 78 Cornell Law Review 371 (on conflicts in Fuller's views on contract as private ordering and contract as a model of reciprocity between rulers and ruled).

Politics and professional responsibility: Ernst Bloch's *Natural Law and Human Dignity* 1986, a wonderfully rich and wide-ranging discussion of European natural law traditions, argues that legal positivism's indifference to moral concerns bred a cynicism about law in Germany which made it easy for the Nazis to dismantle liberal legal institutions. For claims about legal positivism's moral myopia see also M Tushnet, *The American Law of Slavery 1810–1860* 1981, pp 54–65; R M Cover, *Justice Accused* 1975; D Dyzenhaus, *Hard Cases in Wicked Legal Systems* 1991. Among Fuller's writings on law and political values are 'Freedom: A Suggested Analysis' (1955) 68 Harvard Law Review 1305; 'Irrigation and Tyranny' in *Principles of Social Order*, op cit; 'Freedom as a Problem of Allocating Choice' (1968) 112 Proceedings of the American Philosophical Society 101; 'Some Reflections on Legal and Economic Freedoms' (1954) 54 Columbia Law Review 70.

Natural law tamed?: On Hart's 'minimum content of natural law' see also Hart 1958, pp 78–81 and his remarks in *Law, Liberty and Morality* 1963, p 70: 'It is indeed arguable that a human society in which ... [such universal values as individual freedom, safety of life, and protection from deliberately inflicted harm] are not recognised at all in its morality is neither an empirical nor a logical possibility ...'. For commentary and criticism see eg Fuller 1969a, pp 184–186; A P D'Entrèves, *Natural Law* 2nd edn 1970, pp 185–203.

On Finnis see eg D N MacCormick, 'Natural Law Reconsidered' (1981) 1 Oxford Journal of Legal Studies 99; McCoubrey, op cit, pp 179–186; Weinreb 1987, pp 108–115; Covell, *Defence of Natural Law*, op cit, ch 5. R Hittinger, *A Critique of the New Natural Law Theory* 1987 elaborately critiques Finnis' work and that of the theologian Germain Grisez on which he relies substantially; a main criticism is of the idea that natural law theory needs no philosophy of 'nature'. Weinreb 1987 similarly complains (ch 4) that Finnis' theory (like Fuller's) is of 'natural law without nature'. R P George, *In Defense of Natural Law* 1999 (especially pp 31–91) defends the Grisez-Finnis approach. Finnis (ed)

Natural Law, op cit, Vol 2, Parts 3 and 4, reprints articles bearing on this debate. See also the papers in (2000) 75 Notre Dame Law Review No 5, a special issue dedicated to Finnis.

Chapter 6 – The problem of the creative judge

Pound's rejection of the model of rules: Wigdor 1974 is a superb biography of Pound, including an incisive study of the evolution of his ideas. Hull 1997 interestingly explores Pound's relationship with Karl Llewellyn and the American legal realist movement. Paul Sayre's *The Life of Roscoe Pound* 1948, is idiosyncratic, sometimes eloquent, richly anecdotal, warm, personal and unashamedly biased towards its subject. E B McLean, *Law and Civilization: The Legal Thought of Roscoe Pound* 1992 is a straightforward summary of main themes in Pound's work. In 'The Need of a Sociological Jurisprudence' (1907) 19 Green Bag 607, one of Pound's earliest programmatic statements, sociological jurisprudence is advocated as a response to popular disrespect for law and the need to keep legal processes in tune with popular aspirations: if this is not achieved lawyers may lose 'their legitimate hegemony in legislation and politics to engineers and naturalists and economists' (p 612). Pound carefully distinguished sociological jurisprudence from sociology of law which he saw as a social science analysing law as a natural phenomenon in terms of behaviour: see his introduction to G Gurvitch, *Sociology of Law* 1947.

The outlook of sociological jurisprudence: On Pound's 1906 address to the American Bar Association in St Paul, Minnesota, and its consequences, see Wigdor 1974, pp 123–130; Hull 1997, pp 63–66. J H Wigmore's celebrated account of the event is reprinted in Sayre, *Life of Roscoe Pound*, op cit, pp 146–151; and in A Kocourek, 'Roscoe Pound as a Former Colleague Knew Him' in P Sayre, *Interpretations of Modern Legal Philosophies*, op cit, pp 424–427. For Pound's early firm defence of legislation as entitled to full recognition as a source of principle in common law reasoning see also 'Common Law and Legislation' (1908) 21 Harvard Law Review 383; and 'Liberty of Contract' (1909) 18 Yale Law Journal 454.

A theory of interests: Pound acknowledged the influence of the German jurist Rudolf von Jhering in developing a theory of interests as a foundation for legal theory. See on the relationship between Pound's and Jhering's ideas, Reuschlein, *Jurisprudence*, op cit, pp 107–112.

The search for a measure of values: The view that legal philosophy must establish and systematise values is developed in Pound 1940, ch 2. On relationships between Kohler's theories and Pound's sociological jurisprudence see Reuschlein, *Jurisprudence*, op cit, pp 117–120. For statements of the content of the jural postulates of Anglo-American law at various times in Pound's career see Pound 1942, ch 4; Pound 1959 III, pp 8–10 and references there to earlier writings.

The wider context of Pound's jurisprudence: On Pound's essentially conservative political views see Sayre, *Life of Roscoe Pound*, op cit, ch 6. On the reform philosophies of the Progressives see eg R M Crunden, *Ministers of Reform* 1984. M White, *Social Thought in America* 1949 is widely cited as authority for the existence of a general 'revolt against formalism' in American intellectual life from the beginning of the twentieth century and including, as its legal aspect, a rejection by Pound and others of the legal-logical fixations of positivist analytical jurisprudence. But legal formalism is a vague, empty term and the writings considered in this chapter are better seen as specific responses to the inadequacies of positivist analytical jurisprudence's explanations of legal change in the context of the American legal system, especially in periods of rapid social change.

Equally misleading, in my view, is the attempt (in R S Summers, *Instrumentalism and American Legal Theory* 1982) to link Pound with other influential mid-twentieth century American jurists in a relatively unified school of 'pragmatic instrumentalists'. See also W E Rumble, *American Legal Realism* 1968, pp 13–20. It seems no more enlightening to treat Pound's work (as does Hull 1997) as part of a wider, distinctive 'American jurisprudence' characterised by the use of 'bricolage' because, as Kelsen properly insists, most jurisprudence – though not, he claims, his own! – adopts this approach (which Kelsen calls syncretism of methods), whatever its national origins.

Dworkin and Pound: Burnet 1985 is a rare attempt to compare the two writers systematically, although it does not link them specifically as defenders of a particular common law outlook as does the text of this chapter. Dworkin seems more ready to acknowledge a debt to Fuller than to Pound if only in the most general terms: 'But for the example of his [Fuller's] dissatisfaction, others would have been content with the positivist's truism that the validity of law is one thing and its morality another': Dworkin 1965, p 668.

Principles and policies: For commentary on Dworkin see generally M Cohen (ed) *Ronald Dworkin and Contemporary Jurisprudence* 1984; Symposium on Dworkin's *Law's Empire* (1987) 6 Law and Philosophy 281–438; A Hunt (ed), *Reading Dworkin Critically* 1992; S Guest, *Ronald Dworkin* 2nd edn 1997; S Honeyball and J Walker, *Integrity, Community and Interpretation* 1998. After the publication of *Law's Empire* in 1986, Dworkin's writings in legal and moral philosophy have focussed mainly not on normative legal theory, as defined in this book, but on systematically elaborating and defending liberal values in relation to many contexts, including constitutional interpretation, affirmative action, health care, abortion and euthanasia, censorship, civil liberties and ideas of equality.

Dworkin's claim that principles can be part of law although their legal validity is not given by a rule of recognition directly challenges Hart's legal theory which treats such a rule as integral to its model of developed law. In general, legal positivists have responded to Dworkin's challenge with three main arguments: (i) that Dworkinian legal principles depend on a rule of recognition for their identification; (ii) that rules of recognition can (but need not) include reference to moral or other value criteria as part of the test by which legal officials recognise rules as law (see Hart 1961: 204); and (iii) that (contrary to Dworkin's view) the distinction between rule and principle is a matter of degree and legal rules often encompass relatively vague standards so that the model of rules already embraces much of what Dworkin refers to as principles. Hart (1994: 263–268) adopts versions of all of these arguments.

Argument (ii) is the most controversial among contemporary positivists. Usually termed 'inclusive' or 'soft' legal positivism or 'incorporationism', it raises difficult questions about what positivists will now accept as conventional 'tests' of the legal and how far the rule of recognition can be seen as having the task originally assigned to it (Hart 1961: 94–95) of remedying uncertainty in identifying law in a legal system. However, inclusive positivism does preserve the 'social thesis' that law is only what is recognised as such by social practice in a society. So it continues to assert a clear distinction from natural law positions.

For debates around inclusive legal positivism see eg (among supporters) Waluchow 1994; Kramer, *In Defense of Legal Positivism*, op cit, ch 6; J Coleman, *The Practice of Principle* 2001; (and opponents) J Raz, *Ethics in the Public Domain* 1994, ch 10. See also Coleman (ed) *Hart's Postscript*, op cit, especially papers by Shapiro, Coleman, Marmor, Zipursky, Himma and Leiter. The whole debate is discussed, with an attempt at practical reconciliation, in J Eekelaar, 'Judges and Citizens' (2002) 22 Oxford Journal of Legal Studies 497. For a thoughtful early attempt to incorporate Dworkinian ideas about principles into positivist theory see also D N MacCormick, *Legal Reasoning and Legal Theory* 1978. L Alexander and K Kress, 'Against Legal Principles' in A Marmor (ed) *Law and Interpretation* 1995 argues that appeal to legal principles, though widespread in common law interpretation, is misguided and obscures the interpretive task. On the idea that common law 'works itself pure' see Lieberman, *Province of Legislation Determined*, op cit, ch 4.

The closed world of legal interpretation: Dworkin has long recognised the frequent vagueness of the rule-principle distinction. See Dworkin 1977, pp 27–28. On problems of relating Dworkin's idea of community to empirical conditions in contemporary societies see E Lagerspetz, 'Ronald Dworkin on

Communities and Obligations' (1999) 12 Ratio Juris 108; see also N Simmonds, 'Between Positivism and Idealism' (1991) 50 Cambridge L J 308, arguing that Dworkin fails to recognise that 'community is the matrix of interpretation, not its result'.

Dworkin's portrayal of law as a matter of interpretation has helped to stimulate a huge recent literature on legal interpretation. For contrasting approaches see eg B Bix, *Law, Language and Legal Determinacy* 1993; T A O Endicott, *Vagueness in Law* 2000; S Levinson and S Mailloux (eds) *Interpreting Law and Literature* 1989; G Leyh (ed) *Legal Hermeneutics* 1992; P Nerhot (ed) *Law, Interpretation and Reality* 1990; A Marmor, *Interpretation and Legal Theory* 1992; A Marmor (ed) *Law and Interpretation*, op cit; D Patterson, *Law and Truth* 1996; N Stavropoulos, *Objectivity in Law* 1996.

Politics, professionalism and interpretive communities: On citizens as legal interpreters see also J Rawls, *A Theory of Justice* rev edn 1999, especially pp 335–343 (citizen's right in a 'nearly just' society to judge the legal rendering of basic principles on which the political order as a whole is founded). Unlike Dworkin, Rawls sees civil disobedience as breaching law to assert higher principle, not as an alternative interpretation of the legal situation (pp 320–321). His statement that the 'final court of appeal is not the court, nor the executive, nor the legislature, but the electorate as a whole' (p 342) seems to be meant in a looser, more rhetorical sense than Dworkin might argue for. But the two writers' positions are close.

On the Dworkin–Fish debate and Fish's ideas on interpretive communities see S Fish, *Doing What Comes Naturally* 1989, especially chs 4–7, 16 and 17; [R] Dworkin 1985, chs 6 and 7; J M Schelly, 'Interpretation in Law' (1985) 73 California Law Review 158. On the problem of 'fit' in interpretation see T R S Allan, 'Justice and Fairness in Law's Empire' (1993) 52 Cambridge Law Journal 64; A Marmor, *Interpretation and Legal Theory*, op cit, pp 82–84. On the need for sociological understanding of lawyers' interpretive communities and Fish's ultimate lack of interest in such an understanding see A Goldsmith, 'Is There Any Backbone in This Fish?' (1998) 23 Law and Social Inquiry 373. Fish makes clear (eg in 'The Law Wishes to Have a Formal Existence' in A Norrie (ed) *Closure or Critique* 1993) that his view of law does not preclude historical inquiries into how interpretive communities work but (like Dworkin in this respect) he assumes these communities are bounded in such a way that their identity is obvious and the nature of their working in general is understandable without the need for empirical inquiries.

Chapter 7 – Scepticism and realism

Scepticism about normative analysis of law: For parallel Scandinavian literature see especially, A Hägerström, *Inquiries Into the Nature of Law and Morals* 1953;

K Olivecrona, *Law as Fact* 1939, and the completely rewritten (and more guarded) 2nd edn 1971; A Ross, *On Law and Justice* 1958 and *Directives and Norms* 1968.

American legal realism has often been criticised for an indifference to values (eg Pound 1931, p 703), but this hardly applies to some of its most eminent theorists. Most realists denied the existence of moral absolutes. Felix Cohen, however, claimed insistently that the relativity of moral values did not undermine their importance as guides to law in a particular time and place: see his *Ethical Systems and Legal Ideals* 1933; and L K Cohen (ed) *The Legal Conscience* 1960. Karl Llewellyn sympathised with natural law theory's search for legal ideals but rejected its attempts to demonstrate moral absolutes and its claims that law and morality could not be analytically separated. See 'One "Realist's" View of Natural Law for Judges' in Llewellyn 1962; and Twining 1973, pp 185–188. These positions suggest no greater indifference to legal values than is found in the writings of many positivist analytical jurists.

On views of American legal realism in Britain see Twining 1968, pp 5–7 discussing dismissive attitudes at Oxford University and in legal literature in the 1950s. But legal realism helped to inspire the progressive academic lawyers who founded the Modern Law Review in 1937 to invigorate legal scholarship in Britain: see C Glasser, 'Radicals and Refugees' (1987) 50 Modern Law Review 688. For Hart's views on American legal realism see Hart 1961, ch 7; Hart 1977.

For general assessments of American legal realism see N Duxbury, *Patterns of American Jurisprudence* 1995; L Kalman, *Legal Realism at Yale 1927–1960* 1986; Horwitz 1992; Stevens 1983; Twining 1973; Rumble, *American Legal Realism*, op cit.

Pragmatism and realism: C S Peirce introduced pragmatism as a philosophical term and doctrine in the late nineteenth century. For James' doctrines see his *Pragmatism* 1907. Dewey's synthesis of Peirce's and James' ideas is reflected in his *Reconstruction in Philosophy* 1920, *Experience and Nature* 1925 and *The Quest for Certainty* 1929. See generally eg E C Moore, *American Pragmatism* 1961; M Brint and W Weaver (eds) *Pragmatism in Law and Society* 1991; M Alberstein, *Pragmatism and Law*, 2001; B Tamanaha, *Realistic Socio-Legal Theory* 1997, ch 2.

On Felix Cohen's essay see also G Peller, 'The Metaphysics of American Law' (1985) 73 California Law Review 1151, at pp 1227–1232; and on Cohen generally, M P Golding, 'Realism and Functionalism in the Legal Thought of Felix S Cohen' (1981) 66 Cornell Law Quarterly 1032. Close parallels with Cohen's discussion of 'transcendental nonsense' and 'magic solving words' in law can be found in Axel Hägerström's discussions of 'word magic' in his *Inquiries*, op cit, and in the works by Karl Olivecrona cited earlier. On the

Marxist notion of 'reification', appropriated in critical legal studies literature see G Lukacs *History and Class Consciousness* 1971; Gabel 1980; M H Kramer, *Legal Theory, Political Theory and Deconstruction*, op cit, ch 5.

Realism and normative legal theory: For the background to Pound's 'spring offensive of 1931 against the realists' (cf Llewellyn 1931a, p 54) and Llewellyn's reply which supplies the nine generalisations discussed in the text, see Hull 1997, especially ch 4; Twining 1973, ch 5; Horwitz 1992, ch 6. On Moore's approach to empirical research see also eg W U Moore and C C Callahan, 'My Philosophy of Law' in Julius Rosenthal Foundation 1941. Schlegel 1995 is an excellent account of the fate of the most significant legal realist efforts at social scientific research.

On Holmes' hugely influential 1897 speech, 'The Path of the Law', see the symposium '"The Path of the Law" After One Hundred Years' (1997) 110 Harvard Law Review, No 5; S J Burton (ed) *The Path of the Law and Its Influence* 2000. The literature on Holmes' life and work is vast: recent books include A W Alschuler, *Law Without Values* 2000; G E White, *Justice Oliver Wendell Holmes* 1993; H L Pohlman, *Justice Oliver Wendell Holmes and Utilitarian Jurisprudence* 1984; R W Gordon (ed) *The Legacy of Oliver Wendell Holmes, Jr* 1992. On caricatures of Llewellyn's view of rules see Twining 1968, ch 2, and for a clear statement of his actual position, in mid-career, on their importance see Llewellyn 1941.

On the enigmatic Jerome Frank see J Paul, *The Legal Realism of Jerome N Frank* 1959; W Volkomer, *The Passionate Liberal* 1970; R J Glennon, *The Iconoclast as Reformer* 1985; and N Duxbury, 'Jerome Frank and the Legacy of Legal Realism' (1991) 18 Journal of Law and Society 175 (thoughtfully locating Frank's outlook in the context of his times).

A famous source of radical realist claims about subjective psychological factors determining judges' decisions is J C Hutcheson, 'The Judgment Intuitive' (1929) 14 Cornell Law Quarterly 274. Written by an experienced judge, it claimed that intuition (rather than logic) is central to deciding cases. This kind of view naturally suggested that psychology held the main key to explaining judicial and administrative behaviour. Cf E S Robinson *Law and the Lawyers* 1935, p v: 'This book attempts to show that jurisprudence is certain to become one of the family of social sciences – that all its fundamental concepts will have to be brought into line with psychological knowledge'. See also Frank 1949, chs 10 and 11; Frank 1930 (on the importance of psychoanalytic theory); Arnold 1935, pp 269–270 (on the importance of psychiatry).

Peller ('Metaphysics of American Law', loc cit) characterises Llewellyn's approach as 'constructive realism' in contrast to the 'deconstructive realism' exemplified by Cohen's attack on 'transcendental nonsense'. But the constructive-deconstructive opposition seems too stark. Cohen, for example, only deconstructs existing legal doctrine to construct more realistic functional doctrine. It seems better to treat as the basic variable the degree of seriousness with which theorists view orthodox doctrinal reasoning. Realists, like Llewellyn, who see this reasoning as substantially significant can be considered 'constructive' insofar as their efforts aim at a better understanding of its working, or at improving the way legal doctrine is used.

Llewellyn's constructive doctrinal realism: On Llewellyn's work the best general source is Twining 1973, an excellent, deeply sympathetic intellectual biography; see also Hull 1997. Twining 1968, pp 5–23 gives an interesting personal account of Llewellyn. See also W L Twining, 'The Idea of Juristic Method' (1993) 48 University of Miami Law Review 119.

On Llewellyn's work on the Uniform Commercial Code see especially Wiseman 1987; A R Kamp, 'Between-the-Wars Social Thought' (1995) 59 Albany Law Review 325 (considering social scientific influences on Llewellyn's work on the UCC); A R Kamp, 'Uptown Act: A History of the Uniform Commercial Code 1940–49' (1998) 51 Southern Methodist University Law Review 275; J Whitman, 'Commercial Law and American Volk: A Note on Llewellyn's German Sources for the Uniform Commercial Code' (1987) 97 Yale Law Journal 156.

On Llewellyn and Hoebel's Cheyenne studies see S Landers, 'Practising What You Preach Against?' in J R Wunder (ed) *Law and the Great Plains* 1996 (on methodological issues); A K Mehrotra, 'Law and the "Other"' (2001) 26 Law and Social Inquiry 741 (an appreciation of the Cheyenne studies in context); D R Papke, 'How the Cheyenne Indians Wrote Article 2 of the Uniform Commercial Code' (1999) 47 Buffalo Law Review 1457.

The political context of American legal realism: E A Purcell, *The Crisis of Democratic Theory* 1973 illuminatingly links debates around legal realism to broader political and cultural developments (including debates on democratic values and totalitarianism) in the United States. See also, generally, Kalman, *Legal Realism*, op cit; Horwitz 1992; and for legal realism's place in the development of American legal education Stevens 1983 and Twining 1973, Part 1. On lawyers' involvement in the New Deal see P Irons, *New Deal Lawyers* 1982, and for the legal context, G E White, *The Constitution and the New Deal* 2000. The movement for 'free judicial decision' associated with the 'Free Law' jurists was not confined to Germany: see *The Science of Legal Method* 1917 by various authors, especially essays by E Ehrlich and F Gény.

Post-realist policy-science: On the collaboration of McDougal and Lasswell see especially Duxbury, *Patterns*, op cit, ch 3; Kalman, *Legal Realism*, op cit, pp

176–187. On the law and society movement in the United States see L M Friedman, 'The Law and Society Movement' (1986) 38 Stanford Law Review 763; R Cotterrell (ed) *Law and Society* 1994. The standard American text on economic analysis of law is R A Posner, *Economic Analysis of Law* 5th edn 1998.

Post-realist radical scepticism: On judicial behaviouralism see further Cotterrell 1992, pp 218–222, 341–342. On the American Critical Legal Studies movement: see generally, Special issue (1984) 36 Stanford Law Review, no 1; Kelman 1987; R Unger, *The Critical Legal Studies Movement* 1986; M Tushnet, 'Critical Legal Studies: A Political History' (1991) 100 Yale Law Journal 1515; J Boyle (ed) *Critical Legal Studies* 1992; A Altman, *Critical Legal Studies: A Liberal Critique* 1990; Special Issue (1999) 10 Law and Critique No 3; Duxbury, *Patterns*, op cit, ch 6; Goodrich 1996, ch 8 (sharply criticising CLS's limitations arising from its location in elite American law schools). D Kairys (ed) *The Politics of Law* 3rd edn 1998 is the standard introduction to and, in a sense, manifesto of CLS ideas.

For samples of writing charting the mainstream development of broadly critical approaches in Britain see R Fryer et al (eds) *Law, State and Society* 1981; D Sugarman (ed) *Legality, Ideology and the State* 1983; Twining (ed) 1986; P Fitzpatrick and A Hunt (eds) *Critical Legal Studies* 1987; Fitzpatrick (ed) *Dangerous Supplements* 1991.

Legal professionalism and the legacy of realism: A good idea of the bewilderment that realism caused in some sections of the legal profession in America can be gathered from P Mechem, 'The Jurisprudence of Despair' (1936) 21 Iowa Law Review 669. A comparable anguish about the 'nihilism' of critical legal studies is expressed in Carrington 1984. See further Minda 1995, ch 11; and Chapter 9, below. On the implications for professional legal ethics of legal realism's claims about law's indeterminacy see D B Wilkins, 'Legal Realism for Lawyers' (1990) 104 Harvard Law Review 469. On the situation of legal education in Britain at the time of the realist 'ferment' in America see Glasser, 'Radicals and Refugees', loc cit.

Chapter 8 – A jurisprudence of difference: class, gender and race

The ghost of Marx: Marx's main writings on law are collected in M Cain and A Hunt (eds) *Marx and Engels on Law* 1979. For discussion see H Collins, *Marxism and Law* 1982; P Phillips, *Marx and Engels on Law and Laws* 1980. The most sophisticated work of Marxist legal theory is Pashukanis 1978, and see P Beirne and R Sharlet (eds) *Pashukanis: Selected Writings on Marxism and Law* 1980.

Soviet Legal Philosophy 1951, a selection of key works, maps the course of early debates on law in the Soviet Union. P Hirst's *On Law and Ideology* 1979 and *Law, Socialism and Democracy* 1986 relate Marxist ideas on law to a modern Western context, as does B Edelman, *Ownership of the Image* 1979. Sypnowych 1990 discusses relations between law and socialist traditions derived from Marxism, but some of the book's presuppositions (and its emphasis on countering the Marxist thesis that law will wither away with the progressive achievement of socialism) seem anachronistic in the light of historical events since it was written. On social relations as a basic concept in Marxist legal theory see A Hunt, *Explorations in Law and Society* 1993, ch 11.

Equality, difference and liberal feminism: On feminist legal theory generally see eg, apart from sources cited in the text, N Lacey, *Unspeakable Subjects* 1998; M C Nussbaum, *Sex and Social Justice* 2000; M H Kramer, *Critical Legal Theory and the Challenge of Feminism* 1995; H Petersen, *Home Knitted Law* 1996 (essays on various aspects of women's legal experience) ; H Barnett, *Introduction to Feminist Jurisprudence* 1998. Among useful essay collections are K T Bartlett and R Kennedy (eds) *Feminist Legal Theory* 1991; M Fineman and N Thomadsen (eds) *At the Boundaries of Law* 1991; S James and S Palmer (eds) *Visible Women* 2001; L F Goldstein (ed) *Feminist Jurisprudence: The Difference Debate* 1992; M Becker, C G Bowman and M Torrey (eds) *Feminist Jurisprudence* 1994; P Smith (ed) *Feminist Jurisprudence* 1993; F E Olsen (ed) *Feminist Legal Theory* (2 vols) 1995 (reprinting key papers); H Barnett (ed) *Sourcebook on Feminist Jurisprudence* 1997.

For feminist approaches to particular areas of English law see eg A Bottomley (ed) *Feminist Perspectives on the Foundational Subjects of Law* 1996; S Milns and N Whitty (eds) *Feminist Perspectives on Public Law* 1999; A Morris and T O'Donnell (eds) *Feminist Perspectives on Employment Law* 1999; S Scott-Hunt and H Lim (eds) *Feminist Perspectives on Equity and Trusts* 2001.

Different moral voices in law: On implications of Carol Gilligan's work for law see also M Drakopoulou, 'The Ethic of Care, Female Subjectivity and Feminist Legal Scholarship' (2000) 8 Feminist Legal Studies 199; L K Kerber et al, 'On *In a Different Voice*: An Interdisciplinary Forum' (1986) 11 Signs 304, with response by Gilligan; Frug 1992, ch 3, and the response to Frug's paper (as originally published) in J Greenberg, M Minow and E Schneider, 'Contradiction and Revision' (1992) 15 Harvard Women's Law Journal 65; J C Tronto, *Moral Boundaries: A Political Argument for an Ethic of Care* 1994. See also, more generally, S Sevenhuijsen, *Citizenship and the Ethics of Care* 1998; R West, *Caring for Justice* 1997, ch 1; E B Cole and S Coultrap-McQuin (eds) *Explorations in Feminist Ethics* 1992; N Naffine (ed) *Gender and Justice* 2002 (reprinting key papers).

On possibilities for developing a different moral voice of legal practice see also R Jack and D Jack, *Moral Vision and Professional Decisions: The Changing Values of Women and Men Lawyers* 1989 (studying professional experiences and values of US women lawyers in comparison with those of their male counterparts); C Menkel-Meadow, 'Exploring a Research Agenda of the Feminization of the Legal Profession' (1989) 14 Law and Social Inquiry 289; J L Pierce, *Gender Trials: Emotional Lives in Contemporary Law Firms* 1995, ch 5 (arguing that 'a more caring practice' exists among women lawyers); M Thornton, *Dissonance and Distrust: Women in the Legal Profession* 1996. L Guinier, M Fine and J Balin, *Becoming Gentlemen* 1997 (analysing women students' experience at a major US law school) reports 'the disappointments of women as they enter previously male-dominated institutions and, to a surprising extent, remain isolated, marginalised and dissatisfied' (p 2).

Radical feminism and the gender of law: On MacKinnon see D Cornell, 'Sexual Difference, the Feminine and Equivalency' (1991) 100 Yale Law Journal 2247 (arguing that MacKinnon's programme is too limited because it fails to affirm sexual difference as anything other than victimisation); E Jackson, 'Catherine MacKinnon and Feminist Jurisprudence: A Critical Appraisal' (1992) 19 Journal of Law and Society 195. On 'sexually transmitted debt' in the surety cases see also R Mackenzie, 'Beauty and the Beastly Bank' in Bottomley (ed) *Foundational Subjects of Law*, op cit, and K Green and H Lim, 'Weaving Along the Borders' in Scott-Hunt and Lim (eds), *Equity and Trusts*, op cit. On the place of law in feminist strategies see also E Kingdom, *What's Wrong with Rights?* 1991 (essays cautioning against feminist reliance on rights-based arguments). On pornography as a feminist issue see eg Barnett, *Introduction*, above, pp 281–315; Smart 1989, ch 6; Frug 1992, pp 145–153. On the problem of essentialism see A P Harris, 'Race and Essentialism in Feminist Legal Theory' (1990) 42 Stanford Law Review 581.

Postmodern feminism: On Mary Joe Frug's work see the papers by B Johnson, R Colker and M Minow in (1992) 105 Harvard Law Review No 5. See also M Ashe, 'Inventing Choreographies: Feminism and Deconstruction' (1990) 90 Columbia Law Review 1123 (a review essay discussing a range of postmodernist and related ideas bearing on feminism).

Critical race theory: For debates on rights discourse see Symposium on the critique of rights (1984) 62 Texas Law Review No 8; A Hunt, 'Rights and Social Movements' (1990) 17 Journal of Law and Society 309; D Herman, 'Beyond the Rights Debate' (1993) 2 Social and Legal Studies 25. N Milner, 'The Denigration of Rights and the Persistence of Rights Talk' (1989) 14 Law and Social Inquiry 631, argues that rights discourse retains its attractiveness and power in practice even among those who are critical of it.

For wide-ranging surveys of the current concerns and recent intellectual history of CRT see R Delgado and J Stefancic (eds) *Critical Race Theory: The Cutting Edge* 2nd edn 2000; F Valdes, J M Culp and A P Harris (eds) *Crossroads, Directions and a New Critical Race Theory* 2002; A K Wing (ed) *Critical Race Feminism: A Reader* 1997. In this literature specifically legal issues are often inseparable from broader social issues, illustrating the claim in the text (see introduction to Chapter 9) that the jurisprudence of difference is symptomatic of the 'invasion' of law (as a distinct conceptual field) by the social.

See also the 600 page symposium on 'LatCrit Theory' (1997) 85 California Law Review No 5; R Delgado and J Stefancic, 'Critical Race Theory' (1998) 51 Current Legal Problems 467 (usefully summarising the history of CRT and its concerns); P Goodrich and L G Mills, 'The Law of White Spaces' (2001) 51 Journal of Legal Education 15 (relating CRT to British contexts and detailing intemperate and unscholarly reactions to it, reminiscent of those that legal realism and CLS earlier attracted).

For a sample of specific studies see M J Matsuda et al, *Words That Wound* 1993 (on legal control of racist speech in the United States); Lopez 1996 (on law's construction of racial identity); G A Spann, *Race Against the Court* 1993 (claiming that the US Supreme Court perpetuates the subordination of racial minorities); A N Ancheta, *Race, Rights and the Asian American Experience* 1998 (arguing that racial justice will be achieved only by recognising the diversity of ethnic and racial experience); D Cooper and D Herman, 'Jews and Other Uncertainties' (1999) 19 Legal Studies 339 (on the construction of 'Jew' in the racialised discourse of English trusts law).

Politics, professionalism, difference: See M Minow, *Making All the Difference* 1990 (showing how American law creates and confronts social differentiation with regard, for example, to disability, race, ethnicity, religion and gender). On the public-private distinction see also S I Benn and G F Gaus (eds) *Public and Private in Social Life* 1983; M Thornton (ed) *Public and Private: Feminist Legal Debates* 1995; M P D'Entrèves and U Vogel (eds) *Public and Private* 2000; Symposium on the public-private distinction (1982) 130 University of Pennsylvania Law Review No 6 (especially papers by K Klare, C Stone, D Kennedy and M Horwitz).

Chapter 9 – The deconstruction and reconstruction of law

Law as a fractured system of meanings, and all legal thought produced from particular standpoints: These issues have given rise to calls for a focus on the subjectivity of legal understanding (rather than merely assuming the 'objectivity' of what is understood, ie law). See eg Schlag 1991; J M Balkin, 'Understanding Legal Understanding' (1993) 103 Yale Law Journal 105; D Caudill, *Lacan and the Subject of Law* 1997, ch 4.

Postmodernism and deconstruction: Postmodernism and legal theory: see eg Douzinas and Warrington 1991; Davies 1996; C Douzinas et al (eds) *Politics, Postmodernity and Critical Legal Studies* 1994; D Cornell et al (eds) *Deconstruction and the Possibility of Justice* 1992; I Ward, *Kantianism, Postmodernism and Critical Legal Thought* 1997; H M Stacy, *Postmodernism and Law* 2001; Minda 1995, ch 12; A Carty (ed) *Post-Modern Law* 1991.

On Balkin's account of deconstruction see Schlag 1991 (criticising tendencies to treat deconstruction as an analytical tool). Derrida's main discussion of law is Derrida 1992 (discussed in 'Derrida, Justice, Autopoiesis', below).

Recovering minor jurisprudences: On Lacanian psychoanalysis and law see Caudill, *Lacan and the Subject of Law*, op cit; Stacy, *Postmodernism and Law*, op cit, ch 5. On the 'postal rule' see also S Gardiner, 'Trashing with Trollope' (1992) 12 Oxford Journal of Legal Studies 170; C Douzinas and R Warrington, 'Posting the Law' (1991) 4 International Journal for the Semiotics of Law 115. On 'judgments of love' as 'a royal road to questions of the place of law in intimate relationships, of the public in the private, of the juridical as well as the political in the personal' see Goodrich 1996, ch 2. Among recent discussions of courts of love, doubting their historical existence, see A Weir, *Eleanor of Aquitaine* 1999, pp 181–182 ('almost certainly no more than a literary conceit') and D D R Owen, *Eleanor of Aquitaine* 1993, pp 152–156. W A Neilson, *The Origin and Sources of the Court of Love* (1899, reprinted 1967) argues that the practices associated by some writers with courts of love did exist and, although playful rather than serious, were socially significant and influential. A Kelly, *Eleanor of Aquitaine and the Four Kings* 1952 sees 'something ghoulish' in exposing accounts of courts of love 'to the callous scrutiny of an age hostile to sentiment' and claims that these accounts give 'glimpses of a woman's notions of society different in essential respects from the prevailing feudal scheme' (p 164).

Law without foundations: The circularity of legal thought is not a discovery of postmodernist theorists (see eg Cohen 1935, p 45, and N MacCormick, *Legal Reasoning and Legal Theory*, op cit, p 246) but they have made it central to their analyses to show either law's power (as knowledge free of the problems of foundationalism) or its weakness (built on illusory bases of authority).

On postmodernist theory's indifference to empirical inquiries see Teubner 1997. This indifference is founded on postmodernism's denial 'that the culture in which we live can be separated from the rhetorical means by which we represent that culture to ourselves' and 'that our theoretical perspectives stand aloof from the practices we study' (F J Mootz, 'Correspondence: Postmodern Constitutionalism as Materialism' (1992) 91 Michigan Law Review 515, at p 522). However, these views should lead not to an avoidance of empirical inquiries but to a different understanding of their nature.

Derrida, justice, autopoiesis: On Derrida's view of justice see Balkin 1994; D Cornell, *The Philosophy of the Limit* 1992; R Buonamano, 'The Economy of Violence' (1998) 11 Ratio Juris 168; D Litowitz, 'Derrida on Law and Justice' (1995) 8 Canadian Journal of Law and Jurisprudence 325; Stacy, *Postmodernism and Law*, op cit, ch 4. J M Balkin, *Cultural Software: A Theory of Ideology* 1998, ch 7, argues a need to presuppose transcendent values of justice and truth to which any particular culture only imperfectly responds. Douzinas and Warrington 1995 considers issues of ethics and justice in postmodern perspective.

On law and autopoiesis theory see N Luhmann, 'Operational Closure and Structural Coupling' (1992) 13 Cardozo Law Review 1419; Teubner 1993; G Teubner (ed) *Autopoietic Law: A New Approach to Law and Society* 1988; Přibáň and Nelken (eds) 2001; A Febbrajo and G Teubner (eds) *State, Law, Economy as Autopoietic Systems* 1992. Cornell (*Philosophy of the Limit*, op cit, ch 5) compares deconstruction with autopoiesis theory: 'Derrida agrees with Luhmann ... that there is no "real" normative origin from which all the values and norms of the legal system ... can be adequately assessed. But, unlike Luhmann, Derrida does argue that this origin cannot ever be fully displaced by the logic of recursivity ... The endless deconstruction of law destabilises the machine and exposes the cracks in the system. As a result of this destabilisation, the displacement of the origin can never be completed ...' (pp 131–132). Thus, on this view, law cannot be discursively self-sufficient as autopoiesis theory claims.

Law's empty shell: The idea of law as constitutive has gained wide acceptance especially among American sociolegal scholars and is in no way restricted to postmodernist writers. In one form it resembles Marxist understandings of law's ideological functions; in another it correlates strongly with pragmatist ideas about law's instrumental power to shape social life.

Pragmatism: See sources cited in notes to 'Pragmatism and Realism' in Chapter 7, above. For a thoughtful critique of American neo-pragmatism see Luban 1994, ch 3. Schlag 1991, pp 1705–1721 argues that pragmatists rely on a 'conventional depiction of the field of action, of thought, and of plausible political aims' (p 1720) and so cannot escape these conventions. A classic exposition of antifoundationalism, influential in neo-pragmatism, is R Rorty, *Philosophy and the Mirror of Nature* 1980.

Reorienting legal theory: On faith in law see eg S Levinson, *Constitutional Faith* 1988; J M Balkin, 'Agreements with Hell and Other Objects of Our Faith' (1997) 65 Fordham Law Review 1703; Oliver, Douglas-Scott and Tadros (eds) 2000.

Theorising legal communities: The law-and-community approach presented in the text derives from Cotterrell 1997. I have since tried to develop and apply it in various contexts in the following papers: 'Is There a Logic of Legal Transplants?' in D Nelken and J Feest (eds) *Adapting Legal Cultures* 2001; 'Seeking Similarity, Appreciating Difference' in A Harding and E Örücü (eds) *Comparative Law in the 21st Century* 2002; 'Common Law Approaches to the Relationship Between Law and Morality' (2000) 3 Ethical Theory and Moral Practice 9; and 'Transparency, Mass Media, Ideology and Community' (1999) 3 Cultural Values 414. See also Cotterrell 1999, pp 222–227.

Legal theory beyond the nation state: The vast literature on globalisation in relation to particular transnational legal developments, and on current legal issues in relation to groups of various kinds existing within states, is beyond this book's scope. On emergent patterns of transnational authority see eg the provocative analysis of M Hardt and A Negri, *Empire* 2000, arguing that the new form of sovereigny is decentred and deterritorialised, comprising 'a series of national and supranational organisms united under a single logic of rule' (p xii). Among the most important efforts, so far, to theorise the nature of transnational legal processes in relation to current changes in the character of the social are B De S Santos, *Toward a New Legal Common Sense* 2nd edn 2002, and G Teubner (ed) *Global Law Without a State* 1997.

Legal theory and legal professions: For a wide-ranging debate on postmodern politics in legal contexts see J F Handler, 'Postmodernism, Protest and the New Social Movements' (1992) 26 Law and Society Review 697, and commentaries on this paper in the same journal issue. On professional implications of the development of transnational legal practice see eg R Abel, 'Transnational Law Practice' (1994) 44 Case Western Reserve Law Review 737; Y Dezalay and B Garth, *Dealing in Virtue* 1996; J Flood, 'Megalawyering in the Global Order' (1996) 3 International Journal of the Legal Profession 169.

On legal professionalism in contemporary Britain see eg R Abel, 'Between Market and State: The Legal Profession in Turmoil' (1989) 52 Modern Law Review 285; Special issue 'Tomorrow's Lawyers' (1992) 19 Journal of Law and Society No 1; G Hanlon, 'A Profession in Transition?' (1997) 60 Modern Law Review 798.

For recent critiques of the trajectories of legal professionalism in the United States see H Edwards, 'The Growing Disjunction Between Legal Education and the Legal Profession' (1992) 91 Michigan Law Review 34 (law schools are moving towards pure theory while law firms are moving towards the pursuit of profit above all else: 'ethical practice' has been neglected by both); A T Kronman, *The Lost Lawyer* 1993 (American lawyers are losing the traditional values that underpin professional satisfaction and pride); M A Glendon, *A Nation Under Lawyers* 1994 (lawyers' influence in society is greater than ever but professional values are looser, more uncertain and out of touch with public expectations).

References

Dates in brackets after the author's name are those of the original publication of the work or edition cited.

Abrams, K (1990) 'Ideology and Women's Choices' 24 Georgia Law Review 761–801.

Ahdar, R J (ed) (2000) *Law and Religion* (Aldershot: Ashgate).

Allison, J W F (1999) 'Legal Culture in Lon Fuller's Analysis of Adjudication' in Witteveen and Van der Burg (eds) (1999) pp 346–363.

Arnold, T W (1935) *The Symbols of Government* (New York: Harcourt Brace and World edn, 1962).

Arthurs, H W (1985) *Without the Law: Administrative Justice and Legal Pluralism in Nineteenth-Century England* (Toronto: University of Toronto Press).

Auchmuty, R (2001) 'The Fiction of Equity' in S Scott-Hunt and H Lim (eds) *Feminist Perspectives on Equity and Trusts* pp 1–25 (London: Cavendish).

Austin, J (1832) *The Province of Jurisprudence Determined* (Cambridge: Cambridge University Press edn, 1995).

— (1885) *Lectures on Jurisprudence or the Philosophy of Positive Law* 5th edn (London: John Murray).

Balkin, J M (1987) 'Deconstructive Practice and Legal Theory' 96 Yale Law Journal 743–786.

— (1992) 'What is a Postmodern Constitutionalism?' 90 Michigan Law Review 1966–1990.

— (1994) 'Transcendental Deconstruction, Transcendent Justice' 92 Michigan Law Review 1131–1186.

Barker, E (1928) *Political Thought in England 1848–1914* 2nd edn (Westport, Conn: Greenwood Press reprint, 1980).

Beger, N J (2002) 'Putting Gender and Sexuality on the Agenda: Queer Theory and Legal Politics' in R Banakar and M Travers (eds) *An Introduction to Law and Social Theory* pp 173–188 (Oxford: Hart).

Bentham, J (1970) *Of Laws in General* (London: University of London Athlone Press).

— (1977) *A Comment on the Commentaries and A Fragment on Government* (London: University of London Athlone Press).

Blackstone, W (1809) *Commentaries on the Law of England* 15th edn (London: Cadell and Davies). For convenience references in the text are to the original pagination of the 1765–1769 edition as indicated in this later edition.

Bobbio, N (1987) *The Future of Democracy: A Defence of the Rules of the Game*, transl by R Griffin (Cambridge: Polity).

Brunner, H E (1945) *Justice and the Social Order*, transl by M Hottinger (London: Lutterworth Press).

Buckland, W W (1949) *Some Reflections on Jurisprudence* (Hamden, Conn: Archon reprint, 1974).

Burnet, D A (1985) 'Dworkin and Pound' 71 Archiv fur Rechts-und Sozial-philosophie 234–245.

Burrow, J W (1966) *Evolution and Society: A Study in Victorian Social Theory* (Cambridge: Cambridge University Press).

Butler, J (1990) *Gender Trouble: Feminism and the Subversion of Identity* (New York: Routledge).

Campbell, T D (1996) *The Legal Theory of Ethical Positivism* (Aldershot: Dartmouth).

Carrington, P D (1984) 'Of Law and the River' 34 Journal of Legal Education 222–228.

Carter, J C (1907) *Law: Its Origin Growth and Function* (New York: Da Capo reprint, 1974).

Castberg, F (1955) 'Philosophy of Law in the Scandinavian Countries' 5 American Journal of Comparative Law 388–400.

Cocks, R (1983) *Foundations of the Modern Bar* (London: Sweet & Maxwell).

Cohen, F S (1935) 'Transcendental Nonsense and the Functional Approach' reprinted in L K Cohen (ed) *The Legal Conscience: Selected Papers of Felix S Cohen* pp 33–76 (New Haven: Yale University Press, 1960).

Cohen, M R (1933) *Law and the Social Order: Essays in Legal Philosophy* (New York: Archon reprint, 1967).

Collini, S, Winch, D and Burrow, J (1983) *That Noble Science of Politics: A Study in Nineteenth-Century Intellectual History* (Cambridge: Cambridge University Press).

Conklin, W E (2002) 'The Place of the People in John Austin's Structuralism' in M Troper and A Verza (eds) *Legal Philosophy: General Aspects* (ARSP-Beiheft 82) pp 184–200 (Stuttgart: Franz Steiner Verlag).

Cotterrell, R (1992) *The Sociology of Law: An Introduction* 2nd edn (London: Butterworth).

— (1995) *Law's Community: Legal Theory in Sociological Perspective* (Oxford: Oxford University Press).

— (1997) 'A Legal Concept of Community' 12 Canadian Journal of Law and Society 75–91.

— (1998) 'Law and Community: A New Relationship?' 51 Current Legal Problems 367–391.

— (1999) *Émile Durkheim: Law in a Moral Domain* (Edinburgh: Edinburgh University Press. Stanford: Stanford University Press).

— (2001) 'The Representation of Law's Autonomy in Autopoiesis Theory' in Přibáň and Nelken (eds) (2001) pp 80–103.

Daintith, T C (1982) 'Legal Analysis of Economic Policy' 9 Journal of Law and Society 191–224.

Dalton, C (1988) 'Where We Stand: Observations on the Situation of Feminist Legal Thought' 3 Berkeley Women's Law Journal 1–13.

Davies, M (1996) *Delimiting the Law: 'Postmodernism' and the Politics of Law* (London: Pluto).

Derrida, J (1992) 'Force of Law: The "Mystical Foundation of Authority"' in D Cornell, M Rosenfeld and D G Carlson (eds) *Deconstruction and the Possibility of Justice* pp 3–67 (New York: Routledge).

Dewey, J (1924) 'Logical Method and Law' 10 Cornell Law Quarterly 17–27.

Diamond, A (ed) (1991) *The Victorian Achievement of Sir Henry Maine: A Centennial Reappraisal* (Cambridge: Cambridge University Press).

Dicey, A V (1905) *Lectures on the Relation Between Law and Public Opinion in England During the Nineteenth Century* (London: Macmillan).

— (1959) *An Introduction to the Study of the Law of the Constitution* 10th edn (London: Macmillan).

Dinwiddy, J R (1975) 'Bentham's Transition to Political Radicalism, 1809–10' 36 Journal of the History of Ideas 683–700.

Douzinas, C and Warrington, R (1991) *Postmodern Jurisprudence: The Law of Text in the Texts of Law* (London: Routledge).

— (1994) *Justice Miscarried: Ethics, Aesthetics and the Law* (Hemel Hempstead: Harvester Wheatsheaf).

Dowdall, H C (1926) 'The Present State of Analytical Jurisprudence' 42 Law Quarterly Review 451–470.

Dubois, E C et al (1985) 'Feminist Discourse, Moral Values, and the Law – A Conversation' 34 Buffalo Law Review 11–87.

Dworkin, A (1985) 'Against the Male Flood: Censorship, Pornography and Equality' 8 Harvard Women's Law Journal 1–29.

Dworkin, R M (1965) 'Philosophy, Morality and Law: Observations Prompted by Professor Fuller's Novel Claim' 113 University of Pennsylvania Law Review 668–690.

— (1967) 'The Case For Law: A Critique' 1 Valparaiso University Law Review 215–217.

— (1971) 'Philosophy and the Critique of Law' in R P Wolff (ed) *The Rule of Law* pp 147–170 (New York: Simon and Schuster).

— (1977) *Taking Rights Seriously* (London: Duckworth reprint with new appendix, 1978).

— (1982) '"Natural Law" Revisited' 34 University of Florida Law Review 165–188.

— (1985) *A Matter of Principle* (Cambridge, Mass: Harvard University Press).

— (1986) *Law's Empire* (Oxford: Hart reprint, 1998).

— (1989) 'Liberal Community' 77 California Law Review 479–504.

Edwards, S S M (1996) *Sex and Gender in the Legal Process* (London: Blackstone).

Ellickson, R C (1991) *Order Without Law: How Neighbors Settle Disputes* (Cambridge, Mass: Harvard University Press, 1991).

Elliott, G (1987) *Althusser: The Detour of Theory* (London: Verso).

Evans, M O (1896) *Theories and Criticisms of Sir Henry Maine* (London: Stevens and Haynes).

Feaver, G (1969) *From Status to Contract: A Biography of Sir Henry Maine 1822–1888* (London: Longmans, Green).

Fehlberg, B (1997) *Sexually Transmitted Debt: Surety Experience and English Law* (Oxford: Oxford University Press).

Finnis, J (1980) *Natural Law and Natural Rights* (Oxford: Oxford University Press).

Fish, S (1982) 'Working on the Chain Gang: Interpretation in Law and Literature' 60 Texas Law Review 551–567.

—— (1983) 'Wrong Again' 62 Texas Law Review 299–316.

Fitzpatrick, P (1992) *The Mythology of Modern Law* (London: Routledge).

—— (2001) *Modernism and the Grounds of Law* (Cambridge: Cambridge University Press).

Frank, J (1930) *Law and the Modern Mind* (Garden City, NY: Anchor reprint, 1963, including 1948 preface to sixth printing).

—— (1949) *Courts on Trial: Myth and Reality in American Justice* (Princeton: Princeton University Press).

Frug, M J (1992) *Postmodern Legal Feminism* (New York: Routledge).

Fuller, L L (1940) *The Law in Quest of Itself* (Chicago: Foundation Press).

—— (1946) 'Reason and Fiat in Case Law' 59 Harvard Law Review 376–395.

—— (1958) 'Positivism and Fidelity to Law – A Reply to Professor Hart' 71 Harvard Law Review 630–672.

—— (1969a) *The Morality of Law* 2nd edn (New Haven: Yale University Press).

—— (1969b) 'Human Interaction and the Law' 14 American Journal of Jurisprudence 1–36.

—— (1978) 'The Forms and Limits of Adjudication' 92 Harvard Law Review 353–409.

Gabel, P (1980) 'Reification in Legal Reasoning' 3 Research in Law and Sociology 25–51.

Gabel, P and Kennedy, D (1984) 'Roll Over Beethoven' 36 Stanford Law Review 1–55.

Gilligan, C (1982) *In a Different Voice: Psychological Theory and Women's Development* (Cambridge, Mass: Harvard University Press).

—— (1985) Contributions to discussion in Dubois et al (1985).

Gilmore, G (1961) 'Legal Realism: Its Cause and Cure' 70 Yale Law Journal 1037–1048.

Goodrich, P (1987) *Legal Discourse: Studies in Linguistics, Rhetoric and Legal Analysis* (London: Macmillan).

—— (1990) *Languages of Law: From Logics of Memory to Nomadic Masks* (London: Weidenfeld and Nicolson).

— (1994) 'Jani Anglorum: Signs, Symptoms, Slips and Interpretation in Law' in C Douzinas, P Goodrich and Y Hachamovitch (eds) *Politics, Postmodernity and Critical Legal Studies* pp 107–144 (London: Routledge).

— (1995) *Oedipus Lex: Psychoanalysis, History, Law* (Berkeley: University of California Press).

— (1996) *Law in the Courts of Love: Literature and Other Minor Jurisprudences* (London: Routledge).

— (1997) 'Introduction: Psychoanalysis and Law' in P Goodrich (ed) *Law and the Unconscious: A Legendre Reader* pp 1–36 (London: Macmillan).

Goody, J (1977) *The Domestication of the Savage Mind* (Cambridge: Cambridge University Press).

Gough, J W (1955) *Fundamental Law in English Constitutional History* (Oxford: Oxford University Press).

Habermas, J (1974) *Theory and Practice*, transl by J Viertel (London: Heinemann).

Hacker, P M S (1977) 'Hart's Philosophy of Law' in Hacker and Raz (eds) (1977) pp 1–25.

Hacker, P M S and Raz, J (eds) (1977) *Law, Morality and Society: Essays in Honour of H L A Hart* (Oxford: Oxford University Press).

Haines, C G (1930) *The Revival of Natural Law Concepts: A Study of the Establishment and of the Interpretation of Limits on Legislatures with Special Reference to the Development of Certain Phases of American Constitutional Law* (New York: Russell and Russell edn, 1965).

Hamburger, L and Hamburger, J (1985) *Troubled Lives: John and Sarah Austin* (Toronto: University of Toronto Press).

Harno, A J (1932) 'Social Planning and Perspective Through Law' in *Handbook and Proceedings of the Association of American Law Schools 1932 Annual Conference* pp 8–22 (New York: AALS).

Hart, H L A (1953) 'Definition and Theory in Jurisprudence' reprinted in Hart (1983) pp 21–47.

— (1955) 'Introduction' to J Austin, *The Province of Jurisprudence Determined and the Uses of the Study of Jurisprudence* pp vii–xviii (Indianapolis: Hackett reprint, 1998).

— (1958) 'Positivism and the Separation of Law and Morals' reprinted in Hart (1983) pp 49–87.

— (1961) *The Concept of Law* (Oxford: Oxford University Press reissue, repaginated with new postscript, 1994).

— (1963) *Law, Liberty and Morality* (Oxford: Oxford University Press).

— (1965) 'Lon L Fuller: The Morality of Law' reprinted in Hart (1983) pp 343–363.

— (1968) *Punishment and Responsibility: Essays in the Philosophy of Law* (Oxford: Oxford University Press).

— (1970) 'Jhering's Heaven of Concepts and Modern Analytical Jurisprudence' reprinted in Hart (1983) pp 265–277.

— (1972) 'Legal Powers' reprinted in Hart (1982) pp 194–219.

— (1977) 'American Jurisprudence Through English Eyes: The Nightmare and the Noble Dream' reprinted in Hart (1983) pp 123–144.

— (1982) *Essays on Bentham: Studies in Jurisprudence and Political Theory* (Oxford: Oxford University Press).

— (1983) *Essays in Jurisprudence and Philosophy* (Oxford: Oxford University Press).

— (1987) 'Comment' in R Gavison (ed) *Issues in Contemporary Legal Philosophy: The Influence of H L A Hart* pp 35–42 (Oxford: Oxford University Press).

— (1994) 'Postscript' to Hart (1961) pp 238–276.

Hinsley, F H (1986) *Sovereignty* 2nd edn (Cambridge: Cambridge University Press).

Hobbes, T (1651) *Leviathan* (Cambridge: Cambridge University Press edn, 1991).

Holdsworth, W S (1928) *The Historians of Anglo-American Law* (Hamden, Conn: Archon reprint, 1966).

Holmes, Jr, O W (1897) 'The Path of the Law' reprinted in (1997) 110 Harvard Law Review 991–1009.

— (1899) 'Law in Science and Science in Law' 12 Harvard Law Review 443–463.

Honoré, A M (1973) 'Groups, Laws and Obedience' in A W B Simpson (ed) *Oxford Essays in Jurisprudence* 2nd series pp 1–21 (Oxford: Oxford University Press).

— (1987) *Making Law Bind: Essays Legal and Philosophical* (Oxford: Oxford University Press).

Horwitz, M J (1992) *The Transformation of American Law 1870–1960: The Crisis of Legal Orthodoxy* (New York: Oxford University Press).

Howe, M de W (ed) (1953) *Holmes–Laski Letters: The Correspondence of Mr Justice Holmes and Harold J Laski 1916–1935* (London: Geoffrey Cumberlege, Oxford University Press).

Hull, N E H (1997) *Roscoe Pound and Karl Llewellyn: Searching for an American Jurisprudence* (Chicago: University of Chicago Press).

Hunt, A (1990) 'The Big Fear: Law Confronts Postmodernism' 35 McGill Law Journal 507–540.

Julius Rosenthal Foundation (1941) *My Philosophy of Law: Credos of Sixteen American Scholars* (Boston: Boston Law Book Co).

Kelman, M G (1984) 'Trashing' 36 Stanford Law Review 293–348.

— (1987) *A Guide to Critical Legal Studies* (Cambridge, Mass: Harvard University Press).

Kelsen, H (1941a) 'The Law as a Specific Social Technique' reprinted in Kelsen (1957) pp 231–256.

— (1941b) 'The Pure Theory of Law and Analytical Jurisprudence' reprinted in Kelsen (1957) pp 266–287.

— (1945) *General Theory of Law and State*, transl by A Wedberg (New York: Russell and Russell edn, 1961).

— (1955) 'Foundations of Democracy' 66 Ethics 1–101.

— (1957) *What is Justice? Justice, Law and Politics in the Mirror of Science* (Berkeley: University of California Press).

— (1967) *Pure Theory of Law*, transl by M Knight (Berkeley: University of California Press).

— (1973) 'God and the State', transl by P Heath, in O Weinberger (ed) *Hans Kelsen: Essays in Legal and Moral Philosophy* pp 61–82 (Dordrecht: D Reidel).

— (1991a) *General Theory of Norms*, transl by M Hartney (Oxford: Oxford University Press).

— (1991b) 'Sovereignty' in S L and B L Paulson (eds) *Normativity and Norms: Critical Perspectives on Kelsenian Themes* pp 525–536 (Oxford: Oxford Univerity Press).

Kennedy, D (1979) 'The Structure of Blackstone's Commentaries' 28 Buffalo Law Review 205–382.

Kirchheimer, O (1941) 'The Legal Order of National Socialism' reprinted in F S Burin and K L Shell (eds) *Politics, Law and Social Change: Selected Essays of Otto Kirchheimer* pp 88–109 (New York: Columbia University Press, 1969).

— (1961) *Political Justice: The Use of Legal Procedure for Political Ends* (Princeton: Princeton University Press).

Klare, K E (1978) 'Judicial Deradicalization of the Wagner Act and the Origins of Modern Legal Consciousness, 1937–1941' 62 Minnesota Law Review 265–339.

Kocourek, A (1928) *Jural Relations* 2nd edn (Indianapolis: Bobbs-Merrill).

Krygier, M (1986) 'Law as Tradition' 5 Law and Philosophy 237–262.

Kuper, A (1991) 'The Rise and Fall of Maine's Patriarchal Society' in Diamond (ed) (1991) pp 99–110.

Lacey, N (1993) 'Theory into Practice? Pornography and the Public/Private Dichotomy' 20 Journal of Law and Society 93–113.

Larson, M S (1977) *The Rise of Professionalism: A Sociological Analysis* (Berkeley: University of California Press).

Laski, H J (1967) *A Grammar of Politics* 5th edn (London: George Allen and Unwin).

Lasswell, H D and McDougal, M S (1943) 'Legal Education and Public Policy: Professional Training in the Public Interest' 52 Yale Law Journal 203–295.

Levinson, S and Balkin, J M (1991) 'Law, Music and Other Performing Arts' 139 University of Pennsylvania Law Review 1597–1658.

Levy, L W (ed) (1987) *Essays on the Making of the Constitution* 2nd edn (New York: Oxford University Press).

Levy-Ullmann, H (1935) *The English Legal Tradition: Its Sources and History*, transl by M Mitchell (London: Macmillan).

Llewellyn, K N (1930a) 'A Realistic Jurisprudence: The Next Step' reprinted in Llewellyn (1962) pp 3–41.

— (1930b) *Cases and Materials on the Law of Sales* (Chicago: Callaghan).

— (1931a) 'Some Realism About Realism' reprinted in Llewellyn (1962) pp 42–76.

— (1931b) 'Frank's Law and the Modern Mind' reprinted in Llewellyn (1962) pp 101–110.

— (1940) 'On Reading and Using the Newer Jurisprudence' reprinted in Llewellyn (1962) pp 128–165.

— (1941) 'My Philosophy of Law' in Julius Rosenthal Foundation (1941) pp 183–197.

— (1951) *The Bramble Bush: On Our Law and Its Study* 2nd edn (Dobbs Ferry, NY: Oceana).

— (1960) *The Common Law Tradition: Deciding Appeals* (Boston: Little, Brown).

— (1962) *Jurisprudence: Realism in Theory and Practice* (Chicago: University of Chicago Press).

— (1989) *The Case Law System in America*, transl by M Ansaldi (Chicago: University of Chicago Press).

Llewellyn, K N and Hoebel, E A (1941) *The Cheyenne Way: Conflict and Case Law in Primitive Jurisprudence* (New York: Legal Classics Library reprint, 1992).

Lobban, M (1991) *The Common Law and English Jurisprudence 1760–1850* (Oxford: Oxford University Press).

Lopez, I F H (1996) *White By Law: The Legal Construction of Race* (New York: New York University Press).

Luban, D (1994) *Legal Modernism* (Ann Arbor: University of Michigan Press).

Luhmann, N (1982) *The Differentiation of Society*, transl by S Holmes and C Larmore (New York: Columbia University Press).

Lyotard, J-F (1984) *The Postmodern Condition: A Report on Knowledge*, transl by G Bennington and B Massumi (Manchester: Manchester University Press).

MacCormick, D N (1981) *H L A Hart* (London: Edward Arnold).

— (1985) 'A Moralistic Case for A-Moralistic Law' 20 Valparaiso Law Review 1–41.

— (1992) 'Natural Law and the Separation of Law and Morals' in R P George (ed) *Natural Law Theory: Contemporary Essays* pp 105–33 (Oxford: Oxford University Press).

MacKinnon, C A (1985) Contributions to discussion in Dubois et al (1985).

— (1987) *Feminism Unmodified: Discourses on Life and Law* (Cambridge, Mass: Harvard University Press).

— (1989) *Toward a Feminist Theory of the State* (Cambridge, Mass: Harvard University Press).

Maine, H S (1861) *Ancient Law* (London: Dent edn, 1917).

— (1875a) *Lectures on the Early History of Institutions* (London: John Murray).

— (1875b) 'The Effects of Observation of India on Modern European Thought' reprinted in Maine (1876) pp 203–239.

— (1876) *Village Communities in the East and West* 3rd edn (London: John Murray).

— (1883) *Dissertations on Early Law and Custom* (London: John Murray).

– (1885) *Popular Government* (London: John Murray).

Maitland, F W (1893) 'Outlines of English Legal History, 560–1600' reprinted in Maitland (1911) vol 2, pp 417–496.

— (1901) 'The Crown as Corporation' reprinted in Maitland (1911) vol 3, pp 244–270.

— (1911) *The Collected Papers of Frederic William Maitland* (Cambridge: Cambridge University Press).

Manchester, A H (1980) *A Modern Legal History of England and Wales 1750–1950* (London: Butterworth).

Mannheim, K (1956) *Essays on the Sociology of Culture*, transl by E Manheim and P Kekcskemeti (London: Routledge and Kegan Paul).

Manning, C A W (1933) 'Austin Today: or "The Province of Jurisprudence" Re-examined' in W I Jennings (ed) *Modern Theories of Law* pp 180–226 (London: Wildy reprint, 1963).

Marx, K and Engels, F (1888) *The Communist Manifesto*, transl by S Moore (Oxford: Oxford University Press edn, 1992).

Matsuda, M J (1996) *Where Is Your Body? – And Other Essays on Race, Gender and the Law* (Boston: Beacon Press).

McIlwain, C H (1910) *The High Court of Parliament and Its Supremacy: An Historical Essay on the Boundaries Between Legislation and Adjudication in England* (New Haven: Yale University Press).

Menkel-Meadow, C (1985a) Contributions to discussion in Dubois et al (1985).

— (1985b) 'Portia in a Different Voice: Speculations on a Women's Lawyering Process' 1 Berkeley Women's Law Journal 39–63.

Mill, J S (1859) 'On Liberty' in *Utilitarianism, On Liberty, Considerations on Representative Government* pp 69–185 (London: Dent edn, 1993).

Minda, G (1995) *Postmodern Legal Movements: Law and Jurisprudence at Century's End* (New York: New York University Press).

Minow, M (1988) 'Feminist Reason: Getting It and Losing It' 38 Journal of Legal Education 47–60.

Moles, R N (1987) *Definition and Rule in Legal Theory: A Reassessment of H L A Hart and the Positivist Tradition* (Oxford: Basil Blackwell).

Morison, W L (1958) 'Some Myth About Positivism' 68 Yale Law Journal 212–233.

— (1982) *John Austin* (London: Edward Arnold).

Müller, I (1991) *Hitler's Justice: The Courts of the Third Reich*, transl by D L Schneider (London: I B Tauris).

Murphy, P L (1972) *The Constitution in Crisis Times 1918–1969* (New York: Harper and Row).

Neumann, F L (1944) *Behemoth: The Structure and Practice of National Socialism 1933–1944* (New York: Octagon reprint, 1983).

— (1986) *The Rule of Law: Political Theory and the Legal System in Modern Society* (Leamington Spa: Berg).

O'Donovan, K (1985) *Sexual Divisions in Law* (London: Weidenfeld and Nicolson).

Oliver, P, Douglas-Scott, S and Tadros, V (eds) (2000) *Faith in Law: Essays in Legal Theory* (Oxford: Hart).

Olsen, F (1983) 'The Family and the Market: A Study of Ideology and Legal Reform' 96 Harvard Law Review 1497–1528.

Pashukanis, E B (1978) *Law and Marxism: A General Theory*, transl by B Einhorn (London: Ink Links).

Paulson, S L (1975) 'Classical Legal Positivism at Nuremburg' 4 Philosophy and Public Affairs 132–158.

Pocock, J G A (1957) *The Ancient Constitution and the Feudal Law: A Study of English Historical Thought in the Seventeenth Century* (Cambridge: Cambridge University Press reprint with new Postscript, 1987).

Posner, R A (1972) 'A Theory of Negligence' 1 Journal of Legal Studies 28–96.

Postema, G J (1986) *Bentham and the Common Law Tradition* (Oxford: Oxford University Press).

Pound, R (1906) 'The Causes of Popular Dissatisfaction with the Administration of Justice' reprinted in R D Henson (ed) *Landmarks of Law: Highlights of Legal Opinion* pp 180–195 (New York: Harper, 1960).

— (1908) 'Mechanical Jurisprudence' 8 Columbia Law Review 605–623.

— (1911) 'The Scope and Purpose of Sociological Jurisprudence' (Part 2) 25 Harvard Law Review 140–168.

— (1923) *Interpretations of Legal History* (Cambridge: Cambridge University Press).

— (1931) 'The Call For a Realist Jurisprudence' 44 Harvard Law Review 697–711.

— (1940) *Contemporary Juristic Theory* (Littleton, Col: Rothman reprint, 1981).

— (1941) 'My Philosophy of Law' in Julius Rosenthal Foundation (1941) pp 249–262.

— (1942) *Social Control Through Law* (New Haven: Yale University Press).

— (1943) 'A Survey of Social Interests' 57 Harvard Law Review 1–39.

— (1950) *New Paths of the Law* (Lincoln, Neb: University of Nebraska Press).

— (1959) *Jurisprudence* (St Paul, Minn: West Publishing Co).

— (1963) 'Runaway Courts in the Runaway World' 10 University of California at Los Angeles Law Review 729–738.

Přibáň, J and Nelken, D (eds) (2001) *Law's New Boundaries: The Consequences of Legal Autopoiesis* (Aldershot: Ashgate).

Raz, J (1980) *The Concept of a Legal System: An Introduction to the Theory of Legal System* 2nd edn (Oxford: Oxford University Press).

Rumble Jr, W E (1985) *The Thought of John Austin: Jurisprudence, Colonial Reform, and the British Constitution* (London: Athlone Press).

Sartorius, R (1966) 'The Concept of Law' 52 Archiv für Rechts-und-Sozialphilosophie 161–190.

Savigny, F C von (1831) *Of the Vocation of Our Age for Legislation and Jurisprudence*, transl by A Hayward (New York: Arno Press reprint, 1975).

— (1867) *System of the Modern Roman Law*, transl by W Holloway, vol 1 (Westport: Hyperion Press reprint, 1979).

Schlag, P (1991) 'The Problem of the Subject' 69 Texas Law Review 1627–1743.

Schlegel, J H (1995) *American Legal Realism and Empirical Social Science* (Chapel Hill: University of North Carolina Press).

Schmitt, C (1985) *Political Theology: Four Chapters On the Concept of Sovereignty*, transl by G Schwab (Cambridge, Mass: MIT Press).

Schwartz, R D and Miller, J C (1964) 'Legal Evolution and Societal Complexity' 70 American Journal of Sociology 159–169.

Scott, J W (1988) 'Deconstructing Equality-Versus-Difference: Or, the Uses of Poststructuralist Theory for Feminism' 14 Feminist Studies 33–50.

— (1992) 'Experience' in J Butler and J W Scott (eds) *Feminists Theorize the Political* pp 22–40 (New York: Routledge).

Selznick, P (1969) *Law, Society, and Industrial Justice* (New Brunswick: Transaction reprint, 1980).

Shklar, J N (1964) *Legalism* (Cambridge, Mass: Harvard University Press).

Simpson, B (1973) 'The Common Law and Legal Theory' reprinted in Twining (ed) (1986) pp 8–25.

Skinner, Q (1978) *The Foundations of Modern Political Thought Vol 1: The Renaissance* (Cambridge: Cambridge University Press).

Skolnick, J (1975) *Justice Without Trial: Law Enforcement in Democratic Society* 2nd edn (New York: Wiley).

Smart, C (1989) *Feminism and the Power of Law* (London: Routledge).

Sommerville, J P (1999) *Royalists and Patriots: Politics and Ideology in England 1603–1640* 2nd edn (London: Longman).

Stein, P (1980) *Legal Evolution: The Story of an Idea* (Cambridge: Cambridge University Press).

Stephen, L (1900) *The English Utilitarians Volume 3: John Stuart Mill* (London: Duckworth).

Stevens, R (1983) *Law School: Legal Education in America from the 1850s to the 1980s* (Chapel Hill: University of North Carolina Press).

Stoljar, S J (1958) 'The Corporate Theories of Frederic William Maitland' in L C Webb (ed) *Legal Personality and Political Pluralism* pp 20–44 (Melbourne: Melbourne University Press).

Stone, J (1964) *Legal System and Lawyers' Reasonings* (London: Stevens).

— (1966) *Social Dimensions of Law and Justice* (Sydney: Maitland).

Strauss, L (1953) *Natural Right and History* (Chicago: University of Chicago Press).

Sugarman, D (1983) 'The Legal Boundaries of Liberty: Dicey, Liberalism and Legal Science' 46 Modern Law Review 102–111.

— (1986) 'Legal Theory, the Common Law Mind and the Making of the Textbook Tradition' in Twining (ed) (1986) pp 26–61.

Summers, R S (1984) *Lon L Fuller* (London: Edward Arnold).

Sypnowich, C (1990) *The Concept of Socialist Law* (Oxford: Oxford University Press).

Teubner, G (1989) 'How the Law Thinks: Toward a Constructivist Epistemology of Law' 23 Law and Society Review 727–757.

— (1993) *Law as an Autopoietic System*, transl by A Bankowska and R Adler (Oxford: Blackwell).

— (1997) 'The King's Many Bodies: The Self-Deconstruction of Law's Hierarchy' 31 Law and Society Review 763–787.

Tie, W (1999) *Legal Pluralism: Toward a Multicultural Conception of Law* (Aldershot: Ashgate).

Tushnet, M (1983) 'Following the Rules Laid Down: A Critique of Interpretivism and Neutral Principles' 96 Harvard Law Review 781–827.

— (1986) 'Critical Legal Studies: An Introduction to its Origins and Underpinnings' 36 Journal of Legal Education 505–517.

Twining, W (1968) *The Karl Llewellyn Papers* (Chicago: University of Chicago Law School).

— (1973) *Karl Llewellyn and the Realist Movement* (London: Weidenfeld and Nicolson).

— (1984) 'Evidence and Legal Theory' reprinted in Twining, *Law in Context: Enlarging a Discipline* pp 110–130 (Oxford: Clarendon, 1997).

— (ed) (1986) *Legal Theory and Common Law* (Oxford: Basil Blackwell).

Vyshinsky, A Y (1951) 'The Fundamental Tasks of the Science of Soviet Socialist Law', transl by H W Babb, in V I Lenin et al, *Soviet Legal Philosophy* pp 303–341 (Cambridge, Mass: Harvard University Press).

Waluchow, W J (1994) *Inclusive Legal Positivism* (Oxford: Oxford University Press).

Weber, M (1948) 'Politics as a Vocation' in H H Gerth and C Wright Mills (eds and transl) *From Max Weber: Essays in Sociology* pp 77–128 (London: Routledge and Kegan Paul).

— (1978) *Economy and Society* (Berkeley: University of California Press).

Weinreb, L L (1987) *Natural Law and Justice* (Cambridge, Mass: Harvard University Press).

West, R (1992) 'The Difference in Women's Hedonic Lives: A Phenomenological Critique of Feminist Legal Theory' in M J Frug (ed) *Women and the Law* pp 807–825 (Westbury, NY: Foundation Press).

White, G E (1972) 'From Sociological Jurisprudence to Realism: Jurisprudence and Social Change in Early Twentieth-Century America' reprinted in White (1978) pp 99–135.

— (1976) 'The Path of American Jurisprudence' reprinted in White (1978) pp 18–73.

— (1978) *Patterns of American Legal Thought* (Indianapolis: Bobbs-Merrill).

— (1988) *The American Judicial Tradition: Profiles of Leading American Judges* 2nd edn (New York: Oxford University Press).

White, J B (1990) *Justice as Translation: An Essay in Cultural and Legal Criticism* (Chicago: University of Chicago Press).

Whitman, C B (1991) 'Review Essay: Feminist Jurisprudence' 17 Feminist Studies 493–507.

Wigdor, D (1974) *Roscoe Pound: Philosopher of Law* (Westport, Conn: Greenwood Press).

Williams, P J (1991) *The Alchemy of Race and Rights* (Cambridge, Mass: Harvard University Press).

Wiseman, Z B (1987) 'The Limits of Vision: Karl Llewellyn and the Merchant Rules' 100 Harvard Law Review 465–545.

Witteveen, W J (1999) 'Laws of Lawmaking' in Witteveen and Van der Burg (eds) (1999) pp 312–345.

Witteveen, W J and Van Der Burg, W (eds) (1999) *Rediscovering Fuller: Essays on Implicit Law and Institutional Design* (Amsterdam: Amsterdam University Press).

Yale, D E C (1972) 'Hobbes and Hale on Law, Legislation, and the Sovereign' 31 Cambridge Law Journal (supplementary volume) 121–156.

Index

Analytical jurisprudence
  judicial function, and, 132–133,
    143
  lawyers' concerns, and, 129, 146
  legal development, and, 122, 145
  nature of, 83–85, 114–115
  political and moral contexts of,
    130, 146
  rational science, as, 113
Aquinas, Thomas, 121, 140
Aristotle, 140
Arnold, Thurman, 188
Austin, J L, 85, 87
Austin, John
  achievement, 49, 50, 75, 77
  aims, 53, 111–112
  assessments of, 14
  Bentham, differences from,
    50–51, 52, 53, 64
  codification, on, 51, 53–54, 72
  common law, hostility to, 51, 52,
    150
  conceptualist, as, 82
  constitutional law, on, 69
  democracy, on, 72, 209
  duties, on, 58

Austin, John—*contd*
  empiricist, as, 81, 82–83
  fear of revolution, 209, 213
  general jurisprudence, 53, 54, 75
  government, on, 72–74, 76, 79
  Hart's critique, 80, 88, 90, 92, 94
  hostility to ideas of, 76–77
  influence, 50
  influences on, 50, 52, 64, 82
  judges, on, 77, 146, 180
  judicial law-making, on, 51,
    71–72, 99
  law
    command, as, 56, 58
    concept of, 54–56
    customary, 135
    defining, 87
    generality of, 56–57
    government, as, 57–58, 94,
      106
    international, 77, 109–110,
      261
    map of, 75, 155
    morals, separation from, 54,
      114, 115, 125
    persistence and continuity of,
      69, 88

Austin, John—*contd*
law—*contd*
positive, 54–55, 56, 69, 115
science of, 50, 53, 76, 176
legal education, and, 75
legal profession, and, 74–75
legislation, science of, 53, 76
liberty, on, 57–58, 76–77
methods, 81–82, 90
modern state, on, 72–74
natural rights, on, 57
new world order, and, 262–263
obedience, on, 73, 246
political views, 74
positive morality, on, 55, 56,
68–69
Pound's critique. *See* Pound
power-conferring rules, 60–63,
70, 94
rights, on, 58
Roman law scholarship, on, 52,
53–54
Rule of Law, and. *See* Rule of
Law
rules, on, 88
sanctions, on, 56, 58–62, 73
society, view of, 72–73
sovereignty, on, 63–69, 83, 105,
210, 228, 244, 245
tacit commands, on, 70
task of legal theory, on, 6
utility, principle of, 53, 54
Austin, Sarah, 49, 73, 74
Autopoiesis theory, 249–250, 255

Balkin, Jack, 239, 240, 248, 264
Bentham, Jeremy
censorial jurisprudence, 53
codification, on, 51
command, law as, 56
common law, hostility to, 23, 51,
150

Bentham, Jeremy—*contd*
concept of law, 54
constitutionalism, 110–111
democracy, on, 72
expository jurisprudence, 53
individuation of laws, on, 62
influence on Austin, 50, 82–83
judges, on, 51, 71–72
legal reform, commitment to, 76
leges in principem, on, 68
natural rights, on, 57, 117–118
sanctions, on, 58
separation of law and morals,
114, 115
separation of powers, and, 79
sovereignty, on, 64, 68, 210, 244,
245
task of legal theory, on, 6
utility, principle of, 52, 53, 54
Blackstone, William, 24, 25, 28,
33, 38, 54, 68, 114, 117
Brunner, Emil, 137
Buckland, William, 14

Campbell, Tom, 139
Carter, James, 32
Clark, Charles, 182, 200
Codification
ancient codes, 41
Bentham on, 51
common law and, 39
Germany, 36, 39
Maine on, 41
Roman law, 37
Savigny's opposition to, 36–37,
41
Cohen, Felix, 179–180, 183, 188,
203
Coke, Edward, 24, 26, 27, 28,
33–34, 35, 116
Common law
Ancient Constitution, 35, 48

Common law—*contd*
Austin on. *See* Austin
authority of, 25–26, 29, 36
Bentham on. *See* Bentham
community and, 27, 28, 32,
  33–34, 39, 44, 142, 169, 176,
  210
continuity of, 26, 28
custom, as, 27–28, 157
declaratory theory, 25, 29
development of, 26, 27–28, 36,
  145, 157, 176
empiricism of, 101–102
esoteric knowledge, as, 33–34
flexibility of, 23
Fuller on. *See* Fuller
influence of, 21
judges, 25–26, 27, 30, 31, 146,
  168
language, 33
legislation and, 30–31, 36
maxims, 24
natural law and. *See* Natural law
nature of, 22
politics, and, 34–35
Pound and. *See* Pound
precedent, 25–26
principles, as 23, 176
rationality of, 32–33
rules, as, 22–23
social environment, view of, 32,
  36
system, as, 23
theory, 21–22
unwritten law, as, 28–29
Community
abstraction, as, 258
affective, 259
author of law, as, 257
belief, of, 259–261
boundaries of, 258
common law and. *See* Common
  law

Community—*contd*
definition, 259
Dworkin on, 169–170, 171–172,
  210, 257, 258
experience of, 257
Finnis on, 141–142, 143, 170
Fuller on, 141, 169
instrumental, 259, 261
judges and. *See* Judges
law regulating, 256
lawyers and, 38
legal interpretive. *See* Law
nature of, 258
networks of, 259, 263
traditional, 259–260
transnational law and, 263
types of, 259–261, 263
Critical legal studies (CLS), 181,
  203–206, 211, 234, 240, 264
Critical race theory (CRT), 229–
  233, 234

Daintith, Terence, 59
Darwin, Charles, 42–43
Derrida, Jacques, 239–241, 242,
  247–248
Dewey, John, 178
Dicey, A V, 23–24, 111, 118
Douglas, William, 182, 200
Dworkin, Andrea, 222, 224
Dworkin, Ronald
civil disobedience, on, 171
common law thought, and, 30,
  146, 168, 176
community, on. *See* Community
feminist critique of, 223
foundations of law, 245
Hart, critic of, 147
internal/external dichotomy, 10,
  97–98, 164
judges' authority, on, 162
judicial decision-making, on,
  161, 163, 165–166, 168, 170

Dworkin, Ronald—*contd*
   judicial discretion, on, 164–165
   liberal values, defending, 161,
      166
   legal interpretation, on, 10, 167–
      168, 171–174, 192, 258, 260
   legal positivism, on, 162–163
   legal profession, and, 171, 172
   Llewellyn compared, 191
   model of rules, on, 160–162
   organicist view, 166
   policies, on, 165–167
   Pound compared. *See* Pound
   principles, on, 162–164, 165,
      166–167
   reputation, 147
   right answer thesis, 165, 192
   rights, on, 161–162
   science of law, and, 176
   task of legal theory, on, 6–7,
      97–98

Economic analysis of law, 200–
   202
Eleanor of France, Queen, 243
Engels, Friedrich, 209
Equity, 41, 42, 43, 220, 248

Fehlberg, Belinda, 221
Feminist legal theory
   development of, 215
   different moral voices, and, 217–
      221
   effectiveness of, 215
   equality-difference debates, 216–
      217
   essentialism in, 224, 225
   ethic of care, 219–220, 234
   ethic of justice, 219–220, 234
   experience, and, 225, 227, 228
   gender as socially constructed,
      217, 227

Feminist legal theory—*contd*
   law as gendered, 223–224
   legal profession, and, 223
   liberal, 215–216, 228, 232
   normative legal theory, and, 215,
      216, 217, 225, 228–229, 234
   objectivity, on, 224, 225
   patriarchy, 217
   politics, 233–234
   postmodern, 226–228, 233
   public–private dichotomy, 233
   radical, 223–225, 232
   social relationships, emphasising,
      220
   surety cases, 221
Finnis, John, 121, 140–143, 170
Fish, Stanley, 172–173, 192
Frank, Jerome, 184–185, 187, 188,
   189, 196
Frug, Mary Joe, 226–227, 252
Fuller, Lon
   authority of law, on, 126–127
   common law method, on, 133
   common law thought, and, 135
   contractual ordering, on, 135,
      136
   Hart debate, 123–124
   judges, on, 134
   law
      customary, 135, 136
      definition, 132, 136
      enacted, 135
      existence of, 131, 136, 164
      fiat and reason, 133, 138, 145
      internal morality, 126–127,
         131, 134
      natural, 125, 129, 133, 138
      Nazi, 123–130, 136–137
      non-law, demarcation from,
         136
      purposive concept of, 132,
         134

Fuller, Lon—*contd*
law—*contd*
    task of, 134
  legal education, on, 138
  legal obligation, on, 124
  legal positivism, on, 117, 129, 133
  legality, on, 128, 129–130, 132, 142–143
  moral content of law, on, 124–125
  morality of aspiration, 130–132
  morality of duty, 130–132
  polycentric problems, on, 134
  procedural morality, on, 125, 129, 140
  professional responsibility, on, 136–138
  reciprocity, 134, 135
  rules, on, 9

Gabel, Peter, 230
Gilligan, Carol, 217–221, 228, 232, 234
Gilmore, Grant, 195, 197
Goodrich, Peter
  academic law, on, 264
  courts of love, on, 243–244
  methods, 242, 251–252
  postal rule, on, 241–242
  view of law, 253
Goody, Jack, 28

Haines, Charles Grove, 123
Hale, Matthew, 25, 28, 29
Hart, H L A
  Austin compared, 111–112
  Austin, critique of. *See* Austin
  Bentham and, 80, 110–111
  circular analyses, 244–245
  concept of law, 87–88, 129
  conceptualism, rejecting, 87

Hart, H L A—*contd*
  empiricist, as, 82, 83, 85, 87, 91, 98–100, 102, 105
  feminism and, 228–229
  Fuller debate, 123–124
  hermeneutics, 96–98
  judicial decision-making, on, 99–101, 104, 122, 146
  Kelsen contrasted. *See* Kelsen
  legal positivism, on, 124
  legal profession, and, 87
  legal realism, on, 187
  legal system, existence of, 95–96, 98–99
  legal theory, aims of, 98
  linguistic philosophy, 85–87, 97, 98
  methods, 88, 90, 178–179, 188
  natural law, on, 139–140
  Nazi law, on, 123
  obligation, on, 90–91, 228, 229
  officials, on, 90, 95–96, 98–99, 105, 210, 228, 244–245, 246, 257
  political concerns, 94
  pre-legal society, on, 92
  rule(s)
    adjudication, of, 93
    change, of, 93
    concept, 88–89
    core and penumbra, 99–100, 198
    external aspect, 10, 89, 90, 97
    habits and, 90
    internal aspect, 10, 89–90, 95–96, 97, 98
    normative language, 89
    open texture, 99
    power-conferring, 60–61, 62, 88, 93, 95
    predictive approach to, 89
    primary, 92–94

Hart, H L A—*contd*
  rule(s)—*contd*
    recognition, of, 93, 94, 95,
      105, 106, 172, 244
    secondary, 92–94, 95
    self-regulating system, as,
      94–95
    Rule of Law, and. *See* Rule of
      Law
  separation of law and morals, 97,
    114, 115, 124
  sociology, and, 87, 91–92, 97,
    98–99, 100–101, 228
  task of legal theory, on, 7
Historical jurisprudence
  anthropology and, 47–48
  civilisation, view of, 48
  common law methods,
    defending, 36
  Maine's. *See* Maine
  Savigny's. *See* Savigny
  sociology, and, 47
Hobbes, Thomas, 54, 56, 63–64,
  70, 142
Hoebel, E A, 189–190
Hohfeld, Wesley, 84–85
Holmes, Jr, Oliver Wendell, 6,
  148, 183–184, 195–196, 203
Honoré, Tony, 13
Horwitz, Morton, 204

James, William, 178
Judges
  common law. *See* Common law.
  community, and, 25, 29, 31
  role of, 143, 145, 175, 180
  Hart on. *See* Hart
  instrumentalist and organicist
    views of role, 150–151, 165–
    166
  law-making by, 122, 146
  political context of work, 204–
    205

Judges—*contd*
  polycentric problems, and, 134,
    220
  predictability of decisions, 183–
    184
  sovereign's delegates, as, 70, 143,
    146
  styles, 190–192
Judicial behaviouralism, 202–203
Jurisprudence
  analytical. *See* Analytical
    jurisprudence
  definition, 2
  difference, of. *See* Jurisprudence
    of difference
  historical. *See* Historical
    jurisprudence
  legal education, in, 8
  'minor', 243–244
  postmodernist. *See*
    Postmodernism
  sociological. *See* Pound
  See also Legal philosophy
Jurisprudence of difference
  normative legal theory,
    challenging, 237, 244, 255–
    256
  definition, 233
  legal practice, as, 234–235
  legal profession, and, 234
  methods, 234
  politics of, 234
  social relationships, emphasising,
    244, 256

Kelsen, Hans
  achievement, 111–112
  aims, 103, 111
  Anglo-American environment,
    in, 80
  Austin, on, 80
  basic norm (*Grundnorm*), 105–
    106, 244

Kelsen, Hans—*contd*
circular analyses, 245
conceptualist, as, 83, 101–102, 105, 108
democracy, on, 109
empiricism, rejecting, 103
gapless law, on, 106
Hart contrasted, 80–81, 102, 103–106, 111
influence, 80, 101
influences on, 101, 102
international law, on, 109–110, 261–262
judicial law-making, on, 122
justice, on, 110
law's self-regulation, on, 104, 146
methods, 102–104, 106, 108, 147
nation, on, 108, 109–110
norm, concept of, 102
norms, contradiction between, 106
political significance of work, 122, 137
political theory, 108–110, 111
pure theory, 80, 102–103, 104, 106–107, 111, 122
Rule of Law, and. *See* Rule of Law
science of law, 129
sociology of law, on, 103
state, on, 107–108, 110
task of legal theory, on, 7
Kirchheimer, Otto, 127, 128
Klare, Karl, 204, 205
Kocourek, Albert, 84–85
Kohler, Josef, 157

Lacan, Jacques, 241
Lasswell, Harold, 199
Law
ambivalence towards, 231
authority of, 12, 231, 245

Law—*contd*
autonomous realm, as, 15, 18, 107
autopoietic, 249–250
barrenness of, 244
circularity, 244, 255
common. *See* Common law
complexity, 119
compromise of interests, as, 118, 119
constituting social life, 203–204, 252
culture and, 38, 39, 42, 231, 252
distinctiveness of, 17–18, 244
economic analysis of, 200–202
faith in, 256
fiat and reason, 133, 145
focal conception of, 140
foundations of, 244, 256
hermeneutic understanding of, 96
human rights, 260
ideological effects, 204, 213
insiders and outsiders of, 90, 164, 231, 255, 257–258
intellectual field, as, 107
interpretive communities of, 207, 210, 211, 213–214, 215, 232, 237, 246, 257
language of. *See* Legal language
moral or political practice, as, 145
natural. *See* Natural law
Nazi, 123–130, 136–137
normativity, 102
objectivity in, 237–238
pluralistic view of, 255
politics and, 11–12, 107
positive. *See* Austin
postmodern. *See* Postmodernism
professional practice, as. *See* Lawyers

Law—*contd*
sanctions of, 58–62
science of, 45, 103, 106
self-regulating character of, 104, 107, 244, 249
separation from morality, 114–115, 137
steering mechanism, as, 119
system, as, 9, 106, 107, 175
transnational, 262–263
United States, 145, 195, 252
unity of, 8–10, 75, 105, 106, 107, 175, 237
voluntas and *ratio*, 128, 133
written and unwritten, 41
See also Legal doctrine
Law and Society movement, 200, 211
Lawyers
American, 150
changing situation of, 265
common, 39
insiders, as, 10, 257
legal theory, and, 9, 11, 46
professional knowledge and expertise, 11, 45, 75–76, 107, 184
professional organisation, 11, 44–45, 265
professional responsibility, 136–137
radical, 234–235
status, 11
varied outlooks, 265
Legal fictions, 41–42, 43
Legal institutions, 3
Legal language
open texture, 86, 99
normativity of, 89
performatives, 86, 87
realism and, 179–181
social insights from, 86–87

Legal philosophy
academic philosophy, and, 4, 5
conceptual clarification, 4–5, 83–84
conceptualist, 84
corporate personality debates, 84, 85, 87, 178–180, 204
English, 83–84
empiricist, 83, 84, 101–102
lawyers' enterprise, as, 4, 5
legal experience, and, 13–14
political significance, 11
professional legal practice, and, 4–6, 136, 176
scope, 2–3
See also Analytical jurisprudence; Legal theory
Legal positivism
common law and, 176
Fuller and, 129, 132
legal authority and, 116, 120
legal change, and, 122
legal procedure, and, 129
meaning, 115
morality and, 119, 137–139, 145
natural law, rapprochements with, 138–140, 143
Nazi regime, and, 123, 137
rise of, 117, 118
Rule of Law and, 123, 129
Legal realism
American legal system, and, 195–197
American movement, as, 177–178, 181, 195
Britain, in, 194, 198, 207
conceptual analysis and, 179–181
constructive doctrinal, 186, 187
crisis of confidence in law, as, 206–107
doctrinal analysis, and, 186
empirical research, 182

Legal realism—*contd*
fact scepticism, 185
formalism and, 198, 205
Germany, in, 197
instrumental view of law, 178
legal language, and, 179–181
legal practice, and, 234
legal profession, and, 206
method, as, 181
New Deal, and, 196, 197
normative legal theory and, 7,
182, 187, 198–199
predictability of judicial
decisions, and 183–185,
policy analysis, and, 182–183,
196
policy-science, 185, 187, 199
political context, 195–198
political critiques of, 196
pragmatism and, 178–179
radical scepticism, 186, 187, 199,
202, 203
rule scepticism, 185, 187
Scandinavian, 177, 197
tenets of, 181–182
Legal theory
autopoietic, 249–250, 255
behavioural inquiries, and, 176–
177
demystifying role, 7
empirical, 3, 15, 182–183, 200,
263
legal practice, and, 9
normative. *See* Normative legal
theory
realist. *See* Legal realism
sceptical, 7, 203
scope, 3
tasks, 6–8
unity of law, and, 8–9, 175, 231,
237

Legislation
common law and. *See* Common
law
Maine on, 42, 43, 44
Savigny on, 37–39
science of. *See* Austin
Levy-Ullmann, Henri, 22
Llewellyn, Karl
behavioural and normative
analysis, 191
Cheyenne studies, 190
constructive doctrinal realist, as,
187
Dworkin compared, 191
Formal style, 191–193
Grand style, 191–193
judicial craft, on, 189–190
judicial process, on, 189
judicial styles, on, 190–194
juristic method, on, 190
legal concepts, on, 188
legal realism, on, 181–182, 183
method, 189
New Deal, and, 197–198
predictability of decisions, on,
183, 189
rules, on, 183, 184, 187–188
Uniform Commercial Code, and,
189, 194
Locke, John, 142
Luhmann, Niklas, 119, 249

MacCormick, Neil, 94, 97, 139
McDougal, Myres, 199
McIlwain, Charles, 30
MacKinnon, Catharine
essentialism of, 224, 225
Gilligan, critique of, 221
male domination, on, 221, 232
Marx and, 221–222, 223, 224
normative legal theory, on, 224
pornography, on, 222–223

MacKinnon, Catharine—*contd*
  view of law, 222
  women's perspective, 226
Magna Carta, 26
Maine, Henry
  common law, and, 43, 46, 210
  government, view of, 44, 72, 74
  influences on, 42–43
  influence, 45–46, 47
  legal education, on, 45
  legal evolution, on, 40–42, 44
  legal profession, and, 44–47
  obedience, on, 73
  popular will, on, 209
  science of law, 45–46
  society, view of, 44, 74
  status and contract, on, 43
Maitland, F W, 34
Mannheim, Karl, 17
Manning, C A W, 66
Marxism
  law as class will, on, 209
  lawyers and, 234
  legal theory, 212–215, 225
  radical legal critique, 211
Mill, John Stuart, 72
Moore, W Underhill, 182, 200
Morison, W L, 81

Natural law
  authority of law, on, 120–121
  Bentham on, 117
  classical, 118–120, 133
  common law and, 35, 113, 116–117
  decline of, 117–119
  Finnis on, 140–143
  Hart on, 139–140
  Maine on, 42, 43
  method, 140–141
  Nazi experience and, 123–130
  political context of, 121–122

Natural law—*contd*
  political significance, 120, 122
  revival of, 122–123, 138–139
  Rule of Law and, 123
  tradition, 115–116
  United States, in, 117
  unjust laws, 121
  See also Legal positivism
Neumann, Franz, 127–128, 133, 137
Normative legal theory
  aims, 6–8
  behavioural analysis and, 193
  circularity in, 244–247
  community-oriented theories, 211, 256, 257, 262, 263
  contextual study of, 13–14, 16–18
  critique of, 254–255
  development of, 16–17, 113
  empirical legal theory, 263, 265–266
  empiricism-conceptualism dichotomy in, 83
  endless disputes, 13
  foundations of law, and, 238
  imperium-oriented theories, 211, 256, 262
  intellectual fashions in, 14
  internal/external dichotomy, 9–11, 15, 17–18, 231, 255
  jurisprudence of difference and. *See* Jurisprudence of difference
  lawyers' perspectives and, 15
  legal professional significance, 12–13, 113, 264
  legal realism and. *See* Legal realism
  limits of, 15–16
  meaning, 3, 8, 182
  nature of law, and, 15

Normative legal theory—*contd*
political influences on, 113
political significance, 12–13
realism in. *See* Legal realism
scepticism in, 176
social context of law and. *See*
Social
transnational regulation, and,
263
unity and system in law, showing,
8–11, 175, 206, 231, 235, 237
worth of, 254
See also Legal theory

Pashukanis, Evgeny, 214, 232
Philosophy
legal. *See* Legal philosophy
linguistic. *See* Hart
Politics
common law and. *See* Common
law
definition, 12
Postema, Gerald, 32, 71
Postmodernism
antifoundationalism, 238, 239,
244, 247, 255
deconstruction, 239–241, 244
ethics in, 248
feminism, in. *See* Feminism
interpreting postal rule, 241–242
law
authority of, 251, 255
circularity of, 244–245, 251
creating meaning, 251
critique of, 253–254
ethical emptiness, 251, 253,
255, 256
moral meaning of, 255
self-sufficiency of, 250–252,
255
legal authority, and, 245
legal profession, and, 264

Postmodernism—*contd*
legal theory, in, 239, 244, 250
master narratives, challenging,
238–239, 248, 250, 251
meaning, 238, 239
normative legal theory, critique
of, 245–247
politics of, 264–265
recovering minor jurisprudences,
241–244
social science, and, 247
violence, and, 247
Pound, Roscoe
aims, 154–156
analytical jurisprudence, and,
148–149, 156
Austin and, 149–150, 152
common law, and, 30, 146, 150,
153, 156, 157, 160, 168
critic of legal system, as, 151–
153, 196
Dworkin and, 147, 160–162,
164, 165–166, 168, 169
instrumentalism, 151, 159
interests, on, 154–156, 213
judges, on, 160, 174
jural postulates, 157–158, 172
law, concept of, 148–149
legal profession, and, 150, 152,
161
legal realism, and, 181
legislation, on, 152
methods, 147
natural law, on, 122–123, 149
organicism, 151, 159, 165
political outlook, 160, 161, 209
pragmatism, and, 159
reputation, 147
social engineering, 151
sociological jurisprudence, 147,
148, 151, 154, 159, 168
task of legal theory, on, 6

Pound, Roscoe—*contd*
　values in law, on, 149, 157–158
Pragmatism, 159, 252–254

Raz, Joseph, 94, 97
Rights
　critical race theory and, 230–231
　Dworkin on, 161–162
　jurisprudence of difference, in,
　　256
　natural, 118
Roosevelt, Franklin, 196, 198
Ross, Edward, 148
Rule of Law
　Austin and, 57, 70, 79, 94, 112
　Bentham and, 110
　feminism and, 232
　Finnis on, 142–143
　Fuller on, 129, 142
　Hart and, 62, 94–95, 107–108,
　　111, 112, 129
　Kelsen and, 107–108, 112, 129
　legal positivism and. *See* Legal
　　positivism
　Nazi experience and, 123
　Neumann on, 127
Rules
　Austin's approach to, 88
　Hart on. *See* Hart
　social relations and, 256

Savigny, Friedrich Carl von,
　36–39, 41, 42, 44, 47, 51
Schlegel, J H, 182
Schmitt, Carl, 107
Simpson, Brian, 23, 27
Skinner, Quentin, 16
Social, The
　Austin on, 210
　Bentham on, 210
　boundaries of, 232, 236

Social, The—*contd*
　differentiation of, 225, 228, 233–
　　236, 237, 257
　feminism and, 220
　lack of unity of, 214
　legal interpretation and, 232
　legal realism and, 210
　need to analyse, 246
　normative legal theory's
　　exclusion of, 14–15, 18, 210,
　　211, 216, 232, 235, 247
　postmodern views of, 226
　relationships as basis of law, 214,
　　220
　unified, as, 235
Sociology of law, 2–3, 47, 103,
　200
Sovereign
　delegation by, 69, 70
　institution, as, 63, 68–69, 83
　illimitable by law, 65–66, 68–69
Sovereignty
　Austin on. *See* Austin
　Hobbes on, 63–64
　legal, 66, 70–71, 83
　location of, 66–67
　meaning of, 64
　pre-legal, 66, 71
　United States, in, 67
Stone, Julius, 82
Strauss, Leo, 119

Teubner, Gunther, 249
Twining, William, 199

Waismann, Friedrich, 99
Weber, Max, 101, 118, 125, 138,
　142, 259
West, Robin, 216–217
Wigdor, David, 150, 151, 159
Williams, Patricia, 229–230
Wittgenstein, Ludwig, 85, 87